PRESIDENT'S MANAGEMENT AGENDA
A Balanced Scorecard Approach

PRESIDENT'S MANAGEMENT AGENDA
A Balanced Scorecard Approach

James B. Whittaker

Vienna, Virginia

MANAGEMENTCONCEPTS

8230 Leesburg Pike, Suite 800
Vienna, Virginia 22182
Phone: (703) 790-9595
Fax: (703) 790-1371
Web: www.managementconcepts.com

© 2003 Management Concepts, Inc.

All rights reserved. No part of this book may be reproduced or utilized in any form or by any means, electronic or mechanical, including photocopying, recording, or by an information storage and retrieval system, without permission in writing from the publisher, except for brief quotations in review articles.

Printed in the United States of America

Library of Congress Cataloging-in-Publication Data

Whittaker, James B.
    President's management agenda: a balanced scorecard approach / James B. Whittaker.
        p.   cm.
    Includes index.
    ISBN 1-56726-124-8 (hc.)
    1. Executive departments—United States—Management.   2. Administrative agencies—United States—Management.   3. Strategic planning—United States.   4. Performance—Management.   I. Title.

JK421.W4536 2003
352.3'0973—dc21

2003044558

About the Author

James B. Whittaker is a well-known author and lecturer about the Government Performance and Results Act of 1993. His commitment to strategic planning, performance measurement, and leadership in the federal government spans more than 40 years. He has held executive positions in the public sector and currently holds executive positions in the private sector. He retired from the U.S. Navy with the rank of Rear Admiral. He was responsible for developing and implementing strategic plans and performance plans for a variety of organizations, and he has defended these plans before the U.S. Congress. He has used the theories in a practical manner to deal with a variety of oversight agencies, including the Office of Management and Budget, the General Accounting Office, and the General Services Administration. As program manager for four of the largest and most successful automatic data processing projects in the federal government, he was responsible for awarding contracts of more than $4 billion. He was also responsible for the reengineering of three major business processes that procured, stored, and issued an inventory valued at more than $50 billion. He was appointed Acting Deputy Assistant Secretary of Defense for Systems under President Reagan.

Dr. Whittaker is currently a founder and officer in several high-technology companies and a consultant to the General Accounting Office and the Office of Personnel Management. He has been the primary lecturer on strategic planning in the Office of Personnel Management Senior Executive Service development program for more than 10 years and the primary GPRA lecturer since the law was passed. In 1994, he gave several Government Performance and Results Act pilot courses to support the General Accounting Office, the Office of Management and Budget, and the Office of Personnel Management. He is currently engaged in developing and implementing several strategic plans and performance plans in the civil agencies and the Department of Defense. In the past several years, clients have included the Board of Governors of the Federal Reserve System, the United Nations Development Program, the U.S. Department of Agriculture, the Centers for Disease Control, the National Institutes of Health, the World Bank, the Defense Supply Center, the Defense Reutilization and Marketing Service, the Census Department, the U.S. Department of Education, the U.S. Department of the Treasury, the Defense Mapping Agency, the Department of the Army, and the Immigration and Naturalization Service.

He has a Ph.D. and an M.B.A. (with distinction) from the University of Michigan and a B.S. from the University of Kansas. He is the author of *Balanced Scorecard in the Federal Government*, *Strategic Planning in the Federal Government: GPRA Best Practices*, *Strategic Planning in a Rapidly Changing Environment*, *Strategic Planning in the U.S. Government*, *The Government Performance and Results Act of 1993*, and *The Government Performance and Results Act, second edition*. Dr. Whittaker has developed and taught several management seminars on the faculty of the Management Education Department of the Graduate School of Business Administration of the University of Michigan. He has also been an adjunct member of the faculty of The George Washington University, the Catholic University of America, and Georgetown University.

Table of Contents

Preface ix

Chapter 1. Overview 1
   Time for President Bush 2

**Chapter 2. The Balanced Scorecard in the Private Sector:
Measuring Business Strategy** 3
   Financial Perspective 3
   Customer Perspective 4
   Internal Business Perspective 5
   Learning and Growth Perspective 6
   Conclusion 8

Chapter 3. The President's Management Agenda 9

Chapter 4. Merging the Balanced Scorecard and the PMA 41

Chapter 5. The PMA and the FY 2004 Budget 43
   Governing with Accountability 43
   Assessing Program Performance 56

**Chapter 6. The National Aeronautics and Space Administration:
Performance Plan and PMA Action Plans** 65

**Chapter 7. The Defense Finance and Accounting Service:
Strategic Plan and Balanced Scorecard Measures and Targets** 95

**Chapter 8. The Balanced Scorecard at the Federal Aviation
Administration Logistics Center** 121
   FAALC Strategic Plan for 1994 121
   FAALC Strategic Plan for 1997 126
   FAALC Strategic Plan for 1999–2002 136
   FAALC Strategic Plan for 2003–2007 150

**Chapter 9. The Balanced Scorecard at the Naval Undersea
Warfare Center** **165**
Naval Undersea Warfare Center 1998 Strategic Plan 165
NUSC Strategic Management Process 175
NUWC Newport Division 1998 Strategic Plan 177
NUWC Newport Division 1998 Strategic Plan Brochure 193
NUWC Newport Division Five-Year Planning Process 196
"Five-Year Planning Explained in One Easy Lesson" 199
"A Journey of Change" 202

**Chapter 10. The President's Management Agenda and
Balanced Measures at the Internal Revenue Service** **213**
Commissioner's Testimony 213
The IRS Balanced Measurement System 216
Organizational Performance Management and the IRS Balanced
  Measurement System 233

Chapter 11: Best Practices in Performance Measurement **249**
"Balancing Measures: Best Practices in Performance Management" ... 249

**Chapter 12. The Balanced Scorecard in Procurement—
Two Case Examples** **259**
PEA Guide to the Balanced Scorecard 259
Department of Transportation's Procurement Balanced Scorecard 276

**Chapter 13. The Balanced Scorecard in Human Resources
at the Department of Energy** **289**
Strategic Measurement System for DOE Contractor Human Resources (SMS^{HR}):
  A Comprehensive Approach to Tailored Strategic HR Planning 289

**Chapter 14. Utilizing the Balanced Scorecard Tool
in the Public Sector** **299**

**Chapter 15. The Future of the Balanced Scorecard
in the Federal Government** **319**

Appendix A. Balanced Scorecard for a Contractor **321**

Index **329**

Preface

This book is the third in a new series about federal government management. Management in the federal government started to change when President Clinton signed the Government Performance and Results Act (GPRA) into law in August 1993. GPRA required a dramatic difference in federal government operations to achieve full compliance.

Since 1993, federal organizations have been approaching the implementation of GPRA in a variety of ways. Starting in 1994, several hundred GPRA pilot projects were undertaken as various federal organizations prepared for the first full year of implementation in their own ways.

Although the law was signed by President Clinton, it never received strong support from the Clinton administration. Other initiatives such as the National Performance Review, headed up by Vice President Gore, received more support than GPRA and its requirements.

The first book in this series, *Strategic Planning in the Federal Government: GPRA Best Practices*, established a baseline for strategic planning in the federal government. The second book, *Balanced Scorecard in the Federal Government*, described and documented the results of the implementation, with special emphasis on the balanced scorecard and balanced measures.

The federal government is making some progress in using new concepts to implement GPRA. Some organizations and individual functions are using Kaplan and Norton's balanced scorecard, modified for the federal government. Other organizations and individual functions are developing the concept of balanced measures. The strength of these new efforts is that they focus on more than just "bottom line" financial results—recognizing that it is difficult to focus exclusively on such results when the vast majority of federal organizations do not operate in a "profit" environment. It therefore makes sense for the federal government to broaden the balanced scorecard approach that Kaplan and Norton have used in their pacesetting private sector work.

President Bush's President's Management Agenda (PMA) appears to be a good fit. Through the PMA, President Bush is providing focus to federal organizations where their improvement can make the most difference.

This book takes the question of federal government management one step further. With the election of President Bush, many changes have been made. First, and perhaps one of the most important factors, is that the President is interested in results. You only need to listen to President Bush talk about a variety of programs and issues over a period of time to hear his interest in results shine through repeatedly. Next, the PMA is consistent with GPRA and emphasizes results rather than process. Finally, and even more importantly, the PMA will measure the impact of those results on the federal government.

For suggested improvements to future editions or for any detailed questions you have about this book or this series, please e-mail me at JamesBW238@aol.com or call/fax me at (703) 416-8616.

James B. Whittaker
June 2003
Arlington, Virginia

CHAPTER 1
Overview

The U.S. federal government is in the midst of a massive change in the way it does business. For decades, the primary federal government driver has been the budget. Unfortunately, this may never change. However, in August 1993 Congress passed legislation, signed into law by President Clinton, entitled the Government Performance and Results Act of 1993 (GPRA).

This law, which the federal government has been implementing for the past seven years, sets the stage for the federal government to be managed and measured in different ways. First, it mandates new documents. Rather than being driven by the budget, the law requires agencies of the federal government to have long-range strategic plans. These plans must encompass at least five years plus the budget year, or a total minimum of six years. The strategic plans are to be driven by the mission of the agency and developed and implemented in consultation with Congress, stakeholders, customers, and employees of the organizations.

Next, the long-range strategic plans, which might span 15 or even 20 years in duration, are to drive the budget. This is a critical change. Anyone who has been a part of government for even a few months knows how important it is to spend funds allocated to an organization in order to get more funds next year. Clearly, federal government incentives in the past have been flawed. GPRA has the potential to correct these problems.

The primary aims of GPRA are to ensure that strategic planning drives budgeting and that resource decisions reflect strategic priorities, not just any "firestorm" that occurs. Agencies must establish long-term priorities and then accomplish them.

Next, the law sets forth a requirement for another new document—a performance plan—to guide the transition from the strategic plan with its long-term goals that are updated at least every three years, to what needs to be accomplished over the short term—specifically, in the next fiscal year. The performance plan, which is developed for each fiscal year, sets forth the annual goals and objectives that are derived from the long-term strategic plan. It is this annual performance plan that drives the budget of the government organization.

Six months after the end of each fiscal year, government agencies must report on how well they did in accomplishing annual goals and objectives. This report is due each year on the March 31 following the end of the fiscal year. Fiscal Year (FY) 1999, which ended in September 1999, was the first execution year of GPRA across the federal government. On March 31, 2000, performance reports were submitted on performance against the 1999 annual performance plans.

The transition from the old way of doing things to the new, results-oriented planning atmosphere has been varied. In the summer of 1997, the General Accounting Office (GAO) predicted that "the results of the GPRA Implementation will be uneven."[1] GAO was right.

---
[1] General Accounting Office. *The Government Performance and Results Act: 1997 Implementation Will Be Uneven* (Washington, D.C.: GAO, 1997). Report GGD-97-109.

The level of senior management attention, management involvement, and seriousness, as well as the effectiveness of the implementation, varied widely across the federal government. This finding was true not only on the first set of strategic plans analyzed by GAO and graded by Congress, but also on the performance plans. However, progress was achieved across the board.

TIME FOR PRESIDENT BUSH

President Bush has made many changes in the U.S. federal government. One of the most important has been establishing the President's Management Agenda. The PMA is important for a number of reasons. First, it gives high-level, sustained emphasis to the vast changes initiated by GPRA almost ten years earlier. With PMA, the President sent Congress a "bold strategy for improving the management and performance of the federal government. Government likes to begin things—to declare grand new programs and causes. But good beginnings are not the measure of success. What matters in the end is completion. Performance. Results. Not just making promises, but making good on promises. In my Administration, that will be the standard from the farthest regional office of government to the highest office in the land." This was a clear mandate that the bar has been raised.

Second, the PMA approach is the right one for the federal government. The federal government uses the vast resources of this great country—and those resources are limited. The "right things" have to be accomplished. We don't need to start numerous projects that never get finished and we don't need to undertake projects that should not be initiated in the first place. The President must lead this performance management charge; the federal government bureaucracy does not have a chance of long-term change without his leadership. Even with his effective leadership, this will be a long, tough struggle. There are just too many inappropriate incentives in the federal government that must be dealt with. Let us trust that President Bush's leadership will be effective and of a long-standing nature to turn around the "ship of bureaucracy."

This book presents some of the "best practices" in the federal government that support the PMA and thus the President's vision. The President's vision for government reform is guided by three principles: Government should be (1) citizen-centered, not bureaucracy-centered; (2) results-oriented; and (3) market-based, actively promoting rather than stifling innovation through competition.

Although the initial grades of the federal government across the PMA were on the low side, some agencies have made great progress. Those agencies will be noted and referred to throughout this book.

CHAPTER 2

The Balanced Scorecard in the Private Sector: Measuring Business Strategy

Kaplan and Norton[1] deal with a number of important issues in their discussion of measuring business strategy. Their basic point is that to be successful in an increasingly competitive world, businesses must satisfy a variety of benchmarks, not just financial performance. They outline several perspectives that must be achieved, including a financial perspective, a customer perspective, an internal business perspective, and a learning and growth perspective.

FINANCIAL PERSPECTIVE

The financial perspective is key to the balanced scorecard (BSC) approach. In many ways, financial perspectives provide the focus for goals, objectives, and measures and indicators across the scorecard. For most commercial organizations, financial areas of decreasing cost, improving productivity, increasing revenue, enhancing effective asset utilization, and reducing risk provide the required linkage across all BSC perspectives.

Companies can choose from a variety of financial objectives, depending on the stage in their life cycle. Kaplan and Norton simplify the choices and identify three stages of the life cycle: (1) grow, (2) sustain, and (3) harvest. While these concepts are important in the private sector, they are less relevant in the public sector.

In the early stage of the private sector life cycle, commercial companies have products or services with large growth potential. To develop this potential, private sector organizations must invest in these products or services. Their objectives and measures will be tailored to such factors as growth rate percentages in revenue and sales growth rates in various targeted markets or customer groups.

Later in the private sector life cycle, business will be in the *sustain* stage. Most private sector companies are in this stage. Here the strategy of the company changes. In addition to concern about sales growth, firms need to be earning a good return on their invested capital.

Later in the private sector life cycle, firms will want to *harvest* investments made in the two earlier cycles. New investment will be curtailed except when necessary to maintain existing capabilities. Investment projects in this stage would require short-period paybacks and definite, less risky returns. Financial objectives would be operating cash flow (before depreciation) and working capital reductions.

Consequently, as the organization moves though the life cycle in the private sector, different financial performance is required. Financial measures change to align the interest of the shareholders and the investors with the reality of the marketplace to ensure that the firm provides the appropriate financial returns.

---

[1]Robert S. Kaplan and David P. Norton, *The Balanced Scorecard* (Boston: Harvard Business School Press, 1996).

Kaplan and Norton show that three financial themes drive the strategies of grow, sustain, and harvest. The financial themes are (1) revenue growth and mix, (2) cost reduction/productivity improvement, and (3) asset utilization/investment strategy.

Revenue growth and mix refers to how the firm would expand its product and service offerings to reach new customers and markets, and change the products and services toward higher value-added offerings. Measurement would include sales growth by business segment or percent revenue increase from new customers and new product or service offerings. In any theme or strategy, measurement should show what the firm is trying to achieve and then develop the most appropriate, most effective measures and indicators for that theme or strategy.

Cost reduction/productivity improvement refers to efforts to lower the direct costs of products or services and reduce indirect costs. One of the more manageable aspects of the private sector problem, as opposed to the federal government, is the ability to do, measure, and incentivize this behavior. Since the private sector is reporting and measuring these objectives on a daily, weekly, and monthly basis, progress may be much more achievable and measurable. The federal government not only lacks the system capability and the requirements to measure and report these indicators, but also may have political considerations relative to the issue that result in productivity improvement and cost reduction not being major program goals. The ability to apply some of the "best practices" from the private sector becomes more difficult in the federal arena.

The last theme—asset utilization/investment strategy—is also a more difficult one to implement in the federal government. In the private sector, firms strive to achieve higher utilization of their fixed asset base by using scarce resources more efficiently and getting rid of assets that provide inadequate returns. Through the ubiquitous financial controls and objectives, this is a normal way of doing business in the private sector. This approach is not so easily implemented in the federal government, where many disincentives may apply. As a recent example, Congress decided during the budget discussion for FY 2000 that 1 percent of the budget should be reduced to provide a method of reducing fraud, waste, and abuse in the execution of executive branch programs. How much of that 1 percent would have been covered if the various elected officials who have taken care of their constituents withdrew the obvious "pork" already in the budget?

Kaplan and Norton start with financial objectives, recognizing that the private sector firm must achieve above-average financial returns based on the capital invested or it will not exist in the long run. Interestingly, the private sector firm must effectively and efficiently use financial objectives and measures to drive its operations as the federal government has, in the past, been required to spend the budget dollars appropriated and authorized. This federal government requirement has resulted in less than effective and efficient utilization of those dollars. The GPRA requirement mandates that those financial assets be turned into appropriate results across the country.

Financial objectives and measures will continue to increase in importance in the federal government as positive steps are taken to make the federal government more businesslike. However, it will be a difficult task to move government to results-oriented activity rather than a "budget driven/spend your funds to get more" approach.

CUSTOMER PERSPECTIVE

In the customer perspective, the private sector company must identify the customer and in what segment it will compete. These customers and these segments must then deliver the financial results necessary to sustain the business. The customer perspective allows the private sector company to align core customer outcomes such as satisfaction, loyalty, acquisition, retention, and profitability. It also allows the company to measure explicitly the value proposition that the company offers the customer and the segments that it has targeted. Value propositions are the drivers of the core customer outcomes.

Core measurement outcomes are generic across all kinds of organizations. They include measures of (1) market share, (2) customer retention, (3) customer acquisition, (4) customer satisfaction, and (5) customer profitability.

The customer value proposition represents the attributes that private sector companies provide through their products and services. These value propositions create loyalty and satisfaction in the targeted customer segments of the market. Value propositions will vary across different industries and across different segments of various industries. However, Kaplan and Norton noticed a common set of attributes across the industries within which they have worked on the balanced scorecard. These three categories of attributes are (1) product/service attributes, (2) customer relationship, and (3) image and reputation.

Product/service attributes relate to the functionality of the product or service and its price and quality. Some customers want consistently low-cost products while other customers are willing to pay for unique products, services, and quality. The customer approach chosen must be able to provide the financial returns necessary to build and sustain the business over time by yielding a sufficient return on investment assets utilized.

Customer relationship concerns elements such as delivering the product or service to the customer and measuring such things as how responsive the company is and what the time of that response is. It also includes how the customer feels about dealing with the firm. What kind of employees do you want dealing with the customer? How knowledgeable are they? How does the customer feel about the level of service provided by the company? How responsive is the company initially in regular times, and how does it respond when there is a problem? Is there convenient access to the product and service provided by the company? More and more companies today are providing 24/7 service in a variety of industries.

Image and reputation deal with those intangible factors that attract customers to various firms in the private sector. Firms are able to generate customer loyalty beyond the tangible aspects of the products and services provided to the customer. A good example of this concept is the high level of product and service accompanied by a variety of aligned policies that state that the customer is always right. Nordstrom customer service is legendary, and the loyalty of its customers is a vital part of its corporate strategy.

A set of core outcome measures should be developed that target the customer and his or her relationship to the private sector company directly. The product and service delivery should be measured on functionality, quality, and price. The relationship with the customer should be measured on the quality of the purchasing experience and the personal relationship of that experience. Last, the image and reputation of the firm should be developed to strengthen the execution of the strategy in the market and the market segment that has been targeted.

INTERNAL BUSINESS PERSPECTIVE

Internal business perspective means that the firm must identify those processes that are most critical to achieving success. Thus, this analysis must target those processes that are most critical to achieving shareholder and customer objectives. Kaplan and Norton state that this analysis should be conducted as an internal value chain analysis. They start with the front end—the innovation process. Firms start with customers' needs and then develop new products and solutions that will be offered to customers to satisfy those needs. Next they look at the operating process whereby the firm delivers products and services to the customers of the firm. They finish with the post-sale service offering that adds value to the products and services sold to customers to satisfy their needs.

This focus on the internal business process and the derivation of objectives and measures is one of the most distinctive differences between the balanced scorecard and more traditional performance measurement systems. Traditional systems rely more on financial measures and on controlling and improving existing departments and divisions. The BSC puts more emphasis on improvement of the operation as a whole and the integration of results that will achieve both stockholder and customer objectives. This integration direction will be extremely helpful in the federal government where some of the most "ineffective, moat-like silos" exist. There are few incentives in many government operations to drive integration of action for results that will support the customer and the taxpayer rather than support the entrenched incumbents in government operations.

Kaplan and Norton note that all companies are attempting to reduce cycle times, improve quality, maximize throughput, increase yields, and lower costs for their business processes. Therefore, in the private sector this push for improved performance will not necessarily lead to a unique strategy. However, in the federal government this push for performance is not as widespread. Various federal agencies could provide unique contributions to their customers and to the taxpayers by setting objectives and measures in the five areas mentioned above. In fact, there are few federal agencies or departments that should not be doing so.

LEARNING AND GROWTH PERSPECTIVE

The final perspective develops objectives, measures, and indicators to drive organizational learning and growth. Objectives in this perspective provide the foundation to enable objectives in the other three perspectives to be achieved. It is not unusual to find many private sector organizations where it is difficult to invest in the enhancement of employees, processes, and systems. This is particularly true when too much emphasis is placed on short-term financial performance. These investments are usually expensed; therefore, cutbacks in these expenses are a quick way to get a short-term "pop" in earnings. Managers with a short-term outlook hope that this misallocation of short-term investments that flow to the bottom line do not catch up with them before they leave. If the right level of emphasis on investments and attention is not provided to your people, processes, and systems, the downside impact will be felt. This is particularly true in the public sector, where insufficient funds are frequently allocated for personal and professional development of the workforce—and the negative consequences are seen routinely across the federal government.

Kaplan and Norton identify three principal categories for the learning and growth perspective across a wide variety of private sector firms: (1) employee capabilities; (2) information system capabilities; and (3) motivation, empowerment, and alignment.

Employee Capabilities

One of the biggest changes in the past 10 to 20 years involves employee contributions to organizations. Successful organizations require continual improvement over time. Many tasks that were previously assigned to employees have been automated. Jobs that previously were narrow and uncomplicated have given way to automated ways to accomplish that work. Today's employees are consistently asked to do more and think about how they can continually improve their performance and the performance of their work group. This change places more responsibility on the individual employee and his or her capacity to think and respond to a variety of job requirements.

This shift in job requirements demands a change in employees to ensure that their minds and creative abilities are directed and aligned with the objectives of the organization. This will be a particularly important factor in implementing the BSC in the public sector since this transition of employee responsibilities and tasks has occurred but the requisite actions and investments by the public sector organizations have not always accompanied this transition.

Three core employee measurements include (1) employee satisfaction, (2) employee retention, and (3) employee productivity. These measures loomed even more important as the 20th century wound down with some of the lowest unemployment rates in the United States in the past several decades. Private sector employees in many fields and in many geographic areas had wide choices and opportunities for employment. Therefore, these three employee measures became even more critical in many industries.

Employee satisfaction can be measured in surveys conducted annually or on some other schedule. These surveys might address factors such as: (1) job recognition, (2) sufficient access to information, (3) appropriate involvement in decisions, (4) encouragement to be creative and innovative, (5) sufficient staff support, and (6) overall satisfaction with the company.

Employee retention is an increasingly important issue as firms move away from manufacturing to service industries. As the individual is asked to be more creative and deal with more thoughtful, innovative situations, the value of the long-term investment in the employee becomes clear. As the business world develops the concept of knowledge management, much of that asset is what the human component of the organization has learned and passed on for the organization to improve its performance and increase its shareholder value in the future. If organizations do not retain the employees they need to be successful, future success will be more difficult. Moreover, adequate financial returns to the shareholder, and product and service returns to the customer, will be more difficult to achieve.

Employee productivity can be measured in a variety of ways. One of the simplest measures is revenue per employee. However, revenue can increase while the return to invested assets goes down. Therefore, one might measure profit or earnings before interest and taxes (EBIT) per employee as a more appropriate indicator. Employee productivity needs to be measured in ways that are integrated with the key factors of success across the organization even as the organizational environment changes the challenges to the organization.

If the employees of an organization need to be re-skilled, then specific drivers of learning and growth involve staff competencies, the technology infrastructure, and the climate for action in the organization.

Information System Capabilities

Information system capabilities may be one of the most important factors in this system of objectives and measures. Employee motivation and skills are important for high-performance organizations providing substantial returns to shareholders and customers, but they are probably not sufficient in this day and age. Effective employees in this increasingly competitive environment must have fast, accurate information on products and services, on internal business processes, and on the financial consequences of their individual decisions. With the increasing competitiveness of the environment and the growing demands of customers to reduce cost, increase quality, minimize cycle time, and enhance customer satisfaction, many firms will fail or will achieve only minimal success due to the problems in information systems. Some private sector companies have developed objectives and measures focused on a strategic information coverage ratio. These measures of strategic information availability look at the percentage of processes with real-time quality, cycle time, and cost feedback available, and the percentage of customer-facing employees with on-line customer information.

Motivation, Empowerment, and Alignment

Kaplan and Norton suggest a number of measures that can be used in the area of motivation, empowerment, and alignment. They can vary from a simple measure (e.g., the number of suggestions per employee) to a more complex measure (e.g., the number of suggestions implemented) to an even more complex measure that quantifies process improvements (e.g., quality, time, and performance).

Performance drivers for individual and organizational alignment focus on the alignment between company and individuals/departments. This alignment is critical throughout the organization to ensure that the right objectives are achieved. When this alignment is checked throughout the organization, the element of team performance must be effectively addressed. Kaplan and Norton reference a variety of measures for team building and team performance in addition to measures for individual performance.

Kaplan and Norton note that there are fewer examples of measures in the learning and growth perspective because many companies have not yet started to develop them. Companies do not appear to be linking the learning and growth area to their strategy and long-term objectives, and instead assume that the outcomes of these efforts are correct and are ends in themselves. This is a good area for federal government analysis and experimentation since the long-term efficacy of the federal workforce and its information technology systems are key to effective government now and in the future.

CONCLUSION

Kaplan and Norton make several key points in their wrap-up on measuring business strategy. First, they note that their comments relate to an organizational unit in the private sector called a strategic business unit. These units are generally much smaller and less complex than the agencies and departments of the federal government. Therefore, their BSC comments have to be carefully considered and not applied arbitrarily.

Second, a successful BSC is one that communicates a strategy through an integrated set of measurements that includes both financial and non-financial items. The federal government can use this effectively, but the concept of strategy is not one that is used or understood throughout the federal government. A large, long-term training effort will be required to derive the benefits of the BSC.

Third, the BSC needs to be linked to the organizational strategy by three principles: (1) cause-and-effect relationship, (2) performance driver, and (3) financials. Moreover, the outcome and performance driver measures on the balanced scorecard must result from intensive and broad-based discussions between senior- and mid-level management.

Fourth, the best BSCs are those that allow development of the underlying strategy of the business unit from the listing of objectives and measures and the associated linkages among them. Last, the use of the BSC to develop corporate strategy as distinguished from strategic business unit strategy is in the early development stage. Over time, more research information will be available in this complex area.

The Kaplan and Norton book contains many detailed examples explaining how various private sector companies have employed the BSC concept. The book does not delve deeply into particulars but provides the reader with sufficient detail to explore the BSC in more depth.

CHAPTER 3
The President's Management Agenda

This chapter sets forth the details of the PMA. The document can be read in its entirety on the website www.omb.gov.

EXECUTIVE OFFICE OF THE PRESIDENT
OFFICE OF MANAGEMENT AND BUDGET

THE PRESIDENT'S MANAGEMENT AGENDA

FISCAL YEAR 2002

Table of Contents

	Page
President's Message	1
Introduction—Improving Government Performance	3
Government-wide Initiatives	
1. Strategic Management of Human Capital	11
2. Competitive Sourcing	17
3. Improved Financial Performance	19
4. Expanded Electronic Government	23
5. Budget and Performance Integration	27
Program Initiatives	33
6. Faith-Based and Community Initiative	35
7. Privatization of Military Housing	39
8. Better Research and Development Investment Criteria	43
9. Elimination of Fraud and Error in Student Aid Programs and Deficiencies in Financial Management	47
10. Housing and Urban Development Management and Performance	51
11. Broadened Health Insurance Coverage through State Initiatives	55
12. A "Right-Sized" Overseas Presence	59
13. Reform of Food Aid Programs	65
14. Coordination of Veterans Affairs and Defense Programs and Systems...	69

GENERAL NOTES

1. All years referred to are fiscal years unless otherwise noted.

2. Web address: *http://www.whitehouse.gov/omb/budget*

President's Message

I am pleased to send to the Congress a bold strategy for improving the management and performance of the federal government. Government likes to begin things—to declare grand new programs and causes. But good beginnings are not the measure of success. What matters in the end is completion. Performance. Results. Not just making promises, but making good on promises. In my Administration, that will be the standard from the farthest regional office of government to the highest office in the land.

This Report focuses on fourteen areas of improvement where we can begin to deliver on our promises. The recommendations we have targeted address the most apparent deficiencies where the opportunity to improve performance is the greatest. These solutions are practical measures, well within our reach to implement.

These proposals will often require the cooperation of Congress. Congress' agenda is a crowded one, and there is an understandable temptation to ignore management reforms in favor of new policies and programs. However, what matters most is performance and results. In the long term, there are few items more urgent than ensuring that the federal government is well run and results-oriented.

This Administration is dedicated to ensuring that the resources entrusted to the federal government are well managed and wisely used. We owe that to the American people.

GEORGE W. BUSH

Improving Government Performance

> *"Government likes to begin things—to declare grand new programs and causes and national objectives. But good beginnings are not the measure of success. What matters in the end is completion. Performance. Results. Not just making promises, but making good on promises. In my Administration, that will be the standard from the farthest regional office of government to the highest office of the land."*
>
> Governor George W. Bush

To reform government, we must rethink government.

The need for reform is urgent. The General Accounting Office (GAO) "high-risk" list identifies areas throughout the federal government that are most vulnerable to fraud, waste, and abuse. Ten years ago, the GAO found eight such areas. Today it lists 22. Perhaps as significant, government programs too often deliver inadequate service at excessive cost.

New programs are frequently created with little review or assessment of the already-existing programs to address the same perceived problem. Over time, numerous programs with overlapping missions and competing agendas grow up alongside one another—wasting money and baffling citizens.

> *"Congress and the new administration face an array of challenges and opportunities to enhance performance and assure the accountability of the federal government. Increased globalization, rapid technological advances, shifting demographics, changing security threats, and various quality of life considerations are prompting fundamental changes in the environment in which the government operates. We should seize the opportunity to address today's challenges while preparing for tomorrow."*
>
> Comptroller General David M. Walker

Though reform is badly needed, the obstacles are daunting—as previous generations of would be reformers have repeatedly discovered. The work of reform is continually overwhelmed by the constant multiplication of hopeful new government programs, each of whose authors is certain that this particular idea will avoid the managerial problems to which all previous government programs have succumbed. Congress, the Executive Branch, and the media have all shown far greater interest in the launch of new initiatives than in following up to see if anything useful ever occurred.

So while the government needs to reform its operations—how it goes about its business and how it treats the people it serves, it also needs to rethink its purpose—how it defines what business is and what services it should provide.

The President's vision for government reform is guided by three principles. Government should be:

— Citizen-centered, not bureaucracy-centered;

— Results-oriented;

— Market-based, actively promoting rather than stifling innovation through competition.

The President has called for a government that is active but limited, that focuses on priorities and does them well. That same spirit should be brought to the work of reform. Rather than pursue an array of management initiatives, we have elected to identify the government's most glaring problems—and solve them. The President's Management Agenda is a starting point for management reform.

- The Agenda contains five government-wide and nine agency-specific goals to improve federal management and deliver results that matter to the American people.

- It reflects the Administration's commitment to achieve immediate, concrete, and measurable results in the near term.

- It focuses on remedies to problems generally agreed to be serious, and commits to implement them fully.

- The goals in this Agenda are being undertaken *in advance of*, not *instead of* other needed management improvements.

- Additional goals will be undertaken, as tangible improvements are made in this initial set of initiatives.

A COHERENT AND COORDINATED PLAN

The five government-wide goals are mutually reinforcing. For example,

- Workforce planning and restructuring undertaken as part of *Strategic Management of Human Capital* will be defined in terms of each agency's mission, goals, and objectives—a key element of *Budget and Performance Integration*.

- Agency restructuring is expected to incorporate organizational and staffing changes resulting from *Competitive Sourcing and Expanded E-government*.

- Likewise, efforts toward *Budget and Performance Integration* will reflect improved program performance and savings achieved from *Competitive Sourcing* and will benefit from financial and cost accounting and information systems which are part of efforts in *Improved Financial Management*.

IMPLEMENTING THE PLAN

The President has not only set an initial agenda, but is already implementing this plan.

- In July, the President directed Cabinet Secretaries and agency heads to designate a "chief operating officer" to have responsibility for day-to-day operations of departments and agencies.

- At the same time, the President re-established the President's Management Council (PMC) consisting of the chief operating officers. The PMC provides an integrating mechanism for policy implementation within agencies and across government. Importantly, the PMC is a way for the departments and agencies to support the President's government-wide priorities and to build a community of management leadership that learns, solves problems, and innovates together.

> Typically the department's No. 2 official, its "chief operating officer," has agency-wide authority and reports directly to the agency head. This assignment places "management" with Presidential appointed officials, primarily at the deputy secretary level, where policy and management meet.

- First results have already been achieved in several reform categories. See *Competitive Sourcing, Privatization of Military Housing,* and *Elimination of Fraud and Error in Student Aid Programs and Deficiencies in Financial Management* for examples.

FREEDOM TO MANAGE

Federal managers are greatly limited in how they can use available financial and human resources to manage programs; they lack much of the discretion given to their private sector counterparts to do what it takes to get the job done. Red tape still hinders the efficient operation of government organizations; excessive control and approval mechanisms afflict bureaucratic processes. Micro-management from various sources—Congressional, departmental, and bureau—imposes unnecessary operational rigidity.

The Administration will sponsor a three-part Freedom to Manage initiative to clear statutory impediments to efficient management:

- *Statutory cleanup.* As part of the 2003 budget process, OMB has asked departments and agencies to identify statutory impediments to good management. Agencies are reviewing government-wide statutory provisions which, if repealed, would remove barriers to efficient management.

- *Fast-track authority.* We will propose legislation to establish a procedure under which heads of departments and agencies could identify structural barriers imposed by law, and Congress would quickly and decisively consider and act to remove those obstacles.

- *Managerial flexibility and authority.* OMB will package affirmative legislation comprising proposals to free managers in areas such as personnel, budgeting, and property disposal.

> - For years NASA was expressly prohibited by statute from relocating aircraft based east of the Mississippi River to the Dryden Flight Research Center in California for the purpose of the consolidation of such aircraft.
>
> - The 2001 Defense Appropriations Act requires the U.S. military installations in Kaiserslauten, Germany to use U.S. coal as their energy source for heat. The same provision allows U.S. bases at Landstuhl and Ramstein to acquire their heat energy from any source, but they must consider U.S. coal as an energy source in making their selection. The provision restricts use of the most economical energy source and imposes higher costs on the Defense Department as a result.
>
> - The Department of Agriculture is prohibited by statute from closing or relocating a state Rural Development Office.

As the barriers to more efficient management are removed, we will expect higher performance. With Freedom to Manage will come clear expectations of improved performance and accountability.

A SHARED RESPONSIBILITY

All too often Congress is a part of the government's managerial problems. Many members find it more rewarding to announce a new program rather than to fix (or terminate) an existing one that is failing. The Congressional practice of "earmarking" special projects in appropriations bills has exploded—growing more than six-fold in the last four years. Excessive earmarks lead to wasteful spending and hogtie executive decision-making, making it more difficult for agencies to fund higher priorities and accomplish larger goals as needed funds are diverted.

The President has made solving these problems a top priority. Congress can help in a number of important ways, among them:

- actively supporting government management reforms;
- using its oversight powers to insist that agencies fix their problems;
- providing the investments and the tools necessary;
- helping agencies remove barriers to change; and
- not placing limitations on reform efforts.

THE EXPECTED LONG-TERM RESULTS

The impetus for government reform comes, in part, as a reaction to chronic poor performance and continuing disclosure of intolerable waste. Agencies will take a disciplined and focused approach to address these long-standing and substantial challenges and begin the steps necessary to become high performing organizations in which:

- hierarchical, "command and control" bureaucracies will become flatter and more responsive;

- emphasis on process will be replaced by a focus on results;

- organizations burdened with overlapping functions, inefficiencies, and turf battles will function more harmoniously; and

- agencies will strengthen and make the most of the knowledge, skills, and abilities of their people; in order to meet the needs and expectations of their ultimate clients—the American people.

A MANAGEABLE GOVERNMENT

The most difficult, but most important, job of a good leader is to ask tough questions about the institution: Is this program needed? Is it a wise use of the organization's finite resources? Could those resources be used better elsewhere? These are questions that the structure and incentives of government do not encourage. We need to:

- *Shift the burden of proof.* Today, those who propose to shift priorities or adjust funding levels are expected to demonstrate that a program or activity should be changed. It is time, instead, that program proponents bear the burden of proof to demonstrate that the programs they advocate actually accomplish their goals, and do so better than alternative ways of spending the same money.

- *Focus on the "base" not the "increment."* Policy and budget debates focus on the marginal increase (or cut) in a program—failing to look at whether the program as a whole (the base) is working or achieving anything worthwhile. We need to reverse the presumption that this year's funding level is the starting point for considering next year's funding level.

- *Focus on results.* A mere desire to address a problem is not a sufficient justification for spending the public's money. Performance-based budgeting would mean that money would be allocated not just on the basis of perceived needs, but also on the basis of what is actually being accomplished.

- *Impose consequences.* Underperforming agencies are sometimes given incentives to improve, but rarely face consequences for persistent failure. This all-carrot-no-stick approach is unlikely to elicit improvement from troubled organizations. Instead, we should identify mismanaged, wasteful or duplicative government programs, with an eye to cutting their funding, redesigning them, or eliminating them altogether.

- *Demand evidence.* Many agencies and programs lack rigorous data or evaluations to show that they work. Such evidence should be a prerequisite to continued funding.

Over the past three decades, reform initiatives have come and gone. Some genuine improvements have been made. But the record on the whole has been a disappointing one. That must change—and this report is a primer on how that change can be achieved.

GOVERNMENT-WIDE INITIATIVES

1. Strategic Management of Human Capital

> *"We must have a Government that thinks differently, so we need to recruit talented and imaginative people to public service. We can do this by reforming the civil service with a few simple measures. We'll establish a meaningful system to measure performance. Create awards for employees who surpass expectations. Tie pay increases to results. With a system of rewards and accountability, we can promote a culture of achievement throughout the Federal Government."*
>
> Governor George W. Bush

THE PROBLEM

- The federal government has reduced its workforce by 324,580 full-time equivalent employees since 1993, with most of these reductions coming from the Department of Defense. At 1.8 million employees, the federal civilian payroll has been reduced to its lowest level since 1950. The bad news is that this downsizing was accomplished through across-the-board staff reductions and hiring freezes, rather than targeted reductions aligned with agency missions. A consequence is that the average age of the federal workforce has risen to 46 years, compared to 42 in 1990. And even as the workforce shrinks, the number of layers of hierarchy continues to increase, especially near the top. The paradoxical result: a workforce with steadily increasing numbers of supervisors and steadily declining accountability—a workforce that feels more and more overworked at the same time as its skills move further and further out of balance with the needs of the public it serves.

  > Much of the downsizing was set in motion without sufficient planning for its effects on agencies' performance capacity. Across government, federal employers reduced or froze their hiring efforts for extended periods of time. This helped reduce their number of employees, but it also reduced the influx of people with new knowledge, new energy, and new ideas-the reservoir of future agency leaders and managers (GAO Report 01-263, 2000).

  > According to OPM, using the initiation of the improvement period as "notification" of poor performance, and assuming an average improvement period of three to four months plus a 30-day advance notice period, the time from notification to dismissal is about five to six months.

- The managerial revolution that has transformed the culture of almost every other large institution in American life seems to have bypassed the federal workforce. Federal personnel policies and compensation tend to take the same "one-size-fits-all" approach they took in 1945. Excellence goes unrewarded; mediocre performance carries few consequences; and it takes months to remove even the poorest performers. Federal pay systems do not reflect current labor market realities: under current law, the entire General Schedule that covers almost every kind of white-collar occupation must be adjusted by a single percentage in each of the 32 localities in the contiguous 48 states.

- In most agencies, human resources planning is weak. Workforce deficiencies will be exacerbated by the upcoming retirement wave of the baby-boom generation. Approximately 71 percent of the government's current permanent employees will be eligible for either regular or early retirement by 2010, and then 40 percent of those employees are expected to retire. Without proper planning, the skill mix of the federal workforce will not reflect tomorrow's changing missions.

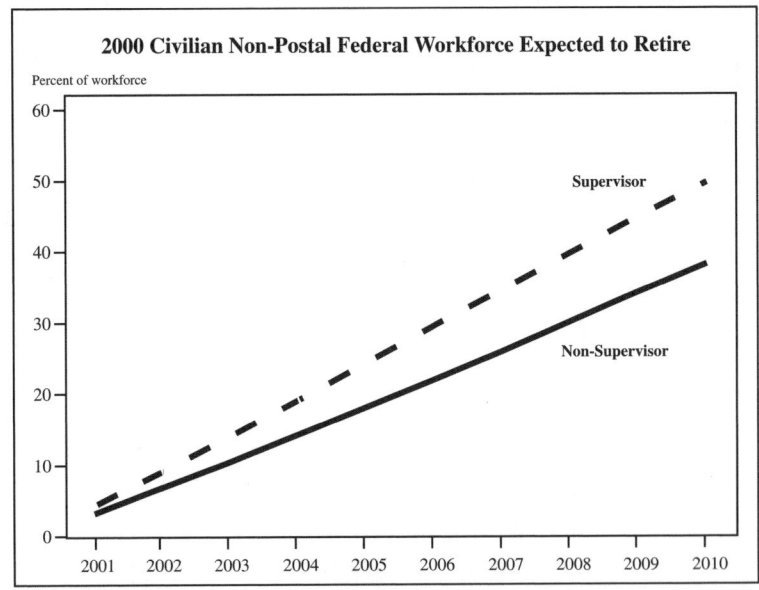

- A survey of nearly 2,000 new employees by the Merit Systems Protection Board (MSPB) revealed that they encountered numerous problems during their job search. For example, 47 percent were not aware that federal job vacancies are posted on the Internet; 14 percent did not think that job announcements provided enough information to decide if they were interested in the position; and 25 percent did not think that hiring decisions were made within a reasonable period of time (MSPB, 2000).

- In February 2001, GAO added human capital management to the government-wide "high-risk list" of federal activities. Inspectors General at nine major federal agencies have listed workforce problems among the top 10 most serious management challenges that their agencies face.

- These realities contribute to the growing consensus that action is required. The federal government has a unique opportunity to redefine the way it manages human capital.

> The Energy Department's staff lack project and contract management skills required to oversee large projects, such as the cleanup of radioactive and hazardous waste sites.
>
> Downsizing at NASA over the last decade through attrition and buyouts has resulted in an imbalance in NASA's skill mix. Through a series of workforce reviews, NASA has identified these imbalances and developed a plan to meet future needs. NASA received extended buyout authority last year to specifically address skill mix imbalances by allowing targeted buyouts in skill areas that exceeded needs, then hiring an equal number in skill areas that needed strengthening for the future.
>
> In a November 1999 report, the Overseas Presence Advisory Panel concluded that the State Department needed to reform its human resource practices because it did not have the flexibility, tools, or strategic organization required to support its mission.

THE INITIATIVE

- The first priority of the President's management reform initiative is to make government citizen-centered. The number of layers in government must be compressed to reduce the distance between citizens and decision-makers, and agencies should redistribute their alloted staff from higher-level positions to front-line service-delivery. Each agency has been asked to prepare a five-year restructuring plan as part of its 2003 budget request, based upon a workforce analysis, to accomplish this important goal.

- Agencies will reshape their organizations to meet a standard of excellence in attaining the outcomes important to the nation. Each agency will identify how it will reduce the number of managers, reduce the number of organizational layers, reduce the time it takes to make decisions, change the span of control, and increase the number of employees who provide services to citizens.

- The Administration will adopt information technology systems to capture some of the knowledge and skills of retiring employees. Knowledge management systems are just one part of an effective strategy that will help generate, capture, and disseminate knowledge and information that is relevant to the organization's mission.

- While the Administration will be seeking some targeted civil service reforms, agencies must make better use of the flexibilities currently in place to acquire and develop talent and leadership. Such authorities are largely underutilized across the federal sector because many agencies are unaware of the existence of such flexibilities. The Administration will assess agencies' use of existing authorities as well as the outcomes achieved under demonstration projects. This assessment will help us determine what statutory changes are needed to enhance management flexibility, permit more performance-oriented compensation, correct skills imbalances, and provide other tools to recruit, retain, and reward a high-quality workforce.

THE EXPECTED NEAR-TERM RESULTS

- Human capital strategies will be linked to organizational mission, vision, core values, goals, and objectives.

- Agencies will use strategic workforce planning and flexible tools to recruit, retrain, and reward employees and develop a high-performing workforce.

> The State Department implemented a recruitment strategy for certain information technology workers using existing pay flexibilities. It pays retention allowances ranging from 5 to 15 percent of an employee's base salary to certain information technology workers who obtain job-related degrees and certificates. After one year of operation, this program has helped to significantly reduce turnover and increase the skills base of State's information technology workforce (GAO Report 01–565T).

- Agencies will determine their "core competencies" and decide whether to build internal capacity, or contract for services from the private sector. This will maximize agencies' flexibility in getting the job done effectively and efficiently.

- The statutory framework will be in place to make it easier to attract and retain the right people, in the right places, at the right time.

> The Bureau of the Census has used technology to significantly reduce hiring time. The agency has an electronic hiring system that provides managers with desk-top, web-based access to an electronic applicant tracking feature that allows managers to see images of applicant resumes and transcripts within twenty-four hours of receipt. The system has helped the Census Bureau reduce the time required to fill computer specialists, statisticians, and mathematical statistician positions from six months to as little as three days. Since September 1998, the agency has filled 1,000 vacancies using this process (GAO Report 01–357T, 2001).

THE EXPECTED LONG-TERM RESULTS

- Citizens will recognize improved service and performance and citizen satisfaction will increase.

- Agencies will build, sustain, and effectively deploy the skilled, knowledgeable, diverse, and high-performing workforce needed to meet the current and emerging needs of government and its citizens.

- The workforce will adapt quickly in size, composition, and competencies to accommodate changes in mission, technology, and labor markets.

- Government employee satisfaction will increase.

- High performance will become a way of life that defines the culture of the federal service.
  - The system will attract and retain talented people who will demand and deliver sustained excellence and high levels of performance.
  - The civil service will use clear and carefully aligned performance incentives for individual employees, for teams, and for its leadership. In turn, these incentives will be tied clearly to reaching their agency's mission objectives.
  - Agencies will meet and exceed established productivity and performance goals.
  - Accountability for results will be clear and meaningful, with positive rewards for success and real consequences for failure.

2. Competitive Sourcing

> *"Government should be market-based—we should not be afraid of competition, innovation, and choice. I will open government to the discipline of competition."*
>
> Governor George W. Bush

THE PROBLEM

- Nearly half of all federal employees perform tasks that are readily available in the commercial marketplace—tasks like data collection, administrative support, and payroll services. Historically, the government has realized cost savings in a range of 20 to 50 percent when federal and private sector service providers compete to perform these functions. Unfortunately, competition between public and private sources remains an unfulfilled management promise. By rarely subjecting commercial tasks performed by the government to competition, agencies have insulated themselves from the pressures that produce quality service at reasonable cost.

- Because agencies do not maintain adequate records on work performed in-house, they have often taken three to four years to define the jobs being considered for competition.

- To compare the cost of in-house performance to private sector performance, detailed estimates of the full cost of government performance to the taxpayer have to be calculated. The development of these estimates has devolved into a contentious and rigid exercise in precision.

THE INITIATIVES

To achieve efficient and effective competition between public and private sources, the Administration has committed itself to simplifying and improving the procedures for evaluating public and private sources, to better publicizing the activities subject to competition, and to ensuring senior level agency attention to the promotion of competition.

- In accordance with the Federal Activities Inventory Reform (FAIR) Act, agencies are assessing the susceptibility to competition of the activities their workforces are performing. After review by OMB, the agencies will provide their inventories to Congress and make them available to the public. Interested parties may challenge the omission or inclusion of any particular activity.

- Agencies are developing specific performance plans to meet the 2002 goal of completing public-private or direct conversion competition on not less than five percent of the full-time equivalent employees listed on the FAIR Act inventories. The performance target will increase by 10 percent in 2003.

- The Administration will adopt procedures to improve and expand competition. As a first step, OMB has proposed that reimbursable (fee-for-service) work involving performance by a federal agency be recompeted every three to five years, similar to standard contract review, renewal, or solicitation procedures.

- The Administration will seek to implement findings of the Commercial Activities Panel, a commission created by Congress to examine the policies and procedures governing public-private competition.

- Finally, the Administration is pursuing administrative and legislative actions to incorporate the full costs of agency work into the daily budget and acquisition process. This will eliminate the complex, after-the-fact calculation of public-sector costs.

THE EXPECTED RESULTS

Increased competition consistently generates significant savings and noticeable performance improvements.

- Recent competitions under OMB Circular A–76[1] have resulted in savings of more than 20 percent for work that stays in-house and more than 30 percent for work outsourced to the private sector.

- From 1995 through 2000, the Department of Defense completed over 550 A-76 initiatives, which resulted in an average 34 percent reduction in cost. DoD expects to achieve $11.7 billion in savings as a result of A-76 competition between 1997 and 2005.

- Numerous studies conducted by the GAO, the Center for Naval Analyses, and others confirm the magnitude of these savings.

- Competition promotes innovation, efficiency, and greater effectiveness. For many activities, citizens do not care whether the private or public sector provides the service or administers the program. The process of competition provides an imperative for the public sector to focus on continuous improvement and removing roadblocks to greater efficiency.

- By focusing on desired results and outcomes, the objective becomes identifying the most efficient means to accomplish the task.

---

[1] Public-private competition is governed by OMB Circular A–76. The Circular establishes federal policy for determining whether commercial activities should be provided through contract with commercial sources, use of in-house government personnel, or through interservice support agreements with other federal agencies.

3. Improved Financial Performance

> *"Without accountability, how can we ever expect results? Under my Administration, we will bring this cycle of failure to an abrupt end. As President, I will hold all affected agencies accountable for passing their audits not later than 2002. I will say to those I put in place, get your audits right."*
>
> Governor George W. Bush

THE PROBLEM

- Federal agencies recently identified $20.7 billion in erroneous benefit and assistance payments associated with just 13 programs. That amount represents more than the total annual expenditures of seven states.

- Examples of erroneous payments:

    — The Medicare Fee-for-Service Program had estimated erroneous payments of $11.9 billion (6.8 percent) in 2000. Erroneous payments included payments for medically unnecessary services, unsupported claims/services, and miscoded claims.

    — The Department of Agriculture estimates $976 million in food stamp overissuances, and $360 million in underissuances, for a total of $1.34 billion in erroneous payments, representing a total error rate of approximately 8.9 percent in 2000.

    — Regional Veterans Benefits Administration offices made erroneous initial VA benefit decisions 32 percent of the time in 1999.

    — In 2000, the IRS reported that $7.8 billion in unrecovered Earned Income Tax Credit claims were erroneously paid to taxpayers for tax year 1997.

> *"It takes the Federal Government 5 months to close our books...This is not the stuff of excellence."*
>
> Paul H. O'Neill, Secretary of the Treasury

> "...accurate and timely information to manage your financial program activities on a day-to-day basis are part of a core value set that world-class organizations have adopted."
>
> Paul H. O'Neill, Secretary of the Treasury

- A clean financial audit is a basic prescription for any well-managed organization, yet the federal government has failed all four audits since 1997. Moreover, most federal agencies that obtain clean audits only do so after making extraordinary, labor-intensive assaults on financial records.

- Without accurate and timely financial information, it is not possible to accomplish the President's agenda to secure the best performance and highest measure of accountability for the American people.

THE INITIATIVE

- The Administration will first establish a baseline of the extent of erroneous payments. Agencies will include in 2003 budget submissions information on erroneous payment rates, including actual and target rates, where available, for benefit and assistance programs over $2 billion. Using this information, OMB will work with agencies to establish goals to reduce erroneous payments for each program.

- To ensure that federal financial systems produce accurate and timely information to support operating, budget, and policy decisions, OMB will work with agencies to:

    — Improve timeliness by:
    - re-engineering reporting processes and expanding use of web-based technologies;
    - instituting quarterly financial statements;
    - accelerating end-of-year reporting; and
    - measuring systems compliance with agencies' ability to meet OMB and Treasury requirements accurately and timely.

    — Enhance usefulness by:
    - requiring comparative financial reporting;
    - reporting specific financial performance measurements; and
    - integrating financial and performance information.

    — Ensure reliability by obtaining and sustaining clean audit opinions for:
    - components of agencies;
    - agencies; and
    - the government as a whole.

— We will make changes to the budget process that will allow us to better measure the real cost and performance of programs.

THE EXPECTED RESULTS

- More accurate benefit and assistance payments to current recipients will enable programs to serve additional eligible recipients without increasing their budgets and will reduce program costs. For example:
    - Reducing erroneous payments in federal housing programs will result in being able to provide housing subsidies to currently eligible people who are not being served due to limited funding.
    - Reducing erroneous payments in entitlement programs, such as Food Stamps or Social Security, will decrease the cost of these programs to the American taxpayer. As an indication, with heightened scrutiny, the estimated erroneous payment rate for the Medicare program was reduced from 14 percent in 1996 to 6.8 percent in 2000.
    - Preliminary data from test matches between the Departments of Education and the Treasury suggest that the Pell Grant program is making over-awards of up to $400 million each year because students or their parents do not report their income accurately on their student aid applications. If those erroneous overpayments were eliminated, the savings could be used to increase the maximum Pell Grant award by up to $100, providing more grant assistance to low-income students to help them afford college.
- Improved accountability to the American people through audited financial reports.
    - Financial systems that routinely produce information that is:
        - timely, to measure and effect performance immediately;
        - useful, to make more informed operational and investing decisions; and
        - reliable, to ensure consistent and comparable trend analysis over time and to facilitate better performance measurement and decision making.

4. Expanded Electronic Government

> "I will expand the use of the Internet to empower citizens, allowing them to request customized information from Washington when they need it, not just when Washington wants to give it to them. True reform involves not just giving people information, but giving citizens the freedom to act upon it."
>
> Governor George W. Bush

The federal government can secure greater services at lower cost through electronic government (E-government), and can meet high public demand for E-government services. This administration's goal is to champion citizen-centered electronic government that will result in a major improvement in the federal government's value to the citizen.

THE PROBLEM

The federal government is the world's largest single consumer of information technology (IT). IT has contributed 40 percent of the increase in private-sector productivity growth, but the $45 billion the U.S. government will spend on IT in 2002 has not produced measurable gains in public-sector worker productivity. At least four major causes for this failure can be discerned.

- Agencies typically evaluate their IT systems according to how well they serve the agency's needs—not the citizens' needs. Systems will often be evaluated by the percentage of time they are working rather than the performance gain they deliver to the programs they support. In general, agencies do not evaluate their IT systems by standards relevant to the work the agency is supposed to do.

- Just as private-sector companies in the 1980s tended to use computers merely as souped-up typewriters and calculators, so government agencies in the 1990s have used IT to automate pre-existing processes rather than create new and more efficient solutions.

- IT offers opportunities to break down obsolete bureaucratic divisions. Unfortunately, agencies often perceive this opportunity as a threat and instead make wasteful and redundant investments in order to preserve chains of command that lost their purpose years ago. Financial systems are often automated separately from procurement systems, which are in turn carefully segregated from human resources systems, significantly increasing costs and minimizing potential savings. Likewise, with rare exceptions—the Department of Defense's Finance and Accounting System being one—agencies shun opportunities to work together to consolidate functions like payroll.

Many agencies do not take care to ensure that their IT systems can communicate with one another. The Department of Veterans Affairs (VA), for example, built a new online form for veterans in one office and then discovered they had to print out the information and mail it to another office of VA because the two systems were not interoperable. VA is now devoted to interoperability—but not all agencies are as zealous.

THE INITIATIVES

The Administration will advance E-government strategy by supporting projects that offer performance gains across agency boundaries, such as e-procurement, e-grants, e-regulation, and e-signatures. It will manage E-government projects more effectively by using the budget process to insist on more effective planning of IT investments by government agencies. A task force of agency personnel in coordination with OMB and the President's Management Council will identify E-government projects that can deliver significant productivity and performance gains across government. The task force will also identify the systematic barriers that have blocked the deployment of E-government advances. The task force will work to:

- Create easy-to-find single points of access to government services for individuals.

- Reduce the reporting burden on businesses—businesses should not have to file the same information over and over because government fails to reuse the data appropriately or fails to take advantage of commercial electronic transaction protocols.

- Share information more quickly and conveniently between the federal and state, local, and tribal governments. We must also do a better job of collaborating with foreign governments and institutions.

- Automate internal processes to reduce costs internally, within the federal government, by disseminating best practices across agencies.

To support the task force's work, OMB will scrutinize federal IT investments to ensure that they maximize interoperability and minimize redundancy. The President's Budget proposes a $20 million E-government fund for 2002 ($100 million over the three years 2002 through 2004) to pay for collaborative E-government activities across agency lines.

The Administration will also improve the federal government's use of the Web.

- It will expand and improve the FirstGov *(www.FirstGov.gov)* web site to offer citizens a convenient entry to government services. OMB will engage the agencies and state and local governments in this venture, to help citizens find information and obtain services organized according to their needs, and not according to the divisions created by the government's organizational chart.

- Agencies will undertake a Federal Public Key Infrastructure (PKI) to promote digital signatures for transactions within the federal government, between government and businesses and between government and citizens. The digital signature initiative should be coordinated with state and local governments as well as the private sector.

- By the end of 2002, all agencies will use a single e-procurement portal, *www.FedBizOpps.gov,* to provide access to notices of solicitations over $25,000. A fully operational government-wide entry point on the Internet represents a first step in capitalizing on electronic business processes and making e-procurement the government-wide standard. The next step: agencies will make use of the single portal to consolidate procurement on the way to the broader E-government goal of supply chain management.

- Agencies will allow applicants for federal grants to apply for and ultimately manage grant funds online through a common web site, simplifying grant management and eliminating redundancies in the same way as the single procurement portal will simplify purchasing.

- Major regulatory agencies will use the Web to inform citizens of the cases before them, allow access to the development of rules, and make more transparent the decisions they make, as the Department of Transportation already does through its Docket Management System.

THE EXPECTED RESULTS

The E-government initiative will make it simpler for citizens to receive high-quality service from the federal government, while reducing the cost of delivering those services. The PKI effort will ensure that electronic transactions with and within government are private and secure. The e-procurement and grant-management portals will make transactions with the government—or obtaining financial assistance from the government—easier, cheaper, quicker and more comprehensible. The work on supply chain management will enable agencies to eliminate redundant processes and save resources. And putting the federal regulatory process on-line will offer citizens easier access to some of the most important policy decisions: better informing the citizenry and holding government more effectively to account. In short, by improving information-technology management, simplifying business processes, and unifying information flows across lines of business agencies will:

- provide high quality customer service regardless of whether the citizen contacts the agency by phone, in person, or on the Web;

- reduce the expense and difficulty of doing business with the government;

- cut government operating costs;

- provide citizens with readier access to government services;

- increase access for persons with disabilities to agency web sites and E-government applications; and

- make government more transparent and accountable.

5. Budget and Performance Integration

> *"Government should be results-oriented - guided not by process but guided by performance. There comes a time when every program must be judged either a success or a failure. Where we find success, we should repeat it, share it, and make it the standard. And where we find failure, we must call it by its name. Government action that fails in its purpose must be reformed or ended."*
>
> Governor George W. Bush

THE PROBLEM

- Improvements in the management of human capital, competitive sourcing, improved financial performance, and expanding electronic government will matter little if they are not linked to better results.

- Everyone agrees that scarce federal resources should be allocated to programs and managers that deliver results. Yet in practice, this is seldom done because agencies rarely offer convincing accounts of the results their allocations will purchase. There is little reward, in budgets or in compensation, for running programs efficiently. And once money is allocated to a program, there is no requirement to revisit the question of whether the results obtained are solving problems the American people care about.

> In May 2001, the General Accounting Office reported that the majority of federal managers are largely ignoring performance information when allocating resources. In only six federal agencies did 51 percent or more of the managers indicate they used this information to a great or very great extent in resource allocation. Of the 28 agencies covered in the survey, fewer than 40 percent of the managers in 11 agencies said they used the information in this manner, and in one agency, only 24 percent of the managers did so.

- In 1993, Congress enacted the Government Performance and Results Act (GPRA) to get the federal government to focus federal programs on performance. After eight years of experience, progress toward the use of performance information for program management has been discouraging. According to a General Accounting Office (GAO) survey of federal managers, agencies may, in fact, be losing ground in their efforts to building organizational cultures that support a focus on results.

- Agency performance measures tend to be ill defined and not properly integrated into agency budget submissions and the management and operation of agencies. Performance measures are insufficiently used to monitor and reward staff, or to hold program managers accountable.

- The single goal for Department of Defense (DoD) procurement is the percentage of procurement funds requested and appropriated by Congress compared to DoD identified needs. This is a measure of inputs and lobbying success, but talks nothing about results achieved.

- The U.S. Fire Administration exists to reduce the loss of life from fire-related incidents. One of the performance indicators used is the quantity of information to constituents and to those who can have a positive impact of targeted populations. This is a description of activity and an input measure.

- The Health Resources and Services Administration provides grants to increase the number of primary care providers, encourage better distribution of health professionals, and increase the number of minorities in the health professions. Program performance has been measured not by the number or distribution of health care professionals, but rather by the number of grants made to academic institutions, hospitals or students.

Managers responsible for producing public services often do not have control over the resources they use or flexibility to use them efficiently; authority is not aligned with accountability. In the GAO survey cited above, in 22 agencies more than half the managers reported they were held accountable for the results of their programs. But only in one agency did more than half the managers report that they had the decision making authority to help the agency accomplish its goals to the same extent.

- Managers do not have timely and complete information with which to monitor and improve their results. Information is collected and filed away for use "somewhere else."

> About the time GPRA was signed into law, President Clinton requested information on the impact of a proposed increase in funding for a children's program. Neither the agency nor OMB was able to calculate this impact.

- The structure of the federal budget makes it impossible to identify the full cost associated with individual programs. Because the budget does not identify full cost, competition for services has been forced to substitute a separate process governed by complex, artificial rules for cost measurement—and this, in turn, has acted as a barrier to competition and a source of constant confusion.

- The American people should be able to see how government programs are performing and compare performance and cost across programs. The lack of a consistent information and reporting framework for performance, budgeting, and accounting obscures this necessary transparency.

> In the mid-1990's, the government could not determine the environmental changes that had resulted from the spending of billions of dollars in federal monies over two decades.

- Public Housing Drug Elimination Program: This program has shown little or no impact on drug activity, is less effective than other approaches in reducing drug traffic, and goes beyond the Department of Housing and Urban Development's (HUD's) core mission by adding a law enforcement role.

- Amtrak is a private company that receives substantial government funding to provide national passenger rail service throughout the country. Amtrak's precarious financial state is well-known; the corporation holds over $3 billion in debt, has never made a profit in its 30 year history, and has extensive long-term capital needs. Many analysts and oversight agencies predict that it will not meet the statutory deadline of December 2002 to be operationally self-sufficient.

- The Department of Labor's (DOL's) current process for certifying foreign workers as eligible for permanent employment in the United States is duplicative, labor-intensive, and unnecessarily complex. It can take up to six years for DOL to complete the certification process that allows the immigrant to petition for a work-based visa.

THE INITIATIVE

- To provide a greater focus on performance, the Administration plans to formally integrate performance review with budget decisions. This integration is designed to begin to produce performance-based budgets starting with the 2003 Budget submission.

- Initially, OMB will work with agencies to select objectives for a few important programs, assess what programs do to achieve these objectives, how much that costs, and how effectiveness could be improved.

- Over time, agencies will be expected to identify high quality outcome measures, accurately monitor the performance of programs, and begin integrating this presentation with associated cost. Using this information, high performing programs will be reinforced and non-performing activities reformed or terminated.

- The Administration is also transmitting legislative changes that will make budgeting and management in the Executive Branch more performance-oriented and improve accountability. The Administration will propose a bill to fully fund employee retirement benefits, taking a step toward simplifying the rules for opening government support services to more competition by substituting a budgetary cost measure for the current complex cost comparison. A second bill will align other costs with results, and provide a framework for a more transparent budget presentation.

- Ultimately, the Administration will attempt to integrate more completely information about costs and programs performance in a single oversight process. This would include budgeting for the full cost of resources where they are used, making budget program and activity lines more parallel with outputs, and, where useful, improving alignment of budget accounts.

THE EXPECTED NEAR-TERM RESULTS

- Starting in 2003, the President's Budget will shift budgetary resources among programs devoted to similar goals to emphasize those that are more effective.

- In the 2003 Budget, the Administration will set performance targets for selected programs along with funding levels.

- In the 2003 Budget, agencies and programs will budget for the full costs of retirement and health care programs that are currently budgeted centrally.

- The 2003 Budget will present to the American people the objectives the Administration seeks to achieve in the coming year and provide better information on the linkage between objectives and the matching cost.

THE EXPECTED LONG-TERM RESULTS

- Better performance, based on an assessment of the expected outcomes relative to what is actually being achieved, including results expected from the President's electronic government initiative.

- Better control over resources used and accountability for results by program managers. This is consistent with the President's strategic management of the human capital initiative, which increases staff and responsibility at the "front line" of service delivery and links rewards to performance.

- Better service as a result of more competition based on full costing of resources used by working capital funds and other support service providers, and a simpler competitive process consistent with the President's competitive sourcing initiative.

- Standard, integrated budgeting, performance, and accounting information systems at the program level that would provide timely feedback for management and could be uploaded and consolidated at the agency and government levels. This would facilitate the goals of the President's initiative to improve financial performance.

- Eventual integration of existing segregated and burdensome paperwork requirements for measuring the government's performance and competitive practices with budget reporting.

PROGRAM INITIATIVES

Program Initiatives

In addition to the five government-wide management initiatives, this Report presents nine agency-specific reforms. While there is a long list of critical management and performance problems facing agencies of the federal government, we have chosen these to begin the effort, based on several criteria:

- severity of the problem and the importance of the problem to those served;
- direct and demonstrable benefit to citizens;
- opportunity to make a dramatic and material difference in program performance; and
- probability of achieving improvements in the near term.

As stated in the introduction, this is the beginning of a comprehensive effort, and these reforms will provide significant improvements. As we begin to see the results, we will focus our attention on additional reform opportunities.

CHAPTER 4
Merging the Balanced Scorecard and the PMA

The balanced scorecard moved industry from a sole focus on financial results to a broader, more effective focus on financial results, the customer, learning and growth, and internal business. This change has different ramifications and nuances in the private sector than it does in the federal government. Now President Bush has presented the PMA, which provides a much broader focus on what needs to be achieved to be an effective federal manager. In adopting a government-wide focus, the President has highlighted several keys areas.

Strategic management of human capital provides several inputs to the balanced scorecard of any federal organization. First, human capital strategies need to be linked to the organization's mission, vision, core values, goals, and objectives. Next, federal organizations need to develop high-performing workforces. They also need to determine whether to build internal capacity or to contract for capability from the private sector. Expected long-term results include citizens recognizing improved service and customer satisfaction increasing. Government employee satisfaction is also expected to increase.

Competitive sourcing will require that government agencies develop specific performance plans to meet ever-increasing goals of completing public-private or direct conversion competition for not less than 5 percent of full-time equivalent employees in 2002 and not less than 10 percent in 2003. Expected results are significant savings and noticeable performance improvements. The objective is to identify the most efficient means to accomplish the task assigned.

Improved financial performance will be achieved through a number of initiatives. A baseline of erroneous payments will be established and goals will then be set to show long-term progress. Emphasis will be placed on federal financial systems producing accurate and timely information by improving timeliness, enhancing usefulness, and ensuring reliability. Expected results include reducing erroneous payments and ensuring more timely, useful, and reliable financial reporting from the federal government.

Expanded electronic government will allow the federal government to provide greater levels of service at lower cost. Expected results include higher quality customer service, a reduction in the expense and difficulty citizens experience dealing with the federal government, and a reduction in government operating costs.

The last major government-wide initiative may be the most critical and difficult to achieve. The budget and performance integration initiative is intended to provide a greater focus on performance. By formally integrating a performance review with budget decisions, performance-based budgets should be used starting in 2003. The expected long-term results include better performance of the federal government, better control over resources used, and accountability for results by program managers.

These five government-wide initiatives give every federal organization a variety of possibilities to use in developing a balanced scorecard. Depending on the mission, vision, and structure of each federal organization, the PMA provides many broad management initiatives.

For those federal agencies that are involved with the nine program initiatives in the PMA, there is even more input for the balanced scorecard for their agencies. All in all, the PMA is a welcome focus for important areas that are going to be measured over the long term and dealt with in the budget process. Mission—not budgets—should drive federal organizations. The intent is that the PMA will be successful in supporting this concept and facilitating its implementation.

CHAPTER 5

The PMA and the FY 2004 Budget

Major thrusts of the FY 2004 budget are (1) governing with accountability and (2) assessing program performance. These are explored in detail on the Office of Management and Budget website, www.OMB.gov.

GOVERNING WITH ACCOUNTABILITY

We want to make sure when we spend money, that it meets needs. . . . that's what the American taxpayer expects. They expect results and I expect results.

President George W. Bush
April 9, 2002

Government-wide Initiatives on the President's Management Agenda

- Strategic Management of Human Capital
- Competitive Sourcing
- Improved Financial Performance
- Expanded Electronic Government
- Budget and Performance Integration

With that plain spoken appeal, President Bush conveyed to his appointed leaders that he had chosen them not to mark time but to achieve real change. His call demands measurable results that matter in the lives of the American people.

This mandate gave birth to the President's Management Agenda, launched in August 2001. As the President has said, the five main challenges he selected represent "the most apparent deficiencies where the opportunity to improve is greatest." The Administration harbors no illusions that leaps forward will come easily. Constant effort must be made to find ways to save and stretch taxpayer dollars, many through small improvements. Breakthrough gains may come only after years of dedicated, even tedious, effort.

Because facing such challenges requires sustained effort, the President's Management Agenda tracks agencies' status against established Standards for Success as well as their progress toward meeting the standards. Status and progress are rated using the familiar symbols of red, yellow, and green. Grades are reported on the Executive Branch Scorecard at the end of this chapter.

Since the scorecard's unveiling in the 2003 Budget a year ago, 26 federal departments and agencies have been working to upgrade their ratings in those areas most in need of improvement. The good news is that signs of progress outnumber distress signals, as 11 departments or agencies show 17 changes for the better, while two agencies slipped in the management of their finances.

Although effort and management attention have been strong at virtually every agency, progress has been uneven.

The Administration will follow closely how and whether agencies put their plans into effect. When shortfalls in results become apparent, we will take corrective action.

Explanation of Status Scores

Green   Agency meets all of the standards for success.
Yellow   Agency achieves some, but not all, of the criteria.
Red   Has any of a number of serious flaws.

Explanation of Progress Scores

Green   Implementation is proceeding according to plans.
Yellow   Slippage in implementation schedule, quality of deliverables, or other issues requiring adjustments by agency in order to achieve initiative on a timely basis.
Red   Initiative in serious jeopardy. Unlikely to realize objectives without significant management intervention.

Some real management advances in the federal government have been racked up over the past year. For example:

- Both the Department of the Treasury and the Social Security Administration (SSA) met—two years early—the goal to produce audited financial statements by November 15th, just 45 days after the end of the year, compared with 151 days under previous administrations.
- The Department of Health and Human Services (HHS) has reduced its personnel offices from 40 to seven, and will eventually move to just one. This and other consolidations will allow HHS to deploy hundreds of employees to the front lines to deliver services directly to the American people.
- The Department of Defense (DoD) reduced headquarters staff by 11 percent, reducing civilian employees by over 3,000 in just the last year.
- Rules for conducting public-private competitions have been slashed by almost 12,000 words, cutting the time for conducting competitions from as much as four years to a maximum of just one year.
- The Department of Veterans Affairs (VA) is opening up the activities of 52,000 employees to competition over the next five years, 25,000 of them in 2003 alone.
- For the first time ever, auditors said the Department of Agriculture's financial statements accurately reflect its financial status.
- Government agencies and employees are paying their credit card bills more quickly. The federal government began 2002 with 10 percent of its individually billed travel accounts delinquent. That amount has been reduced to six percent, bringing total delinquent dollars for individually billed accounts down by over $310 million.
- The number of government-owned vehicles will decline by more than 10,000, from 586,450 in 2001 to 576,039 in 2004. (See the motor vehicles table later in the chapter.)
- Citizens are now only three clicks from transactions and services on the redesigned

website www.Firstgov.gov, which Yahoo!© rated one of the "world's 50 most incredibly useful websites."
- The GovBenefits.gov website provides, with a minimum of red tape, an online tool for citizens to learn about federal benefit programs for which they may qualify.
- Free Filing, debuting in 2003, will enable 60 percent of taxpaying Americans to prepare and file their taxes online and without cost.

While progress to date is encouraging, agencies, by and large, have been moving to address more easily corrected problems. The challenges will undoubtedly increase in 2003. The coming year will be critical to sustaining the agenda's momentum and achieving the goals envisioned by the President.

The Department of Homeland Security—A Starting Point for Managerial Flexibility

When the President proposed a new Department of Homeland Security (DHS), the debate focused to a large extent on whether the Department would be able to execute its mission under the constraints of a decades-old statutory management framework. The President sought significant flexibility in hiring processes, compensation systems and practices, and performance management to recruit, retain, and develop a motivated, high-performance, and accountable workforce. After a vigorous debate on the subject, the Congress and the Administration adopted these and other managerial flexibilities for the new Department.

The law governing DHS also includes important, but limited, government-wide authority. For example, agencies will have the ability to offer pay incentives to individuals who want to retire or leave government early if theirs are not the agencies' most needed skills. The law also provides that agencies may use an expedited hiring process if a shortage or critical hiring need exists. It's a start well worth continuing.

Yet the success in obtaining managerial flexibility for the new Department stands in contrast to the inaction of the Congress on other common sense management proposals the President submitted more than a year ago. As it has before, the Administration will seek to reflect program costs more accurately by assigning all employee costs, including those relating to the accrued costs of retirement and retiree health care benefits, to the appropriate program. The Administration also seeks greater flexibility in managing and disposing of property held by the government.

If nothing else, the debate surrounding the creation of DHS reinforced the need for broad management reform for the entire executive branch. The Administration will work with the new Congress to reform systems and policies so that the government can better protect Americans, as well as improve services the federal government delivers.

A discussion of overall achievement in the five government-wide areas follows. Individual agencies' success or lack of it in the government-wide initiatives, as well the program specific initiatives are presented in subsequent chapters and in the Performance and Management Assessments volume. As implementation continues, the focus will sharpen on actions that demonstrate real change.

Strategic Management of Human Capital

The federal government faces a crisis in personnel management. Federal agencies, for too long, have not managed themselves well enough to know whether they had the right people with the right skills to do their work. Making the federal workforce challenges even greater, 40 percent of all federal workers and 71 percent of senior executives will be eligible to retire by 2005.

The Strategic Management of Human Capital initiative gives agencies the tools they need to get the workers with the right skills to do the federal government's work in the 21st Century. Over the past year, agencies have devoted considerable time to developing human capital plans to make their organizations more citizen-centered, ensure that their staff have the necessary skills to achieve the agency's mission, and hold managers and employees accountable for results.

The Human Capital initiative must now move beyond the planning stage. While thoughtful analysis had to precede significant workforce restructuring, progress assessments in the coming year will be based on concrete action that agencies take, such as reforming their performance appraisal systems, developing succession plans, and streamlining their organizations toward more citizen- centered service.

Several agencies already have taken action like DoD's headquarters reorganization. Other examples include:

- SSA has moved almost 300 employees from staff positions to front-line service delivery to provide better assistance to its customers.
- The Department of Justice will pull its multiple performance appraisal systems together into a single system.
- The Departments of Energy, HHS, and Labor are among agencies that have placed all managers under a performance management system that links their assessments to meeting organizational goals.

But it's not easy. Consider the Office of Personnel Management (OPM) Director Kay James' effort to make senior government executives more accountable. She learned that in 2000, federal agencies gave 85 percent of their senior executives the highest possible performance rating—an assertion that virtually everyone in Washington is way above average. Despite James' urging agencies to begin distinguishing the best performers from others, almost nothing changed. In 2001, more than 83 percent of senior executives received the highest possible rating. Five agencies gave 100 percent of their senior executives the highest rating and six more gave it to 90 percent of their senior ranks. Such figures let the public know that federal managers are not yet serious about holding themselves or their staffs accountable.

The government's human capital problems derive in large part from our antiquated civil service laws, which were designed for a workforce that exists only in the history books. In 1950 when the GS system was implemented, the largest concentration of employees was in clerical positions at the GS-3 through GS-5 pay level. Today, over half of federal staff is at the GS-11 level or above, reflecting changes in business processes and skill requirements in the federal workforce over a period of decades.

The rigidity of the current civil service system makes it difficult to attract and retain more highly skilled employees. Hiring commonly takes six months or more, much of it spent by managers navigating around rules that overwhelm the process. Pay and performance are generally unrelated. Exceptional employees find themselves locked in "time-in-grade" pay prisons, as requirements dictate that performers stay at least one year at, say, a GS-12 level before moving, and then only as high as a GS-13. Even worse, pay over the course of a federal career is heavily determined by the level at which a civil servant begins working.

Meanwhile, mediocre employees benefit, receiving the same pay raises as their harder working colleagues. The federal government's termination rate for poor performance is less than one-tenth of one percent.

For 2004, the Administration proposes to allow managers to increase pay beyond annual raises for high-performing employees and address other critical personnel needs. A new fund of $500 million will be established at OPM for a stable of pay-for-performance plans. Rewarding top employees and those with unusually important skills is preferable to the traditional method of evenly spreading raises across the federal workforce regardless of performance or contribution.

Competitive Sourcing

The Competitive Sourcing initiative, despite its enormous potential for savings to taxpayers, has registered the least progress so far. All agencies are rated red for status. None has opened up a sufficient number of commercial activities to competition. Because this initiative in many ways represents such a significant departure from the old way of running the government, it faces the greatest obstacles.

For example, the General Services Administration (GSA), an organization whose mission is to help federal agencies by performing what most would view to be commercial services—buying goods and services, acquiring and managing properties, and offering related support services—categorized only 44 percent of its staff as commercial.

On the other hand, DoD has traditionally led the government in putting its commercial activities up for competition. The Department is currently conducting competitions on approximately 30,000 civilian positions, including cafeteria services, facilities maintenance, aircraft maintenance, and supply functions. Further progress rests on a strong commitment to start new competitions.

The Department of Transportation's (DOT's) Federal Aviation Administration (FAA) is moving forward on an ambitious competitive sourcing initiative on its Flight Service Stations, which provide a range of services available from private industry such as weather briefings for pilots. In spite of the challenges that its nationwide, 58-location scope presents, the FAA is moving forward methodically to ensure that high-quality service continues to be provided to the American traveling public and that all potential service providers are dealt with fairly. The Department of Energy also has started public-private competition on information technology and financial systems across the Department.

Competitive Sourcing and the 2004 Budget

The promise of competition was on display in the printing of this budget. The Office of Management and Budget (OMB) decided that the traditional practice of using the Government Printing Office (GPO) as the mandatory source for printing the President's Budget was neither fair nor economical and, as advised by the Department of Justice, not required by law. For the first time, OMB requested bids and received several, which would not have happened prior to OMB's new policy. On a comparable basis, the GPO cost estimate for printing this budget was 23 percent less than the previous year, and the lowest cost in at least 20 years—just one example of how competition saves the taxpayer money and, in many cases, produces better business processes along the way.

The competitive sourcing initiative also seeks to provide managers with additional options for providing services more cost-effectively or acquiring skills or service that may not be available in-house.

One of the roadblocks holding back agencies is the long-standing process guiding public-private competitions. As defined in OMB Circular A-76, the process has been unnecessarily bureaucratic and lengthy, sometimes taking up to four years. To help agencies implement the Presidential initiative and building on the recommendations of the Commercial Activities Panel chaired by the Comptroller General, the Administration is simplifying the A-76 process. The new process will be quicker and easier. The number of pages of instructions has been slashed by almost 12,000 words, or more than 30 percent. The timeframe for conducting competitions should be no more than a year in almost all cases. Agencies will compete on a level playing field with the private sector and no longer have extended timeframes or other advantages over the private sector.

Improved Financial Performance

The Improved Financial Performance initiative is enhancing the quality and timeliness of financial information so that it can be used to manage federal programs more effectively, while preventing waste, fraud, and abuse. The financial management challenges facing the government are longstanding. Progress in many cases depends on installing new computer systems that in some cases will require several years. Making progress will be hard.

One of the major changes the Administration instituted at the outset of this initiative was to accelerate the due date of agencies' financial statements. If financial information is only available five months after the fiscal year ends, it is of limited use to anyone. So, as a first step, 2002 financial statements were due February 1, 2003, or nearly a month earlier than the statutory due date of February 28th.

The Administration also has required agencies to produce interim financial statements to establish the practice of preparing financial statements on a regular basis. All agencies provided six-month interim 2002 financial statements by the June 30 deadline. We have required them to combine their financial statements with their performance reports. Information about agency finances and program performance in one document will be available this year.

Soon, bigger tests will come. For 2004, agencies will be required to produce audited financial statements by November 15th. This acceleration means that agencies will no longer be able to use manual processes to prepare statements once a year. They will need to change the way they collect and compile financial information so that it will be more timely, reliable, and useful. The Department of the Treasury and SSA's production of audited financial statements within 45 days of the year's close prove that these goals are within reach.

Challenges, though, have grown more demanding. This initiative was launched in an environment of enhanced scrutiny of financial management practices everywhere. The credibility of some financial auditors was appropriately called into question, causing entities and their auditors to tighten the standards they applied in their audits. It was in this environment that new auditors of the National Aeronautics and Space Administration (NASA) downgraded their opinion of the agency's financial statements. This resulted in the deterioration of NASA's status rating from yellow to red, but indications are that NASA will be able to demonstrate substantial improvement in its 2002 audited financial statements.

Credit Card Abuse in the Federal Government

The federal government sponsors more than 2.5 million credit cards for employees to use in purchasing goods and services or when traveling on official government business. Audits and press reports have highlighted abuses of these cards by federal employees.

- Over $4 million in inappropriate transactions by employees at one agency appear to have been made with pawn shops, jewelry stores, and antique shops.
- The Director and the head of audits and assessments at Los Alamos National Laboratory resigned amid charges that lab employees made nearly $5 million in questionable credit card purchases.

- One federal employee used the names of legitimate companies on falsified invoices to conceal $14,000 in personal purchases.
- At one agency, purchases for over $439,000 were processed for card accounts that were no longer approved for use.

As an initial step at improving controls over government-issued credit cards:

- DoD has targeted 300,000 infrequently used travel cards for cancellation, more than 10 percent of the total issued by the federal government.
- The Department of Education now prohibits official credit card use at about 300 types of businesses, like casinos, limousine rental companies, and veterinarians, among others that should have been prohibited in the first place.
- The Department of Housing and Urban Development (HUD) has reduced unpaid travel card account balances from $389,000 to $15,000.

The Administration will continue to monitor credit card usage by federal employees, requiring quarterly reports by agencies of the number of cards in use, the controls in place to monitor them, and any abuses discovered.

Reducing Erroneous Payments

The Administration has launched a major effort to reduce erroneous payments—in other words, payments the government makes in error. In most instances, they are overpayments. But in all cases, taxpayers are shortchanged.

For the first time ever, agencies were required to report the extent of erroneous payments made in their major benefit programs. Initially, just a few agencies voluntarily reported erroneous payments in their annual financial statements. Now, 15 agencies have estimated their erroneous payment rates. But programs like Medicaid and School Lunch will have to design from scratch a methodology to examine the integrity of program payments.

Fifteen agencies reported making more than an estimated $30 billion in erroneous payments in 2001. The largest amounts are:

Medicare	$12.1 billion
Earned Income Tax Credit	$9.2 billion
Housing Subsidy Programs	$3.3 billion
Supplemental Security Income	$1.6 billion

During the past year, the Administration expended considerable effort to prevent a further erosion of controls over payments from federal programs. The Department of Agriculture's Food and Nutrition Service, for instance, pursued cash sanctions against states with above-average error rates. During the Congress' recent reauthorization of the Food Stamp Quality Control program, attempts were made to dilute the accountability of states and erode the federal government's ability to maintain fiscal accountability. The Administration opposed and will continue to oppose efforts to weaken financial controls and program integrity.

Congress endorsed the President's effort to reduce erroneous payments when it passed the Erroneous Payments Information Act of 2002. This bill requires an estimate of the extent of erroneous payments from all federal programs. Program-wide erroneous payment estimates can only help stem the loss to the federal government in waste, fraud, and abuse—too much of which is taking place without an accounting.

Strengthening Asset Management

In another area of deficiency, the Administration will monitor agency asset management practices as part of the Improved Financial Performance initiative. The federal government's asset management practices have been shown to be particularly weak.

According to its financial statements, the federal government owns $307 billion in property, plant, and equipment, $209 billion in loans receivable, and $184 billion in inventories and related property. But the assets reported on the balance sheet are only a small portion of the assets actually owned by the federal government. DoD property and the government's immense land holdings do not show up on government financial statements. For instance, the federal government holds title to 28 percent of the United States' entire land mass. It owns sites and structures, monuments, memorials, cemeteries, as well as the items in its museums and libraries, including major works of art and historical documents.

Agency management of vehicle fleets will also be monitored as part of agency asset management practices. The government owns more than half a million cars and trucks and spends over $2 billion annually to operate them. In April 2002, the Administration asked agencies to take a closer look at their motor vehicle fleets and to report any planned reductions and cheaper leasing arrangements by the end of the fiscal year. The military agencies and several civilian agencies, notably the Departments of Energy, HHS, the Interior, and GSA projected reductions ranging from five percent to 15 percent. These reductions were offset, however, by equally significant increases in agencies with expanded law enforcement and security-related missions. For example, the new bureaus within the DHS estimated a 21-percent rise in their vehicle fleets, from 28,502 to 34,460 vehicles. Justice projected that its fleet would increase nine percent, from 31,981 vehicles in 2001 to 34,847 in 2004.

The Administration will demand that assets be justified and accounted for and that plans be made for purchases, management, maintenance, and operation.

Vehicle Inventories to Drop from 2001–2004

	2001	2004	Change
Army	73,209	62,531	–15%
Air Force	46,890	40,065	–15%
GSA	1,470	1,286	–13%
HHS	3,388	2,977	–12%
Energy	16,655	15,082	–9%
Defense Contract Management Agency	1,058	984	–7%
Interior	34,397	32,660	–5%
Defense Agencies	4,263	4,029	–5%
Navy	40,005	39,141	–2%
Labor	4,118	4,034	–2%
Agriculture	39,588	39,105	–1%
NASA	2,261	2,235	–1%
Marine Corps	11,141	11,107	—
Environmental Protection Agency	1,105	1,109	—
US Postal Service	210,102	211,650	1%
Commerce	1,916	1,979	3%
Treasury	3,679	3,772	3%
Agencies with under 1,000 vehicles	3,228	3,384	5%
Corps of Engineers	4,508	4,763	6%
Transportation	5,920	6,345	7%

Veterans Affairs	8,403	9,029	7%
Justice	31,981	34,847	9%
State	6,521	7,104	9%
Defense Logistics Agency	2,142	2,361	10%
Homeland Security	28,502	34,460	21%
Total	586,450	576,039	–2%

Expanded Electronic Government

The Internet and the electronic age have made more information accessible at the touch of a button. Government information should be at the forefront of this new revolution. That's where the combination of the Internet and E-Gov come in. Twenty-four high-payoff E-Government initiatives that will maximize government productivity have been launched. Many are already on line and serving citizens. They include:

- *Recreation.gov* allows people to log onto the Internet to find information about publicly owned federal, as well as state and local recreation sites.
- *Business.gov* provides businesses access to information about laws and regulations where they can use a series of interactive tools to help them understand how those laws and regulations apply to their business.
- The *GoLearn.Gov* portal provides online training for tens of thousands of government employees for pennies per course, teaching thousands of government workers for a fraction of traditional costs.
- The E-Grants initiative is creating a single electronic grant application that allows applicants to enter identifying information once—like a single, unique identifier—which would untangle the process for them and the agencies that track them.

Analysis reveals that few federal information technology investments have significantly improved service to the taxpayer. Many major information technology projects do not meet cost, schedule, and performance goals. To address this, the Administration is scrutinizing funding of projects that are "at risk" of failing. Those projects that failed this trio of tests either were not recommended for support for 2004 or will remain on an "at risk" list. Many of those projects either didn't adequately address security risks or make business sense.

OMB is now requiring agencies to submit business cases for over $34 billion in proposed spending, up from less than $20 billion a year ago. For those projects that made an adequate case, the quality of justifications has gone up. (Total Information Technology (IT) spending across the government is now almost $60 billion.)

Implementation of the Government Information Security Reform Act has provided a baseline for agency IT security performance, an audit trail of what has been secured, and the identification of what still needs to be done. Because too many agencies propose funding for IT projects without adequately addressing important security issues, the budget process is being used to redirect funding to address these critical security issues.

To succeed in making the government a modern, electronic enterprise, we must continue to address these chronic problems. The passage of the E-Government Act of 2002 codifies the Office of Electronic Government, which was set up in 2001 to spearhead the Administration's efforts in this area. It also creates an E-Gov fund to help leverage agency investments in cross agency initiatives and promotes the Administration's efforts to ensure computer security. The bill enhances the Administration's ongoing support for specific initiatives like on-line rulemaking, which allows interested parties to comment on draft regulations over the Internet.

Budget and Performance Integration

The Budget and Performance Integration Initiative follows through on the President's commitment to build a results-oriented government that funds what works and reforms or ends failing federal programs, redirecting or recapturing their funding. This initiative has shown the most improvement since September 2001. While no green status scores have been achieved yet, gains in a half-dozen departments and agencies can point to concrete results to justify why programs deserve additional resources.

For example, DOT's Federal Highway Administration has justified additional budget resources by linking highway safety gains to planned use of rumble strips and reflectors to prevent run-off-the-road crashes, which kill thousands of motorists every year.

The Department of Labor shows the full cost of the many training programs it funds; the sources of federal funding; and the extent to which participants get jobs, keep them, and increase their earnings. Presentations like these help policymakers get results for citizens, shifting funds to programs that work best and away from those that do not.

Many other agencies are also working to present their budgets with information telling how well they're doing. However, program performance information is still often unclear or not measured at all. And when programs are measured, more often than not there is little or no connection between performance data and budget decisions. The Administration is using the Program Assessment Rating Tool (PART) to correct this shortcoming.

With the PART, this year OMB along with its colleagues in the agencies reviewed about 20 percent of all federal funding, or some 234 programs. The process of completing the evaluations was sometimes contentious. Nonetheless, it generated a great deal of constructive dialogue about program strengths and weaknesses, as well as the importance of demonstrating program results. Only about half of federal programs evaluated were able to demonstrate results; as a consequence, the detailed findings from the assessments, rather than the overall rating, helped inform budget decisions.

Another key aspect of this initiative has been the development of a set of common performance measures for programs that deliver the same service. Dozens of programs offer job training services in one form or another. The question is: Which ones work well? But even more importantly, which ones help people land and keep solid jobs? Common measure data will allow for comparisons that may reveal opportunities for improvement and increased efficiency. While this first year of efforts focused on six areas—housing, job training, wildfire management, flood mitigation, health, and environment—it will be expanded in the coming year.

Discussions of these specific initiatives can be found in the chapters of agencies chosen to lead each effort. Highlights on how agencies fared in the President's Management Agenda can be located near the close of their respective chapters. A compendium of performance information, including data on PART evaluations conducted this year, is contained in the *Performance and Management Assessments* volume.

The Scorecard

The Executive Branch Management Scorecard that follows is the device the Administration uses to track agencies' efforts in implementing the agenda. Throughout the year, agencies are monitored and ratings are given at the end of each quarter on each initiative. Status ratings are evaluated against the standards for success included in the *Performance and Management Assessments* volume. The standards were developed in consultation with federal agencies through the President's Management Council, the group of agency leaders charged by the President to implement the agenda. Progress ratings assess the agencies' work in developing viable, ambitious plans for achieving the standards and their efforts to implement the plans.

Since July 2002, ratings for each quarter have been posted on the *Results.gov* website. The scorecard published here includes ratings for the quarter that ended December 31, 2002, and shows changes in status since the Administration conducted the first evaluation of September 30, 2001. Since then, a single green light has been added to the one that appeared on the original scorecard. And the second green shows up in the agency that earned the first—the National Science Foundation (NSF). This scorecard includes status scores only for DHS, due to its newness. The second scorecard reports progress on the nine program initiatives.

Executive Branch Management Scorecard

	Current Status as of December 31, 2002					Progress in Implementing the President's Management Agenda				
	Human Capital	Competitive Sourcing	Financial Perf.	E-Gov	Budget/ Perf. Integration	Human Capital	Competitive Sourcing	Financial Perf.	E-Gov	Budget/ Perf. Integration
AGRICULTURE	R	R	R	Y	R	G	R	G	G	Y
COMMERCE	R	R	R	Y	Y↑	G	G	G	Y	G
DEFENSE	Y↑	R	R	R	Y↑	G	Y	G	G	G
EDUCATION	R	R	R	Y↑	R	G	G	G	G	G
ENERGY	Y↑	R	Y↑	Y↑	R	G	G	G	G	Y
EPA	R	R	Y↑	Y	Y	G	G	G	G	G
HHS	R	R	R	R	R	G	G	Y	Y	G
HOMELAND	R	R	R	R	R					
HUD	R	R	R	R	R	Y	Y	G	G	G
INTERIOR	R	R	R	R	R	G	G	R	G	G
JUSTICE	R	R	R	R	R	G	G	G	G	G
LABOR	Y	R	Y↑	Y	Y↑	G	Y	G	G	G
STATE	R	R	R	R	R	G	Y	G	Y	G
DOT	R	R	R	R	Y	G	G	G	G	G
TREASURY	R	R	R	R	R	G	G	G	Y	G
VA	R	R	R	Y↑	Y↑	G	G	G	G	G
AID	R	R	R	R	R	R	R	Y	Y	G
CORPS	R	R	R	R	R	G	R	G	Y	Y
GSA	R	R	Y	R	R	R	G	G	Y	Y
NASA	Y↑	R	R↓	R	Y↑	G	G	G	G	G
NSF	R	R	G	G↑	R	G	R	G	G	Y
OMB	R	R	R	R	R	Y	G	Y	G	Y
OPM	Y	R	Y↑	Y	R	G	G	G	G	G
SBA	R	R	R↓	Y	Y	G	G	R	G	Y
SMITHSONIAN	R	R	R	Y	R	Y	Y	Y	G	Y
SSA	Y	R	Y	Y	Y↑	G	Y	G	G	G

Arrows indicate change in status since baseline evaluation on September 30, 2001.

Program Initiative Scorecard

Initiative	Status	Progress
Faith-Based and Community Initiative	Y↑	G
Privatization of Military Housing	Y	G
Better R&D Investment Criteria	R	Y
Elimination of Fraud and Error in Student Aid Programs and Deficiencies in Financial Management	R	G
Housing and Urban Development Management and Performance	R	Y
Broadened Health Insurance Coverage Through State Initiatives	Y	G
A "Right-Sized" Overseas Presence	R	Y
Reform of Food Aid Programs	G↑	G
Coordination of VA and DoD Programs and Systems	Y	G

Arrows indicate change in status since baseline evaluation on June 30, 2002.

ASSESSING PROGRAM PERFORMANCE

The Office of Management and Budget has developed a systematic, consistent process for developing program performance ratings in the FY 2004 budget. The following pages present that process and list the programs that are being assessed in FY 2004.

Assessing Program Performance for the FY 2004 Budget

The Administration has taken unprecedented steps to reform the budget process by establishing a systematic, consistent process for developing program performance ratings and then using that information to make budget decisions. To enhance the practical use of performance information, OMB, in collaboration with other federal agencies, has developed the Program Assessment Rating Tool (PART), comprised of assessment criteria on program performance and management. The PART establishes a high, "good government" standard of performance and will be used to rate programs in an open, public fashion. Ratings for 20 percent of programs will be published in the FY 2004 budget, and the basis for the rating will be made available to the public.

The PART and other guidance regarding program performance assessments for the FY 2004 budget may be obtained by clicking on the appropriate bullets on the website www.whitehouse.gov/omb/budintegration/part_assessing2004.html:

- Memorandum from OMB Director to Agency Heads on "Program Performance Assessments for the FY 2004 Budget"
    - Attachment I—Programs to Be Assessed for FY 2004

- Instructions for the Program Assessment Rating Tool (PART)

- PART Worksheets
    — competitive grant programs
    — block/formula grant programs
    — regulatory-based programs
    — capital assets and service acquisition programs
    — credit programs
    — research and development programs
    — direct federal programs

- Training on the Program Assessment Rating Tool (PART)

- OMB Circular A-11, Part 6, Preparation and Submission of Strategic Plans, Annual Performance Plans, and Annual Program Performance Reports, particularly Sections 220 and 221.

The following pages present the memorandum from the OMB director to agency heads and the list of programs to be assessed for FY 2004.

EXECUTIVE OFFICE OF THE PRESIDENT
OFFICE OF MANAGEMENT AND BUDGET
WASHINGTON, D.C. 20503

July 16, 2002

M-02-10

MEMORANDUM FOR HEADS OF EXECUTIVE DEPARTMENTS AND AGENCIES

FROM: Mitchell E. Daniels, Jr.
Director

SUBJECT: Program Performance Assessments for the FY 2004 Budget

Improving programs by focusing on results is an integral component of the President's budget and performance integration initiative. OMB's April 24, 2002 FY 2004 Budget planning memorandum emphasized the importance of program effectiveness ratings in formulating the FY 2004 Budget. It informed you that formal effectiveness ratings would be conducted for approximately 20 percent of Federal programs, and that the results of these ratings would be published in the FY 2004 Budget. Since then, and with valuable assistance from agency staff, we have progressed in this effort.

For instance, OMB and agencies have identified the programs that will be rated for FY 2004 (see Attachment). Programs listed total approximately $480 billion, or over 24 percent of Federal spending, and reflect a diverse mix of discretionary and mandatory programs. Thank you for your serious commitment to this effort and for helping develop this list.

A critical goal for the FY 2004 Budget is to improve the program rating process by making ratings more consistent, objective, credible and transparent than they were for FY 2003. To this end, OMB, with advice from the President's Management Council's (PMC) subgroup on Budget and Performance Integration, developed the draft program assessment rating tool (PART). On May 17, 2002, the draft PART and instructions were officially provided to agencies through the PMC.

The PART was thoroughly tested by OMB and agency staff during OMB's Spring Review process. We also received excellent feedback from agencies, informal comments from Congressional and General Accounting Office staff, and advice from outside experts, including OMB's Performance Measurement Advisory Council of experts from outside the government. As a result, we have concluded that the PART is a useful and informative instrument that will help us achieve our objective for FY 2004.

The comments we received also identified improvements that could be made to the PART. In response to these comments we have revised the PART. PARTs for all program types, and revised guidance, can be found at http://www.whitehouse.gov/omb/budintegration.

The revised PART will be used by OMB, working closely with agency staff, to complete program effectiveness assessments for the FY 2004 Budget by September 30, 2002. I have asked my staff to complete the PARTs by September 9, 2002, so that any issues regarding completed PARTs can be addressed by September 30.

Major Changes in Final PART

The revised PART includes the following major changes from the draft PART:

- *Four point scale in Section IV, Results* – We received many comments on the "Yes/No" format for responses. Many parties liked the certainty and forced choice of "Yes/No." Others felt the format did not reveal adequate distinction between the performance of various programs, especially in the results section. In response, the PART has been revised to include four choices of responses in the results section (Section IV) only. Now, a program that achieves some of its goals, or that shows reasonable, but not complete progress toward goals, will receive partial credit in the results section, the most heavily weighted section. For Sections I – III, which focus more on processes than results, the "Yes/No" format is retained.

- *Questions Added in Sections II and III for corrective actions* – Many parties commented that the draft PART does not distinguish between programs that were taking action to address planning and management deficiencies, and those that were not. While the PART is primarily a snapshot of the current status of programs, it is important to recognize when significant efforts are underway to address deficiencies in a program. The revised PART contains new questions in sections II and III to address this issue. These new questions, combined with the new format for section IV described above, will result in more refined and meaningful distinctions between programs.

- *Better focus on performance and performance measures* – The PART format for Section IV has also been revised to explicitly require display of performance targets and actual performance on the key measures identified by the agencies and OMB. Guidance has also been revised to require that at least one of the key measures identified for the program be an efficiency measure.

- *Critical Federal Role question to be examined separately from the PART* – We received comments that question 3 in the Section I of the draft PART ("Is the Federal role critical?") was too subjective and could vary depending on philosophical or political viewpoints. We also received many comments that this question is so important that it should not only be retained, but be elevated in importance in the overall score.

    To keep the PART as objective as possible, this question has been eliminated, and the remaining questions in Section I have been adjusted to focus on objective, evidence-based criteria about program purpose and program design. The appropriateness of the Federal Role in addressing national interests, problems or needs will be specifically examined during OMB's Fall Budget Reviews, but will not be included in the PART.

The new PART includes additional revisions to specific questions in response to comments we received. In general, we have tried to reduce the number of questions, especially in Section III, without losing important information.

Subjectivity of PART Responses

During the PART testing and comment period, the issue of the subjectivity of PART responses, either on the part of OMB or agency staff, was raised repeatedly. While subjectivity can be minimized, it can never be completely eliminated regardless of the method or tool. In providing advice to OMB Directors, OMB staff have always exercised professional judgment with some degree of subjectivity. That will not change. As one of our Advisory Council members stated, the PART makes public and transparent the questions OMB asks in advance of making judgments, and opens up any subjectivity in that process for discussion and debate. The PART is a necessary step forward in systematizing and revealing OMB's deliberations.

Nonetheless, we are taking several steps to minimize subjectivity:

- *Clarified Guidance* - We have strengthened and clarified the PART instructions including the evidence required to support a "Yes" or "No" answer, with the specific goal of reducing the subjectivity of responses. Revised guidance can be found at http://www.whitehouse.gov/omb/budintegration.

- *Training* - OMB's Performance Evaluation Team (PET) will conduct training over the next several weeks for OMB examiners and agency staff aimed at achieving consistency of approaches and standards applied in answering questions. Additional information is available through your OMB RMO contact.

- *Review of Completed PARTs for Consistency* - OMB will initiate a process to selectively review questions on completed PARTs for consistency in application of instructions and standards. We will provide additional information on this process at a later time.

- *Potential Involvement of IGs, GAO or other third parties in the assessment* – We have met with the Inspector General community, the General Accounting Office, and other groups with expertise in program evaluation. All of these groups expressed interest not only in the process, but also in assisting OMB and agencies in completing the assessments. Knowledgeable third parties can help identify relevant information for consideration in the assessments. In addition, third parties can provide an objective viewpoint if disputes arise in considering PART questions. We will continue to discuss with these groups how they can most effectively participate in this process, including providing some level of independent review. I encourage all agencies to make the PART assessment process as open and inclusive as feasible.

Finalizing PARTs

As with many other aspects of the budget development process, disagreements between OMB and agency staff may remain after staff work on the PART is complete, and after a technical review for consistency. In these cases, agencies and OMB should resolve disagreements in the traditional manner, i.e., first through OMB branch chief and division director, and then through the OMB Program Associate Director. As noted above, all issues, questions and disagreements must be resolved and finalized by September 30.

Presentation of PART Results in the FY 2004 Budget

Final decisions have not yet been made regarding presentation of PART results in the FY 2004 Budget. We received good advice from the Performance Measurement Advisory Council (PMAC) on making sure the presentation highlights separately the results score and key measures. We also believe sections I – III scores should be displayed in some fashion, and an overall assessment (e.g., "effective" or "ineffective") will be shown. One outstanding question is if or how to show the overall weighted numeric PART score for the program. Since this score will determine the overall assessment, we will almost certainly make the score and the basis for it (i.e., the completed PART) available to the public. The PMAC will discuss presentation options further at their September meeting.

Relationship to GPRA

Agencies expend considerable time and effort developing and updating their Government Performance and Results Act (GPRA) plans and reports on an annual basis. The program assessment effort presents an opportunity to inform and improve agency GPRA plans and reports, and establish a meaningful, systematic link between GPRA and the budget process. This effort will also help identify specific performance measures that could support budget and management recommendations and efforts. Through this process, OMB will work with agencies to maintain measures in GPRA materials that are useful and eliminate reporting burdens that have no utility.

How Ratings Will Be Used

Finally, many agencies expressed concern over how the ratings would be used during the Fall Budget Review, and specifically that a low PART score would automatically result in a funding reduction. OMB does not view the PART as an automated approach to making budget decisions. A low PART score does not, in itself, signify whether a program needs more or less funding. The PART provides a tool for diagnosing how programs can be improved and it is from such diagnosis, as well as other information regarding the program, that budget and management decisions will be made. FY 2004 decisions will be fundamentally grounded in program performance, but will also continue to be based on a variety of other factors, including policy objectives and priorities of the Administration, and economic and programmatic trends.

Program Assessments for FY 2004

CABINET AGENCIES:

Department of Agriculture
APHIS Agricultural Quarantine and Inspection
APHIS Animal Welfare
CCC Direct Payments
CCC Farmland Protection Program
CCC Wildlife Habitat Incentives Program
FAS Food Aid Programs
FNS National School Lunch
FS Wildland Fire Management
FS Capital Improvement and Maintenance
FSIS Food Safety and Inspection Service
RHS Multifamily Housing Direct Loans and Rental Assistance Grants
RMA Crop Insurance
RUS Electric Loan
RUS Rural Water and Wastewater Grants and Loans

Department of Commerce
Advanced Technology
Bureau of Economic Analysis
Economic Development Administration
Manufacturing Extension Partnership
Minority Business Development Agency
National Marine Fisheries Service
National Weather Service
Pacific Coastal Salmon Recovery Grants
U.S. Patent Trademark Office—Patents
U.S. Patent Trademark Office—Trademarks

Department of Defense
Air Combat
Airlift
Basic Research
Chemical Demilitarization
Communications Infrastructure
Defense Health
Energy Conservation Improvement
Facilities Sustainment, Restoration, Modernization, and Demolition
Housing
Missile Defense
Recruiting
Shipbuilding

Department of Education
Adult Education State Grants
Americas Career Resource Network
Comprehensive School Reform
Even Start
Federal Family Education Loan
Federal Pell Grants
GEAR UP
IDEA Grants for Infants and Families
IDEA Grants to States
IDEA Preschool Grants
National Assessment
National Center for Education Statistics
Safe and Drug Free Schools State Grants
Student Aid Administration
Tech-prep Education State Grants
Tribally Controlled Vocational and Technical Institutions
TRIO Student Support Services
TRIO Upward Bound
Vocational Education State Grants
Vocational Rehabilitation State Grants
William D. Ford Direct Student Loans

Department of Energy
Advanced Scientific Computing Research
Advanced Simulation and Computing (ASCI)
Advanced Fuel Cycle Initiative
Basic Energy Sciences
Biological and Environmental Research
Building Technologies
Environmental Management
Environmental Management (R&D)
Energy Efficiency and Renewable Energy
Facilities and Infrastructure
Fuel Cells
Fusion Energy Sciences
Gas Exploration and Production
Gas Infrastructure
Generation IV Nuclear Energy Systems Initiative
Geothermal Technology
High Energy Physics
Hydrogen Technology
Material Protection Control and Accounting

Methane Hydrates
Nuclear Energy Research Initiative
Nuclear Physics
Nuclear Power 2010
Office of Science
Oil Exploration and Production
PMA Bonneville Power Administration
PMA Southeastern Power Administration
PMA Southwestern Power Administration
PMA Western Area Power Administration
Presidents Coal Research Initiative
Safeguards and Security
Solar Energy
Weatherization Assistance
Wind Energy

Department of Health and Human Services
AoA State and Community-Based Services Programs on Aging
ACF Foster Care
ACF Head Start
ACF Refugee and Entrant Assistance
AHRQ Data Collection and Dissemination
AHRQ Translating Research into Practice
BioT Health Alert Network
BioT Metropolitan Medical Response System
CDC Chronic Disease—Breast and Cervical Cancer
CDC Chronic Disease—Diabetes
CDC Domestic HIV/AIDS Prevention
CDC Immunizations
CMS Medicare Integrity
CMS State Children's Health Insurance (SCHIP)
FDA Center for Biologics Evaluation and Research
FDA Center for Devices and Radiologic Health
FDA Center for Drug Evaluation and Research
FDA Center for Food Safety and Applied Nutrition
FDA Center for Veterinary Medicine
HRSA Consolidated Health Center
HRSA Health Professions
HRSA Maternal Child Health (MCH)
HRSA National Health Services Corps
HRSA Nursing Education Loan Repayment
HRSA Ryan White
IHS Federally-Administered Activities
IHS Sanitation Facilities
OIG Health Care Fraud and Abuse Control (HCFAC)
SAMHSA Children's Mental Health Services
SAMHSA Projects for Assistance in Transition from Homelessness
SAMHSA Substance Abuse Treatment Programs of Regional and National Significance

A PART is currently under development for the National Institutes of Health and is targeted for completion in Spring 2003.

Department of Housing and Urban Development
Disabled Housing Grants
Elderly Housing Grants
HOME Investment Partnership (HOME)
Housing Vouchers
Native American Housing Grants
Section 8 Project-Based Rental Assistance

Department of the Interior
BIA School Construction
BIA School Operations
BLM Restoration Activities
BOR Hydropower
BOR Rural Water Supply Projects
BOR Title XVI Water Reuse and Recycling
DOI Wildland Fire Management
FWS National Fish Hatchery System
FWS Partners for Fish and Wildlife
MMS Environmental Studies
NPS Facility Management
NPS Natural Resource Challenge
OSM Abandoned Mine Land
OST Tribal Land Consolidation
USGS National Mapping

Department of Justice
Drug Enforcement Administration
FBI Cybercrime
FBI White Collar Crime
FPS Bureau of Prisons
INS Immigration Services
OJP Community Oriented Policing Services
OJP Drug Courts
OJP Juvenile Accountability

OJP Residential Substance Abuse Treatment
OJP Weed and Seed

Department of Labor
Bureau of Labor Statistics (BLS)
Community Service Employment for Older Americans
Dislocated Worker Assistance
Federal Employees Compensation Act (FECA)
Occupational Safety and Health Administration (OSHA)
Office of Federal Contract Compliance Programs (OFCCP)
Pension and Welfare Benefits Administration (PWBA)
Trade Adjustment Assistance (TAA)
Youth Activities

Department of State and Other Related Agencies
Department of State:
Anti-Terrorism Assistance
Border Security—Visa and Consular Services
Broadcasting to Near East Asia and South Asia
Educational and Cultural Exchange Programs in Near East Asia and South Asia
Embassy Security Construction
Military Assistance to new NATO and NATO Aspirant Nations
PKO—including East Timor and OSCE
Refugee Admissions to the United States
Refugees to Israel
Security Assistance to Sub-Saharan Africa

Other Related Agencies (International Assistance Programs):
Export Import Bank—Long Term Guarantees
International Development Association
Overseas Private Investment Corporation—Finance
Treasury Technical Assistance
USAID Climate Change
USAID Development Assistance—Population
USAID Food Aid Programs (including Public Law 480 Title II)

Department of Transportation
FAA Grants in Aid for Airports (Airport Improvement)
FHWA Highway Infrastructure
FMCSA Highway Safety
NHTSA Highway Safety
USCG Aids to Navigation
USCG Drug Interdiction
USCG Search and Rescue

Department of the Treasury
ATF Consumer Product Safety Activities
Bank Enterprise Award (BEA)
Earned Income Tax Credit (EITC) Compliance
Federal Law Enforcement Training Center (FLETC)
IRC Collection
Mint Coin Production
OCC Bank Supervision
Office of Foreign Assets Control (OFAC)
OTS Thrift Supervision

Department of Veterans Affairs
Burial
Compensation
Medical Care

INDEPENDENT AND OTHER AGENCIES:

Corps of Engineers (Civil Works)
Corps Hydropower
Emergency Management
Flood Damage Reduction
Inland Waterways Navigation
Wetlands (non-regulatory)

Corporation for National and Community Service
AmeriCorps

Consumer Product Safety Commission
Consumer Product Safety Commission

Environmental Protection Agency
Air Toxics
Civil Enforcement
Drinking Water State Revolving Fund
Existing Chemicals
Leaking Underground Storage Tanks

New Chemicals
Non-Point Source
Pesticide Registration
Pesticides Re-registration
Superfund Removal
Tribal General Assistance

Federal Emergency Management Agency
Disaster Relief Fund—Public Assistance
Hazard Mitigation Grant
National Flood Insurance

General Services Administration
Asset Management of Federally—Owned Real Property
Multiple Award Schedules
Supply Depots and Special Order
Vehicle Acquisition
Vehicle Leasing

National Aeronautics and Space Administration
Mars Exploration
Space Shuttle
Space Station

National Science Foundation
Geosciences
Tools

Office of National Drug Control Policy
High Intensity Drug Trafficking Area— (HIDTA)
Youth Anti-Drug Media Campaign

Office of Personnel Management
Federal Employees Group Life Insurance— (FEGLI)
Retirement

Small Business Administration
Business Information Centers
Section 504 Certified Development Corporation Guar. Loan
Service Corps of Retired Executives
Small Business Development Centers

Social Security Administration
Disability Insurance
Supplemental Security Income for the Aged

Tennessee Valley Authority
TVA Power
TVA Resource Stewardship (Non-Power)

CHAPTER 6

The National Aeronautics and Space Administration: Performance Plan and PMA Action Plans

The National Aeronautics and Space Administration (NASA) has had an effective strategic management system for many years. This chapter presents excerpts of that system (details of which are available on the NASA website, www.NASA.gov). The first section is an excerpt from NASA's FY 2003 Performance Plan and the second section presents the PMA action plans for NASA. This second section provides a wealth of information on how a major agency implements the PMA.

FY 2003 Performance Plan
Background and Introduction

The Government Performance and Results Act

The Government Performance and Results Act (GPRA) was passed by Congress and signed by the President in 1993. GPRA was enacted to improve the efficiency of all Federal agencies, with the following specific goals:

Improve Federal program management, effectiveness, and public accountability
Improve Congressional decision making on where to commit the Nation's financial and human resources
Improve citizen confidence in Government performance

GPRA directs Executive Branch agencies to develop a customer-focused strategic plan that aligns activities with concrete missions and goals. The Act directs agencies to manage and measure results to justify Congressional appropriations and authorizations. One hundred and eighty days after the completion of the fiscal year, agencies report on the degree of success in achieving the goals and performance measures defined in the strategic and performance plans. NASA's third Annual Performance Report will be furnished to the Congress in March 2002, covering performance in FY 2001.

NASA's Strategic Management System

Processes within NASA's Strategic Management System provide the information and results for GPRA's planning and reporting requirements. This system is defined in the NASA Strategic Management Handbook (NASA Procedures and Guidelines 1000.2, February 2000). Strategic Management Elements are depicted in the handbook (Figure 1-2) illustrating the hierarchy of documentation for the Strategic Management System (Agency–Enterprise–Centers–Program/Project–Employees).

The NASA Strategic Plan (NASA Policy Directive 1000. ib) defines the vision, mission, and fundamental questions of science and research that provide the foundation of the Agency's goals. The Plan describes five Strategic Enterprises that manage the programs and activities to implement our mission, answer fundamental questions, and provide service to identified customers. These Strategic Enterprises are the: *Space Science Enterprise, Earth Science Enterprise, Human Exploration and Development of Space Enterprise, Biological and Physical Research Enterprise and Aerospace Technology Enterprise.* The support systems for the Strategic Enterprises, defined as Crosscutting Processes, are: *Manage Strategically, Provide Aerospace Products and Capabilities, Communicate Knowledge and Generate Knowledge.* Interested readers may access NASA's Strategic Plan at the following website: http://www.hc.nasa.gov/office /codez/new.

The FY 2003 Performance Plan reflects the recent Strategic Plan. In the NASA Strategic Plan, the vision and mission statements of the Agency are articulated. We reprint them here for the convenience of the reader.

NASA Vision Statement

NASA is an investment in America's future. As explorers, pioneers, and innovators, we boldly expand frontiers in air and space to inspire and serve America and to benefit the quality of life on Earth.

NASA Mission Statement

- **To advance and communicate scientific knowledge and understanding of the Earth, the solar system, and the universe;**
- **To advance human exploration, use, and development of space;**
- **To research, develop, verify, and transfer advanced aeronautics, space, and space technologies.**

Outcomes of NASA's Activities

Government investment decisions on funding for space and aeronautics research and technology cannot be made knowing in advance the full benefits ("outcomes") that will accrue from making the investments. Nor can the exact timetable be known as to when these benefits will be realized. However, we can identify how the outcomes of NASA's activities contribute significantly to the achievement of America's goals in five key areas:

Economic growth and security—NASA conducts aeronautics and space research and develops technology in partnership with industry, academia, and other federal agencies to keep America capable and competitive.

Increased understanding of science and technology—NASA communicates widely the content, relevancy, and excitement of our mission and discoveries to inspire and increase the understanding and the broad application of science and technology.

Protection of the Earth's Environment—NASA studies the Earth as a planet and as a system to understand global climate change, enabling the world to address environmental issues.

Educational Excellence—NASA involves the educational community in our endeavors to inspire America's students, create learning opportunities, and enlighten inquisitive minds.

Peaceful Exploration and Discovery—NASA explores the Universe to enrich human life by stimulating intellectual curiosity, opening new worlds of opportunity, and uniting nations of the world in this quest.

Annual performance goals (APGs) supporting the first three outcomes can be found in all of the Enterprises and Crosscutting Processes. APGs supporting the preservation of the environment can be found in the Earth Science Enterprise.

NASA's Fiscal Year 2003 Budget

The NASA FY 2003 budget request to OMB supports the President's commitment to support NASA's space and aeronautics program. This budget supports NASA's near-term priorities to fly the Space Shuttle safely and build the International Space Station. NASA's longer-term investments in America's future—developing more affordable, reliable means of access to space and conducting cutting-edge scientific and technological research—are also supported.

The successful execution of NASA's strategic goals and objectives is contingent on receipt of the requested appropriations, as well as the provision of funds, materials, or services which have been committed to the cooperative agreements or partnerships that are referenced in this document. The parties to these agreements include: foreign governments, other Federal Agencies or Departments, and commercial entities.

NATIONAL AERONAUTICS AND SPACE ADMINISTRATION
FISCAL YEAR 2003 ESTIMATES
(IN MILLIONS OF REAL YEAR DOLLARS)
FEDERAL RETIREES COST DISTRIBUTED BY ENTERPRISE

For Display Purposes Only

	FY 2001	FY 2002 Excludes Emergency Response Funds	FY 2002 Includes Emergency Response Funds	FY 2003
Human Space Flight	7,198.5	6,797.1	6,873.1	6,172.9
International Space Station	2,127.8	1,721.7	1,721.7	1,492.1
Space Shuttle	3,118.8	3,272.8	3,272.8	3,208.0
Payload & ELV Support	90.0	91.3	91.3	87.5
HEDS Investments and Support	1,292.8	1,181.5	1,257.5	1,220.2
Space Communications & Data Systems	521.7	482.2	482.2	117.5
Safety, Mission Assurance & Engineering	47.4	47.6	47.6	47.6
Science, Aeronautics & Technology	7,134.5	8,082.3	8,114.8	8,918.5
Space Science	2,617.6	2,872.7	2,880.1	3,428.3
Biological & Physical Research	365.2	823.5	828.0	851.3
Earth Science	1,771.2	1,631.2	1,635.7	1,639.4
Aerospace Technology	2,247.8	2,527.6	2,543.7	2,855.6
Academic Programs	132.7	227.3	227.3	143.7
Inspector General	23.9	24.7	24.7	25.6
Subtotal Agency	14,357.2	14,904.2	15,012.7	15,117.0
Emergency Response Fund		108.5		
Total Agency		15,012.7		

*FY 2001 restructured to reflect new FY 2002 Two Appropriation Structure

Fiscal Year 2003 Estimates (In millions of Dollars)

	FY 1999	FY 2000	FY 2001*	FY 2002[1]	FY 2003
NASA Total Including Federal Retirees Cost			(14,357)	(15,013)	15,117
NASA Total Excluding Federal Retirees Cost	13,653	13,602	14,253	14,902	15,000
Space Science	2,119	2,194	2,321	2,867	3,414
Earth Science	1,414	1,443	1,485	1,626	1,628
Human Exploration and Development of Space**	6,345	6,302	5,973	6,830	6,131
Aerospace Technology	1,339	1,125	1,404	2,508	2,816
Biological & Physical Research***			313	820	842
R&PM/CoF/OIG/Academic Programs	2,436	2,538			
OIG/Academic Programs				251	169
Federal Retirees Cost			(104)	(111)	117
Civil Service FTEs**	18,469	18,375	18,711	19,005	19,050

*Reflects 9/28/01 Operating Plan

** Includes Human Space Flight, Biological & Physical Research, Mission Communications and Space Communications Services, Space Operations, and Safety, Mission Assurance & Engineering.

***Beginning in FY 2001, Biological & Physical Research is a separate Enterprise.

****FTE's reflect total Agency including Office of Inspector General (OIG).

[1]Includes $108M for Emergency Response Fund

The mission support line in the preceding table (FY 1999–2001) provides funding for mission support and includes: safety, mission assurance, engineering and advanced concepts activities supporting agency programs; salaries and related expenses in support of research in NASA field installations; design, repair, rehabilitation and modification of institutional facilities and construction of new institutional facilities; and other operations activities supporting conduct of agency programs such as the OIG and Academic Programs.

NASA is making progress towards full cost management. Beginning in FY 2002, NASA is implementing a two-appropriation budget (excluding the Inspector General account). The two-appropriation budget includes Human Space Flight (HSF) and Science, Aeronautics and Technology (SAT). The budget for Mission Support and other select elements have been allocated against the Enterprises contained in the two-appropriation budget that began in FY 2002.

For informational purposes, the Enterprise sections of this plan will display: 1) Enterprise FY funding levels for FY 1999-2003 and, 2) Civil Service staffing levels assigned to each Enterprise.

Additional detail on the means and strategies for accomplishing these performance targets is included in the budget narrative sections of this document. The NASA FY 2003 Budget will be available through the NASA homepage at the following internet address: http://ifmp.nasa.gov/codeb/budget2003/.

NASA's Performance Plan

The performance plan describes performance measures for program activities requested in the FY 2003 budget. FY 2003 Performance goals and objectives are defined for NASA's Strategic Enterprises and for Crosscutting Processes in the NASA Strategic Plan (NPD 1000.lb).

The FY 2003 Plan provides information on how NASA plans to verify and validate performance data. Enterprises/Crosscutting Processes also include a description of the individual means that they will use to verify and validate measured values in performance reporting. These added features are provided to communicate various approaches used in the verification and validation of performance data and to support the credibility of reported performance.

Strategic goals and objectives are provided along with annual performance goals and indicators in the introductory section for each Enterprise and Crosscutting Process. The annual performance goals and indicators used in performance tracking are integrated with the strategic goals and objectives to provide a better linkage between the Strategic Plan and the Performance Plan. This format provides greater performance context and eliminates the necessity for a separate performance table to demonstrate the linkage between the Strategic Plan and the Annual Performance Plan that was a duplicative effort.

Generate Knowledge, a crosscutting process, is central to NASA's mission and is the primary means through which we seek the answers to our fundamental questions. Based on a NASA Advisory Council recommendation, Generate Knowledge was not included in the FY 2002 Performance Plan. The NAC's recommendation was based on the potential duplication of science research metrics across the Enterprises. As a result, NASA has been exploring alternative ways to effectively communicate this performance. Beginning with FY 03, an alternative method for reporting Generate Knowledge, in lieu of using performance metrics, will be provided in the Agency Performance Report. Based on the input provided by the Committee on Science, Engineering, and Public Policy (COSEPUP) report titled *Implementing the Government Performance and Results Act for Research* (2000), NASA will take a new approach to reporting the knowledge generated by the Agency's funded research. The NASA Research Results report will be an annual compilation of research highlights and most important discoveries made possible by the Generate Knowledge process via NASA funding. This report will augment the enterprise metrics that are detailed in the Agency Performance Plan. This report will not measure performance, but will describe research products resulting from NASA investments.

In accordance with OMB Circular A-11 requirements, annual performance goals for FY 1999-2003 are displayed by Enterprise/ Crosscutting Process. Multi-year formats help to demonstrate cumulative progress towards achievement of strategic goals and objectives. Each annual performance goal also has an associated color assessment to facilitate trend analysis.

The following color key is used to assess performance:

Blue: Significantly exceeded performance

Green: Achieved performance target

Yellow: Did not achieve performance target, progress was significant and achievement is anticipated within next fiscal year

Red: Failed to achieve performance target, do not anticipate completion within the next fiscal year

Each Enterprise or Crosscutting Process section continues to include a budget link table that recaps the relationship of budget account and annual performance goals. To facilitate configuration management, control numbers have been assigned to all performance targets. The numbering sequences may not be contiguous, as targets may have been dropped out as the formulation process progressed.

The Performance Evaluation Process

NASA uses a process of extensive internal and external reviews to evaluate our progress against established plans. Enterprises and functional managers conduct reviews on a periodic basis. There are regular reviews for functional management activities, such as procurement, finance, facilities, personnel, and information resources management. There are also programmatic reviews of science, engineering, and technology plans and performance. The NASA Inspector General conducts independent reviews and provides recommendations for corrective actions.

NASA has established management councils, as described in the NASA Strategic Management Handbook, which conduct internal oversight reviews. Throughout the year, Program Management Councils (PMCs) at Headquarters and the Centers assess program schedules, cost, and technical performance against established programmatic commitments. The Senior Management Council (SMC) brings together both Headquarters and Field Installation Directors to conduct assessment reviews twice a year of the progress being made in meeting the Enterprise and Crosscutting Process performance targets.

NASA's extant management review processes provide appropriate forums for internal reporting and reviewing of project and program performance data. The recent streamlining of agency processes provides confidence that new data collection and oversight processes need not be created for compliance with GPRA. Our mission oriented organizational structure and established management processes are well suited to assessment of this type of performance evaluation.

There are also significant external review processes in place. The external reviews typically begin with the peer review processes in which NASA uses panels of outside scientific experts to ensure that science research proposals are selected strictly on the merits of the planned research. This process takes into account past performance for selection and/or continued funding. NASA requests assistance from other federal agencies to provide expert advice and council. In some cases, the organizations are advisory bodies of experts from the public and private sectors that work with NASA to establish priorities in particular scientific disciplines. For example, NASA has requested that its senior advisory body, the NASA Advisory Council (NAC), independently review NASA's annual performance. Since FY 1999, the NAC has reviewed reported performance and provided a qualitative assessment of the Agency's progress that is included in the Agency Performance Report. In other cases, reviews are conducted by organizations such as the NASA Advisory Council, the Aerospace Safety Advisory Panel, and the National Academy of Sciences, which share responsibility for oversight of the Agency.

Additionally, the General Accounting Office reviews both the Performance Plan and Performance Report in their annual report "Status of Plans for Achieving Key Outcomes and Addressing Major Management Challenges."

The use of these external reviews allows NASA to receive a report card on whether we are making the anticipated progress towards accomplishing the priorities established by the Administration, the Congress, and our advisory bodies. When necessary, these external assessments result in the revision of either implementation plans or strategic plans.

The GPRA Performance Evaluation and Report Process

For the purposes of the GPRA performance reporting process, NASA uses advisory committees as the critical input when assessing performance. These committees provide inputs on NASA's Strategic

Plan, individual Enterprise Strategic Plans, and budgetary priorities. NASA furnishes program performance status information, and in turn, the committees render advice and council. NASA uses this process to generate an independent "scorecard report on our annual performance.

NASA has historically been one of the most open federal agencies in terms of performance measurements. Public attention is drawn quickly to program successes, and particularly to program failures. Press conferences on scientific results and program technical status are commonplace. The technical measurement of program progress is a management imperative due to the heavy emphasis on development programs, and within the programs, the specific projects. Flight programs such as the International Space Station compile thousands of technical performance metrics, schedule milestones, and cost performance data.

However, the GPRA requires a heavier focus on outcome metrics rather than NASA's ubiquitous input and output metrics. Like other federal agencies engaged in science and technology, NASA has difficulty in quantifying outcomes and, especially, relating current outcomes to current fiscal expenditures. This is appropriate since NASA's development programs are multi-year in character. In some cases, past expenditures began more than a decade ago. For example, the Hubble Space Telescope that entered into development in the mid-1970's. More recently, NASA has focused on programs and projects with much shorter development periods, on the order of 3-5 years. Yet, the science outcomes are dependent on scientists analyzing the information gathered in the years after launch. Therefore, in measuring the incremental annual performance of a multi-year research or development activity, where an outcome is not realized for several years, output metrics are the most appropriate way to measure the progress towards the achievement of strategic goals and objectives.

The stated objectives of programs within NASA's Enterprises are long-term in character. Annual performance evaluations assess whether appropriate progress is being made in obtaining the scientific or technical data that was believed necessary to achieve these objectives at the time they were developed. By obtaining such information, NASA provides the outputs necessary to achieve outcomes such as answering scientific questions or implementing new aerospace technologies. However, in many cases, NASA cannot guarantee that such outcomes will be achieved since other factors outside NASA's direct control (like breakthroughs in scientific understanding or private sector investments in technology) may be required to achieve a given outcome.

It is particularly important in our view to avoid evaluating actual output performance in R&D organizations solely by counting the number of planned events for the year with the number that actually occurred. The "beancount" approach is more appropriate to a known manufacturing environment. In the high-performance, high-risk R&D environment that characterizes NASA's programs, it is inadvisable to incentivize on-time performance at the expense of safety, budget, quality, high performance and appropriate risk-taking.

NASA has worked hard to maintain the highest emphasis on safety; this value applies not only to safety of personnel but also to preservation of high value facilities, equipment, experimental hardware, and related capabilities. Quality goes hand-in-hand with safety, but extends well beyond it. For example, taking credit for completing a critical design review (CDR) for a spacecraft is only appropriate when the CDR process has been thorough, complete, and meets performance standards. Great care must be taken that quality does not suffer when contract fee incentives call for a milestone payment upon completion of the CDR. Other examples abound, and give rise to our constant vigilance to avoid rushing to launch in order to achieve a given date.

It is possible, of course, to emphasize safety and quality and achieve little of lasting significance or have the achievement take an inordinate amount of time. Building spacecraft that do not test new designs, but rely only on proven designs, is appropriate for operational, mission agencies or commercial entities. It is not the appropriate role for an R&D agency like NASA. Conducting basic and applied research involves experimentation. When exploring new methods and new technologies in these high-performance ventures, it is acceptable to take risks, to push the envelope, and to fail. The tolerance of failure puts NASA and other R&D agencies into a different category than other federal agencies involved in the delivery of services to the public. Note, however, that this does not translate into an acceptance of failures that result from taking an inappropriate level of risk. The level of appropriate risk is tailored to the environment. The distinction is critical, particularly in high-value, high-cost environments, such as human space flight, the maintenance of the Hubble Space Telescope, and the launch of research spacecraft. The risk of failure in those venues is limited by all practicable means.

Thus, output measures are best used in suitable context. For these reasons, NASA management encourages Space Shuttle program managers to set aside metrics dealing with launches planned vs. launches achieved during a given fiscal year. If by waiting, one less launch is achieved than planned, but the result is better safety or quality or enables improved performance or reduces risk, then the latter result is what NASA wants to incentivize.

NASA's Verification and Validation of Performance Data

NASA is committed to ensuring that reported performance information is valid and reliable. Data credibility is a critical element in the Agency's ability to manage for results and to be accountable for the accuracy of performance data. NASA's performance in developing and delivering products and services is evaluated at the Agency, Strategic Enterprise, functional office, program and project, crosscutting process, and individual levels. Each level has responsibility to execute requirements and to measure, evaluate, and report results. Methods and procedures for collecting this information are evaluated and validated by program managers who are responsible for data collection and reporting. As each part of the organization completes its measurement process, data are used to validate that performance meets or exceeds planned goals, objectives and performance targets. In those situations in which performance does not meet expectations, opportunities for continuous improvement are identified.

Communicating our verification and validation approaches provides greater confidence that reported performance information is credible while enhancing the usefulness of the information. In an audit of the FY 2000 Performance Report, GAO stated that NASA's validation and verification reporting efforts provided greater confidence that results were credible. Specific documentation of achievement was provided for each annual performance goal. This effort will continue as demonstrated by individual enterprise/crosscut verification and validation efforts summarized in the Plan and verification/validation/data source information by APG reported in the Report. Data sources that were used included, but were not limited to, databases used for other purposes, third-party reviews, and certification by managers and/or contractors. Changes or improvements to existing data collection and reporting systems or processes were included in the verification methodology. As appropriate, reliance upon external sources was identified in the data sources section of each target's performance. With regards to external data sources, NASA relies on the individuals responsible for the performance to validate and verify the information provided for GPRA compliance.

For the purpose of assessing NASA's overall performance, we will continue to ask our Advisory Committees to evaluate accomplishments at the Enterprise level. Their assessments not only integrate quantitative output measures but also provide balance in the context of safety, quality, high performance, and appropriate risk. The NAC evaluates annual performance for both the Enterprises and the Crosscutting Processes, assessing both actual performance and progress towards strategic goal and objective achievement. In addition, the Office of the Inspector General (OIG) has conducted validation audits of reported performance data used to support the Agency's actual results on selected performance targets to ensure that underlying performance data are accurate and reliable.

PRESIDENT'S MANAGEMENT AGENDA

ACTION PLANS FOR THE

NATIONAL AERONAUTICS AND SPACE ADMINISTRATION

May 9, 2002

Initials of NASA   **Initials of OMB**
Representative: _____   **Representative:** _____

TABLE OF CONTENTS

HUMAN CAPITAL 3

COMPETITIVE SOURCING 12

FINANCIAL MANAGEMENT 14

EXPANDING ELECTRONIC GOVERNMENT 16

BUDGET/PERFORMANCE INTEGRATION 19

PMA SCORECARD 21

HUMAN CAPITAL

CURRENT STATUS

OMB reports NASA's status as "red" for human capital. NASA is in the process of developing an agency-wide human capital plan, has proposed new authorities to improve management of its human capital, and has committed to improving its workforce tracking. However, NASA has yet to approve an agency-wide human capital plan, fully utilize its existing human capital management authorities, or implement an improved workforce tracking system. Also, NASA needs to complete and submit to OMB a Transformation Workforce Restructuring Plan based on the Strategic Resources Review. This will be critical, in conjunction with the Strategic Human Capital Plan, to ensuring that no skill gaps/deficiencies exist in mission critical occupations.

NASA PLANS TO ACHIEVE YELLOW STATUS

Develop and Approve Agency Strategic Human Capital Plan

NASA will develop and approve an agency-level human capital plan and associated implementation plans. NASA will submit its first full, Strategic Human Capital Plan to OPM and OMB no later than June 30, 2002. At a minimum, this plan will address three key areas.

1) Strategic Management of Critical Workforce Needs

NASA's critical workforce competencies are not permanent or static, but are a portfolio of skills that changes over time as NASA's needs change, with new competencies coming in and competencies no longer needed transitioning out. To greatly improve the agility and flexibility of NASA's workforce, NASA's human capital plan will:

- Define the critical workforce competencies NASA needs to execute its approved programs over the next ten years—including permanent and non-permanent civil servants, and contracted workforce in industry and academia.

- Develop an agency-wide capability to track, project, and analyze critical workforce competencies that enables strategic management

- Identify imbalances in current and projected workforce of today, relative to what is needed for the future (oversupply/undersupply of key skills)

- Identify those workforce competencies that can or could be supplied through academia, industry or other organizations and those competencies that can only be met through a civil servant workforce.

- Identify the limited number of truly critical civil servant personnel needed for those competencies that NASA must retain in-house as well as those needed to oversee competencies supplied through academia, industry or other organizations.

- Identify and plan out the reforms needed to enable the competitive sourcing of those competencies that can or could be supplied through academia, industry or other organizations, including a schedule for each reform and an estimated range of the number of civil servant positions that could be affected each year (to be outlined in the NASA Competitive Sourcing Plan).

- Develop a lifecycle model for NASA's workforce competencies to aid in their strategic management that includes three distinct phases: 1) identifying the need for then establishing new competencies; 2) assessing and maintaining the health of mature competencies; and 3) determining whether NASA no longer needs to provide a competency (either with in-house personnel or at all), and the process for transitioning NASA away from that competency.

2) Creating and Expanding Organizational Agility

NASA must improve its agility as an organization, to adapt to the changing needs of the future. This can be done with more institutional flexibility, more flexibility in the ability to shape the workforce, and more flexibility within the workforce itself at the individual employee level.

Management Authorities and Flexibility—To improve the recruitment, retention, competency and flexibility of NASA's civil servant workforce, NASA's human capital plan will:

- Identify new authorities necessary to implement the reforms contained in NASA's Competitive Sourcing Plan. These authorities could include (but proposals are not limited to): benefits portability, extended buyout authority, retraining expenses for involuntarily separated employees, and waiver of reduction of annuity when reemploying civil servants (a menu of options will be attached to the Strategic Human Capital Plan).

- Identify new authorities that could improve the recruitment, retention, competency and flexibility of NASA's civil servant workforce. These authorities could include: excepted service and distinguished scholar hiring authorities, scholarship for service, expanded use of term appointments and IPAs, simplified candidate evaluation, pay broad-banding, critical pay authority, and industry and academic exchange programs (a menu of options will be attached to the Strategic Human Capital Plan).

Civil Service Mix—Permanent and Non-Permanent—To improve agility of the workforce, NASA's plan will:

- Develop a strategy—tied to information from NASA capabilities in strategic management of human capital—that will enable the identification of the appropriate mix, over time, between permanent and non-permanent civil servants.

- Ensure that mechanisms and incentives are available for achieving the appropriate mix of non-permanent civil servants and IPAs (e.g. terms, temps, NEX, IPAs, etc.).

Employee Agility—To improve agility of the individual employee, NASA's human capital plan will:

- Include a plan that ensures that the norm is for employees to broaden their experience and skill base, as part of career advancement at NASA.

- Incorporate training and education activities to help make employees more agile.

3) **Assuring Future Leadership, Management and Technical Expertise**

<u>Recruitment and Retention</u>

- Define strategies for improving ability to recruit and retain

<u>Training and Education</u>

- Define training and education priorities that assure NASA's future needs can be met

<u>Mentoring and Succession Planning</u>—To improve and ensure successful management of NASA's programs, NASA's plan will:

- Provide methods for identifying NASA civil servant program/project leaders and experts that are most critical to NASA executing its approved programs.

- Establish mentoring and knowledge sharing approaches and programs—driven by strategic needs—that enable current leaders to transfer their expertise to future project leaders.

- Identify and use lessons learned from successes and failures to mentor and transfer critical knowledge and skills to future project leaders who need this development and knowledge.

Begin Implementation of Human Capital Plan: To begin implementation of its Plan, NASA will complete the following actions.

1) **Strategic Management of Critical Workforce Needs**

- Provide a progress report and quarterly accomplishments relative to OPM's Human Capital scorecard by June 30, 2002

- Complete Competency pilot at KSC by June 30, 2002

- Develop an Agencywide competency dictionary by July 30, 2002

- NASA has developed a phased approach to establishing and Agencywide workforce planning capability. The first phase will involve updating and integrating the existing SRR workforce competency database by September 30, 2002.

- Identify critical competencies across the agency, those at risk, and potential skill mix adjustments between Centers by November 30, 2002.

- As a first step to assuring that employee rewards, recognition, and performance are linked to Agency key goals, the Agency will assess the current state of linkage using the OPM survey (December 2002).

2) **Creating and Expanding Organizational Agility**

- NASA will develop HR tools and strategies that support major Agency transformation implementation plans—including competitive sourcing goals—and, as necessary, will offer legislative proposals to facilitate reforms (ongoing).

- By December 31, 2002 complete a study to evaluate the need for expanded mobility and rotational assignments to expand knowledge and experience of the workforce.

- By October 1, 2002 provide Enterprises/Centers mechanisms and incentives for hiring non-permanent employees.

- To support increasing the utilization of HR flexibilities to recruit, hire and retain a highly productive workforce, NASA Headquarters will delegate NEX authority to Centers (June 2002) and will identify critical positions where incentives are required (September 2002).

- NASA will roll out an automated classification system within the Integrated Financial Management Program (IFMP) (September 2002).

- The Agency will establish a NASA Education program linkage system that tracks students in NASA Education programs in order to link students in these programs to NASA hiring efforts for future workforce needs (September 2002).

3) **Assuring Future Leadership, Management and Technical Expertise**

- By October 2002 develop a project leadership knowledge sharing and mentoring plan including strategic areas of priority, identification of critical leaders and experts who can share knowledge and mentor future project leaders, and begin pilot activities.

- By June 3, 2002 identify positions requiring critical position pay authority.

- Implement an enhanced agency-wide strategy to recruit and retain in critical competencies.

- Establish by November 30, 2002, key strategic skill area targets to shape recruitment of college hires for the summer of 2003 (feeding pipeline through middle of decade).

NASA PLANS TO ACHIEVE GREEN STATUS

The OMB Core Criteria for Achieving Success are to achieve all of the following:

- Agency human capital strategy is aligned with mission, goals, and organizational objectives: 1) integrated into Budget and Strategic Plans; 2) consistent with OPM's human capital balanced scorecard (issued by December 1, 2001); and 3) complies with standards for internal accountability systems to ensure effective merit-based HRM.

- Agency has a citizen-centered organizational structure that is delayered and oriented toward performing the mission assigned to it.

- Agency 1) sustains high-performing workforce that is continually improving in productivity; 2) strategically uses existing personnel flexibilities, tools, and technology; and 3) implements effective succession plans.

- No skill gaps/deficiencies exist in mission critical occupations.

- Agency differentiates between high and low performers through appropriate incentive and rewards.

- Changes in agency workforce skill mix and organizational structure reflect increased emphasis on e-government and competitive sourcing.

Fully Implement Human Capital Plan

To ensure full implementation of its Human Capital Plan and meet all criteria for achieving green status, NASA will undertake the following actions:

1) **Strategic Management of Critical Workforce Needs**

   - Complete rollout of KSC competency model Agencywide and resolve gaps and surplus competencies in mission critical occupations by September 30, 2003.

2) **Creating and Expanding Organizational Agility**

   - NASA will continue to incorporate human resources tools and strategies in major Agency transformation implementation plans, including legislative proposals, where necessary, to facilitate reforms (ongoing)

   - By October 2003 evaluate results of mobility/rotation study, and pilot/implement actions to expand development activities as indicated by study results

   - Identify strategically-derived goals for permanent/non-permanent mix, and implement a plan for achieving those goals.

   - NASA will verify or—where FY 2002 assessment results indicate its absence—establish a linkage between employee rewards, recognition, and performance and Agency key goals (May 2003).

   - NASA Headquarters will verify that delegation of NEX authority to the Centers has resulted in increased use of this flexibility (June 2003).

   - NASA Headquarters will survey Agency managers to assess satisfaction with the automated hiring system module of the IFMP (September 2003).

3) **Assuring Future Leadership, Management and Technical Expertise**

   - Implement by October 1, 2003 new positions subject to critical position pay authority

   - By October 2003 implement agencywide program and products—driven by strategic needs—related to mentoring and transferring knowledge from critical project leader experts to mentor future project leaders.

- Implement by October 1, 2003 a training and education program that is aligned with strategic priorities based upon training needs
- NASA will incorporate the Strategic Human Capital Plan into the Agency's strategic and performance planning processes (September 2003).

BACKGROUND

- NASA reduced its overall civil service workforce by 26 percent between FY 1993 and FY 2000 and reduced the Headquarters staff by 50 percent. Organizational restructuring and reductions resulted in a 52 percent reduction in supervisory positions and a 15 percent reduction in SES. On an Agencywide basis, the supervisor to employee ratio went from 1:6 to 1:10.

- Less than 13 percent of Agency authorized funding is spent on civil service salaries and benefits. NASA accomplishes its work through the combined efforts of civil servants, contractors, and individuals from the academic world who contribute through post-doctoral fellowships, grants programs, Intergovernmental Personnel Assignments, and other partnerships.

- NASA has transferred major and critically important functions, such as the transfer of space launch and operations to an industry partnership and a consolidated contract with an industry team to handle space communications. NASA established a contracting vehicle that outsources ownership and management of desktop computers, local servers, and other communications assets and services.

- Annual guidance for preparation of SES performance plans reflects ongoing requirement that all such plans be aligned with the NASA Strategic Plan.

- Three NASA Centers have been involved in the pilot of an automated tool to link NASA Strategic Plan goals and objectives to the individual's performance plan.

- NASA has established partnerships with academia to provide fellowships in leadership and project management development, including partnership with the Massachusetts Institute of Technology in Project Management and with the University of Virginia's Darden Business School to develop a Business Education Program.

- The Agency leadership model has been updated. It specifies the latest cutting edge skills and behaviors required for effective leadership, and is linked to NASA's Strategic Plan.

- NASA is addressing the critical "pipeline" issue to ensure a future pool of talent in science, engineering, math, and technology disciplines. An Agency-wide Undergraduate Student Research Program pilot phase was initiated in FY 2001 with 107 students (55 male and 52 female students with 41 percent minority participation from 29 states and Puerto Rico, and represent 70 institutions).

- To enhance capability and reduce time away from work, NASA created and implemented additional on-line capabilities. In FY 2001, the Agency increased training *opportunities* in technology-based learning by 127 percent from the FY 1999 baseline and increased employee *use* of technology-based learning opportunities by 122 percent.

NASA'S ACTIONS SINCE 9/30/01

- NASA began a Strategic Resources Review (SRR) in FY 2001 based on NASA's future vision and mission to ensure that resources are prioritized and directed at the most critical Agency requirements and to focus on the Agency's fundamental roles and missions. There are many activities/actions being studied/explored under the SRR, with three major ones being actively explored. They are Shuttle competitive sourcing, International Space Station (ISS) non-government organization (NGO), and Consolidated Business Services.

- NASA has developed a "menu" of legislative proposals for civil service reforms that may be needed to accomplish SRR transformational activities and to ensure NASA can recruit and retain top science, engineering, and management talent.

- NASA developed a human capital functional leadership plan to support the Agency Strategic Plan. This plan is being superseded by a comprehensive Agency Strategic Human Capital Plan that conforms to the OMB and OPM scorecard criteria. A team of senior NASA managers is currently developing a draft plan, to include goals, strategies, tactical plans, and success measures.

- NASA utilizes recruitment bonuses and retention allowances—a trend the Agency expects to continue because of an increasingly competitive job market and high cost of living in some areas.

- The Agency is re-establishing its recruitment networks and rebuilding once extensive Cooperative Education Program. It continues to utilize the Presidential Management Intern Program and student employment programs as sources for entry-level hires.

- NASA is one of the first Federal agencies to hire individuals under new Federal Career Intern Program—a useful tool for hiring recent graduates in engineering and science.

- NASA has implemented a paperless hiring and competitive promotion system—greatly improving the speed of filling vacancies and improving the job-seeking experience for the public. It has been nominated for Agency and Government-wide awards.

- The Agency established a National Recruitment Initiative to develop Agency-wide recruitment strategies to attract and hire a highly technical S&E workforce focusing on the candidate instead of the hiring process; leveraging partnerships and alliances with universities; and coordinating Agency-wide recruitment opportunities and outcomes. The report was issued in March 2002, with tools to facilitate achieving an agile, flexible hiring model identified. Three such tools are currently in the development stage.

- NASA was the first agency to implement the new Federal-wide program to repay student loans to attract or retain employees in critical positions.

- A variety of awards and performance recognition programs are in place. The Agency is currently conducting a study on how recognition programs foster behaviors that lead to mission success. Internal and external benchmarking is being used to identify critical factors for developing, using, communicating, and assessing recognition practices.

- The Agency continues to emphasize quality of work-life initiatives such as alternative work schedules, family-friendly leave programs, and employee assistance programs.

- NASA funds a minimum investment in learning of more than 3 percent of salary and plans continued investment at or above this percentage.

- NASA has enhanced the system architecture of the Site for Online Learning Resources (SOLAR) to support 50,000 learners.

- To improve project team competencies, emphasis has been placed on "just in time" training opportunities for project leaders and team members.

- Learning through simulations, as well as coaching and mentoring opportunities, are being pursued.

- The NASA Integrated Action Team (NIAT) identified actions to provide systems solutions to improve NASA's ability to effectively execute its mission, ensuring application of best practices across spectrum of Agency programs and projects. These actions are now underway.

- The Agency redesigned its Fellowship Program, which now requires Center management to document a reentry strategy to ensure learning acquired is applied to Agency-mission needs. It includes a process to track related mission impacts resulting from the investment.

- Programs have been added to provide knowledge sharing forums and deliver targeted development workshops geared at assisting intact project teams in performing quality project management, incorporating lessons learned on other projects.

- NASA has long-term developmental processes in place that provide a critical tool for succession planning, including the Senior Executive Service Candidate Development Program and the Professional Development Program. With a goal toward ensuring a strong, diverse candidate pool of potential future leaders, increased emphasis is being placed on assuring the right people are nominated for such programs.

- The Agency is developing program linkages/data system to link students supported by NASA Education Programs to Agency human capital requirements.

COMPETITIVE SOURCING

CURRENT STATUS

OMB reports NASA's status as "red" for competitive sourcing. NASA has not completed public-private or direct conversion competition on 15 percent of the FTEs listed on the approved FAIR act inventories of commercial activities. NASA is in the process of developing a plan for achieving competitive sourcing goals, and has agreed to undertake some key competitive sourcing reforms. However, NASA has yet to complete its strategic resources review that may identify competitive sourcing opportunities, or lay out a concrete plan for meeting the government-wide 50 percent competitive sourcing goal. NASA's FAIR Act inventory may not reflect some of the FTEs that would be subject to planned competitive sourcing activities, therefore it is critical to get an updated FAIR Act inventory that accurately reflects commercial activities as soon as possible.

NASA PLANS TO ACHIEVE YELLOW STATUS

Develop a Competitive Sourcing Plan to transform the 40-year old national lab organizational model NASA uses to execute its programs and greatly improve the agility and flexibility of NASA's workforce, NASA's plan will:

- Clearly articulate the reasons for pursuing competitive sourcing and make the case why competitive sourcing is in the best long-term interest of NASA.

- Revise NASA's FAIR Act Inventory to be consistent with the workforce competencies and classifications provided in the Human Capital Plan (i.e., all positions not classified as inherently governmental will be classified as commercial on the Inventory) by June 30, 2002.

- By June 30, 2002, provide an interim competitive sourcing plan that lays out NASA's specific competitive sourcing activities with the exception of Space Shuttle competitive sourcing and a non-government organization for managing Space Station research. This plan should provide an estimate of the specific FTE associated with and schedule for each activity.

    o At a minimum, the interim plan for these reforms should include: a University Affiliated Research Center (UARC) at Ames Research Center, competitive sourcing for technicians at NASA's research centers, and, potentially, one consolidation effort with another government agency (e.g., DOD).

    o Reforms can include (but are not limited to): traditional OMB Circular A-76 competitions, conversions excepted from A-76 competition, consolidation with DOD or other federal agencies, and rehiring after attrition into new or existing contractor or partner organizations such as federally funded research and development centers (FFRDCs) or university affiliated research centers (UARCs).

- By September, 2002, provide a complete, integrated, agency-wide competitive sourcing plan that includes Space Shuttle competitive sourcing and a non-government organization

(NGO) for Space Station in addition to the reforms provided in the interim plan. This plan should, at a minimum, meet the long-term, government-wide 50-percent competitive sourcing goal and provide an estimate of the specific FTE associated with and schedule for each activity.

Begin Implementation of Competitive Sourcing Plan

To begin implementation of its plan, NASA will move beyond planning to implementation of key activities including Shuttle competitive sourcing and Station NGO. The plan should identify any necessary and appropriate exceptions to full competition per OMB Circular A-76.

Begin Extending Competitive Sourcing Reform to Contracted Activities

To begin ensuring that both civil servant and contracted activities are subject to regular, recurring review and competition, NASA will initiate the following actions.

- Create a consolidated list of all Federally Funded Research and Development Centers (FFRDCs), University Affiliated Research Centers (UARCs), Commercial Centers for the Development of Space (CCDSs), University Research, Engineering and Technology Institutes (URETIs), and similar contracts and partnerships providing reimbursable support services by October 1, 2002.

- Put in place plans for reviews and recompetition of these contracts and partnerships by September 30, 2003. At a minimum, plans will include mid-term review dates for any options to extend and a hard termination date of no greater than ten years with provisions for granting exceptions as appropriate.

NASA PLANS TO ACHIEVE GREEN STATUS

Fully Implement Competitive Sourcing Plan

To ensure full implementation of its plan, NASA will take the following actions:

- Achieve Phase I of NASA's competitive sourcing plan as approved by OMB (to be submitted on June 30, 2002) by September 30, 2003.

- Be on schedule for achieving Phase II of NASA's approved competitive sourcing plan by September 30, 2003.

Final target commitments for Phase I and Phase II (e.g., 15% and 50%) will be based on the 2000 FAIR Act Inventory baseline and analysis to be completed by June 30, 2002.

Fully Extend Competitive Sourcing Reform to Contracted Activities

To ensure that both civil servant and contracted activities are subject to regular review and competition, NASA will complete or have underway reviews and recompetitions for all contracts and partnerships that have reached their mid-term review date or their mandatory re-compete date.

FINANCIAL MANAGEMENT

CURRENT STATUS

OMB reports NASA's current status as "red" for financial management. NASA had received a "clean" audit opinion for seven consecutive years and the auditors concluded that NASA had no material financial management weaknesses. PricewaterhouseCoopers (PWC), an independent public accounting firm, audited NASA's FY 2001 financial statements, and concluded that it could not express an opinion on the financial statements because NASA did not provide sufficient evidence, on a timely basis, to support certain amounts on the financial statements. PWC also state that it identified a material weakness resulting from NASA's lack of adequate controls to reasonably assure that property, plant, and equipment and materials are presented fairly in financial statements.

NASA is implementing a new, Integrated Financial Management (IFM) system. However, the most critical component, the Core Financial module has not been fully implemented at the nine NASA field Centers and Headquarters.

NASA PLANS TO ACHIEVE YELLOW STATUS

NASA's overall strategy to fully achieve the objectives of the financial management initiative is to (1) successfully implement its new IFM system and (2) resolve its material weakness and regain a "clean" audit opinion on its financial statements.

Implement IFM System

Due to the use of individual, non-integrated systems at Headquarters and field Centers to meet statutory and regulatory reporting requirements, NASA reports its financial systems as a significant area of management concern in its annual report pursuant to the requirements of the Federal Managers' Financial Integrity Act. The IFM program consists of a series of projects such as core finance, including budget execution; travel, and budget formulation. While all components of the IFM Program are important, the successful completion of the Core Financial project is particularly critical to achieving the objectives of the improved financial management initiative and to implementation of full cost budgeting and management. To continue progress towards full implementation of NASA's IFM, NASA will achieve the following IFM implementation milestone:

- Successfully implement the IFMP Core Financial module at five field Centers and Headquarters (February 1, 2003)

Obtain "Clean" Opinion on FY 2002 Financial Statements

A team consisting of CFO Office staff, Center finance staff, and technical staff to address Station and Shuttle matters is addressing each of the problems identified by PWC in its FY 2001 financial statement audit. To achieve a "clean" opinion on its FY 2002 financial statements, NASA will meet the following milestones:

- Resolve all outstanding issues resulting from the audit of NASA's FY 2001 financial statements (July 31, 2002);

- Close FY 2002 financial records (November 15, 2002);
- Obtain "clean" audit opinion on FY 2002 financial statements (February 1, 2003)

NASA PLANS TO ACHIEVE GREEN STATUS

Implement IFM System

NASA will complete full implementation of the IFM Core Financial module by achieving the following milestone:

- Successfully implement the IFMP Core Financial module at all nine field Centers and Headquarters (June 1, 2003) while continuing on schedule for implementing the remaining modules.

EXPANDING ELECTRONIC GOVERNMENT

CURRENT STATUS

OMB reports that NASA current status as "red" for e-government. NASA has: completed all business cases for IT investment for FY 2002; made progress on its Enterprise Architecture (EA); begun to transition to the Information Technology Investment Portfolio System (I-TIPS); assessed IT security program and developed an action plan for correcting weaknesses; and is participating in seven E-gov initiatives (Geospatial Information One Stop, Recruitment One Stop, Enterprise HR Integration, E-authentication, Integrated Acquisition, and e-grants).

However, NASA's business cases have historically been delivered late, NASA's EA is not yet adequately integrated with its Capital Planning and Investment Control (CPIC) process, and NASA has weaknesses in some areas of security including program management and implementation at both the agency level and within Centers. Additionally, there is inconsistent testing and evaluation of agency security effectiveness.

NASA PLANS TO ACHIEVE YELLOW STATUS

- Capital planning and investment control process must include the necessary provisions to submit business cases that are complete and on time—September 2002.

- Revise remaining unsatisfactory 2002 business cases as identified by OIRA.

- Provide Exhibit 53 and IT business cases on time—September 2002.

- Create the FY 2004 President's budget Information Technology schedule using the Information Technology Investment Portfolio System (I-TIPS)—September 2002.

- Per updated corrective action plans, complete GISRA IT security actions for all systems with security weaknesses—September 2002.

NASA PLANS TO ACHIEVE GREEN STATUS

Ensuring the Strategic Value of IT Investments, justify IT investments and integrate planning into agency decision-making processes and strengthen capital planning and investment control process

- Provide Exhibit 53 and IT business cases on time—September 2002.

- Complete updated corrective action plans for all systems with security weaknesses by September 2002.

- For the baseline IT projects, conduct evaluation and monitor program performance. Metrics include; on average, operating within 90% of "OMB 300" cost, schedule, and performance targets by October 2002

- Plan and implement comprehensive Capital Planning and Investment Control (CPIC) process that integrates IT investments decisions with NASA's Enterprise Architecture for selecting, managing, and evaluating IT investments by December 2002

- Collaborate with US Dept of Education and NSF in establishing a Federal e-Partnership Plan for delivering theme-based educational web campaigns in support of the President's Education Agenda by July 2002. Deliver and evaluate pilot campaign by December 2002.

- Establish an Agency level Enterprise Architecture office towards developing the next phase of NASA's Enterprise Architecture. Phase 1 to include major business operations by September 2002; Phase 2 adds 3 mission areas by July 2003. This agency-level framework will address managing all IT investments and greater centralization of IT security functions. Implement configuration management function by October 2002.

Achieving Internal Efficiency and Effectiveness by Leveraging Technology

- Transition and strengthen common IT infrastructure and shared services based on industry best practices to support "one NASA" - a move from distributed business processes to federated, shared services for accelerated IFMP deployment—February 2003.

- Ensure Agency participation as a partnering agency in implementing 3 OMB E-Government Initiatives (e-training, Enterprise HR Integration) - Ongoing

- For the eTraining initiative, provide support, technical assistance and advice to OPM. Assist in the development of OPM's initiative based on NASA's development and implementation efforts on the "Solar" electronic training site.

Delivery of Information Services to the American Citizen

- Become the managing partner for a government-wide e-education project. Submit e-education plan and business case for OMB approval by July 2002.

- E-Authentication—NASA has provided a full-time technical manager to GSA. Chair the CIO Council Committee to oversee the project.

Improving Intergovernmental Efficiency through E-government

- Geospatial Information—NASA is partnering with Department of Interior to ensure our data products are compliant with the Geospatial Information One Stop initiative.

- EGrants
  - Coordinating the interagency activity under the initiative to expand previous efforts by NSF to pilot their electronic grant application system. Partners include NSF/NIH/Agriculture/NOAA/ONR. On going activity

- o Initiated and led a pilot project to create an Internet portal to search across the Catalog of Federal Domestic Assistance and the FedBizOpps for grant programs and opportunities to be used in pre-populating the grant application. Pilot to be integrated with E-Grants project for coordination of user training and testing by April 30, 2002.
- o NASA is also the lead on the group tasked by OMB to determine the best single identifier to be used across all Federal grant recipients by October 30, 2002.

Reduce the burden on Business through E-Government

- Integrated Acquisition—provide technical guidance and support for the government-wide initiative. NASA led the technical development of FedBizOpps thru the early deployment of the NASA electronic posting system—NAIS. Ongoing activity.

ACTIONS TO DATE

- Developed an e-NASA strategy to provide a strategic framework for NASA e-government investments—July 2001

- Assessed IT security program and developed corrective action plan—November 2001

- Completed an assessment of NASA-wide IT infrastructure to support core business and mission requirements—January 31, 2002

- Implementing an on-line Information Technology Investment Portfolio System (I-TIPS) and created an agency wide Information Technology call—March 15, 2002

- Submitted to OMB all remaining "major" systems business cases for FY 2002 President's budget submission—March 15, 2002

- Drafted Governance Paper for Agency discussion that incorporates strategic management of IT assets and robust implementation of CPIC—April 30, 2002

- Developing plan and business case as the Managing Partner for a new cross agency initiative on E-education.

- Initiated a series of Pilot Projects in the Agency that support the use of technology to more efficiently performs missions. (Web-based collaboration tools, and internal and external portal pilots)

BUDGET/PERFORMANCE INTEGRATION

CURRENT STATUS

OMB reports NASA's status as "red" for budget/performance integration. NASA has made efforts in recent years to move forward towards full cost budgeting and publish its budget justification and performance plan in a single document. However, NASA has yet to implement full cost budgeting and management. NASA's performance planning is also inadequate to support performance budgeting. OMB's Spring Review will require all agencies, in concurrence with OMB, to select programs for evaluation in the President's FY 2004 Budget and the criteria that will be used to evaluate those programs.

NASA has already taken the necessary steps to define its full cost budgeting, management, and accounting approaches in a formal Implementation Guide, which has been in use for planning purposes over the past two years, is assembling a representative full cost recast of its FY 2003 budget submission, and has initiated activities for formulating its FY 2004 Budget in full cost. Also, NASA has been, for at least the past two budget cycles, using an integrated Agencywide budget formulation process with a single Agency-wide database to collect and review budget recommendations from the project level through the Center, Enterprise, and Agency management decision levels and ultimately produce all budget submission information.

NASA PLANS TO ACHIEVE YELLOW STATUS

Implement Full Cost Budgeting

- NASA will submit to OMB a full cost recast of its FY 2003 budget submission, in order to identify the changes attributed to the transition to full cost and act as a baseline for identifying programmatic-driven changes in the FY 2004 budget request.

- By September 2002, NASA will submit a five year, full cost budget for its FY 2004 budget request to OMB that distributes personnel, overhead, and related costs to the program level, for use by OMB in developing the FY 2004 President's Budget.

Prepare for Performance Budgeting

- By May 15, 2002, NASA will reach agreement with OMB on the outline for a Performance Budget Document that integrates theme area goals, funding estimates, schedule, and related performance plan material. This will be backed up by the appropriate Exhibit 300B's; along with a list of programs to be covered through the OMB Spring Review and criteria for evaluating those projects based on the Administration's R&D criteria.

- By mid-June 2002, NASA will reach agreement with OMB on the formats to be used in the Performance Budget Document.

- By August 2002, a shared data file will be established as to where all formally cleared budget-process related documents to be used by OMB and NASA will be kept.
- By September 2002, NASA will submit to OMB an initial draft of its Performance Budget Document with

    o 100% of pre-defined Exhibit 300B's,

    o at least the measures for 20% of the theme areas agreed to in the OMB Spring Review

NASA PLANS TO ACHIEVE GREEN STATUS

Implement Full Cost Management

- By December 2003 NASA will demonstrate that full cost budgeting, management, and accounting are routinely being used across the Agency and that program resources management decisions include the integrated consideration of personnel, overhead, and related programmatic costs and/or funding requirements.

Implement Performance Budgeting

- By February 2003, NASA will provide the completed Performance Budget Document for submission to Congress.

President's Management Agenda

4/16/2002

	Human Capital	Competitive Sourcing	Financial Management	E-Gov	Integrated Budget & Performance
OMB Baseline Score	●	●	●	●	●
OMB Progress (as of 31 March 2002)	○	○	●	●	○
Agreed OMB-NASA Plan	◐	◐	●	●	◐

Human Capital
- ○ Complete Strategic Human Capital (HC) Plan
- ● Link employee rewards, recognition and performance to Agency key goals.
- ● Establish strategies for leadership/knowledge mgmt continuity
- ○ Increase the utilization of HC flexibilities to recruit, hire and retain a highly productive NASA workforce (e.g. recruitment, retention, NEX)
- ○ Utilize HC technologies to maximize the productivity of human capital. (e.g. e-hiring, e-classification, E-Learning, E-Gov, etc.)
- ● Develop HC tools and strategies that support major Agency transformation implementation plans
- ● Identify skills gaps in mission critical areas via an Agency-wide Competency Mgmt Model

Competitive Sourcing
- ○ Submit FAIR Act inventory to IMB
- ● Submit competitive sourcing plan to OMB
- ● OMB approval of FAIR Act inventory
- ● OMB Approval of Competitive Sourcing Plan Phase I (15%)
- ● OMB Approval of Competitive Sourcing Plan Phase II (50%)
- ● Begin implementation of OMB approved competitive sourcing (Phase I)
- ● Begin implementation of OMB approved competitive sourcing (Phase II)
- ● Complete inventory of Inter-service Support Agreeement (ISSAs)
- ● Implement OMB plan for ISSA competitions

IFMP Implementation
- ○ IFMP core finance at pilot center
- ○ Wave 1 Centers
- ● Wave 2 Centers
- ● Wave 3 Centers
- ○ Interim MIS

Audited Financial Statements
- ● Resolution of all outstanding FY2001 issues
- ● Closing of FY02 books
- ● "Clean" audit opinion

Capital Planning
- ○ Implement agency enterprise architecture
- ○ Provide IT business cases to OMB (Form 300s)
- ● PMC evaluation of IT performacne within 90% of target (for baseline IT programs)

E-Gov Implementation
- ● Provide necessary IT infrastructure for accelerated IFMP deployment
- ● Complete e-Education business case
- ● Participation in 5 partnerships of the "OMB 24"

IT Security
- ○ Fully addresses corrective action requirements of 2001 GISRA Plan

Full Cost
- ◐ Provide guidance on full cost implementation
- ● Recast FY2003 budget in full cost
- ● Develop FY2004 full cost budget
- ● Demonstrate Agencywide use of full cost budgeting and mgmt

Performance Budgeting
- ● Define "programs/theme areas" for OMB Spring Review
- ● Develop Performance Budget Document Concept with OMB
- ● Submit Performance Budget Document to OMB
- ● Submit NASA Budget using Performance Budget Document concept

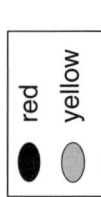

Legend: ● red ○ yellow ◐ green

CHAPTER 7
The Defense Finance and Accounting Service: Strategic Plan and Balanced Scorecard Measures and Targets

The Defense Finance and Accounting Service (DFAS) was created in 1991 to reduce the cost of Department of Defense finance and accounting operations. DFAS has a complex, effective strategic management system, which employs one of the most effective balanced scorecards in the federal government. The first section of this chapter presents excerpts from the DFAS strategic plan and the second section explains the FY 2002 corporate balanced scorecard measures and targets.

The Defense Finance and Accounting Service

Annual Report FY 2001

**YOUR
FINANCIAL
PARTNER
@
WORK**

Table of Contents

DFAS Highlights — 4
A Message to Our Customers — 6
Our Mission — 9
Our Operation — 11
Military and Civilian Pay Services — 13
Commercial Pay Services — 15
Accounting Services — 17
Transforming Financial Management — 19
A Strategy-based Organization — 21
Our Board of Advisors — 22
Here to Serve You — 23

DFAS Highlights
The world's largest finance and accounting operation

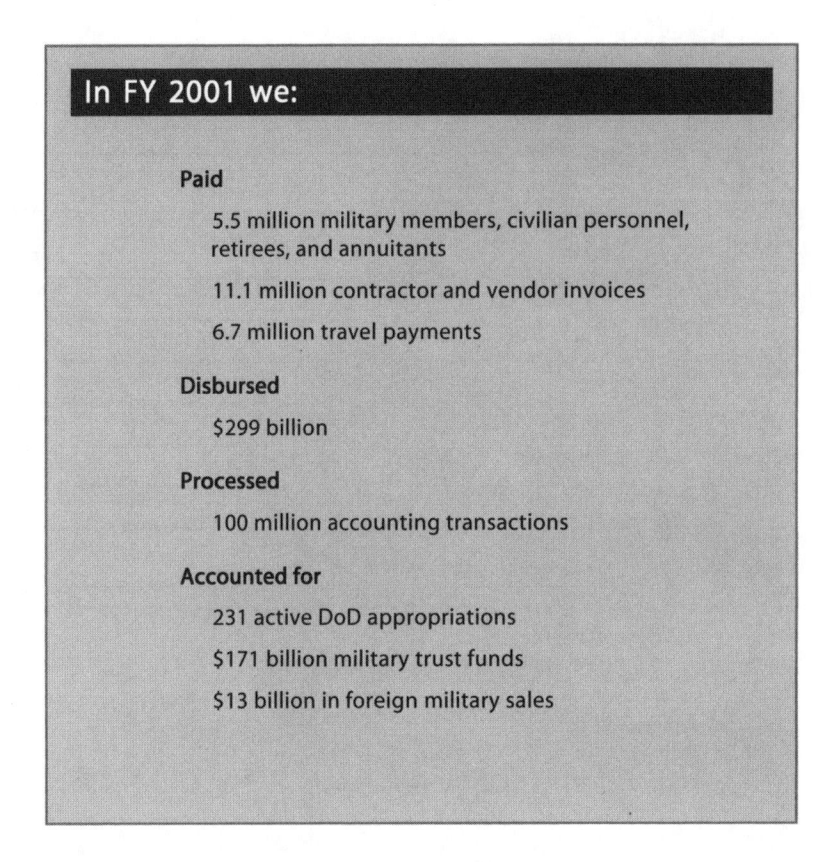

In FY 2001 we:

Paid
- 5.5 million military members, civilian personnel, retirees, and annuitants
- 11.1 million contractor and vendor invoices
- 6.7 million travel payments

Disbursed
- $299 billion

Processed
- 100 million accounting transactions

Accounted for
- 231 active DoD appropriations
- $171 billion military trust funds
- $13 billion in foreign military sales

The Defense Finance and Accounting Service was created in 1991 by the Secretary of Defense to reduce the cost of Department of Defense finance and accounting operations and to strengthen DoD financial management through consolidation of finance and accounting activities. Since inception, DFAS has consolidated over 300 installation-level finance and accounting offices into 26, and trimmed the work force from more than 27,000 to just over 17,000.

While streamlining our operations, we continually seek to improve and enhance our customer service through systems standardization, process improvements, and expanding employee competence. These improvements yield results that eliminate redundant processes, increase operational efficiencies, and reduce costs.

DFAS is a Working Capital Fund activity, which means we are not funded by direct appropriations. Rather, we operate on revenue received by charging customers for services provided. In effect, the military services and defense agencies have contracted out their finance and accounting work to DFAS. Our billing rates are set two years in advance and adjusted annually based on an analysis of the previous year's operations and future expectations for management initiatives, work force trends, and workload volumes. DFAS has steadily reduced its operating costs. *Correspondingly, customer bills have decreased dramatically.*

Read more about DFAS on our website at http://www.dfas.mil

DFAS Annual Report: FY 2001

Customers benefit from lower costs and smaller work force

Cost of Operations ($M)

	FY01	FY00	FY99
Salaries and wages	$869	$892	$844
Systems	385	408	409
Operations support	157	160	198
Rent, communications, facilities	70	68	64
Materials and services	66	82	108
Total	$1,547	$1,610	$1,623

Work Force End Strength

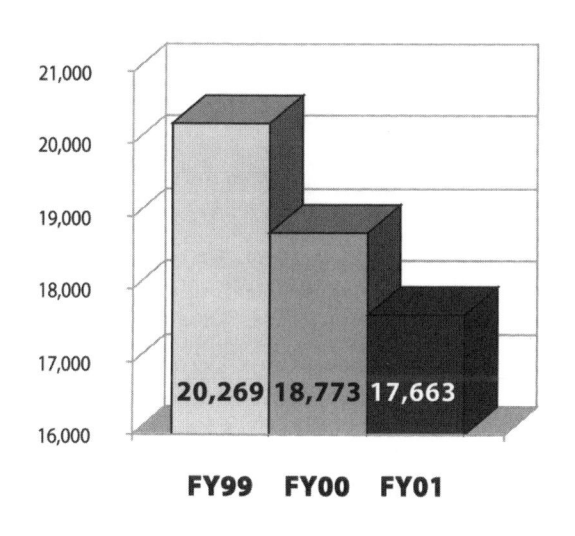

FY99	FY00	FY01
20,269	18,773	17,663

Cost to Customers ($M)

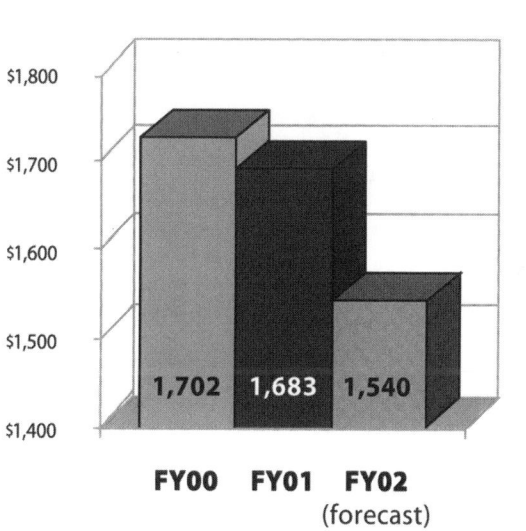

FY00	FY01	FY02 (forecast)
1,702	1,683	1,540

Your Financial Partner @ Work

A Message to Our Customers

During FY 2001, we took major steps toward achieving our vision of providing best value to our customers by being:

- A world-class provider of finance and accounting services
- A trusted, innovative financial partner
- One organization, one identity
- An employer of choice, providing a progressive and professional work environment

This vision—coupled with reinvigorated strategic focus—has driven pivotal accomplishments, including a corporate realignment focused on our customers, a restructuring along business lines, and a significant reduction in operating costs for the second consecutive year.

Best Value to Our Customers

FY 2001 was a good performance year for DFAS and our customers. As a strategy-based, metrics-driven, customer-focused organization, we came together to deliver top quality services at reduced costs. Our operating costs were below budgeted levels for the second year in a row. This cost reduction translates into future savings to our customers through lower billings. As a result, the bill for our customers in

Cost to Customers ($M)

	FY01	FY02	Savings
Army	$613	$566	$47
Navy	389	344	45
Air Force	334	306	28
Marine Corps	83	81	2
Other Agencies	264	243	21
Total	$1,683	$1,540	$143

FY 2002 is forecast to be $143 million less than it was in FY 2001. We will deliver better quality service at lower cost. Our billing rates have been reduced to return prior year savings to our customers, consistent with Working Capital Fund business practices. We want our customers to view us as their best value.

A World-Class Provider

Just as our nation has a world-class defense, DFAS strives to provide world-class finance and accounting services to those who defend America. Our customers deserve no less. We want to do nothing less.

For the second consecutive year, we surpassed DoD's goal of reducing problem disbursements by achieving a 78 percent reduction. This results in more accurate accounting and leads to better decision making. We reduced overaged invoices for both vendor and contract pay to the lowest percentage in the history of DFAS. By paying DoD commercial partners on time, we help preserve our customers' fiscal resources and facilitate better business relationships.

Our abilities are proven in other ways. We met all 45 key indicators on our FY 2001 performance contract with the Department. We use performance metrics to drive best business practices and achieve high quality results. In FY 2001, we earned a second consecutive unqualified—or "clean"—opinion from Deloitte & Touche LLP, independent auditors, on our annual consolidated financial statements. Verifying that our books are in line with accepted accounting standards strengthens our credibility as we advise our customers on obtaining their own clean opinions. For further information regarding our audit, please go to http://www.dfas.mil.

A Trusted, Innovative Partner

We want to build consultative relationships with our customers. We will earn customer trust and confidence through delivering business intelligence and providing more accurate, timely, and useful financial information for better decisions. We are committed to bringing together innovative ideas, technologies, and solutions as we work to improve DoD finance and accounting. Our e-commerce innovations include Employee/Member Self Service, Electronic Leave and Earnings Statements, an electronic Thrift Savings Plan program, Electronic Data Access, and Electronic Document Management. These solutions reduce process cycle times, improve accuracy, and increase our customers' spending power by lowering the cost of our products and services. They also ensure that our customers' financial records provide confidence on accurate availability of resources.

We partnered with the Army to implement the Single Stock Fund, a business process reengineering initiative to improve secondary item logistics and financial processes in their Working Capital Fund. The Army

DFAS Annual Report: FY 2001

has called this "one of the most sweeping changes to logistics and business processes in the past 25 years."

We teamed with the U.S. Special Operations Command to leverage the DFAS Corporate Information Infrastructure to provide world-class support. This truly "purple" DoD financial management system replaced a multistep, multilayered process that produced data four to six weeks old. Today, the headquarters USSOCOM financial management team can query accounting information as current as two business days via a Web browser.

One Organization, One Identity

We implemented a new organizational structure making individual senior executives personally accountable for each major customer and for each major business line. Known as the DFAS Business Evolution, it shifted our focus away from geographic silos to customer-focused delivery of business services: military and civilian payrolls, commercial bill paying, and accounting. This realigned, customer-centric structure allows us to progressively improve our internal operations, implement best practices across all business lines, and reduce cost to our customers. Coming together as a strategy-based organization and establishing linkages through our Balanced Scorecard, we ensure that everyone is working towards the same vision and can connect what they're doing to make the vision a reality. Most importantly, we continue to improve our performance, quality, and value, demonstrating that DFAS is truly Your Financial Partner @ Work.

An Employer of Choice

Since our people are key to making our vision a reality, it is important that we are viewed as an employer of choice, providing a progressive and professional work environment. We are on course. Enhancing employee competence, increasing professional credentials, and building the next generation of DFAS leadership are among our top priorities.

We enable continuous learning and development of critical high quality skills through a training budget that is among the most robust in government. We continually encourage professional development and certification in our staff and look for similar credentials as we attract new talent. DFAS values its employees and is committed to ensuring that professional opportunities exist to acquire, nurture, and sustain a work force with the highest quality skill sets.

The Way Ahead

The state of DFAS is good and getting better each day. We are confident we have built the right foundation to continue to drive down costs. We will remain on track to achieve our quality and productivity goals. Our investment strategy will give us modern, labor-saving information systems at increasingly lower costs. Our customers will reap the benefits through increased quality, better service, and lower bills as we steadily reduce our cost of operations over the next several years.

DFAS: Decreasing Costs

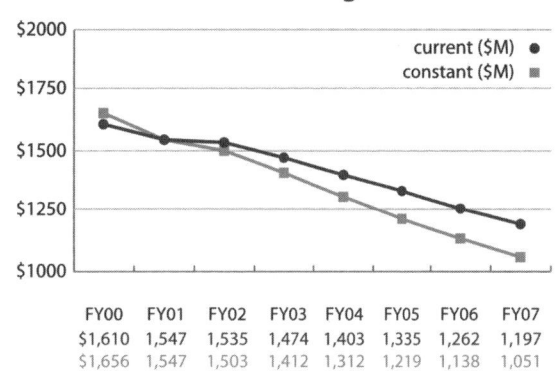

	FY00	FY01	FY02	FY03	FY04	FY05	FY06	FY07
current ($M)	$1,610	1,547	1,535	1,474	1,403	1,335	1,262	1,197
constant ($M)	$1,656	1,547	1,503	1,412	1,312	1,219	1,138	1,051

As we look ahead and as our footprint gets smaller, our business model will evolve. By achieving the optimum mix of civil service, military, and contractor resources and solidifying the strongest customer partnership, together we will transform financial management for the Department.

We know our customers, we know how our products and services support their mission, and we know our support role in their success. Our customers can trust that we will remain focused on our commitment to deliver world-class support for the men and women serving on the front lines of freedom.

Thomas R. Bloom
Director

Mark A. Young
RADM, SC, USN
Deputy Director

DFAS: Our Mission

Provide responsive, professional finance and accounting services for the people who defend America

Nothing matters more to our professionals than serving the men and women of America's Armed Forces. This commitment to serve is what drives our passion to be a world-class finance and accounting organization and to become, as our motto states, Your Financial Partner @ Work.

We pay the people who defend America. It is our mission to ensure warfighters have the peace of mind that their financial entitlements are paid accurately and on time, whether at home or abroad, and that they will have access to the information needed to conduct their financial affairs.

We pay the contractors who provide the products and services that support the warfighters who defend America. It is our mission to ensure the commercial partners of our warfighters are paid accurately and on time.

We process the accounting transactions and maintain the records to deliver business intelligence for decision makers to plan and conduct mission operations with fiscal integrity. It is our mission to provide timely, accurate, and useful financial information.

We pay the people who defend America

We pay the contractors who support the warfighters

We provide financial information to DoD decision makers

Your Financial Partner @ Work

DFAS: Our Operation

Serving our customers with dedicated professionals

Internally, our organizational structure created by the DFAS Business Evolution established a corps of leaders, called Client Executives, who provide single points of contact for DFAS services. They are devoted to anticipating and fulfilling the needs of our customers.

Working in concert with the Client Executives are our three Business Line Executives:

- The Military and Civilian Pay Services Business Line Executive manages all aspects of payments to individuals - paychecks, travel reimbursements, and garnishments.
- The Commercial Pay Services Business Line Executive provides payment services to contractors both large and small.
- The Accounting Services Business Line Executive provides departmental and field level accounting, disbursing, and financial accounting services.

A variety of internal service organizations ensure that the business lines have the support they need to fulfill their roles. Internal financial operations and agency-wide support services are managed by the Corporate Resources Executive.

Organizationally, DFAS reports to the Under Secretary of Defense (Comptroller) and Chief Financial Officer. Headquartered in Arlington, Va., DFAS operates from 25 additional locations.

While we are located worldwide, DFAS has invested in a secure information technology infrastructure linking our employees with each other and with our customers via their desktop computers. This robust infrastructure augmented with e-government solutions enables us to provide service delivery on a 24-7 basis.

Our core values—Integrity, Service, and Innovation—guide the 17,000 members of DFAS as we improve and transform DoD financial management.

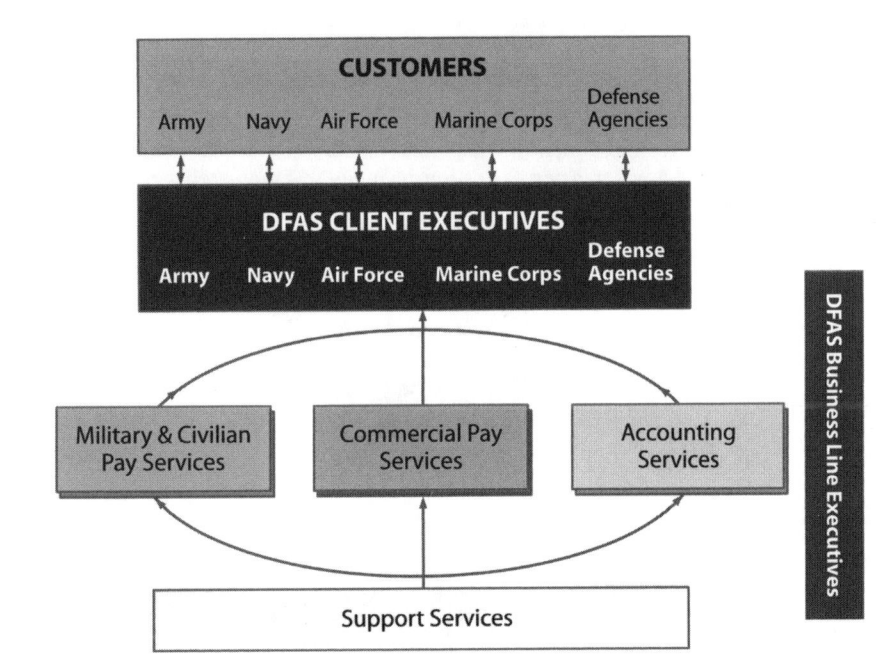

CUSTOMERS: Army, Navy, Air Force, Marine Corps, Defense Agencies

DFAS CLIENT EXECUTIVES: Army, Navy, Air Force, Marine Corps, Defense Agencies

DFAS Business Line Executives: Military & Civilian Pay Services, Commercial Pay Services, Accounting Services

Support Services

Your Financial Partner @ Work

DFAS Military and Civilian Pay Services
Improving accuracy and timeliness while reducing costs

5.5 Million military and civilians paid $114 billion in 135 million payroll payments annually

The Military and Civilian Pay Services Business Line provides all forms of payments to individuals. Almost all pay is delivered via electronic funds transfer.

- we pay...Members of the Army, Navy, Air Force, Marine Corps
- we pay...Civilians in the DoD work force and the Executive Office of the President
- we pay...Military retirees and annuitants

Auxiliary support includes manning call centers and help desks to answer individual inquiries; defining and testing changes to automated pay systems; processing garnishment, debt, and waiver applications; and working with federal, state, and local taxing authorities.

Our FY 2002 priorities are to improve pay accuracy and timeliness, expand Web-based capabilities for pay and benefit information, support the integration of personnel and financial data, and reduce cycle times for fielding new capabilities.

We pay the people who defend America

Your Financial Partner @ Work

DFAS Commercial Pay Services

Streamlining processes to reduce operating costs

11.1 Million invoices paid annually, timeliness increased to 94.8% from 91.7%

The Commercial Pay Services Business Line is responsible for all payments to contractors. Our contractors range from the small business vendors to the large-scale weapons system developers.

Commercial Pay Services disburses approximately $150 billion annually through two product lines—Contract Pay and Vendor Pay.

In Contract Pay, approximately $72 billion is paid annually to contractors primarily associated with major weapons system delivery and support. While only 48 percent of the invoices we receive from contractors are electronic, we make 96 percent of our payments to contractors via electronic funds transfer.

Vendor pay involves payment for day-to-day goods and services, such as supplies, utilities, and transportation support. The total annual payments for these vendor products are approximately $78 billion.

Our FY 2002 priorities are to improve payment accuracy and timeliness, expand end-to-end electronic work flow and invoicing, and reduce interest penalty payments.

We pay the contractors who support the warfighters

Your Financial Partner @ Work

DFAS Accounting Services

Increasing accounting services value for our customers

$517 Billion accounted for annually in 231 active appropriations

The Accounting Services Business Line represents almost 45 percent of our internal business base. This business line is responsible for providing our clients with timely, meaningful financial information to meet their management needs and delivering modern business solutions for accounting requirements.

This business line performs accounting operations at the field and departmental levels for appropriated funds, working capital funds, and trust fund activities, including foreign military sales. In addition, our accounting professionals develop procedures to implement federal accounting requirements mandated by Congress, OMB, Treasury, and DoD, and maintain current operational accounting systems.

A business solutions focus initiated this past year delivers business intelligence that adds true value for our customers. Early successes include teaming with the U.S. Transportation Command to develop a systems architecture framework as well as collaborating with the Army, Navy, and Defense Logistics Agency to evaluate and implement Enterprise Resource Planning systems.

Our FY 2002 priorities are to increase the value of accounting services for our customers, improve the timeliness and accuracy of accounting reports, and streamline end-to-end processes with our customers.

We provide financial information to DoD decision makers

Your Financial Partner @ Work

DFAS: Transforming Financial Management

Innovative solutions provide our customers the best value

The people of DFAS process payments to the Department's military and civilian personnel, retirees, annuitants, and contractors. DFAS accountants record, accumulate, and report financial activity. We have steadfastly introduced new ways of doing business that yield positive results. Use of electronic technologies and the transformation to e-government have modernized operations for our customers.

The integrity of our customers' data is ensured through the secure electronic exchange of financial information. We take pride in operating a modern information infrastructure and introducing new technologies.

Employee/Member Self Service - available at http://www.dfas.mil/emss/ - has enabled both military members and DoD civilians to make payroll changes online and view their leave and earnings statements from their own desktops—improving customer service while cutting costs.

Use of Electronic Funds Transfer significantly reduces costs by eliminating the printing, processing, and mailing of checks. Today, over 98 percent of DoD personnel paid by DFAS enjoy the greater convenience and security of having their pay directly deposited into their accounts.

DFAS uses Electronic Document Management and World Wide Web applications to facilitate access to information and improve operations. Documents are stored securely and shared among activities. Converting documents to an electronic format for online processing not only eliminates the printing of reports but also enables smoother communication flow. We use Electronic Data Management to process over 160 thousand garnishment orders and the majority of our 11 million vendor and contract vouchers annually.

We are connected to our customers' commercial partners through use of Electronic Data Interchange, which sends remittance information directly to vendors and electronically passes data from contracts and modifications to finance and accounting systems. A Web-based invoicing system enables contractors to electronically submit invoices to DFAS.

We use a single Web-based database of basic business information from contractors who want to do business with DoD to preclude the need for submitting recurring, redundant data. This Central Contractor Registration provides all DoD procurement and payment offices with a single source of valid and reliable contractor data. It also facilitates electronic exchange of financial information.

We seek to deliver the best products and services through optimizing the mix of our military, civilian, and contractor work force. We promote competition with private sector companies to improve service delivery and reduce costs. In 2001, a contract was signed with a commercial firm to provide pay services to the 2.5 million military retirees and annuitants. This business relationship recognizes the strategic partnership of our private sector providers in DoD finance and accounting operations.

We will continue to employ the best products and systems available so that our customers will benefit from innovative finance and accounting solutions.

We deliver business intelligence to enable better decision making

Your Financial Partner @ Work

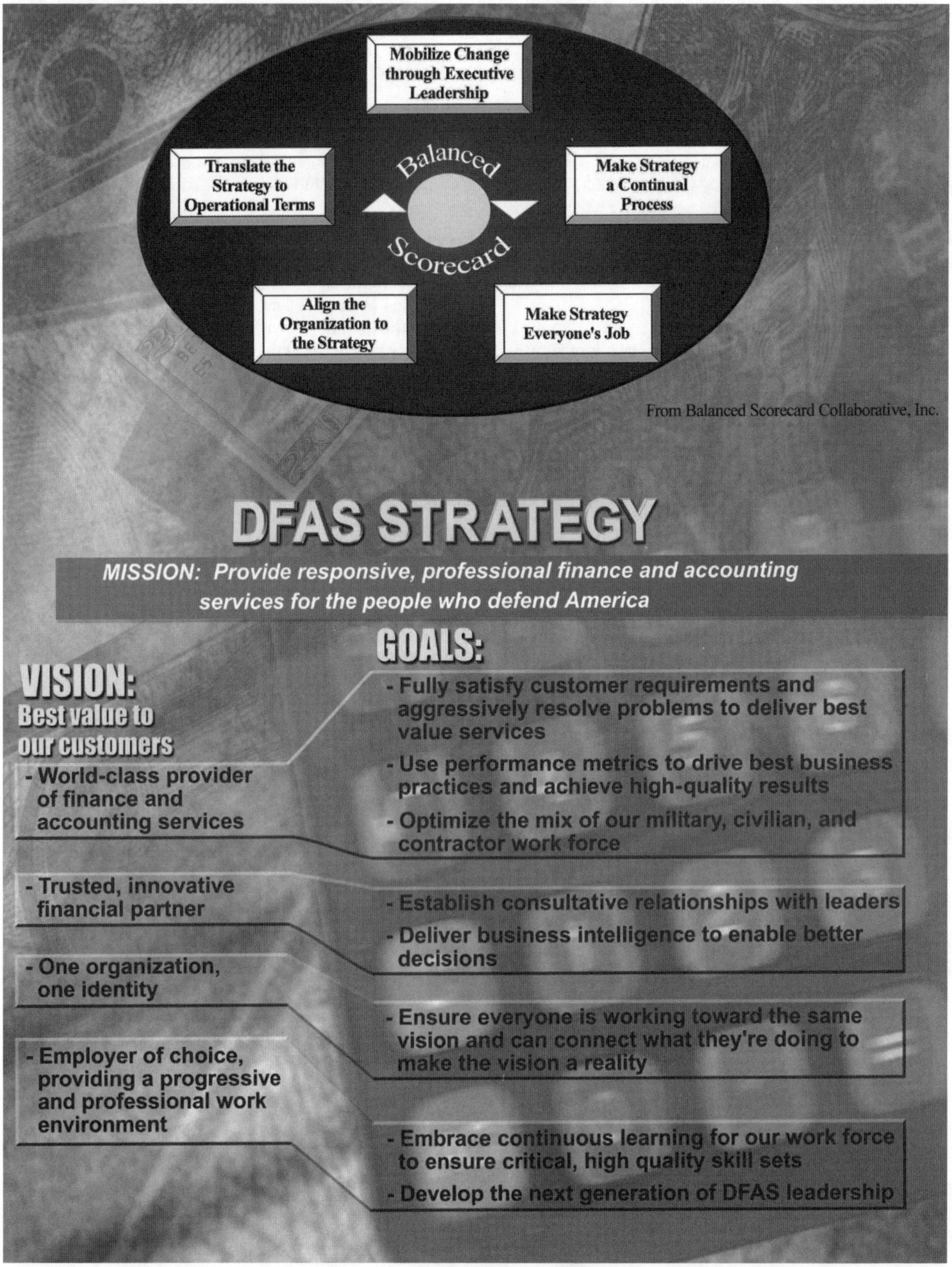

Balanced Scorecard

- Mobilize Change through Executive Leadership
- Translate the Strategy to Operational Terms
- Make Strategy a Continual Process
- Align the Organization to the Strategy
- Make Strategy Everyone's Job

From Balanced Scorecard Collaborative, Inc.

DFAS STRATEGY

MISSION: Provide responsive, professional finance and accounting services for the people who defend America

VISION: Best value to our customers
- World-class provider of finance and accounting services
- Trusted, innovative financial partner
- One organization, one identity
- Employer of choice, providing a progressive and professional work environment

GOALS:
- Fully satisfy customer requirements and aggressively resolve problems to deliver best value services
- Use performance metrics to drive best business practices and achieve high-quality results
- Optimize the mix of our military, civilian, and contractor work force
- Establish consultative relationships with leaders
- Deliver business intelligence to enable better decisions
- Ensure everyone is working toward the same vision and can connect what they're doing to make the vision a reality
- Embrace continuous learning for our work force to ensure critical, high quality skill sets
- Develop the next generation of DFAS leadership

DFAS: A Strategy-based Organization

A metrics-driven, customer-focused support agency

Strategy is everyone's job at DFAS. We are a strategy-based organization that requires all levels working together to make our vision a reality. The DFAS Leadership Council, chaired by the DFAS Director, meets monthly to refine strategy, share information, assess progress, discuss issues, and make decisions to move us forward.

DFAS Strategy

In support of the DFAS mission and vision, we have developed goals to guide our overall strategic direction and shape our decision making. Key components are customer satisfaction, best value services, measured accountability, and work force proficiency.

Balanced Scorecard

We use the Balanced Scorecard methodology, developed by leading industry experts, to align the DFAS organization with our mission and vision and to measure progress. With the Balanced Scorecard, we are better able to articulate our strategy, communicate that strategy, and synchronize individual, organizational, and cross-functional initiatives to achieve common goals.

We have an overall corporate Balanced Scorecard with cascading scorecards for the three business lines and eight support services. Built around four perspectives—Customer, Financial, Internal, and Growth & Learning—and using up and down linkages, the scorecards keep us focused and enable employees at every level to understand their individual roles.

The Balanced Scorecard is not an end in itself but an important tool for measuring our progress and service delivery success against our strategy.

Objectives and Measures

While we have always measured our DFAS processes and outputs, those historic measures have applied primarily to the outcomes now categorized under the Customer and Financial perspectives. Through the use of the Balanced Scorecard, we have extended our reach to the Internal and Growth & Learning perspectives, yielding a more comprehensive view of total operations and enabling us to execute our strategy. The Internal perspective focuses on quality, innovation, and system solutions. The Growth & Learning perspective targets employee competence and satisfaction, succession planning, and fostering a climate of action.

A Contract for Performance

Another way we measure our performance is through a contract with the Defense Resources Board. Our performance contract is a result of the 1997 Defense Reform Initiative, which specifies that directors of Defense Agencies will have a contract with an overall theme of improving efficiencies and decreasing costs. The Defense Resources Board and our director established an annual performance contract to make DoD financial management more affordable and efficient by measuring performance against a set of clearly defined objectives. Our performance indicators measure performance against accuracy, quality, responsiveness, and timeliness objectives. These performance metrics have been carefully selected to holistically ensure that actions are underway to achieve the DFAS mission.

Your Financial Partner @ Work

**Defense Finance and
Accounting Service (DFAS)**

**DFAS FY02 Corporate Balanced Scorecard
Measures and Targets**

Version 1.0

October 01, 2001

DFAS FY02 Corporate Balanced Scorecard Measures and Targets
As of 10/01/01

PERSPECTIVE	OBJECTIVE	MEASURE	
Customer	Improve Client/Customer Satisfaction	1.	Client/Customer Satisfaction
		2.	Commitments Met – Performance Contracts
		3.	Commitments Met – Client Executive Contacts
		4.	Specific Billing Rates
Financial	Reduce Cost to Client/Customer	5.	Total Costs
	Expand the Use of Competitive Sourcing	6.	Competitive Sourcing Performance
		7.	Total Workforce Ratio
Internal Business Processes	Improve and Leverage Quality	8.	Quality Index
		9.	Rework Identified
		10.	Rework Eliminated
		11.	Best Business Practices Adopted
	Encourage Innovation	12.	New Products or Services Delivered
	Deliver Systems Solutions	13.	Commitments Met – System Milestones
Learning & Growth	Enhance Employee Competence	14.	Employees in Developmental Assignments
	Increase Employee Satisfaction	15.	Employee Satisfaction
	Enhance Ability to Recruit and Retain DFAS Talent	16.	Core Competency Profile
	Develop a Climate for Action	17.	Climate for Action

Version 1.0

DFAS FY02 Corporate Balanced Scorecard Measures and Targets
As of 10/01/01

PERSPECTIVE:	CUSTOMER
OBJECTIVE:	Improve Client/Customer Satisfaction

MEASURE #1:
 	
Client/Customer Satisfaction
	Target: 5% or higher increase in satisfaction ratings on customer satisfaction surveys. [Annually]
	
	Target Profile: Customer satisfaction surveys will be conducted annually. Surveys for Military Pay, Civilian Pay, Travel Pay, Accounting and Contract Pay were conducted in FY01. All product lines will be surveyed beginning FY02.
	
	Dimensions Satisfaction Ratings
	
	              FY 01 **FY02 Goal** **FY03 Goal**
	Courtesy 75% 80% 85%
	Quality 71% 76% 81%
	Reliability 69% 74% 79%
	Timeliness 68% 73% 78%
	Tangibles 66% 71% 76%
	Access 64% 69% 74%
	Knowledge 63% 68% 73%
	Choice 55% 60% 65%
	Recovery 51% 56% 61%
	
	Guidelines for Interpreting Results (% Favorable)
	Excellent 90% and above
	Good 80-89%
	Acceptable 66-79%
	Marginal 51-65%
	Critical 50% and below
	
	This measure will reflect a green, yellow, or red status as follows:
	    Green = ≥ 5% improvement
	    Yellow = ≤ 5% improvement
	    Red = decrease from previous year

PERSPECTIVE:	CUSTOMER
OBJECTIVE:	Improve Client/Customer Satisfaction
MEASURE #2: Commitments Met - Performance Contracts	**Target:** Successfully meet all 36 Agency Performance Contract deliverables. [Monthly] **Target Profile:** The DFAS agency performance contract is with the Defense Resources Board and represents its charter to the DOD to provide accurate and timely financial accounting and finance services. This contract is reviewed and updated annually. Meeting these metrics signifies that we have fulfilled our charter. Failure to meet any one of the metrics signifies that we have not met our charter. Each metric is measured monthly. All metrics have a different goal. This measure will reflect a green, yellow, or red status as follows: Green = all green; Yellow = any in yellow; Red = any in red

Version 1.0

DFAS FY02 Corporate Balanced Scorecard Measures and Targets
As of 10/01/01

PERSPECTIVE:	CUSTOMER
OBJECTIVE:	Improve Client/Customer Satisfaction
MEASURE #3: Commitments Met - CE Contacts	**Target:** 112 Client executive contacts per quarter. [Quarterly] **Target Profile:** Target computed as follows. Four (4) CE contacts per quarter by each CE in the Agency (28 CEs x 4 contacts = 112 contacts per quarter). CE contacts can include site visits, VTCs, telephonic contacts, client conference attendance or any other means used to contact and discuss business with our customers. To be considered customer contact there must be two-way feedback. CE contacts do not include sending marketing materials. This measure will reflect a green, yellow, or red status as follows: Green = 112 CE Contacts; Yellow = 100-111 CE Contacts; Red = 99 or below CE Contacts

PERSPECTIVE:	CUSTOMER
OBJECTIVE:	Improve Client/Customer Satisfaction

MEASURE #4:
 	
Specific Billing Rates
	Target: Establish more tailored and/or client-specific billing rates for all applicable DFAS outputs (nine) by FY03. [Annually]
	
	Target Profile: Baseline Target for FY02:
	   FY 00 Baseline - one of nine (output 011)
	   FY 01 - three of nine (outputs 011 plus 02 and 03)
	   FY 02 - six of nine (outputs 011, 02, 03 plus 05, 09, and 029)
	   FY 03 - nine of nine (outputs 011, 02, 03, 05, 09, 029 plus 07, 027, and 010.
	
	Client specific rates will be developed for the following outputs:
	   001 – Civilian Pay (paper vice electronic LES rates)
	   003 – Active Military Pay (client-specific rates)
	   005 – Reserve Pay (client-specific rates)
	   007 – Travel Vouchers Paid (client-specific rates)
	   027 – Travel Vouchers Paid-Disburse Only (client-specific rates)
	   009 – Commercial Pay (client-specific rates)
	   029 – Commercial Pay – EC (client-specific rates)
	   010 – Out of Service Debt (individual vice contractor debt)
	   011 – Direct Billable Hours (client-specific rates)
	
	RM/CBO will develop client specific billing rates for Reserve Pay (output 05) and Commercial Pay (outputs 09 and 29) during FY 02 for implementation in FY 04. Accomplishment is expected in the last quarter of FY 02 during FY 04 budget formulation.
	
	This measure will reflect a green, yellow, or red status as follows: Green = 3 rates established; Yellow = 2 rates established; Red = $\leq$ 1 rate established.

DFAS FY02 Corporate Balanced Scorecard Measures and Targets
As of 10/01/01

PERSPECTIVE:	FINANCIAL
OBJECTIVE	Reduce Cost to Client/Customer
MEASURE #5: Total Costs * The FY 02 reduction will be less than 5 percent when compared to actual FY 01 (currently projected at $1,546 billion) ** FY 02-04 targets exclude new missions (OSD PMO) and policy changes (FASAB #10 impact)	**Target:** 15% reduction in total operating costs (including depreciation) over the next three years from the FY 2001 baseline budget of $ 1.616 billion. [Monthly] **Target Profile:** FY 2001 President's Budget baseline - $1.616 billion (Rate-base: $1.550 billion) (STO: $66 million) FY 2002 target – $1.535 billion* (or 5 percent) FY 2003 target – $1.458 billion** (or 5 percent) FY 2004 target – $1.385 billion** (or 5 percent) This measure will reflect a green, yellow, or red status as follows: Green = $\leq 0.4\%$ above target Yellow = $> 0.4\%$ and $< 1.4\%$ above target Red = $\geq 1.4\%$ above target

PERSPECTIVE:	FINANCIAL
OBJECTIVE:	Expand the use of Competitive Sourcing
MEASURE #6: Competitive Sourcing Performance	**Target:** Announce Competitive Sourcing studies on at least 7% of the eligible positions each year for the next 3 years. [Quarterly] **Target Profile:** The number of Full Time Equivalents (FTEs) to be studied under A-76 Cost Comparison during the FY to meet a goal of 7% of the number of coded as "subject to competition" in the DFAS Commercial Activities and Inherently Governmental Inventory FY 2000. Targets by FY follow: FY02 - 1092 FY03 - 1016 FY04 - 944 This measure will reflect a green, yellow, or red status as follows: Green = $\geq 7.0\%$ Yellow = $< 7.0\%$ and $\geq 1.4\%$ announced Red = $< 1.4\%$ announced

PERSPECTIVE:	FINANCIAL
OBJECTIVE:	Expand the use of Competitive Sourcing
MEASURE #7: Total Workforce Ratio	**Target:** Identify the progress made in competitive sourcing of commercial activities within DFAS. [Quarterly] **Target Profile:** The ratio is the number of DFAS positions competed and won by a MEO or Contractor divided by the number of DFAS civilian and military workforce positions. This measure does not reflect a green, yellow, or red status.

Version 1.0

DFAS FY02 Corporate Balanced Scorecard Measures and Targets
As of 10/01/01

PERSPECTIVE:	INTERNAL BUSINESS PROCESS
OBJECTIVE:	Improve and Leverage Quality

MEASURE #8:
 	
Quality Index
	Target: Achieve a DFAS FY 2003 average quality index rating of 1.00 in FY2001, 1.20 in FY2002, and 1.50 in FY2003. Current baseline is .99 [Monthly]
	
	Target Profile:
	• A single index that provides a numeric value that indicates the perceived quality of DFAS products and services as focused by our external customer(s). The "make-up" of the corporate index is a roll-up of DFAS primary business line indices. All individual, business line, and corporate indices will be evaluated against a standard of 100%.
	
	• The corporate index is a composite of DFAS primary business lines, which includes Accounting, Military and Civilian Pay, Travel Pay, and Commercial Pay. Each of those organizations indices will be equally averaged to form the corporate index. The methods used to calculate business line, product line and corporate indices must be consistent in order to maintain the integrity of interpreting the index numeric value.
	
	• The index provides an organizational quality level and insight as to how frequently we are meeting our customer's requirements. For example, an index of 0.5 = 93.3%, 1.0 = 99.8%, 2.0 = 99.9999999% meeting overall customer requirements.
	
	• The business line indices are subject to change as management teams determine additional metrics to comprise their organizations external customer perceived quality. Changes should be implemented on a quarterly basis and will be noted on the appropriate charts.
	
	This measure will reflect a green, yellow, or red status as follows:
	    Green = ≥ 1.20
	    Yellow = < 1.20 and ≥ 1.10
	    Red = < 1.10 for the year ending FY02

DFAS FY02 Corporate Balanced Scorecard Measures and Targets
As of 10/01/01

PERSPECTIVE:	INTERNAL BUSINESS PROCESS
Objective:	**Improve and Leverage Quality**
MEASURE #9: Rework Identified	**Target:** The measure will track the quantity of inventoried systems/processes that are suspect of costly rework. [Quarterly] **Target Profile:** The quantity of systems/processes selected for improvement within this PMI will be used for 'Rework Eliminated', which tracks rework reduced/eliminated. Rework is identified as Systems/Processes, External Rework, or Internal Rework. • <u>Systems/Processes</u> - This can be an organization or product line, or a specific process that has a relatively high cost of operations for each business line and support service area. • <u>External Rework</u> - Work and or corrections that are performed on a returned product or service from a customer. Defects of products and services to DFAS customers. • <u>Internal Rework</u> - 1) Work that has to be redone inside of an organization to a service due to insufficient information, inadequate tools and/or methods, poorly trained personnel, or other reasons causing a service to incur additional effort. 2) Any extra work required to complete a service beyond a straight-line, non-interrupted product flow. 3) Typically drawn as a diamond in a flowchart where an outcome of the decision is to go backwards in the process to redo work due to missing information, inadequate tools, etc. This measure will reflect a green, yellow, or red status as follows: Green = the business unit has identified rework; Red = business unit has not identified rework.

PERSPECTIVE:	INTERNAL BUSINESS PROCESS
OBJECTIVE:	**Improve and leverage quality**

MEASURE #10:
 	
Rework Eliminated
	Target: Reduce/eliminate rework in the systems/processes selected for improvement by at least 10%. [Quarterly]
	
	Target Profile: The target will be the percentage of systems/processes that have had rework reduced/eliminated over the total quantity selected to be investigated for rework. (i.e. Rework Identified). A significant reduction of product/service flow through process rework steps is also a success indicator.
	
	This measure will reflect a green, yellow, or red status as follows:
	    Green = $\geq$ 10% rework reduction/elimination
	    Yellow = < 10% and $\geq$ 8% rework reduction/elimination
	    Red = < 8% rework reduction/elimination

Version 1.0

DFAS FY02 Corporate Balanced Scorecard Measures and Targets
As of 10/01/01

PERSPECTIVE:	INTERNAL BUSINESS PROCESS
OBJECTIVE:	Improve and leverage quality

MEASURE #11:
 	
Best Business Practices Adopted
	Target: Increase the number of best business practices adopted and implemented to 20 per year. [Quarterly]
	
	Target Profile: Number of best business practices adopted/implemented. The BLs, CR, and IT will identify, share and adopt 20 best business practices per year as follows: Commercial Pay = 2; Accounting = 12 (6 CEs x 2); Military & Civilian Pay = 2; Corporate Resources = 2; IT/Technology Services Organization = 2.
	
	An adopted DFAS Best Practice is a recommended candidate that has been approved, first by the DFAS Strategic Plan Steering Group and then by the DFAS Leadership Council. A Best Practice candidate must be implemented before it can be considered as an Agency Best Practice.
	
	DFAS Best Business Practice candidates are implemented concepts or processes and originate from recommendations made by the Business Lines and/or Support Services. Best business practice candidates are strategies and tactics identified and implemented to produce superior operational results. The term best business practice may be used to identify any method, practice or process that leads to exceptional operational performance. A best business practice is a proven, documented result of an organization's daily business activity - or, it is an outcome of the performance of an individual's or team's duties or responsibilities. The key is that it may have applicability for DFAS entities or DFAS as a whole.
	
	This measure will reflect a green, yellow, or red status as follows:
	    Green = 5 or more adoptions/implementations per quarter
	    Yellow = 4 adoptions/implementations per quarter
	    Red = 3 or less adoptions/implementations per quarter

PERSPECTIVE:	INTERNAL BUSINESS PROCESS
OBJECTIVE:	Encourage Innovation

MEASURE #12:
 	
New Products or Services Delivered.
	Target: Deliver 9 new products/services each reporting year. [Quarterly]
	
	Target Profile: Each Business Line Executive (BLE) and Service CE will deliver one new product or service each year over the next 3 years. (3 BLEs + 6 Service CEs = 9 new products/services per year). The BLEs and CEs will submit new products and services that have been delivered to Clients/Customers to the Strategic Plan Steering Group. This group will then either approve or disapprove the classification of the product or service as a new product or service.
	
	This measure will reflect a green, yellow, or red status as follows:
	    Green = 9 or more products or services delivered during the reporting year
	    Yellow = 8 products or services delivered during the reporting year
	    Red = 7 or less products or services delivered during the reporting year

DFAS FY02 Corporate Balanced Scorecard Measures and Targets
As of 10/01/01

PERSPECTIVE:	INTERNAL BUSINESS PROCESS
OBJECTIVE:	Deliver System Solutions

MEASURE #13:
 	
Commitments Met
- System Milestones
	Target: Complete four major milestones per quarter for each designated system. There will be 60 major milestones tracked each quarter for the 15 systems identified below. [Quarterly]
	
	Target Profile: The following systems will be covered by this objective/measure: DIMHRS, DPPS, DCD/DCW, DSDS, DDS, DJAS, DCAS, GAFS-R, BMR, DIFMS, DWAS, DDRS, SMAS, TRANSCOM, and DIFS-R.
	
	Note: DIFS-R is one of the 15 designated systems; however, we are not progressing with DIFS-R at this time. We are awaiting a decision from DSCA on replacement alternatives for Security Assistance. Based on this, the number of milestones that will be tracked each quarter will be 56 vs. 60.
	
	This measure will reflect a green, yellow, or red status as follows:
	    Green = 52 to 56 milestones met
	    Yellow = 48 to 51 milestones met
	    Red = 47 or less milestones met

PERSPECTIVE:	LEARNING AND GROWTH
OBJECTIVE:	Enhance Employee Competence

MEASURE #14:
 	
Employees in Developmental Assignments
	Target: Have 1.5% of our employees each month participating in developmental assignments (DA). [Monthly]
	
	Target Profile: Enhance breadth of employee competence by targeting a percentage of employees with developmental assignments. Baseline is the total number of DFAS civilian and military employees (18,500). Target calls for 3330 employees participating in developmental assignments each year, or 278 involved in a DA each month.
	• DA should have an associated learning objective
	• DA may range from 1 week to 1 year and may include cross training, job exchanges, shadow assignments, details, and temporary promotions.
	• The intern rotation assignments will be included in the appropriate BL/SS
	
	This measure will reflect a green, yellow, or red status as follows:
	    Green = ≥ 1.5% in DAs
	    Yellow = < 1.5% and ≥ 1.0% in DAs
	    Red = < 1.0% in DAs

Version 1.0

DFAS FY02 Corporate Balanced Scorecard Measures and Targets
As of 10/01/01

PERSPECTIVE:	LEARNING AND GROWTH
OBJECTIVE:	Increase Employee Satisfaction

MEASURE #15:
 	
Employee Satisfaction
	Target: DFAS will achieve 3% less (57.7%) than the 90th percentile of OPM Performance America Benchmark (60.7%) by 2003. In 2002, the goal is to increase from the 2001 score of 50.6% to 54.1% [Annually]
	
	Target Profile: The Employee Satisfaction Index (ESI) is a compilation of 20 questions determined to give the best indicator of employee satisfaction. The Performance America high score average is 66.3% for ESI. The Performance America average 90 percentile score is 60.7%.
	    FY02 Goal 54.1%
	    FY03 Goal 57.7%
	This measure will reflect a green, yellow, or red status as follows:
	    Green = $\geq$ 54.1 %
	    Yellow = < 54.1 % and > 50.6 %
	    Red = $\leq$ 50.6 %

PERSPECTIVE:	LEARNING AND GROWTH
OBJECTIVE:	Enhance ability to recruit and retain DFAS talent
MEASURE #16: Core Competency Profile	**Target:** An increased number of employee critical competencies, optimizing the skill mix of DFAS employees [Quarterly] **Target Profile:** Monitor hiring and attrition to identify the aggregate change in staffing levels by major occupational series. The measure will track the quality of those employees who are hired and those who leave. This measure does not reflect a green, yellow, or red status.

PERSPECTIVE:	LEARNING AND GROWTH
OBJECTIVE:	Develop a climate for action

MEASURE #17:
 	
Climate for Action
	Target: DFAS will achieve 3% less (52.3%) than the 90th percentile of the OPM Performance America Benchmark (55.3%) by 2003. In 2002, the goal is to increase from the 2001 score of 46.9% to 49.3% [Annually]
	
	Target Profile: For FY01 the target equals the 90 percentile score in 2000 (55.3%) – 3% by 2003 for the Climate for Action Index (CAI).
	    Goal **Score**
	    2000 43.5% Benchmark
	    2001 46.4% 46.9% Average score of CAI questions in the 2001 survey vs. goal
	    2002 49.3% TBD Average score of all CAI questions in the 2001 survey.
	    2003 52.3% TBD Average score of all CAI questions in the 2001 survey.
	
	This measure will reflect a green, yellow, or red status as follows:
	    Green = $\geq$ 49.3 %
	    Yellow = < 49.3 % and > 46.9 %
	    Red = $\leq$ 46.9 %

Version 1.0

2002 BALANCE SCORECARD METRICS
OCT 1 - JUNE 30, 2002

9/20/02

CORPORATE BALANCED SCORECARD	GOAL	OPR	Report Cycle	Corporate	ACCT	Comm Pay	Mil & Civ Pay	Corp Res	I&T	TSO	GC	SI	IR	DC	Finance
CUSTOMER PERSPECTIVE															
(500) Client/Customer Satisfaction	5%	C	ANNUAL	○	○	○	○	○							
(501) Commitments Met - Performance Contract	100%	C	MONTH	◐	●	●	◐	◐							
(502) Commitments Met - CB Contacts	108	C	QTRLY	●	●										
(503) Percent of Outputs with Specific Billing Rates	3%	C	ANNUAL	●	●	○	●	●							
FINANCIAL PERSPECTIVE															
(504) Total Costs - FYTD Cost Variance from Target	-5%	C	MONTH	●	●	●	●	●	●	●	●	●	●	●	●
(505) A-76 Competitive Sourcing Performance	>7%	C	QTRLY	◐				◐							
(506) Total Competitive Performance Percentage	8.30%	C	QTRLY												
INTERNAL BUSINESS PROCESS PERSPECTIVE															
(507) Quality Index	Quality Index > or = to 1.1	Q	MONTH	●	●	●	●	●	●						
(508) Rework Identified	1	Q	QTRLY	N/R	●	N/R	●	N/R	●	N/R	N/R	●	N/R		●
(509) Eliminate Rework	-10%	Q	QTRLY	N/R	○	N/R	●	N/R	●	N/R	N/R	●	N/R		●
(510) Best Business Practices Adopted	20%	C	QTRLY	○	●	○	○	○	○						
(511) New Products or Services Delivered	9	BLEs	QTRLY	●	●	N/R	●	●							●
(512) Systems Cost		BLEs	QTRLY	●	●			●	●	●	●	●	●	●	●
(512) System Milestones Delivered	56	BLEs	QTRLY	●	●			◐	●	●	●	●			●
GROWTH AND LEARNING															
(513) Employees in Developmental Assignments	1.5%	H	MONTH	●	●	◐	●	●	●	●	●	●	●	●
(514) Employee Satisfaction	54.1%	H	ANNUAL	◐	●	●	○	●	◐	●	◐	●	●	◐
(515) Core Competency Profile		H	QTRLY	○	○	○	●	○	○	○	○	○	○	○
(516) Climate for Action	49.3%	H	ANNUAL	●	●	●	●	●	●	●	●	●	●	◐

● Red ● Green ◐ Yellow ○ In progress N/R = No Response to date.

DFAS June Corp BSC Results

CHAPTER 8

The Balanced Scorecard at the Federal Aviation Administration Logistics Center

The Federal Aviation Administration Logistics Center (FAALC) in Oklahoma City provides one of the best organizational examples of the effective use of the BSC over a period of years. This chapter first details how the organization dealt with strategy in the 1993 to 1994 period. It then recounts how the BSC was discovered and used in the strategic plan published in 1997. Then, it demonstrates how the strategic plan for 1999 through 2002 reflects even more maturity in the use of the BSC. Last, it presents the FAALC strategic plan for 2003–2007.

Some of this material can viewed on the FAALC Web site, www.logistics.faa.gov.

FAALC STRATEGIC PLAN FOR 1994

The material that follows is adapted from the Federal Aviation Administration Logistics Center, *Strategic Planning, Vision of the Future,* August 1992. It reflects how FAALC's 1994 plan dealt with strategy at much too high a level to drive day-to-day performance.

INTRODUCTION

"Nine tenths of wisdom consists of being wise in time."
"Keep your eyes on the stars; keep your feet on the ground."

—Theodore Roosevelt

Theodore Roosevelt spoke the words above around the beginning of the twentieth century at a time when this country was experiencing enormous changes associated with the industrial revolution. Mr. Roosevelt himself is credited with one of the most remarkable and foresighted accomplishments in the history of America, building the Panama Canal. Undoubtedly, his successes during those times of rapid change can be attributed to the philosophy embodied in these statements.

Just as during Teddy Roosevelt's lifetime, we are witnessing rapid social, economic, political, and technological changes. New and improved technology, the availability of information, and a new global economy are a few of the factors driving changes in the aviation system. Changes in management philosophy, increased public interest in how tax dollars are being used, and cultural diversity are factors driving the "reinvention" of government. All of these changes and other factors will influence the future of the FAA and the FAA Logistics Center.

Our guiding vision is to be the preferred choice throughout the FAA and non-FAA organizations for logistics support of the National Airspace System. The changes we face may present either an opportunity or a threat to making that vision a reality. The more eminent the change the greater likelihood the change will be a threat. On the other hand, given time to prepare and plan for a change we can often create an opportunity for growth or improvement. Through the strategic planning process we can stay in touch with those changes which will influence our future, anticipate the impact of those changes, and build a set of strategies to ensure the changes we face present opportunities which support our vision.

This publication summarizes the results of the FAALC strategic planning efforts to date. This version is provided for internal use by the FAALC employees in order to document the strategic planning process and publicize the FAALC management team's view of the future and strategies for meeting the challenges of the future. As we continue in the implementation of this plan we will learn more and develop a clearer picture of the future. Our strategic plan will be adjusted accordingly. This plan should, therefore, be viewed as a living document, growing, evolving, and changing, as we continue to gather information.

PART I

Strategic Plan Summary

I. Purpose: The FAALC strategic plan provides a direction for the future based on analysis of factors that will affect current FAALC business operations.

II. Process: FAALC management team analyzed current environment, external factors that could change the environment, projected how the FAALC will look in the future, and identified strategies to meet challenges of the future. Employees will take a more active role in development of action plans and implementation.

III. Key Elements of the Plan:
A. Major Factors Affecting the Future
  1. Replacement of traditional ground based systems by Global Positioning Satellite (GPS). GPS will mean less hardware in the field = reduction in required depot level support.
  2. Increased use of Non-developmental Items (NDI) and Commercial Off-the-Shelf (COTS) equipment and systems. NDI/COTS means more contractor support for field maintenance.
C. FAALC Vision: The FAALC is the preferred choice for logistics support to the NAS. Our strategy is to remain a viable, cost effective part of the FAA.
D. Key Issue Areas Addressed in Future Business Model
  1. NAS Logistics Support in FAA
    a. Current: Decentralized functions. Numerous FAA activities have some responsibility.
    b. Future: Integrated—Life Cycle Management common goal/mission of various players.
  2. FAALC Mission
    a. Current: Depot Level Supply Support—Equipment focus.
    b. Future: Life Cycle Management Support—System focus.
  3. FAALC Customers
    a. Current: AAF, AVN, MMAC, AXA, other government agencies, international.
    b. Future: Same basic customers, expanded partnerships.
  4. Lines of Business—In the future we will assume new lines of business. We will continue to perform current lines of business but there will be changes.

5. Resources (Financial)
   a. Current: Fragmented budget process.
   b. Future: Life Cycle Management budget process. Our funds based on ability to "sell" our products and services.
6. People
   a. Current: Specialized skills, functional focus.
   b. Future: Multi-skilled, product team focus.
7. Organization
   a. Current: Functional alignment "stovepipe."
   b. Future: Product/service alignment, fewer layers, team concept.
E. Primary Strategies—"The Foundation of the Strategic Plan"
   1. Streamline Current Operations—Improve processes, customer service.
   2. Increase Competitiveness—Become cost conscious, improve productivity, prepare to compete with contractors for maintenance on systems.
   3. Enter New Lines of Business—Management of AF Field level contracts, Centralized Field level maintenance, Configuration Management, National Logistics Information Service.
   4. Utilize New Business Method—Life Cycle Management
F. Summary: We can meet challenges of the future through teamwork and maximum utilization of our knowledge, skills, abilities, and experience.

PART 2

Designing Our Future—"The Process"

The FAALC Management Team began the strategic planning process in November 1992 by planning to plan and outlining a strategic planning process. Since that time the process has evolved as the team and its understanding of the potential changes in the FAA has matured. In simple terms the process utilized consists of six major steps:

1. Describing our current situation—Where we are today?
2. Painting a picture of where we want to be in the future
3. Identifying the "gaps" between "today" and "tomorrow"—What is different between our picture of today and tomorrow?
4. Mapping out broad strategies to bridge the gaps—How (in very broad terms) can the FAALC get to tomorrow?
5. Developing action plans to accomplish strategies—Specifically what steps should we take, who will lead the effort, when will it be accomplished?
6. Implement the action plans, track progress, measure results, and adjust gaps as necessary.

There are numerous steps that must be taken within each phase of the strategic planning process we have described, as well as a great deal of information to be considered. Figure 3–1 provides a diagram of the strategic planning process utilized by the FAALC management team. A more detailed discussion of each step follows Figure 3–1.

The FAALC management team has completed the first four steps in the process. The result of this first strategic planning cycle is summarized in this document.

A number of employees have already been involved in initiatives which grew out of the strategic planning process. However, we are now ready to enter the Action Plan and Implementation phases of the process on a broader, more structured basis.

Process Discussion

1. **Environmental Assessment**—The process of describing our current situation and identifying possible factors that may influence our future. Identification of mandates, defining our mission and organizational values, conducting an external and internal scan are part of the environmental assessment.

    a. Mandates—Laws, orders, policies, agreements, or commitments that set a boundary on what you can do now and in the future.

    b. Mission/Value—Purpose of the organization and the operating values that the organization will use.

    c. Internal Scan—The process of identifying what resources we have available to shape our future.

    d. External Scan—The process of identifying those forces acting on the FAALC from the outside. Primary focus is on identifying any opportunities that will exist and any threats to the FAALC current operations. Information is gathered from customers, suppliers, and other stakeholders regarding their expectations. The FAA Strategic Plan, our key stakeholders' strategic plans, and political, economic, social and technological trends also provide critical information.

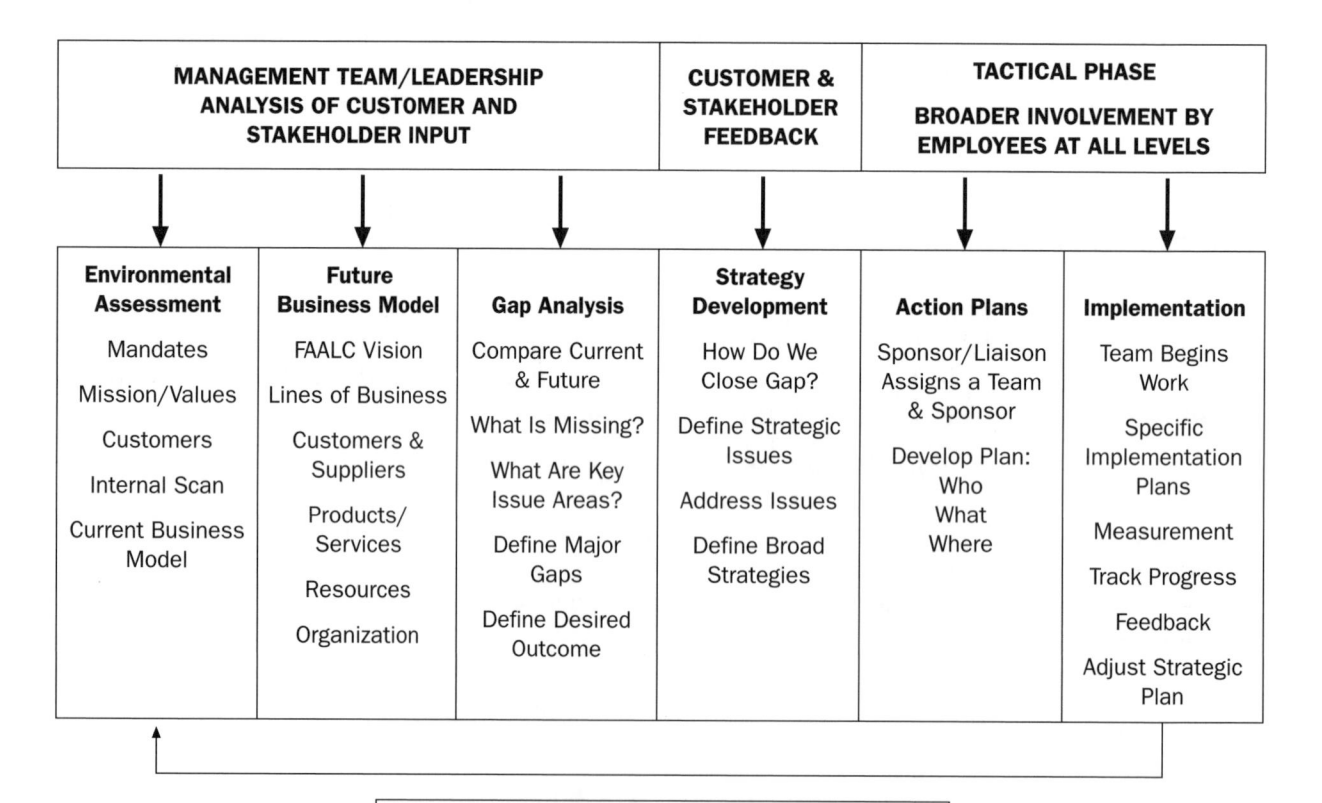

MANAGEMENT TEAM/LEADERSHIP ANALYSIS OF CUSTOMER AND STAKEHOLDER INPUT			CUSTOMER & STAKEHOLDER FEEDBACK	TACTICAL PHASE BROADER INVOLVEMENT BY EMPLOYEES AT ALL LEVELS	
Environmental Assessment	**Future Business Model**	**Gap Analysis**	**Strategy Development**	**Action Plans**	**Implementation**
Mandates	FAALC Vision	Compare Current & Future	How Do We Close Gap?	Sponsor/Liaison Assigns a Team & Sponsor	Team Begins Work
Mission/Values	Lines of Business	What Is Missing?	Define Strategic Issues	Develop Plan: Who What Where	Specific Implementation Plans
Customers	Customers & Suppliers	What Are Key Issue Areas?	Address Issues		Measurement
Internal Scan	Products/ Services	Define Major Gaps	Define Broad Strategies		Track Progress
Current Business Model	Resources	Define Desired Outcome			Feedback
	Organization				Adjust Strategic Plan

STRATEGIC PLANNING IS A CONTINUOUS PROCESS

It never ends, therefore the product of this process, THE STRATEGIC PLAN, will be adjusted and revised as the process evolves and the passage of time generates additional information upon which to make decisions regarding the future.

Figure 8–1. Strategic Planning Process. *Source:* Adapted from Federal Aviation Administration Logistics Center, *Strategic Planning, Vision of the Future,* August 1992.

e. Current Business Model—A description of the key elements of our current business model, i.e., how we do business today. The key elements were identified as NAS Logistics Support in the FAA, the FAALC mission, Customers, Lines of Business, Resources, People and Organization. This is based on information gathered in the Environmental Assessment, and analysis of that information.

2. **Future Business Model**—Describes the FAALC Vision of the Future. Includes a statement, which describes the direction of the FAALC that indicates success in accomplishing our mission in the future. We also describe our future lines of business, the customer base served by that line of business, and the products and/or services provided to that customer. For comparison purposes the key elements defined in the Future Business Model were the same as those defined in the Current Business Model. This is based on analysis of information gathered in the environmental assessment.

3. **Gap Analysis**—During this step in the process we compare our current situation to our overall vision for the FAALC. The framework for accomplishing this is comparison of the current business model to the future business model. By systematically comparing each key element of the current and future business models we discuss the differences, identify potential issues or problems, and finally identify the major gap areas which must be closed to get to our future business model. In our analysis there was a major gap in each of the seven key elements of the model, these then became the key issue areas used to focus our strategy development.

4. **Strategy Development**—At this step we define in very broad terms how the FAALC can achieve the model of the future. First we write a vision for each of the major gaps, i.e., what the FAALC will do, how it will operate, or what characteristic will change if the gap is closed. We also define key strategic issues that must be addressed or considered in the action plans. This will serve as the ultimate goal for the team, or teams, assigned to work this gap.

5. **Action Plan (or Strategy Prospectus) Development**—The development of action plans marks the initial transition of the strategic plan to tactical or operational planning and implementation. This step requires broader employee and management participation. Sponsorship for each major gap is assigned to a member of the management team. In some cases sponsorship may be shared between two members. The sponsor is responsible to establish a team of FAALC employees to begin studying the major gap and develop an action plan. The information generated by the management team through the first four steps will be provided to each team, along with any additional guidance the sponsor deems appropriate. This information is provided in what is referred to as a "Strategy Prospectus." Teams will typically be comprised of employees from various functional areas, i.e., different AML Divisions, and may require membership from outside the FAALC depending on the nature of the assignment. Action plans will outline primary goals and objectives that must be accomplished to realize the vision of the closed gap, and a timetable for accomplishing these goals. Additional "sub-teams" may be required to work specific goals and objectives.

6. **Implementation**—At this step the management team begins to track and monitor the implementation of the Action Plans. Additional or new information may be gained during this phase which will necessitate adjustment to the future business model, may change the nature of focus of a gap, point to a new gap, or require new priorities be placed on action plans.

FAALC STRATEGIC PLAN FOR 1997

Much positive change is evident In the FAALC 1997 strategic plan. The BSC is implemented through four different areas: (1) the customer perspective, (2) the financial stakeholder perspective, (3) the internal business perspective, and (4) the learning and innovation perspective. These areas are laid out as several strategic goals in each perspective into several measures in each perspective and finally into multiple targets in each perspective. This allows the plan to be driven throughout the organization in order to implement the organization strategy effectively.

The following material is adapted from the Federal Aviation Administration Logistics Center, *Strategic Plan: Our Guide to the Future,* 1997.

Introduction

Purpose

The FAA Logistics Center's strategic plan provides a direction for the future based on analysis of factors affecting current Logistics Center business operations.

Process

A group comprised of Logistics Center managers, labor representatives, and employees projected how the Logistics Center will look in the future. The FAA Logistics Center management team analyzed the current environment, external factors that could change that environment, and identified strategies to meet future challenges.

In March 1997, the strategic planning group revised the strategic goals and applied the "Balanced Scorecard Approach" to develop measures and targets for each strategic goal.

Environmental Assessment

"The National Performance Review is about change -- historic change -- in the way government works." This is the first line of "From Red Tape to Results, Creating a Government that Works Better and Costs Less, Report of the National Performance Review," published in September 1993. The FAA Logistics Center's strategic planning group not only sees change in our future, but wants to lead the way in making historic changes in the way we work.

The following factors are some of the most significant changes affecting our future:

Major Factors Affecting the Future

- Replacement of traditional ground-based systems by Global Positioning System (GPS).

- Increased use of non-developmental items and commercial off-the-shelf (COTS) equipment and systems.

- The National Performance Review — a challenge to create a government that works better and costs less.

- New flexibility in the areas of human resource management and acquisition.

- Increased competition for shrinking budget allocations.

Vision

The FAA Logistics Center is a world-class, customer-driven logistics organization whose quality services are in demand throughout the FAA and worldwide.

Mission

The FAA Logistics Center provides comprehensive logistics support and high quality products, assuring safety of the flying public, and satisfies the needs of the National Airspace System (NAS) and other valued customers.

Key Business Processes

Key business processes are those processes cutting across FAA Logistics Center divisional or functional lines. All Logistics Center employees play a role in delivering products or services produced by one or more of these processes.

- Contractor Maintenance Logistics Support (CMLS)
- Contractor Depot Logistics Support (CDLS)
- Organic logistics support
- Site depot services
- Acquisition planning
- Refurbishment

Organizational Values

We Believe In and Are Committed To...

- Customer and Employee Satisfaction
- Quality and Teamwork
- Leadership and Communications
- Loyalty, Commitment, and Trust
- Diversity and Corporate Citizenship
- Innovation and Risk-Taking

Organizational Values Will Be Achieved Because Our Culture Says...

- Everyone understands the vision and priorities of the organization.
- People enjoy coming to work and take pride in their job.
- Everyone is treated with respect.
- Leaders model the value of employee involvement and customer satisfaction.
- People are committed and loyal to this organization.
- Everyone knows their customers and their needs.
- People have the opportunity to influence how the work is done.
- We know and measure how well we're doing in satisfying customers.
- Ideas are exchanged openly.
- We systematically analyze and improve how the work is done.
- Decisions are usually made by consensus.

Strategies

The FAA Logistics Center will employ two broad strategies to achieve our vision:

- Focus on the customer to become a customer-driven organization.
- Increase and/or sustain business for the FAA Logistics Center.

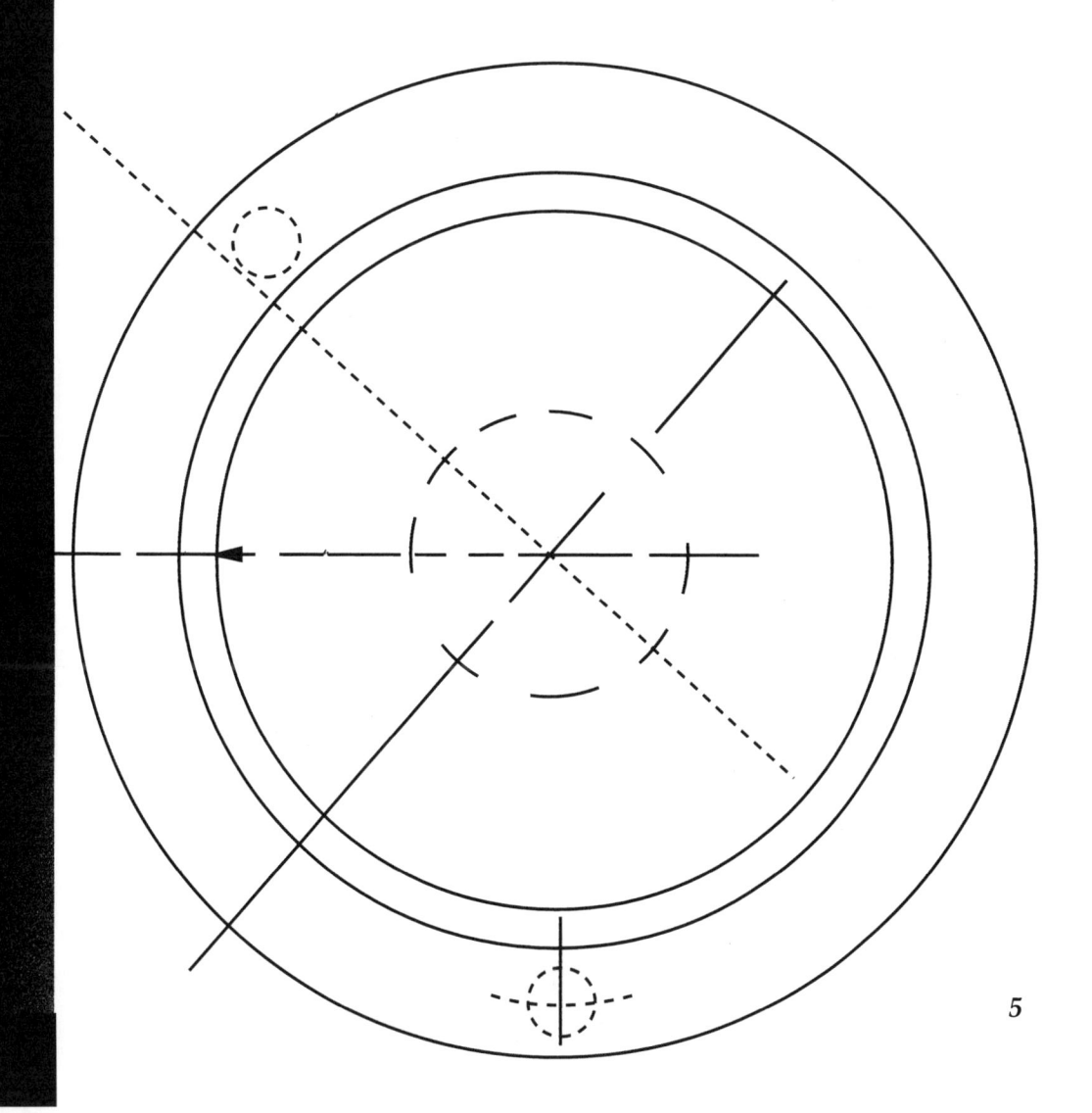

Strategic Goals, Measures, & Targets

The FAA Logistics Center's strategic goals, measures and targets were developed using the "Balanced Scorecard Approach." The Balanced Scorecard Approach says the success of an organization is dependent upon balancing various aspects of the organization to achieve overall success. Managers must look at the organization from four basic perspectives:

- **The Customer Perspective** - What must we do to satisfy, retain, and attract new customers?

- **The Financial Stakeholder Perspective** - What must we do to increase business and ensure financial success?

- **The Internal Business Perspective** - What internal processes must we excel at to satisfy our customers and assure financial success?

- **The Learning and Innovation Perspective** - What must we do to develop employee skills and technology to continue adding value to our customers and improve our capabilities?

The FAA Logistics Center's **Balanced Scorecard** consists of the following:

- **Strategic goals** translate our broad strategies into actionable goals to achieve our vision of the future.

- **Measures** describe what we will measure to determine whether or not we have met our goals.

- **Targets** for the measures are set 3 to 5 years out and are designed to s-t-r-e-t-c-h our performance. If we achieve these targets, we will transform the FAA Logistics Center and achieve our vision.

The FAA Logistics Center's Strategy

To achieve the FAA Logistics Center's vision, we have two broad strategies. These are to be "customer driven" and to "increase or sustain business for the Logistics Center." These two strategies must be balanced. Our financial stakeholders influence our ability to increase our business. We must balance their requirements with our customers' needs and expectations. The following diagram shows the **FAA Logistics Center's** strategic goals established to provide this balance.

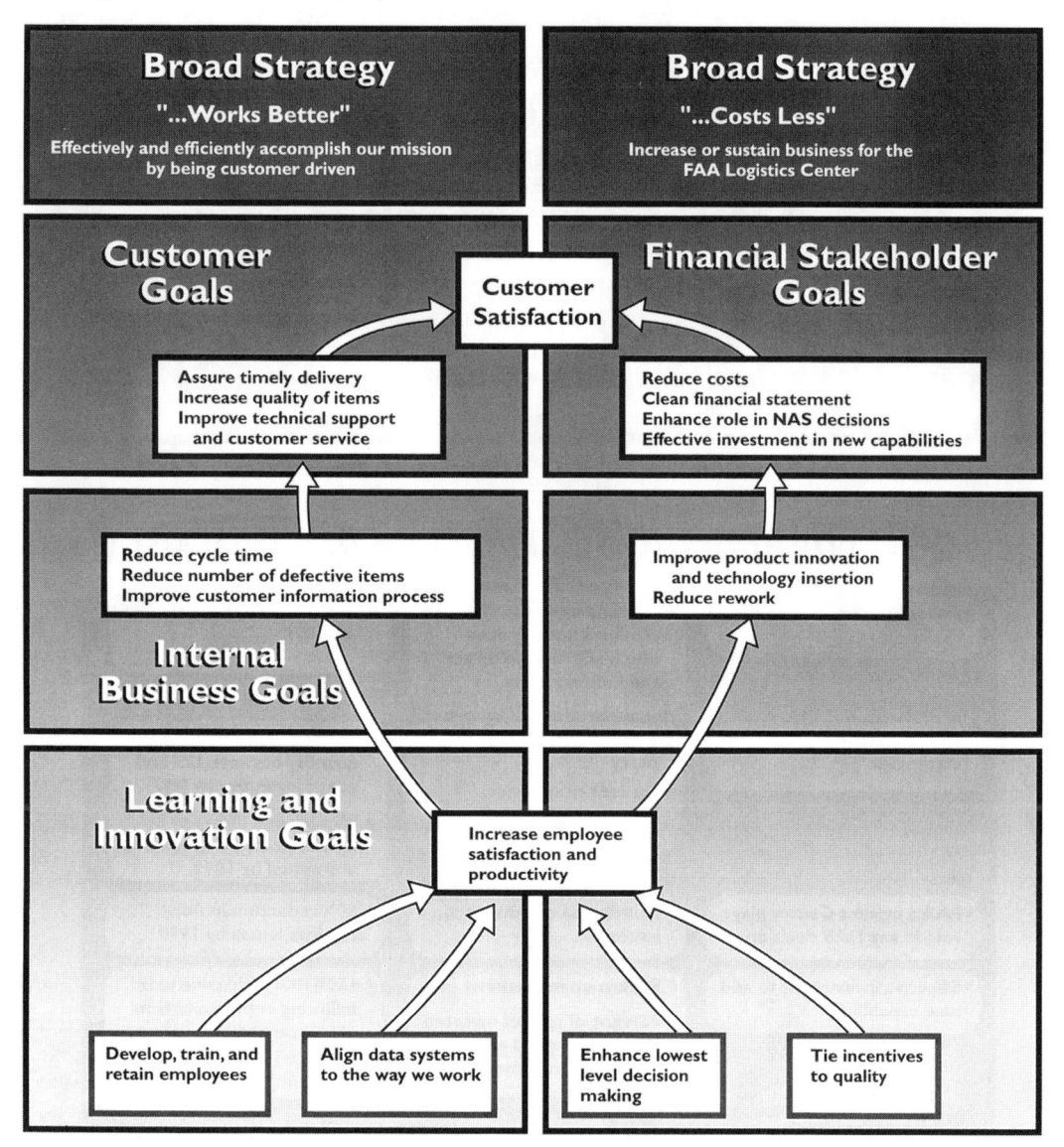

Broad Strategy
"...Works Better"
Effectively and efficiently accomplish our mission by being customer driven

Broad Strategy
"...Costs Less"
Increase or sustain business for the FAA Logistics Center

Customer Goals
- Assure timely delivery
- Increase quality of items
- Improve technical support and customer service

Customer Satisfaction

Financial Stakeholder Goals
- Reduce costs
- Clean financial statement
- Enhance role in NAS decisions
- Effective investment in new capabilities

Internal Business Goals
- Reduce cycle time
- Reduce number of defective items
- Improve customer information process

- Improve product innovation and technology insertion
- Reduce rework

Learning and Innovation Goals

Increase employee satisfaction and productivity

- Develop, train, and retain employees
- Align data systems to the way we work
- Enhance lowest level decision making
- Tie incentives to quality

THE CUSTOMER PERSPECTIVE

STRATEGIC GOAL	MEASURE	TARGET
• Increase customer satisfaction	• Customer satisfaction rating	• Improve overall rating to max rating in 90% of categories by end of 1999
• Assure timely delivery	• Percent of on-time deliveries as defined by customer	• 100% on-time by end of 1999
• Increase quality of items delivered	• Percent of defective shipments (product defective) • Percent of defective shipments (quantity, pkg, marking, or wrong item basis for defective shipment)	• Zero defective shipments by end of 1999
• Increase quality of technical support and customer service	• # of customer queries satisfied the first time • # of customer complaints regarding technical support and customer service	• Increase from current to 100% by end of 1999 • Zero by end of 1999

THE FINANCIAL STAKEHOLDER PERSPECTIVE

STRATEGIC GOAL	MEASURE	TARGET
• Reduce cost	• Average unit cost of products and services which will include direct and indirect costs	• 30% Reduction in unit cost by 2001
• Produce clean financial statement	• Clean assessment by 3rd party • Percent of variance between DAFIS, LIS, and actual inventory value	• Less than 5% variance in quantity between LIS and actual inventory by 9/97 • 0% variance between LIS, agency accounting system, and actual by 1999
• FAA Logistics Center plays role in key NAS decisions	• Number of non-support issues	• 50% reduction in non-support issues by 1999
• Effective investment to add new capabilities	• Return on investment • Percent of budget invested in human capital and capital improvements	• 150% ROI within one year following implementation of new capability • Allocate 15% of budget to capital improvement by 2001

8

THE INTERNAL BUSINESS PERSPECTIVE

STRATEGIC GOAL	MEASURE	TARGET
Reduce cycle time	Cycle time	50% reduction in cycle time by 1999
Improve product delivery time	Delivery time (incrementally)	Delivery in 6 hours by 1999
Reduce rework	Percent of items reworked	.00001% of items reworked by 1999
Reduce number of defective items received	Number of discrepant items received	One complaint per 10,000 received by 1999
Improve product innovation and technology insertion	Number of NSN's that are support condition red	75% reduction by 1999
Improve process for customer information	Customer satisfaction survey	Overall customer rating in this category of 4 or higher (scale of 1-5) by 1999

THE LEARNING AND INNOVATION PERSPECTIVE

STRATEGIC GOAL	MEASURE	TARGET
Develop, train, retain current workers. Attract, develop, and retain knowledge workers	Employee skills assessment	Complimentary mix with broad-based knowledge and technical skills
Align data systems to the way we work to meet employee and customer needs	User satisfaction survey; System access availability time	Survey indicates average rating of 4 or higher (scale of 1-5) in this category by 1999; 75% improvement in system availability time by 1999
Tie incentives to quality	Percent of employee awards related to quality; Number of quality award nominations	50% increase in number of awards related to quality by 1999; Achieve DOT Quality Award by 1999, 3rd place for Baldrige by 2000
Enhance lowest level decision-making	Employee satisfaction/ organization climate survey; Leadership skills assessment	Survey and assessment indicates 100% of assessed leaders' performance above satisfactory in this category by 1999

FAALC STRATEGIC PLAN FOR 1999–2002

The 1999–2002 strategic plan is yet another refinement on the application of the BSC. This plan lays out multiple strategic objectives for each Balanced Scorecard perspective followed by multiple measures and targets for each perspective.

The following material is adapted from the Federal Aviation Administration Logistics Center, *Strategic Plan: Our Guide to the Future: 1999–2002,* Oklahoma City, Oklahoma, FAA Information Media Division.

Introduction

Purpose

The Federal Aviation Administration Logistics Center (FAALC) strategic plan describes the strategic direction and business focus for the next 2 to 3 years. The Logistics Center is organizationally aligned under the Mike Monroney Aeronautical Center and the Assistant Administrator for Region and Center Operations within the FAA. As is the case with many organizations that are part of a larger government Agency, strategic priorities may change with little notice due to factors beyond our control or influence. Envisioning the future is never easy, however, under these circumstances it is particularly challenging. Our planning horizon was by necessity shorter than most strategic plans, and the plan is subject to change or modification in the near term.

Process

Consistent with our commitment to continuous improvement in all areas of the FAA Logistics Center, the strategic planning process was modified with the objective of enhancing the usefulness of this plan. The primary planning team, comprised of the senior managers, mid-level supervisors, and non-supervisory employees, commissioned a planning support team to conduct pre-planning research and analysis and revise the planning process. The planning support team membership included managers and staff support personnel. The support team reviewed the FAA Strategic Plan, primary customers' strategic plans, and even some potential competitors' strategic plans to assess external factors and ensure consistency with the Agency's strategic direction. A comprehensive analysis of future workload demand, completed by the FAALC Business Systems Group, was used extensively by the support group to predict future markets for Logistics Center services.

The support group also gathered feedback from internal users of the strategic plan. The feedback identified gaps in the previous plan that, if filled, would improve the plan's value as a framework for supplemental business plans developed by the FAALC divisions, groups, and teams. As a result new concepts, such as the "Strategy Statement," are included in this version. A "Supplemental Strategic Guide" is being published. The supplement is intended primarily for internal use and contains background information, definitions, explanations, and other information useful to the FAALC employees as they develop business plans in support of this plan.

Vision

The FAA Logistic Center is a world-class customer-driven organization whose quality services are in demand throughout the FAA and worldwide.

Mission

The FAALC ensures the safety of the flying public by providing material support, high quality electronic equipment repair, engineering services, inventory management, and other related services for the National Airspace System (NAS) and other valued customers.

How We Accomplish Our Mission

The FAALC is organizationally aligned by product lines and major support services. Each division is essentially a distinct business unit, capable of providing end-to-end services to a specific customer or segment of customers. The internal support functions are called systems groups. All divisions and groups report directly to the Logistics Center Program Director.

Business Units

Product Divisions

- Radar Products Division
- Communications Products Division
- Automation Products Division
- Navigation Landing and Weather Products Division
- Aircraft Products Division

Service Divisions

- Distribution Services Division
- Product Services Division

Support Groups

The primary mission of the support groups is to provide business services and related support to the business units, however, they may have some functions that are self-sustaining business operations.

- Business Systems Group

- Information Systems Group

- Quality Systems Group

Key Business Processes

Each business unit performs one or more of the key processes itemized below. These processes singularly, or in combination with others, are the key processes required to deliver products or services to our customers.

- Repair, fabrication, and overhaul of NAS equipment and systems which includes both centralized repair and site overhaul, as the customer requests

- Storage, distribution, and transportation of NAS parts and supplies

- Consulting services

  - Technical consulting services related to sustainment of NAS systems and equipment

  - Life cycle planning consulting services related to acquisition, supply support, maintenance, and decommissioning

- Inventory management

Organizational Values

We Believe In and Are Committed To...

- Customer and Employee Satisfaction

- Quality and Teamwork

- Leadership and Communications

- Loyalty, Commitment, and Trust

- Diversity and Corporate Citizenship

- Innovation and Risk-Taking

- Best Value Support for our Customers

Organizational Values Will Be Achieved Because Our Culture Says...

- Everyone understands the vision and priorities of the organization.

- People enjoy coming to work and take pride in the job they do.

- Everyone is treated with respect.

- Leaders model the value of employee involvement and customer satisfaction.

- People are committed and loyal to this organization.

- Everyone knows who their customers are and their needs.

- Everyone has the opportunity to influence how the work is done and what it costs.

- We know and measure how well we are doing in satisfying customers.

- Ideas are exchanged openly.

- We systematically analyze and improve how the work is done.

- Decisions are usually made by consensus.

Assumptions

This strategic plan is predicated on the following assumptions:

- The FAA Logistics Center will receive authorization to operate under a franchise fund during FY-2001.

- The FAA, and specifically Airway Facilities, will continue to be our primary customer.

- The FAA modernization program will retain some ground based navigation systems.

Environmental Assessment

Major Factors Affecting the Future

- FAA modernization including a phased replacement of many traditional ground based navigation systems by Global Positioning Satellite (GPS)

- The need for FAA to operate as a business and our responsibility to give the American public the best value for their dollar

- Customer behavior changes in a fee-for-service or similar environment

Strategies

The FAALC will employ three key strategies to achieve our vision, and position the Logistics Center for future success:

- Position the FAALC to rapidly respond to new customer demands by improving the flexibility and versatility of the organization.

- Work with agency product teams and the private sector to lower the cost of system ownership for our customers.

- Establish the FAALC as the fastest delivery source of quality products in the government sector.

Strategy Statement

Background

The FAALC Strategy Statement is a new feature of our strategic plan. It is included in response to feedback from our workforce. The strategic plan is intended as a tool to guide managers, supervisors, and employees throughout the organization in making business and operational decisions. Feedback regarding the previous plan indicated the plan would be a more useful tool if the Vision and Mission Statements were supplemented by clarifying the Logistics Center's strategic focus, or more clearly describing our direction. The Vision Statement clearly defines our key characteristics and how we want to be viewed by our customers and external stakeholders. The Mission statement describes in broad terms our primary function and ultimate responsibility. Both are necessary segments of our plan and serve to frame the picture of our future. However, a clear picture of what the FAALC will be is necessary for the plan to provide maximum value as a guide to our workforce. The strategy statement is intended to fill this gap.

Our objective is for the workforce to be able to know our strategy and use it as they would any other tool at their disposal.

FAALC Strategy Statement

The FAALC will continue to provide logistics support to our customers, and our primary thrust will continue to be the repair and distribution of NAS equipment and systems.

Our business focus for the near future will be on positioning the FAALC for rapid response to new customer demands, working to reduce the cost of system ownership for the FAA and other customers, and taking action to provide faster delivery service.

Each focus area has common strategic themes, specifically, growth and expansion of the Logistics Center's capabilities and business activities, achievement of operational excellence, and providing value to the customer.

We will constantly seek to improve the quality of our products and services, and be alert to new business opportunities that will add value to the service we provide to our primary customer, the FAA, and ultimately the flying public. We will demonstrate our pride and commitment as public servants dedicated to provide unique products and services that are second to none. Providing the best value to our customer will be a prime objective, and we recognize lowest cost does not always represent the best value.

Linkage to FAA Strategic Plan

FAA Strategic Goals, Key Initiatives, and Performance Goals

- The FAA has three key mission goals:

  - Safety—By 2007 reduce aviation fatal accident rates by 80 percent from 1996 levels.

  - Security—Prevent security incidents in the aviation system.

  - System Efficiency—Provide an aerospace transportation system that meets the needs of users and is efficient in the application of FAA and aerospace resources.

The FAALC in some way will contribute to the accomplishment of all of these goals; however, our mission is most directly related to the System Efficiency goal. The clear connection between our mission and this goal is illustrated in the FAA FY-2000 President's Budget Submission and Performance Plan. In that submission, the Agency's funding is linked to one of the three agency strategic goals. The source of our primary FAA customers' funding is tied directly to the System Efficiency goal. As a result, FAALC strategic goals and performance targets are aimed at improving the utilization of resources and achieving results that will improve operational availability of the NAS.

Strengths Weaknesses Opportunities and Threats Analysis Summary

FAALC strategies were developed based on a situational analysis considering current environmental factors, both internal and external, that could affect the future of the FAALC. The strengths, weaknesses, opportunities, and threats (SWOT) associated with each were also analyzed. The results of this SWOT analysis formed the basis for identification of our strategic objectives. We established objectives that leverage our strengths, eliminate our weaknesses, neutralize threats, and take advantage of opportunities.

A detailed discussion of the critical strengths, weaknesses, opportunities, and threats is provided in the Supplemental Strategic Guidance document.

Strategic Objectives, Measures and Targets

The FAALC Strategic objectives, measures, and targets were developed using the "Balanced Scorecard Approach." The Balanced Scorecard Approach says the success of an organization is dependent upon balancing various aspects of the organization to achieve overall success. Managers must look at the organization from four basic perspectives:

- **The Customer Perspective**—What must we do to satisfy and retain current customers and attract new customers? Customers in this context are primarily the end user of our products or services.

- **The Financial Stakeholder Perspective**—What must we do to satisfy our financial stakeholders? Our key financial stakeholders are the individuals and organizations that control or influence the appropriation, allocation, or utilization of Federal funds. Under the current financial management system, our financial stakeholders typically are not the end user of our products and services.

- **The Internal Business Perspective**—What core internal business processes drive the results we want to achieve under the customer perspective and the financial stakeholder perspective? For these processes, what level of performance must we achieve?

- **The Learning and Innovation Perspective**—What must we do to develop people and technology to support our internal business processes and improve our capabilities so that we can continue to add value to our cusotmers and our financial stakeholders?

The FAALC Balanced Scorecard consists of the following:

Strategies objectives translate our broad strategies into actionable goals in order to achieve our vision of the future.

Measures describe what we will measure to determine whether or not we have met our goals.

Targets for the measures are set 1 to 3 years out and are designed to s-t-r-e-t-c-h our performance.

The Customer Perspective

STRATEGIC OBJECTIVE	MEASURE	TARGET
• Increase customer satisfaction.	• Customer Satisfaction Rating.	• Close 15% of the gap between the April 1999 baseline of 3.66 and maximum rating of 5.0 for each 18-month rating cycle through 2002.
• Increase product availability for our customers.	• Customer Satisfaction Rating.	• Close 50% of the gap between the April 1999 baseline of 4.1 and importance to the customer rating of 4.5 for each 18-month rating cycle through 2002.
• Increase quality of items delivered.	• % Defective shipments (product defective). • Customer survey rating for technical reliability. • % Defective shipments (quantity, packing, packaging, marking, or wrong item basis for defective shipment). • Customer survey rating for delivery accuracy.	• 50% decrease in reported defective products by 2002 based on FY99 defects per 1,000 issues. • Close 33% of the gap between April 1999 baseline of 3.9 and importance rating of 4.5 for each 18-month rating cycle through 2002. • 50% decrease in reported defective products by 2002 based on FY99 defects per 1,000 issues. • Close 33% of the gap between the April 1999 baseline of 4.3 and importance rating of 4.6 for each 18-month rating cycle through 2002.
• Viewed by Agency as best value Logistics Support provider for life cycle support.	• Gross sales attributable to new systems workload.	• 5% increase in gross sales is attributable to new systems workload by 2002.

The Financial Stakeholder Perspective

STRATEGIC OBJECTIVE	MEASURE	TARGET
• Reduce cost.	• Repair cost.	• Reduce repair cost 10% over FY-99 baseline by 2002.
	• Inventory (stock) turn-over rate.	• Stock turnover rate improves by 10% each year through 2002.
	• PC&B as a ratio to gross margin.	• PC&B is 25% of gross margin by 2002.
	• Distribution cost per issue.	• 3% reduction in distribution cost per issue from baseline of $51.77 per issue by end of FY-2000.
• Achieve a return on investment for the Agency when selected to provide Logistics Support for new systems.	• Return on Investment (ROI) to Agency.	• ROI of at least 10% on new business.
• Increase gross sales.	• Volume of sales for products, services, and consulting.	• Increase gross sales 25% by 2002 using FY99 as a baseline.

The Internal Business Perspective

STRATEGIC OBJECTIVE	MEASURE	TARGET
• Reduce average repair time for LRU repair.	• Average repair time.	• Reduce average repair time for LRU in repair facilities 10% by FY-2002 over FY-99 baseline.
• Improve product delivery processes and systems.	• Number of customer orders filled in 24 hours.	• Increase number of customer orders filled in 24 hours by 50%. Include orders filled from FAALC Distribution Center stock only, not PDS shipments.
	• Customer returns receipted to stock within 24 hours.	• 100% of customer returns receipted to stock within 24 hours by 2002.
	• Inventory accuracy for quantity and location.	• 99% inventory accuracy by 2002.
	• Warehouse refusal rate.	• .1% refusal rate by 2002.
• Improve product innovation and technology insertion.	• ROI on obsolescence driven replacements at form, fit, and function.	• ROI greater than 10% per project.
• Improve internal cost analysis process and capabilities.	• Availability of valid financial information necessary to achieve financial objectives and targets related to cost reduction.	• Cost reduction goals under financial perspective are met. (Note: If goals are not met, the inability to meet the goals cannot be attributed to lack of valid financial reports or analyses.)

The Learning and Innovation Perspective

STRATEGIC OBJECTIVE	MEASURE	TARGET
• Develop, train, and retain current workers. Attract, develop, and retain knowledge workers. Skills necessary to ensure product/service delivery are available.	• Percentage of current competency inventories completed and training/development completed.	• All occupations have a current competency inventory reflecting new competencies needed to meet future demands, and training matrix by end of FY 2000. All employees have completed identified training or development within 1 year after assuming current position or receiving new training matrix, providing funding for training is available.
• Implement total asset tracking system, to include bar coding and other state of the art technology.	• Implementation of total asset tracking system. (This measure tied to inventory accuracy, and other process measures in internal business perspective.)	• Total asset tracking system implemented by end of FY-2000, and system produces real time asset location and movement information.
• Implement effective internal cost accounting and financial management information system.	• Availability of current cost information. • Feedback from users.	• 100% of managers and supervisors have cost data available to them through an automated system by end of FY-2000. • 100% of managers and supervisors indicate automated system is a useful tool for making operational decisions.
• Encourage and facilitate self-development of managers.	• Managerial 360 degree assessment.	• Assessment indicates composite scores for all managers improved by .75 points over 1999 assessment by 2002. (Composite score is special report that summarizes scores for all managers into one value for the management team. Individual scores are not identifiable.)
• All employees (including supervisory and non supervisory) are motivated and job satisfaction is high.	• Employee attitude survey results.	• FAALC results show an increase of at least .3 points in all measured categories for all employees over EAS conducted in 1998.
• Implement effective shop production control system.	• Production control efficiency index.	• System is implemented and 100% of identified requirements in the index are rated satisfactory or higher by end of FY-2000.

Strategic Plan Deployment and Action Plans

Each Division and Group will develop annual business plans to describe how their organization will contribute to the achievement of the Strategic Objectives. Preparation of business plans is contingent upon having adequate cost and performance data to make projections and establish measurable goals and targets.

At a minimum business plans will include:

- Financial projections based on projected cost of operations, investments, and revenue.

- Resource utilization plan.

- Production plan indicating anticipated changes in existing workload, and any new workload the Division may be planning to assume or pursue with appropriate business case justification.

- Annual Division or Group goals. These goals must be tied to FAALC strategic objectives or FAALC annual goals.

- Results based performance measures and targets for each annual division goal.

- Outline of key milestones for any projects associated with FAALC strategic goals.

- Explanation regarding how Division or Group annual goals will be cascaded through all levels of the organization.

FAALC STRATEGIC PLAN FOR 2003–2007

The FAALC strategic plan for 2003–2007 was developed with the objective of enhancing its usefulness and applicability. The plan presents FAALC's organizational values and key business processes. It can be viewed at www.logistics.faa.gov.

The FAA Logistics Center Strategic Plan

Introduction

Purpose

The Federal Aviation Administration (FAA) Logistics Center Strategic Plan describes the strategic direction and business focus for the next five years within the FAA. The Logistics Center is organizationally aligned under the Mike Monroney Aeronautical Center and the Assistant Administrator for Region and Center Operations. As is the case with many organizations that are part of a larger government Agency, strategic priorities may change with little notice due to factors beyond our control or influence. Envisioning the future is never easy under these circumstances, however, it is always challenging.

Process

Consistent with our commitment to continuous improvement in all areas of the Logistics Center, the strategic planning process was modified with the objective of enhancing the usefulness and applicability of this plan. The primary planning team, comprised of the senior managers, mid- level supervisors, and non-supervisory employees conducted pre-planning research and analysis in order to develop a Strategic Planning Model, and to revise the planning process. An Executive Strategic Planning Team was commissioned with membership comprised of Logistics Center Managers, Union representatives, and Center of Excellence representatives. The Executive Strategic Planning Team reviewed the FAA Strategic Plan, primary customers' strategic plans, and even some potential competitors' strategic plans to assess external factors and ensure consistency with the Agency's strategic direction. A comprehensive analysis of future workload demand, completed by the Logistics Center Business Systems Group, was used extensively by the support group to predict future markets for Logistics Center services. The Strategic Planning Executive Team also utilized feedback from internal users. The feedback identified gaps in the previous plan that, if filled, would improve the plan's value as a framework for supplemental business plans developed by the Logistics Center divisions, groups, and teams.

Vision

The preferred provider for tomorrow's solutions today to aviation and the nation.

Mission

Provide rapid distribution and supply chain management, maintenance, repair, and other industrial and business services, for the nation's aviation and airspace systems, and to world-wide aviation related customers by offering innovative solutions, consulting expertise, and project management services.

Organizational Values

We Believe In and Are Committed To...

- **Results Oriented**—The Logistics Center constantly drives for results and success. We drive issues to closure, persist despite obstacles and opposition, and maintain a high energy level. Our employees readily put in the needed time and effort to achieve results.

- **Innovation**—The future of the Logistics Center is assured only as long as it welcomes and rewards innovation, creativity, and resourcefulness. We recognize "trial and error" as being elements of innovation and continuous improvement. Innovation has been the cause of success for the Logistics Center.

- **Customer**—Customer Service is our driving force. Our wish is to continually strive to satisfy our customer by delivering results, providing quality products and services, and exceeding our customers' expectations.

- **Quality**—We provide the best quality in all of our products and services. Our goal is to exceed industry benchmarks.

- **People**—People are our most important resource. We respect the individual's dignity and value their contributions. We invest in training and education to give our employees the tools to make the Logistics Center a world-class organization.

- **Teamwork and Collaboration**—The Logistics Center provides a positive and challenging environment that supports the achievement of mission goals and fosters team spirit. We are partners with our customers, stakeholders, suppliers, and are committed to union/management partnerships.

- **Integrity and Openness**—The Logistics Center values trust, sincerity, honesty, and candor in relationships both personally and organizationally. We encourage our employees to express ideas, opinions, and thoughts in an honest and genuine manner.

- **Corporate Citizenship**—The Logistics Center values a positive corporate image and is sensitive to our corporate responsibilities to the community. We actively participate and support community involvement.

Organizational Values Will Be Achieved Because We Strive to Achieve...

- Everyone understands the vision and priorities of the organization

- People enjoy coming to work and take pride in the job they do

- Everyone is treated with respect

- Leaders model the value of employee involvement and customer satisfaction

- People are committed and loyal to this organization

- Everyone knows who their customers are and their needs

- Everyone has the opportunity to influence how the work is done and what it costs

- We know and measure how well we are doing in satisfying customers

- Ideas are exchanged openly

- We systematically analyze and improve how the work is done

- Decisions are usually made by consensus

- Employees are encouraged to participate in center-sponsored health programs

Key Business Processes

These key business processes singularly, or in combination with others, are the key processes required to deliver products or services to our NAS and aviation-related customers. Each strategic business unit or support group performs one or more of the following key processes:

- Repair, fabrication, and overhaul of NAS and aviation-related systems and equipment which includes both centralized repair and site overhaul

- Storage, distribution, and transportation services

- Supply chain management for NAS parts and supplies

- Consulting services

    - Technical consulting services related to sustainment of NAS and equipment

    - Life cycle planning consulting services related to acquisition, supply support, maintenance, and decommissioning

    - Provider of a sub-contractor base comprised of professional, technical and management service providers

- Liaison and advisory service to Washington, DC headquarters customers, field activities and other governmental agencies

- Support to aviation-related customers providing engineering, contract management and acquisition, project management, and sustainment expertise

- Provider of advanced system and technology solutions

How We Accomplish Our Mission

The Logistics Center is organizationally aligned by product lines and major support services. Each division is essentially a distinct business unit, capable of providing end-to-end services to a specific customer or segment of customers. All divisions and groups report to the Chief Operating Officer or Chief Financial Officer who act in close coordination on day-to-day operations. The Program Director provides overall direction and vision for the organization.

*Strategic Business Units**

- Distribution Center Division
- Radar Product Division
- Aircraft Product Division
- Product Services Division
- Navigation, Landing, and Weather Product Division
- Automation/Communications Product Division
- Projects and Consulting Group

*Support Groups**

The primary mission of the support groups is to provide business services and related support to the strategic business units, however, they may have some functions that are self-sustaining business operations.

- Business Systems Group
- Quality Systems Group
- Information Systems Group
- Customer and Business Development Staff

---

*As a market-based organization, we are constantly responding to the rapid changes and shifts in our environment. Therefore, our business units and support groups may change to meet emerging priorities, mission objectives, and customers needs.

Assumptions

This strategic plan is predicated on the following assumptions:

1. The FAA will continue to require core logistics from the Logistics Center.

2. The Logistics Center will generate increased revenue through development of new lines of business.

3. The FAA will continue to support a revolving fund environment.

4. The aviation industry and FAA will continue to undergo rapid changes.

Environmental Assessment

Major Factors Affecting the Future

- FAA modernization including a phased replacement of many traditional ground-based navigation systems by Global Positioning Satellite (GPS)

- The need for the Logistics Center to operate as a business and give the American public the best value for their dollar

- Customer behavior changes as funding is distributed and decentralized in a revolving fund

- Emergence of national business units such as the Terminal Business Service (ATB) and other performance-based organizations will change decision makers and relationships

- Changes in program funding and direction due to national interests

- Political, legal, technological, environmental, and economic barriers to entering new markets

- Competition will continue to put pressure on the operating strategies of the Logistics Center

- Trend toward outsourcing governmental functions will continue

Strategies

The Logistics Center will employ three key strategies to achieve our vision and position the Logistics Center for future success:

- Grow the Logistics Center as the provider of choice for aviation-related equipment through reengineering, repair, and supply chain management of future and legacy systems

- Enable our customers to address fast-paced needs by generating and marketing innovative solutions such as the Logistics Center Results vehicle

- Provide project management and consulting solutions to expedite NAS facility modernization

Strategy Statement

Background

The Logistics Center Strategy Statement is a recurring feature of our Strategic Plan. The Strategic Plan is a tool to guide managers, supervisors, and employees throughout the organization in making business and operational decisions. The Vision Statement clearly defines our key characteristics and how we want to be viewed by our customers and external stakeholders. The Mission Statement describes in broad terms our primary function and ultimate responsibility and serves as a guide to our workforce. Our objective is for the workforce to know our strategy and use it as they would any other tool at their disposal.

Logistics Center Strategy Statement

The Logistics Center will continue to provide logistics support to our customers, and a primary thrust will continue to be the repair and distribution of NAS equipment and systems.

Our business focus is multi- faceted encompassing three distinct areas of emphasis represented by our strategies outlined on Page 9. Each focus area has common strategic themes, specifically, growth and expansion of the Logistics Center's capabilities and business activities, continued improvements in the core business functions, and continuing to provide value added service to our customers.

We will constantly seek to improve the quality of our products and services, and be alert to new business opportunities that will add value to the service we provide to our primary customer, the FAA, and ultimately the flying public. We will demonstrate our pride and commitment as public servants dedicated to provide unique products and services that are second to none. Providing the best value to our customer will be a prime objective, and we recognize lowest cost does not always represent the best value.

Linkage to FAA Strategic Plan

FAA Strategic Goals, Key Initiatives and Performance Goals

The FAA has three key mission goals:

- Safety—By 2007, reduce U.S. aviation fatal accident rates by 80 percent from 1996 levels

- Security—Prevent security incidents in the aviation system

- System Efficiency—Provide an aerospace transportation system that meets the needs of users and is efficient in the application of FAA and aerospace resources

The Logistics Center will contribute to the accomplishment of all of these goals. The clear connection between our mission and these goals is illustrated in the FAA FY-2000 President's Budget Submission and Performance Plan. In that submission, the Agency's funding is linked to one of the three agency strategic goals. The source of our funding as well as, our primary FAA customers' funding is tied directly to the System Efficiency goal. As a result, the Logistics Center strategic goals and performance targets are aimed at improving the utilization of resources and achieving results that improve the operational availability of the NAS.

Strengths, Weaknesses, Opportunities, and Threats Analysis Summary

The Logistics Center strategies were developed based on a situational analysis considering current environmental factors, both internal and external, that could affect the future of the Logistics Center. The strengths, weaknesses, opportunities, and threats (SWOT) associated with each were analyzed. The results of this SWOT analysis formed the basis for identification of our strategic objectives. We established objectives that leverage our strengths, eliminate our weaknesses, neutralize threats, and take advantage of opportunities.

Strategic Objectives, Measures, and Targets

The Logistics Center's strategic objectives, measures, and targets were developed using the "Balanced Scorecard Approach." The Balanced Scorecard Approach says the success of an organization is dependent upon balancing various aspects of the organization to achieve overall success. Managers must look at the organization from four basic perspectives:

- The Customer Perspective—What must we do to satisfy and retain current customers and attract new customers? Customers in this context are primarily the end –user of our products or services.

- The Financial Stakeholder Perspective—What must we do to satisfy our financial stakeholders? Our key financial stakeholders are the American public, taxpayers, and those in government concerned with the impact of our actions and services. Our stakeholders are interested in the value we bring to the nation through our business.

- Internal Business Perspective—What core internal business processes drive the results we want to achieve under the customer perspective and the financial stakeholder perspective? For these processes, what level of performance must we achieve?

- Learning and Innovation Perspective—What must we do to develop people and technology to support our internal business processes and improve our capabilities so that we can continue to add value for our customers and our financial stakeholders?

The Logistics Center Balanced Scorecard consists of the following:

Strategic goals translate our broad strategies into action goals to achieve our vision of the future. Measures describe what we will measure to determine whether or not we have met our goals. Targets for the measures are set 1-3 years out and are designed to s-t-r-e-t-c-h our performance. *If* we achieve these targets, we will transform the Logistics Center and achieve our vision.

---

*Definitions of major innovations are that warrant a significant customer-wide announcement through letters, web, and other open means. Minor innovations are those determined by the CFO and COO to be innovations.

THE CUSTOMER PERSPECTIVE

Strategy 1: Grow the Logistics Center as the provider of choice for aviation-related equipment through re-engineering, repair, and supply chain management of future and legacy systems.

STRATEGIC OBJECTIVE	MEASURE	TARGET
• Increase Customer Satisfaction	• Customer Satisfaction Rating SOs	• Establish the customer satisfaction baseline by FY03 and improve rating by 10% by FY07
• Increase Quality Ratings	• Number of LSF supplied E&R parts reported defective per 1000 E&R Sales (*Customer Reported) • Number of LSF supplied parts reported shipping errors per 1,000 sale	• Increase LSF supplied overall parts Quality Rating by 10% per year, based on FY02 baseline of 97.9% • Increase LSF supplied parts shipping Quality Rating by 15% per year based on FY02 baseline of 99.5%
• Increase customer support to enhance system availability	• Response time, backorders, and issue effectiveness	• Establish the baseline by FY03 and improve 25% by FY07 for each measure

Strategy 2: Enable our customers to address fast-paced needs by generating and marketing innovative solutions such as the Logistics Center "Results" vehicle.

STRATEGIC OBJECTIVE	MEASURE	TARGET
• Increase innovative outcomes to be adopted and used by customers	• Number of innovations; scope of innovations	• Minimum of one major innovation per year and at least three (3) minor innovations to achieve $100M revenue by FY07

Strategy 3: Provide project management and consulting solutions to expedite NAS facility modernization.

STRATEGIC OBJECTIVE	MEASURE	TARGET
• Complete projects on time and within budget	• Universal Service Agreement (USA) requirements	• Meet 100% of USA requirements according to customer satisfaction
• Establish baseline for customer satisfaction on USA/SOs	• Customer Satisfaction Survey	• Improve by 10% by FY04

Definitions of major innovations are that warrant a significant customer-wide announcement through letters, web, and other open means. Minor innovations are those determined by the CFO and COO to be innovations.

THE FINANCIAL STAKEHOLDER PERSPECTIVE

Strategy 1: Grow the Logistics Center as the provider of choice for aviation-related equipment through re-engineering, repair, and supply chain management of future and legacy systems.

STRATEGIC OBJECTIVE	MEASURE	TARGET
• Increase revenue and margin	• Revenue and cost entries in DAFIS/Delphi general ledger account	• Achieve $250M in revenue and obtain 4% margin from operations annually by FY07 • Increase Margin from Operations to a minimum of 2.5% by FY03
• Achieve a return on investment (ROI) for the Agency when selected to provide Logistics Support for new systems	• Margin divided by inventory from operations	• ROI of at least 10% on new business
• Decrease or stabilize core product prices	• Reduction in overhead burden assigned to Product Divisions	• Reduce overhead by 5%

Strategy 2: Enable our customers to address fast-paced needs by generating and marketing innovative solutions such as the Logistics Center "Results" vehicle.

STRATEGIC OBJECTIVE	MEASURE	TARGET
• Increase new business sales	• Revenue and cost entries in DAFIS/ Delphi general ledger account	• Achieve $100M in revenue in FY07 and obtain 1% margin from operations annually
• Maintain cost-effective service fee structure for Results vehicle	• Fee schedule at or below competition	• Annual comparative analysis yields Results at/or better than competition
• Obtain/maintain profitable Results business	• Net margin over operations	• Direct and overhead costs decrease each year to minimal sustainment requirement
• Decrease or stabilize core product prices	• Amount of corporate overhead covered by new business	• New business covers 15% of corporate overhead

Strategy 3: Provide project management and consulting solutions to expedite NAS facility modernization.

STRATEGIC OBJECTIVE	MEASURE	TARGET
• Increase project sales	• Revenue and cost entries in DAFIS/Delphi general ledger account	• Achieve $150M in revenue in FY07 and obtain 4% margin from operations annually

THE INTERNAL BUSINESS PERSPECTIVE

Strategy 1: Grow the Logistics Center as the provider of choice for aviation-related equipment through re-engineering, repair, and supply chain management of future and legacy systems.

STRATEGIC OBJECTIVE	MEASURE	TARGET
• Reduce the number of reds and yellows in the Supportability Report and the number of bad actor Line Replaceable Units (LRUs) in the R&M report	• Current number of systems reported in the Supportability Report • Number of bad actors	• Decrease the number of nonsupportable, unreliable and maintainable LRUs
• Increase the number of projects organically supported	• Volume and value of touch labor vs. Contractor Depot Level Support (CDLS) contracts • Number of systems selected for Logistics Center support • Volume of non-FAA business	• Increase the volume of touch labor sales by 10% per year through FY07 • Add one system per year for Logistics Center support • Increase volume of non-FAA business by $10M per year
• Reduce average repair time for LRU repair and establish an improved methodology for standard repair times	• Average repair time	• Reduce average repair time for LRU in repair facilities by 10% over FY01 baseline
• Improve product delivery processes and systems	• Percent of time to fill a customer requisition on cataloged items within the customer's expected timeframe • Warehouse Management System (WMS) Exception Closure Report	• Establish fill-rate baseline by the end of FY03. Increase number of customer orders filled by 50% by FY07. Include orders filled from Distribution Center stock only, not Planned Direct Ship (PDS) shipments • Achieve 100% receipt closure within 48 hours by end of FY-04
• Improve internal cost analysis process and capabilities	• Availability of valid financial information necessary to achieve financial objectives and targets related to cost reduction • Number of analysts with financial management skills and analytical tools developed	• Cost reduction goals under financial perspective are met • Establishment of cost analysis capability in each PD and Group by FY03

Strategy 2: Enable our customers to address fast-paced needs by generating and marketing innovative solutions such as the Logistics Center "Results" vehicle.

STRATEGIC OBJECTIVE	MEASURE	TARGET
• Improve qualified vendor base to provide additional vendor (or incumbent) opportunities	• Number of new "incumbent" vendors*	• Increase NQVL (National Qualified Vendors List) by 10% per year for customer's recommended incumbents
• Improve marketing and communications of Results vehicle	• Number of new or repeat customer Results orientations per year	• Increase number of new or repeat customer orientations by 10% per year

Strategy 3: Provide project management and consulting solutions to expedite NAS facility modernization.

STRATEGIC OBJECTIVE	MEASURE	TARGET
• Increase customer base	• Revenue and cost entries in DAFIS/Delphi general ledger account	• Increase revenue from nontraditional customers annually by 20%

*Incumbents = vendors not currently on the Results vehicle, but highly recommended by customers.

Note: In the event goals are not met, the cause cannot be attributed to a lack of valid financial reports or analyses.

THE LEARNING AND INNOVATION PERSPECTIVE

Strategy 1: Grow the Logistics Center as the provider of choice for aviation-related equipment through re-engineering, repair, and supply chain management of future and legacy systems.

STRATEGIC OBJECTIVE	MEASURE	TARGET
• Develop workforce strategies that will guide the Logistics Center to identify and train to competencies; acquire technical certifications; recruit, develop, retrain; develop leadership and plan for succession	• Strategic Workforce Action Plan • Managerial 360 degree assessment • Percentage of current competency inventories completed and training and development completed • Number of certifications • Percent of increase in Individual Development Plans (IDP) teams	• 100% implementation of Strategic Workforce Action plan by end of FY05 • Leadership Development Program and Succession Planning Programs are implemented by end of FY04 • Competency inventory based on future state of the Logistics Center and training matrix by the end of FY03. • Certifications for selected series achieved by the end of FY04 • Increase IDPs by 10% per year

STRATEGIC OBJECTIVE	MEASURE	TARGET
• Integrate an automated warehouse management system	• Implementation of automation	• Automation implementation by the end of FY03

Strategy 2: Enable our customers to address fast-paced needs by generating and marketing innovative solutions such as the Logistics Center "Results" vehicle.

STRATEGIC OBJECTIVE	MEASURE	TARGET
• Increase number of annual technology or tool innovations	• Number of innovations; scale of innovations	• Minimum of one major innovation per year and (2) minor innovations to achieve $50M in additional acquisition volume per year
• Improve formal sales/CSR skills of sales and production teams	• Number of formal training courses completed annually per team member	• 2 relevant courses per team member per year

Strategy 3: Provide project management and consulting solutions to expedite NAS facility modernization.

STRATEGIC OBJECTIVE	MEASURE	TARGET
• Increase project management and consulting capability. (performance, schedule, cost)	• Number of certified project managers and engineers	• 85% of project management and consulting workforce certified by end of FY07

Strategic Plan Deployment and Action Plans

Each Division and Group will develop annual business plans to describe how their organization will contribute to the achievement of the Strategic Objectives. Preparation of business plans is contingent upon having adequate cost and performance data to make projections and establish measurable goals and targets. At a minimum business plans will include:

- Financial projections based on projected cost of operations, investments, and revenue

- Resource utilization plan

- Production plan indicating anticipated changes in existing workload, and any new workload the Division may be planning to assume or pursue with appropriate business case justification

- Annual Division or Group goals must be tied to Logistics Center strategic objectives or Logistics Center annual goals

- Results based performance measures and targets for each annual division goal

- Outline of key milestones for any projects associated with Logistics Center strategic goals

CHAPTER 9

The Balanced Scorecard at the Naval Undersea Warfare Center

The Naval Undersea Warfare Center (NUWC) in Newport, Rhode Island, and the Newport Division, a subordinate command, have been using planning as a key business process for almost 20 years. Since 1981, the Newport Division has used a five-year planning process as the cornerstone of its management process.

NUWC's 1998 strategic plan is presented in its entirety in the pages that follow. The plan, which ends with a discussion of balanced performance measures (BPMs), is one of the earliest examples of the use of this concept in a federal organization. Starting with this strategic plan, NUWC began assessing progress toward its strategic goals by looking at five perspectives: (1) customer perspective, (2) business perspective, (3) financial perspective, (4) employee perspective, and (5) learning and growth perspective. These performance measures are then reflected in five-year plans throughout the divisions. On a quarterly basis, the commander and executive director review the performance of the organization on the basis of these five balanced performance measures.

The plan is followed by Figure 9–3, which illustrates NUWC strategic management. The 1998 strategic plan for the Newport Division of NUWC is then presented. The plan includes a detailed section on BPMs.

Following the Newport Division strategic plan is the text of a three-fold handout explaining the major portions of the strategic plan and highlighting the five BPMs. Every large federal organization should publish a similar handout and send it to their employees. Its brevity will encourage workers to learn more about the strategic management process and heighten their interest in it.

The chapter continues with Figure 9–4, which illustrates the Fiscal Year (FY) 2001–2005 five-year planning process at NUWC, Newport Division. It is followed by the five-year planning schedule (Figure 9–5) and the five-year planning plan of action and milestones (Figure 9–6).

The chapter continues with a March 2000 article from the NUWC newspaper. The article explains the five-year planning history and the relation of performance measurement and the balanced scorecard to this process.

The chapter concludes with an article that presents a case study of how NUWC managed change through use of a balance scorecard.

NAVAL UNDERSEA WARFARE CENTER 1998 STRATEGIC PLAN

The following material is adapted from the Naval Undersea Warfare Center, *The NUWC Strategic Plan,* Newport, Rhode Island, NUWC, 1997.

Commander and Technical Director Message

We are witnessing a new era in national security where the phrase "Post-Cold War" is losing its relevance. The promise of technology and the Revolution in Military Affairs (and the accompanying Revolution in Business Affairs) have brought us to the threshold of a new era, one where we have unprecedented opportunity to forge our future. Since the previous version of our Strategic Plan was published in January 1996, we have seen significant changes in DoD and Navy policy guidance and considerable progress in government reinvention and acquisition reform. These changes and the unfolding challenges of the future have precipitated a renewed assessment of our strategic planning processes and led us to publish this document, our 1998 Strategic Plan.

In our previous plan, we discussed the challenges associated with the shift in Undersea Warfare emphasis from open ocean to the littoral and emphasized our responsibilities to lower our costs to the taxpayer while implementing cutting-edge Undersea Warfare technologies. These imperatives remain and have been underscored in new military strategy documents, including *Joint Vision 2010* and *Forward . . . from the Sea*. Our joint warfighting role is integral to the concepts in these and other documents, and our contributions to Joint Warfighting Capability Objectives are continually expanding. Our broadening responsibilities and the constrained funding environment demand our vigilance in accomplishing every aspect of our mission.

The Naval Undersea Warfare Center, its Divisions, and its components are well situated to meet the complex challenges ahead. We have the right mix of highly trained and motivated employees, state-of-the-art facilities and world-class processes to sustain our reputation for excellence that has been cultivated since our beginnings. Our record of accomplishment in support of the Naval Sea Systems Command and the end-users of our products in the Fleet stand as a tribute to the people who make up our workforce. As the pressures to provide more affordable and technologically effective products and services continue apace, we will rise to the challenge, using innovative approaches and learning from the successes of others. Keeping pace with the rapid advances in a broad array of technologies and processes, we will play a vital role in preserving our Navy's Undersea Warfare superiority well into the next millennium.

This Strategic Plan provides a conceptual framework for success in the 21st century. It requires the support of every NUWC employee to be effective. As a team that is focused on the future, we can provide the utmost support to NAVSEA, and more importantly, to the men and women of the finest Navy in the world.

RADM John F. Shipway
Commander

Dr. John E. Sirmalis
Technical Director

Introduction

The Naval Undersea Warfare Center (NUWC) is the Navy's full-spectrum research, development, test & evaluation (RDT&E), engineering, and fleet support center for submarines, autonomous underwater systems, and offensive and defensive weapons systems associated with Undersea Warfare. Having refined the roles of our two Divisions in supporting the operating forces of the Navy over the past five years, we are positioned to improve and expand our contributions in Undersea Warfare. We are revising our planning approach and our processes to provide high quality, affordable RDT&E, in-service engineering, and total life cycle support for the Navy's Undersea Warfare systems and capabilities.

We must break down internal and external barriers to productivity and better understand our individual and collective roles in meeting the challenges ahead.

The NUWC Divisions today are lean, efficient, and focused on our customers' needs. We have evolved to adapt to diminishing resources and a diverse, diffused set of military threats; emphasized technologies that enable the Navy's Undersea Warfare operating forces to make better contributions in joint campaigns; and have established a position of leadership in government reinvention and acquisition reform. Nonetheless, the uncertainties ahead demand that we redouble our efforts to provide effective and affordable products and services to our customers. In the absence of a single, highly capable and well-defined threat, we must establish a flexible technological vision to drive our Undersea Warfare capabilities in the future. With technology and innovation as our primary tools, we have the opportunity to develop processes, products, and services that will further enhance the value of the Navy's Undersea Warfare capabilities. To achieve the necessary progress, we will have to look beyond our own organizations for good ideas and best practices from industry and academia, and to forge mutually beneficial cooperative alliances with other organizations. We must break down internal and external barriers to productivity and better understand our individual and collective roles in meeting the challenges ahead.

As the challenges of the future unfold, we must assess our progress toward our vision and goals and adjust our strategic plans accordingly. Therefore, we have revised our Strategic Plan to incorporate a new set of goals and action strategies to attain them. Our Strategic Plan complements national military strategy, the precepts of the National Performance Review (NPR), and the eight strategic goals outlined in NAVSEA's strategic plan. We fully embrace these strategic goals and will continue to integrate them into all aspects of internal planning. The NUWC Senior Management Team—consisting of the NUWC Commander and Technical Director; and the Division Commanders and Executive Directors—routinely meets to review NUWC's Strategic Plan, its implementation, and its effectiveness. These reviews have reinforced the validity of our planning and have served as a forum to develop objective measures of effectiveness.

Balanced Performance Measures

An important feature of our Strategic Plan is the establishment of a set of balanced performance measurements that allow[s] us to assess our progress toward achieving our strategic goals. Our performance will be appraised in five key perspectives: our customer perspective, our employee perspective, our internal business perspective, our financial perspective, and our learning and growth perspective. Within each of these areas, we have developed a list of more specific factors or requirements that provide standards against which we can better determine our progress. By integrating the performance measurements obtained in each of the five perspectives, we can adjust our processes or plans as necessary to stay on the appropriate path to the future.

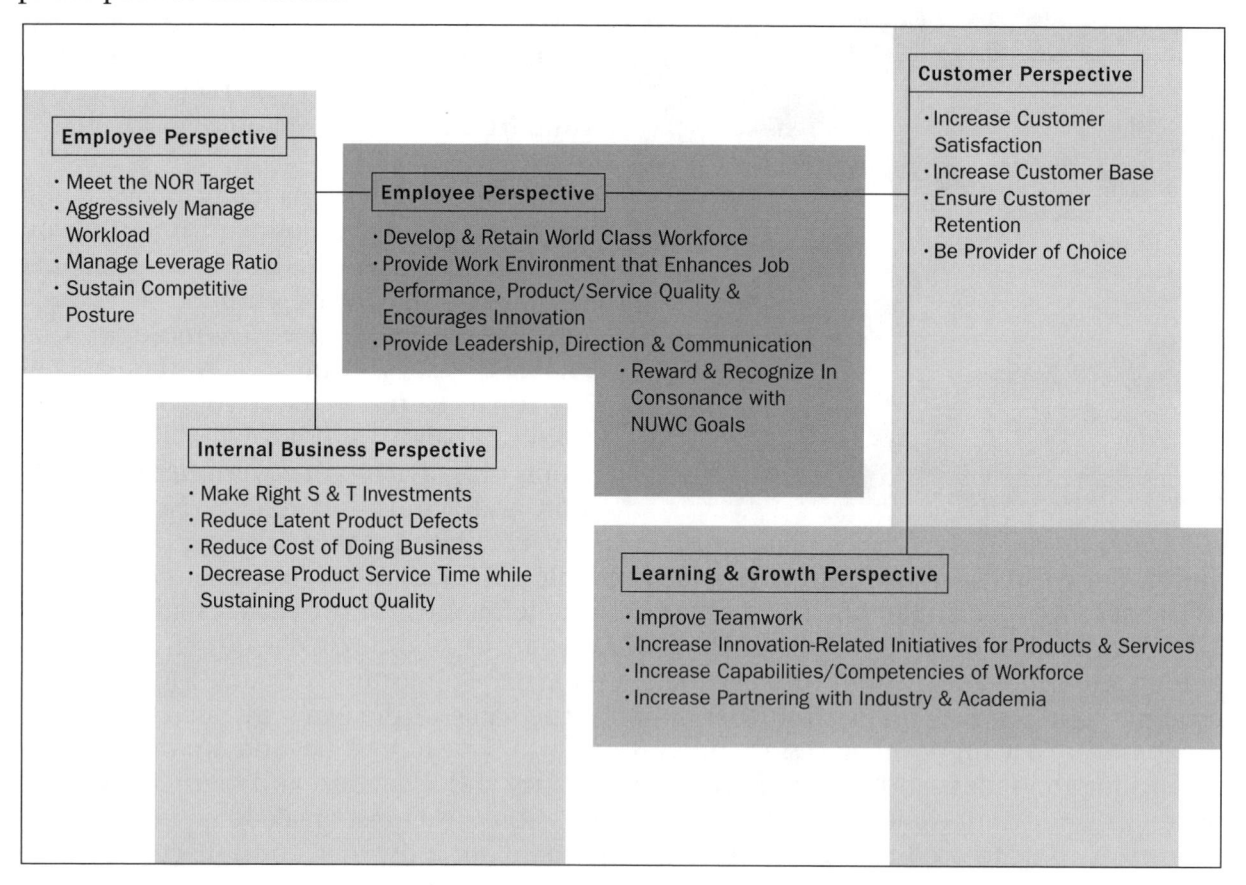

Employee Perspective
- Meet the NOR Target
- Aggressively Manage Workload
- Manage Leverage Ratio
- Sustain Competitive Posture

Employee Perspective
- Develop & Retain World Class Workforce
- Provide Work Environment that Enhances Job Performance, Product/Service Quality & Encourages Innovation
- Provide Leadership, Direction & Communication
- Reward & Recognize In Consonance with NUWC Goals

Customer Perspective
- Increase Customer Satisfaction
- Increase Customer Base
- Ensure Customer Retention
- Be Provider of Choice

Internal Business Perspective
- Make Right S & T Investments
- Reduce Latent Product Defects
- Reduce Cost of Doing Business
- Decrease Product Service Time while Sustaining Product Quality

Learning & Growth Perspective
- Improve Teamwork
- Increase Innovation-Related Initiatives for Products & Services
- Increase Capabilities/Competencies of Workforce
- Increase Partnering with Industry & Academia

Strategic Overview

The NUWC Strategic Plan is published for our employees and stakeholders to keep them informed of our general direction and guidance. It details our vision for the future and the strategic goals we have set to attain that vision. It is intended to focus our collective efforts on a common approach to meet future challenges and it defines our corporate philosophy.

The five strategic goals contained in this document are aligned with NAVSEA's strategic goals and support the spirit and intent of the Government Performance and Results Act (GPRA) and the National Partnership for Reinventing Government (NPR) by directing the establishment of measures that improve performance and reduce costs. Additionally, this plan's Operating Principles are related to and supportive of NAVSEA's Guiding Principles.

Our Strategic Plan is the cornerstone of our strategic planning process. In response to a broad array of external factors, including military strategy, funding constraints, and, most importantly, the Navy's warfighting requirements, we must routinely evaluate our strategic approach and adjust our plans and processes to most effectively accomplish our mission. Based upon DoD, Navy, and NAVSEA guidance and anticipated resources, our plan assesses how best to accomplish our mission and achieve our vision. Our strategic goals and their associated action strategies were developed with the needs and expectations of our customers as primary considerations. Our plan also incorporates a key aspect of the GPRA by addressing performance measurement. By using a Balanced Scorecard approach, we will have defined performance metrics that help us assess our progress toward attaining each goal.

The NUWC Strategic Plan plays a fundamental role in our strategic planning processes. Figure 9–1 illustrates the overall strategic planning process, and demonstrates how the cycle is influenced continually by obtaining feedback and adjusting our processes or plans accordingly.

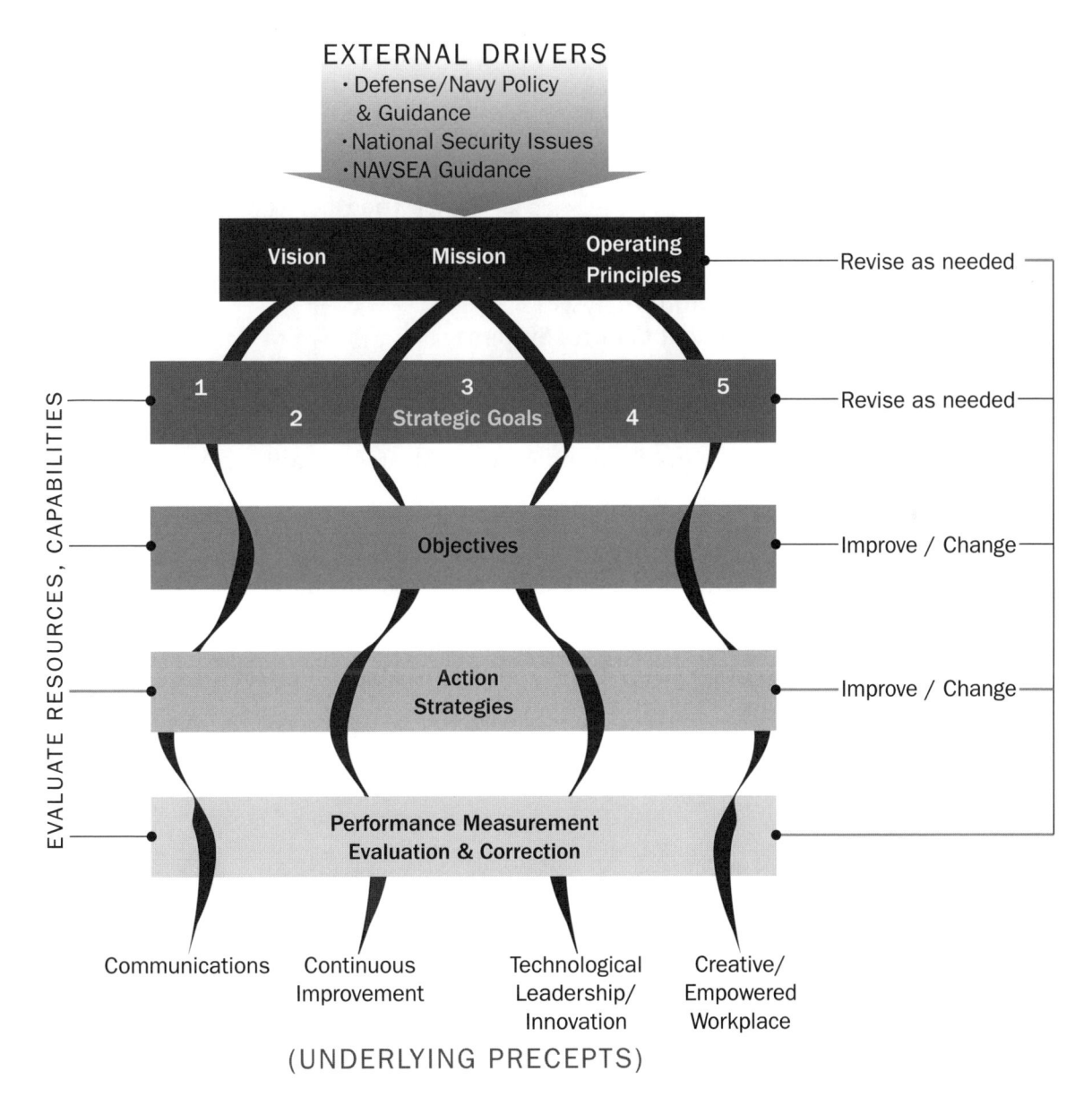

Figure 9–1. NUWC Strategic Planning Process. *Source:* Adapted from Naval Undersea Warfare Center, *The NUWC Strategic Plan*, Newport, Rhode Island, NUWC, 1997.

Vision/Mission/Charter Leadership Areas

Vision

Be our Nation's provider of choice for Undersea Superiority, satisfying today's needs and meeting tomorrow's challenges.

Mission—Undersea Superiority: Today and Tomorrow

We provide the technical foundation, which enables the conceptualization, research, development, fielding, modernization, in-service engineering, and maintenance of systems that ensure our Navy's undersea superiority.

Corporate Charter

The NUWC Charter, promulgated in December 1992, established the top-level organizational relationships (Figure 9-2) and technical leadership areas for NUWC and expertise in the following technical areas:

Technical leadership areas

As assigned by SECNAVINST 5400.16 of 18 December 1992, NUWC provides the Navy with leadership in:

- Undersea Warfare Modeling and Analysis
- Submarine Combat and Combat Control Systems
- Surface Ship and Submarine Sonar Systems
- Submarine Electronic Warfare
- Submarine Unique On-Board Communications Systems and Communications Nodes
- Submarine Launched Weapons Systems (except Strategic Ballistic Missile Systems, Cruise Missiles, and Related Systems)
- Undersea Ranges
- Torpedoes and Torpedo Countermeasures
- Submarine Vulnerability and Survivability (except Hull, Mechanical & Electrical Ship's Equipment—HM&E)
- Undersea Vehicle Active and Passive Signatures (except HM&E)
- Submarine Electromagnetic, Electro-optic and Nonacoustic-effects Reconnaissance, Search and Track Systems

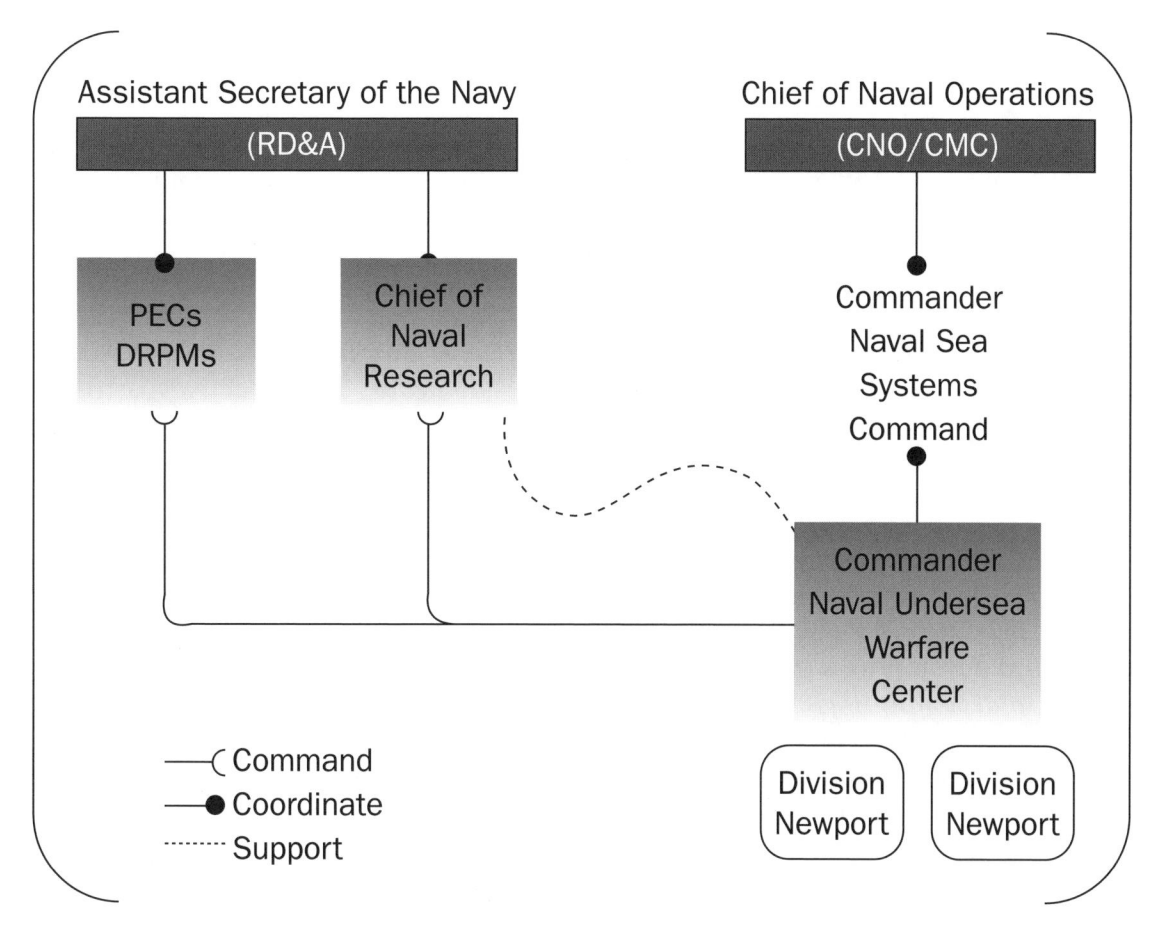

```
                Assistant Secretary of the Navy          Chief of Naval Operations
                         (RD&A)                                 (CNO/CMC)
                   |          |                                      |
              ┌────┴──┐  ┌────┴────┐                           Commander
              │ PECs  │  │ Chief of│                          Naval Sea
              │ DRPMs │  │  Naval  │                           Systems
              │       │  │Research │                           Command
              └───┬───┘  └────┬────┘                              │
                  │           │                            Commander
                  │           └ ─ ─ ─ ─ ─ ─ ─ ─ ─ ─ ─ ─ ─ Naval Undersea
                  │                                          Warfare
                  └──────────────────────────────────────    Center

        ──( Command                              ( Division )  ( Division )
        ──● Coordinate                           ( Newport  )  ( Newport  )
        ······ Support
```

Figure 9–2. Naval Undersea Warfare Center Organizational Structure & Operating Relationships. *Source:* Adapted from Naval Undersea Warfare Center, *The NUWC Strategic Plan,* Newport, Rhode Island, NUWC, 1997.

Operating Principles

Our Operating Principles provide a foundation that governs our approach to daily operations. They are interrelated by several underlying precepts that should influence everything we do:

- Open communications, internally and externally;
- Continuous improvement;
- Technological leadership and innovation; and
- A creative, empowered workforce.

NUWC's operating principles are:

Our customers come first. Understanding and responding to their current and emerging needs are our top priorities. We will collaborate closely with our customers and other stakeholders to ensure we meet their requirements for performance, affordability, and timeliness.

Our employees are the key to our success. Our employees are our most valuable resource. We will provide them with a productive work environment and the necessary skill set, knowledge, and incentives to accomplish our mission.

We are committed to continuous improvement of products, processes, and services. Using the best management practices, we will make improvement decisions based on fact and knowledge. We will measure our performance and, using benchmarking, continuously evaluate our progress toward our goals.

Teamwork is essential. We work as dedicated and effective partners with our family of customers, suppliers, and stakeholders. We will share and pursue the NUWC vision as a unified team.

Innovation and creativity are critical to our success. We seek new and imaginative approaches in creating technologically advanced products and in developing effective business processes to meet our customers' current and future needs.

We value diversity. We recognize and respect the benefits of diversity and are committed to recruiting and developing a diverse workforce.

Environmental stewardship and safety are crucial. Our practices will foster a safe work environment for our employees, provide safe and environmentally sound products for our customers, and ensure we are prudent stewards of the environment.

We conduct ourselves in an ethical manner. We are accountable to the American public and are committed to the highest ethical standards.

Strategic Goals, Objectives, and Strategies

This plan provides a blueprint that charts how we will make our vision a reality. The five goals presented below establish the direction we will take in accomplishing our mission and fulfilling our obligations to the Navy, DoD, and the taxpayer over the next several years. Each goal is supported by more specific objectives and strategies, which help to further refine how we will satisfy current and future undersea superiority requirements. The objectives represent "what" NUWC intends to accomplish with respect to its overarching strategic goal, and the strategies indicate "how" we will achieve each goal. Pursuing these objectives and strategies will allow us to use the appropriate combination of best practices, in both our business and technical processes, and team spirit to enable our delivery of products and services that are effective, affordable, and timely.

Strategic Goal 1

Customer satisfaction

Objectives:

- Refine our ability to anticipate customer needs and expectations.
- Maintain an open, frank relationship with customers to enhance our responsiveness.
- Work closely with our customers to determine their needs.

Strategies:

- Enhance cooperative alliances with customers, sponsors, and suppliers to improve communication of expectations and needs and to encourage increased participation among stakeholders.

- Assign NUWC personnel where appropriate to improve customer satisfaction.
- Develop methods to systematically survey customer satisfaction in our performance as well as their anticipated needs and concerns.
- Foster a spirit of dedication to customers throughout NUWC.

Strategic Goal 2

Enhance the effectiveness of the NUWC workforce by providing opportunity for all employees to realize their full potential

Objectives:

- Develop the tools to ensure a well-informed, skilled, and innovative workforce that is empowered and best equipped to seek new opportunities while accommodating change.
- Expand cross-training, improve internal communications, and promote sharing of ideas throughout NUWC.
- Provide a work environment that enhances productivity, safety, and quality of life.

Strategies:

- Refine human resources plans to achieve a flexible organization based on anticipated work requirements and critical technical capabilities and supporting skills.
- Provide for the professional development of a diverse and highly capable, right-sized workforce.
- Pursue innovative human resources policies to improve productivity through Reinvention Laboratory and Personnel Demonstration programs.
- Recognize and reward employee achievements.
- Encourage employee participation in decision processes that shape the future of the workforce and the organization.
- Detect and break down barriers to communications.

Strategic Goal 3

Improve the responsiveness, performance, and efficiency of NUWC in the conduct of all processes

Objectives:

- Implement process improvements and better business practices.
- Develop and implement cutting-edge acquisition reform and government reinvention measures.
- Improve our ability to provide decisive and prompt action in responding to short-fused requirements.

Strategies:

- Identify technical and business process improvements to achieve better performance, effectiveness, and efficiency.
- Explore internal and external sources for best practices, and implement those that will improve NUWC's performance.
- Eliminate redundant and non-value-added practices.
- Encourage sharing of ideas and lessons learned by promoting strong intra- and inter-divisional reliance programs.
- Pursue technologies that affordably enhance processes and business practices and add product and service value to the customer.

Strategic Goal 4

Develop affordable products and services that fully address Navy needs and lower total ownership costs

Objectives:

- Maintain leadership in enabling the development and maintenance of technologically superior, affordable, and effective products and services.
- Sustain the capability to rapidly and affordably upgrade or correct problems in existing fleet systems.
- Provide best value products and services that meet customers' needs.
- Improve maintenance capabilities and lower costs by improving work practices.
- Sustain capability to meet emergent customer requirements.

Strategies:

- Implement innovative processes that will eliminate inefficiencies and will improve overall cost effectiveness.
- Consider total ownership costs as a primary factor in all acquisition endeavors.
- Use applicable commercial practices and technologies and enhance our knowledge of best practices by capitalizing upon collaborative alliances with industry and academia.
- Strive to lower total life cycle costs without sacrificing warfighting capabilities.
- Encourage increased communications and collaborations across the Divisions to cultivate and share relevant undersea warfare technologies and best practices.
- Work with customers to explore alternative methods to address their needs and resource constraints.

Strategic Goal 5

Apply innovative approaches to meet future challenges

Objectives:

- Aggressively seek and deploy innovative new technologies, which will sustain the Navy's Undersea Warfare competitive advantage.
- Eliminate technical insularity and promote free exchange of ideas.
- Build on successful innovative approaches used by other organizations.
- Provide affordable, high-quality technical, support, and industrial facilities that are unique and essential to Submarine and Undersea Warfare.
- Develop advanced concepts in Undersea Warfare to meet future needs.

Strategies:

- Anticipate undersea superiority emerging needs and their potential implications.

- Consider current and projected customer needs in assessing innovative technologies or processes.
- Pursue advanced concepts that will lead to breakthrough technologies.
- Develop processes to quickly deploy new technologies that accelerate development cycles, improve performance, and lower costs.
- Expand our knowledge base in Undersea Warfare and joint warfighting mission areas.
- Pursue cooperative alliances with industry, academia, other government agencies, and allies to identify and capture technology insertion opportunities.
- Ensure our key technical and support facilities are appropriately used, refined, and revitalized to meet current and future requirements.

NUSC STRATEGIC MANAGEMENT PROCESS

Figure 9–3 depicts the NUWC strategic management process.

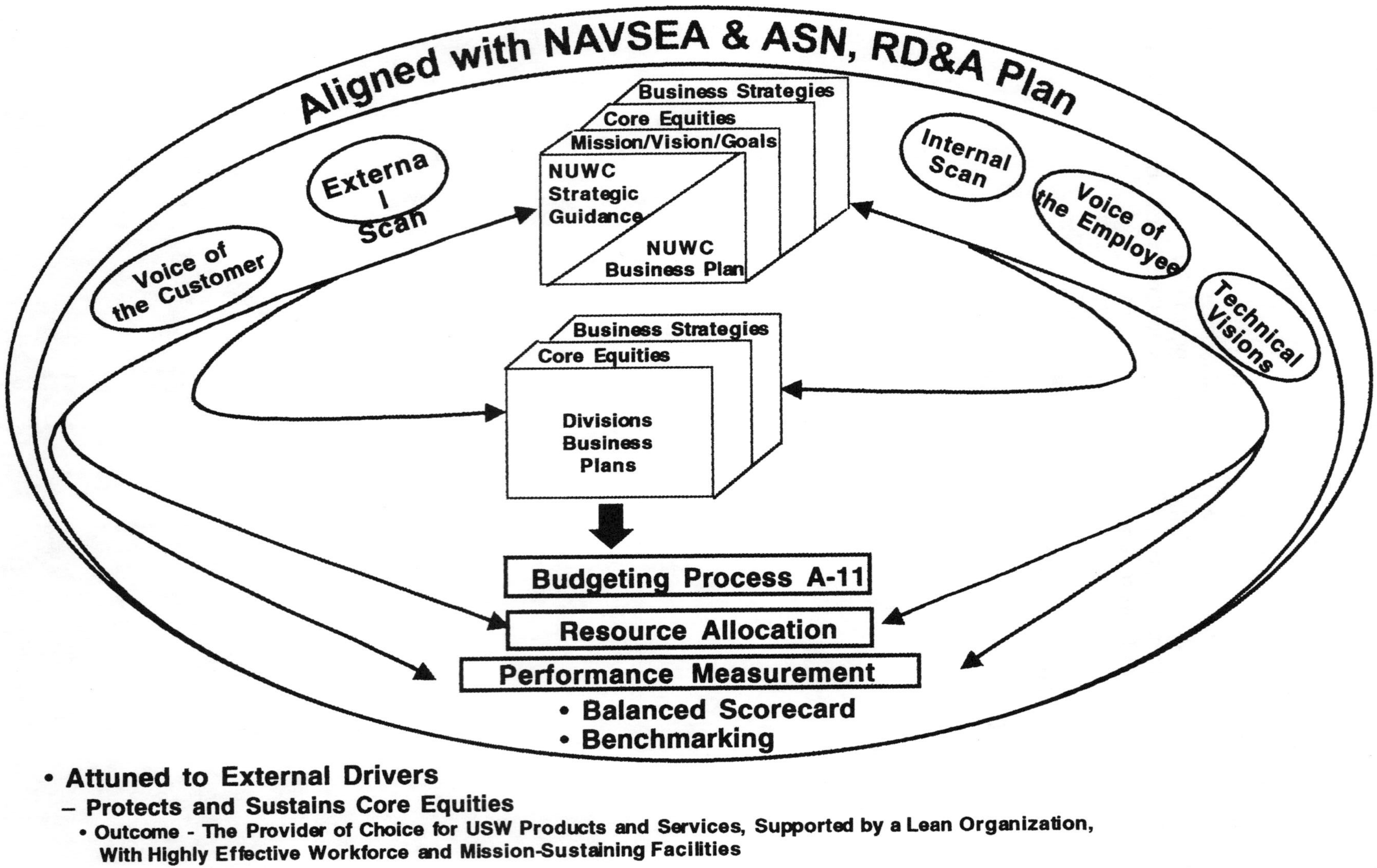

176   PRESIDENT'S MANAGEMENT AGENDA

Aligned with NAVSEA & ASN, RD&A Plan

- Voice of the Customer
- External Scan
- Internal Scan
- Voice of the Employee
- Technical Visions

NUWC Strategic Guidance
- Business Strategies
- Core Equities
- Mission/Vision/Goals

NUWC Business Plan

Divisions Business Plans
- Business Strategies
- Core Equities

Budgeting Process A-11
Resource Allocation
Performance Measurement
- Balanced Scorecard
- Benchmarking

- **Attuned to External Drivers**
  - Protects and Sustains Core Equities
- **Outcome** - The Provider of Choice for USW Products and Services, Supported by a Lean Organization, With Highly Effective Workforce and Mission-Sustaining Facilities

Figure 9–3. NUWC Strategic Management Process. *Source:* Head, Strategy Development Staff (Code 011), Naval Undersea Warfare Center, Division Newport, Newport, Rhode Island.

NUWC NEWPORT DIVISION 1998 STRATEGIC PLAN

The following material is adapted from *Strategic Plan 1998: Naval Undersea Warfare Center Division Newport,* Newport, Rhode Island, Naval Undersea Warfare Center Division Newport, 1997, Report No. NUWC-NPT-AP10,852-1.

Strategic Plan

1998

we enable undersea superiority,

SATISFYING TODAY'S *needs*

and meeting tomorrow's CHALLENGES...

Naval Undersea Warfare Center
Division Newport

Commander and Executive Director Message

The dedication and resourcefulness of our workforce has resulted in a rich legacy of achievement in effective undersea warfare products and services. As a result, we have a great heritage in which we can take great pride and satisfaction. However, tremendous changes have occurred in the past five years since we formed the Naval Undersea Warfare Center, and new changes continue at an increasingly intense pace. In this demanding environment we cannot let our proud past distract us from addressing the challenges of change. We must continue our tradition of excellence, but we must also adapt so we can sustain it in a much different world. This strategic plan provides a framework for building our future. It describes the strategic foundation and our strategic management processes that are built upon it; explains our strategic goals, what they mean to us, and how we will attain them; and it relates the plan to our five-year planning process and the balanced performance measures system for evaluating our progress.

Our future is one of continued changes, constraints, and heightened competition for increasingly scarce national security resources. We must fully understand and satisfy our customers' needs of today while anticipating and preparing for future needs. Our technical and business practices must be fine-tuned so we can provide capable and affordable products and services more quickly. Continued rapid advances in technology throughout the marketplace challenge us to forge new relationships with others and to build new competencies and learn new skills.

When faced with the challenges of the future, we should frame our actions in the form of four underlying precepts: we should communicate with whomever appropriate to exchange knowledge and ideas; we must remember that each of us has leadership and accountability responsibilities that we cannot ignore; we should strive for innovation and new ideas to help us work smarter, faster, and more affordably; and we must establish productive collaborations that optimize use of scarce resources and maximize product quality.

Our greatest strength continues to be you, our employees. This plan provides a conceptual blueprint for our evolution, and the key to its success lies in each of you. We ask that you read and embrace this plan. If we are to continue to be successful, each of you must take a proactive role in crafting the solutions to the challenges and changes that we face. Our success demands that each of you assume an active role in forging our future. We look forward to working with you in our journey of change and, as always, welcome your ideas and feedback.

S. J. LOGUE
CAPTAIN, U.S. NAVY
COMMANDER

J. G. KEIL
EXECUTIVE DIRECTOR

Table of Contents

Strategic **Framework** — 2

Cultural Values/Operating Principles — 4

Strategic GOALS — 6
- *Increase Customer Loyalty*
- *Invest in Our People*
- *Improve the Way We Work*
- *Provide Capable and Affordable Products*
- *Innovate for the Future*

BALANCED **Performance** *Measures* — 12

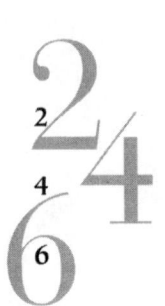

STRATEGIC FRAMEWORK

Our Mission

UNDERSEA SUPERIORITY: TODAY AND TOMORROW.

We provide the technical foundation that enables the conceptualization, research, development, fielding, modernization, and maintenance of systems that ensure our Navy's undersea superiority.

Our Vision

Be our Nation's provider of choice for undersea superiority, satisfying today's needs and meeting tomorrow's challenges.

OUR MISSION IS OUR REASON FOR BEING... *our responsibility for fulfilling the Navy's and the Nation's defense needs.* Our Vision represents the future state we strive to achieve in accomplishing our mission. In working toward our vision, we consider a number of external and internal factors: we conduct a continuous External Scan to determine what conditions or actions are currently influencing or will influence our ability to meet our mission, including policy, resources, competitors, and developments in industry; Customer Feedback gives us important information regarding our customers' view of our performance and provides insight into means for improving; and Employee Feedback conveys our employees' perspective on how we can improve ourselves. These factors shape and drive our approach to the future, and our actions are "filtered" through our system of Cultural Values and our Operating Principles (see following pages). This process results in establishment of our STRATEGIC GOALS, which when attained will permit us to *achieve our vision and accomplish* We develop strategies for meeting each Strategic Goal and use a balanced set of performance measures to continually assess our progress toward goal attainment.

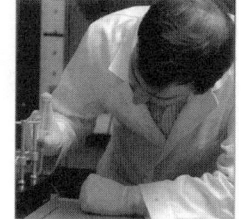

Strategic Goals

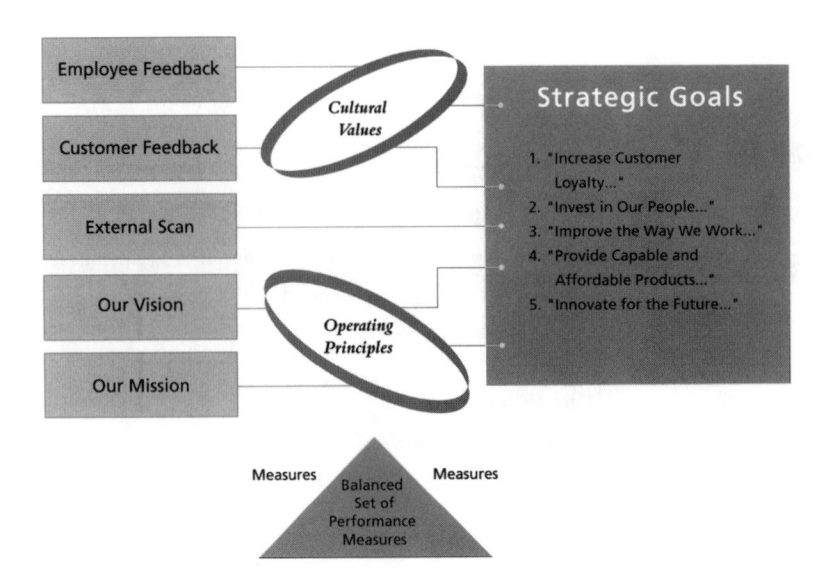

1. "Increase Customer Loyalty..."
2. "Invest in Our People..."
3. "Improve the Way We Work..."
4. "Provide Capable and Affordable Products..."
5. "Innovate for the Future..."

In implementing our action strategies, we will continually measure our progress through systematic assessments of performance against goals and their supporting operating targets. This allows us to make adjustments to our management processes to ensure we are headed toward the goal. The strategies that we refine and pursue at the Division Newport level serve as the basis for the five-year plans that are developed and deployed throughout our departments.

Our strategic management process is supportive of the strategic plans and the mission attainment of both the Naval Sea Systems Command (NAVSEA) and the Naval Undersea Warfare Center (NUWC). This "co-missioning" ensures that our efforts are aligned with and fully support NAVSEA and NUWC strategic goals.

our mission. In the following pages, we explain our cultural values, operating principles, and strategic goals. Each of our strategic goals and the strategies we will use to achieve them are explained in terms of both our employees' perspective and Division management's perspective.

OUR CULTURAL VALUES

Our cultural values influence everything we do; they make up our fundamental system of beliefs, which describe how we approach our responsibilities.

"Our Commitment is to Our CUSTOMERS"	Team Members Sponsors Fleet Citizens
"Our Strength is in Our PEOPLE"	Responsive Creative Open Empowered
"Our Contribution is in Our PRODUCTS"	Innovative Timely Capable Affordable

OUR OPERATING PRINCIPLES

Our operating principles reinforce and refine our cultural values, describing in more detail our "corporate philosophy." They are meant to serve as general guidelines for how we conduct our day-to-day business, and they provide a philosophical linkage between the way we carry out our routine activities and achieve our strategic goals. The following are our operating principles:

Our CUSTOMERS *come first.* — Working with our customers, we respond to the needs of the Fleet to ensure we provide the most effective and affordable undersea warfare products and services in a timely manner.

Our WORKFORCE *is critical to our success.* — We provide our workforce with the skill set, knowledge, motivation, and work environment to effectively accomplish our mission. We rely on our workforce to forge the future of the Division.

DIVERSITY *strengthens our creativity and teamwork.*	We respect each other and our differences and recognize the value of our diverse backgrounds.
IMPROVEMENT *must be continuous.*	We have a passion for excellence! We understand and support quality programs, and constantly work to enhance our processes, products, and services.
TEAMWORK *is essential.*	We cooperate, communicate, and collaborate, both internally and externally, to achieve the most effective products and services.
INNOVATION *and creativity are crucial.*	We seek new and innovative approaches to old problems and attack new challenges with imagination. We look outward for creative ideas to adapt to our use. We take manageable risks to field new technologies for effective solutions.
We are ACCOUNTABLE.	We are honest, ethical, and accountable for all our actions.
We are COMMITTED *to environmental stewardship and safety.*	We promote practices and attitudes that respect our environment and make our workplace safe and productive.
We are good CITIZENS *of our community.*	We recognize our economic and social impact on the stakeholders in our communities. We adhere to the highest standards of citizenship and participate in charitable, educational, and community outreach programs.

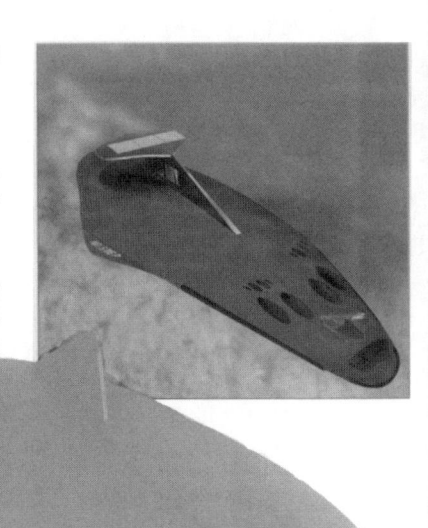

5

STRATEGIC GOAL 1

Increase Customer Loyalty ...

We will achieve this Goal by

- Fostering a spirit of dedication to customer satisfaction and service throughout Division Newport.
- Working closely with customers, maintaining frank and open relationships.
- Recognizing that each employee is an agent of the Division who carries our message to current and future customers.
- Initiating processes to improve customer loyalty and better address their concerns.
- Producing and providing best value products and services.

What this Means to Us

We must achieve and sustain high levels of customer loyalty if we expect to thrive as the Navy's primary provider of undersea warfare products and services. We can accomplish this only if we understand our customers' requirements and satisfy their needs. A second critical element of our strategy is to respond quickly to customer requests, questions, and comments. Additionally, we must constantly evaluate whether we are meeting customers' needs by asking them, through both formal survey processes and ongoing informal communications, how our performance compares with their expectations. Every one of us has the potential to positively (or negatively) impact customer loyalty. In all our customer interactions, we must be sensitive to and manage the image we project, both individually and collectively, to ensure it accurately portrays our capabilities and potential. This means

- Being honest, straightforward, and attentive with customers and sponsors.
- Seeking and sharing important information about customers that could impact our ability to meet their present and future needs.
- Keeping abreast of technological and warfighting issues that are important to our customers and stakeholders.
- Acting as positive representatives of the Division, keeping customers informed of our technical accomplishments, innovations, awards, and other relevant information that will increase their confidence in our products and services.
- Taking prompt action to address causes of customer concern or dissatisfaction.
- Creating opportunities to exceed customer expectations.

6 CUSTOMER *Loyalty*

Strategies

- Conduct periodic surveys of customers, analyzing and internally disseminating results; take prompt, decisive action to address customer concerns.

- Conduct open and frank discussions of expectations, concerns, ideas, and opportunities with customers and stakeholders; follow up with appropriate actions.

- Anticipate and position for emergent customer needs.

- Develop cooperative alliances with customers, sponsors, and suppliers to enhance customer satisfaction.

- Celebrate and share our successes with our customers.

- Assign personnel to field positions with customers.

Invest in Our People...

STRATEGIC GOAL 2

We will achieve this Goal by

- Providing challenging work and development opportunities to all members of our organization at every level.

- Establishing a work atmosphere that promotes loyalty, trust, cooperation, productivity, and innovation.

- Placing high priority on addressing employee challenges and concerns.

- Developing an agile, flexible, and effective workforce.

- Encouraging our people to become well-informed and innovative, to look beyond traditional boundaries for solutions, and to welcome the opportunities and challenges associated with the processes of continuous, adaptive, or breakthrough change.

What this Means to Us

Employee knowledge, skill, and team spirit are essential to our success. Each of us must possess a strong and enduring desire to improve individual and organizational performance. Our workforce will be characterized as energetic, spirited, agile, proactive, and future-focused. This means

- Pursuing challenging opportunities to develop professional and managerial knowledge and skills.

- Mentoring fellow employees.

- Being familiar with and supporting Division management initiatives.

- Communicating openly, sharing information, and listening for understanding.
- Taking responsibility for job performance.

Strategies
- Enhance workforce professional development through training, challenging field assignments and educational programs, and by encouraging employee participation in development processes.
- Conduct employee surveys and use results to generate improvements.
- Keep each other well informed.
- Implement hiring and retention strategies that meet strategic skill set needs.
- Provide the necessary tools and facilities to enable workforce effectiveness.
- Pursue innovative human resources policies and plans.
- Foster among supervisors a heightened appreciation of the present and future challenges facing employees.
- Hold employees accountable for work performance, recognizing and rewarding individual and team contributions.

STRATEGIC GOAL 3

Improve the Way We Work...

We will achieve this Goal by
- Questioning what we do and why we do it.
- Making continuous improvements in technical and business processes.
- Measuring results and improving/adapting processes from measurement and facts.
- Streamlining or eliminating inefficient or wasteful processes/practices.
- Managing total ownership costs.
- Doing more with less and working better/cheaper/faster.
- Infusing cost-consciousness into all business decisions to balance technical positioning for the future.

What this Means to Us

This goal is important to every part of our organization, product lines as well as business departments. Each of us must improve our overall performance while reducing bottom-line costs to our customers. To succeed at this difficult task, each of us has to constantly re-examine how we approach every aspect of our work. Although measures that enhance our effectiveness can be initiated from the top down, workers at local levels know best how to improve performance, and therefore we must be actively involved in helping achieve the National Performance Review goal of more effective operations. This means

- Examining local processes and practices continuously to determine if and how they might be improved, asking "How can I do my job better?" every day.
- Working as a team.
- Supporting Division-wide management initiatives introduced to increase effectiveness and/or reduce costs.
- Seeking and sharing good ideas/best practices that could be adopted across departmental lines.
- Communicating ideas up and down the chain of command, and across the Division.

Strategies
- Find, share, and implement new ideas and best practices from other organizations.
- Capitalize on government initiatives and reinvention laboratory status.
- Work closely with NUWC Division Keyport to draw from each other's strengths.
- Apply new organizational effectiveness concepts to make the Division more effective and efficient.
- Use cross- and intra-departmental reliance to capitalize on our strengths throughout the Division.
- Use performance measurement to assess cost-effectiveness and overall performance.
- Create incentives to eliminate wasteful, duplicative, and no-consequence work.
- Realize technical process improvements to enhance performance and achieve targeted cost/schedule reductions.
- Maintain competitive costs to customers.
- Establish and manage to appropriate business operating targets.
- Pursue technologies that enhance effectiveness.

Continuous IMPROVEMENT

9

Strategic Goal 4

Provide Capable and Affordable Products...

We will achieve this Goal by

- Understanding thoroughly the Fleet's operating environment and requirements to ensure effective products and solutions.
- Seeking and adopting innovative processes that will improve overall performance, reliability, and affordability.
- Providing prompt and comprehensive responses to short-fused Fleet requests.
- Generating new ideas to complement our technical capabilities and improve cost-effectiveness.

What this Means to Us

The warfighters in the Fleet depend upon us to provide undersea warfare systems that ensure unchallenged naval supremacy. To accomplish this vital part of our mission with constrained resources, we must use the most effective and affordable technologies available, and must refine our system concepts and implementation approaches to ensure that the total ownership costs of our products are kept to an absolute minimum. This means

- Seizing opportunities to interact with our customers and the Fleet.
- Responding quickly and completely to customer requests.
- Developing "out of the box" solutions to the Navy's near-term challenges.
- Being creative, using and sharing ideas that lead to more effective and affordable products and services.
- Anticipating and meeting customer requirements, never losing sight of end-user needs.
- Capitalizing on commercial practices and technologies.

Strategies

- Support OPNAV and the Fleet in defining technical requirements.
- Exploit emergent technologies (e.g., simulation-based design, synthetic training environments, etc.) that enhance product quality.
- Improve communications with customers to quickly ascertain emergent Fleet requirements and to provide faster response.
- Devise and implement engineering practices and approaches that decrease cycle times and costs while enhancing product performance.
- Streamline or eliminate practices and processes that cause unnecessary delays in deployment or reduce effectiveness of our products.

10

- Pursue cross-departmental and external collaborations as a means to derive solutions that drive down costs and development times while improving product performance.

- Use a total systems engineering perspective in developing and applying technical processes.

STRATEGIC GOAL 5
Innovate for the Future...

We will achieve this Goal by
- Engaging customers to understand and anticipate their future needs.

- Seeking the knowledge and mastery of technologies that will address long-term Fleet needs and sustain the Navy's competitive advantage in undersea warfare.

- Developing a global perspective and a corporate culture that foster innovation, eliminate technical insularity, and promote free exchange of ideas with our partners.

- Developing advanced concepts and processes to accelerate the transition of relevant, affordable new technologies to Fleet products.

- Ensuring our facilities and other resources are appropriately used, refined, and revitalized to support our customers' technology requirements.

What this Means to Us
The dynamic defense acquisition environment and rapidly advancing technology have brought us increasing opportunities for change. We are being provided with greater freedom and more tools with which we can address challenges and stretch our technical imagination. As we seek new and innovative options to expand the "art of the possible" in undersea warfare, we must channel our efforts into developing the right technologies and practices to achieve our technical visions. This means

- Building broader and deeper understanding of current and expected undersea warfare military needs through education, professional development, and meaningful assignments.

- Broadening our technical horizons by increasing contacts with industry, academia, and other government agencies, and by looking beyond traditional bounds for ideas and information (i.e., developing a global perspective).

- Expanding the "art of the possible" by being creative and imaginative in developing technical visions for the future and identifying opportunities for technology insertion into current and future platforms and systems.

- Learning which tools and resources are available and applying them to address technological requirements.

Strategies

- Refine and apply warfare analysis methods and advanced concepts to better anticipate and assess military requirements.

- Create and deploy technical visions that drive and shape technology insertion opportunities.

- Collaborate with agencies and organizations that have strong potential to contribute to our technical knowledge.

- Pursue internal and external opportunities to leverage investments in technology.

- Encourage innovative technological approaches to undersea warfare challenges, allowing managed "risk-taking."

- Devise and utilize an employee development strategy that fosters the Division's growth as a learning organization.

- Develop a revitalization strategy for our facilities.

Balanced Performance Measures

Division Newport will assess its progress toward the strategic goals by using a set of balanced performance measurements. We have determined five key perspectives that serve as focal points for measuring our progress.

- Our customers' perspective, which examines how well we are meeting their needs.

- Our business perspective, where we examine our internal processes.

- Our financial perspective, or how we are managing our resources.

- Our employees' perspective, which will gauge adequacy of the work environment and whether we are giving employees the tools they need to meet expected demands.

- Our learning and growth perspective, where we examine our ability to learn and grow as an organization.

For each of these five interrelated perspectives, we have developed a list of performance criteria or goals that we intend to satisfy (see following page). At the Division level, these performance measures are deliberately broad to address strategic issues. As they are deployed throughout our product lines and business departments, they will provide a link between our high-level strategic goals and desired outcomes at the operational level. To serve their purpose, these performance measures, tailored to department needs, should be reflected in five-year plans throughout the Division.

192 PRESIDENT'S MANAGEMENT AGENDA

Photo Credit
Cover Ship - Ingalls Shipbuilding

BALANCE Measures

Internal Business Perspective

- Increase Science & Technology funding
- Increase advanced development funding
- Reduce cost of doing business
- Reduce latent Fleet defects
- Bring technical processes under process management
- Achieve seamless information flow

Customer Perspective

- Increase customer satisfaction
- Increase customer base
- Ensure customer retention
- Be provider of choice

Financial Perspective

- Meet the Net Operating Result target
- Sustain high efficiency
- Sustain/increase employee work base
- Manage leverage ratio

Learning and Growth Perspective

- Improve teamwork
- Increase innovation-related initiatives for product and services
- Increase capabilities/competencies of workforce
- Increase partnering with industry and academia

Employee Perspective

- Recruit, develop, and retain a world-class workforce
- Provide work environment that enhances job performance, product/service quality, and encourages innovation
- Provide leadership, direction, and communication
- Reward and recognize in consonance with Division goals

NUWC NEWPORT DIVISION 1998 STRATEGIC PLAN BROCHURE

The material that follows is adapted from *Strategic Plan 1998: Naval Undersea Warfare Center Division Newport,* Newport, Rhode Island, Naval Undersea Warfare Center Division Newport, 1997, Report No. NUWC-NPT-AP10,852-2.

Mission
Undersea Superiority: Today and Tomorrow.
We provide the technical foundation that enables the conceptualization, research, development, fielding, modernization, and maintenance of systems that ensure our Navy's undersea superiority.

Vision
Be our Nation's provider of choice for undersea superiority, satisfying today's needs and meeting tomorrow's challenges.

Cultural Values
Our cultural values influence everything we do; they make up our fundamental system of beliefs, which describe how we approach our responsibilities.

"Our commitment is to our customers"

"Our strength is in our people"

"Our contribution is in our products"

Our Goals

Increase Customer Loyalty...
- Conduct periodic surveys of customers, analyzing and internally disseminating results; take prompt, decisive action to address customer concerns.
- Conduct open and frank discussions of expectations, concerns, ideas, and opportunities with customers and stakeholders; follow up with appropriate actions.
- Anticipate and position for emergent customer needs.
- Develop cooperative alliances with customers, sponsors, and suppliers to enhance customer satisfaction.
- Celebrate and share our successes with our customers.
- Assign personnel to field positions with customers.

Invest in Our People...
- Enhance workforce professional development through training, challenging field assignments and educational programs, and by enhancing employee participation in development processes.
- Conduct employee surveys and use results to generate improvements.
- Keep each other well-informed.
- Implement hiring and retention strategies that meet strategic skill set needs.
- Provide the necessary tools and facilities to enable workforce effectiveness.
- Pursue innovative human resources policies and plans.
- Foster among supervisors a heightened appreciation of the present and future challenges facing employees.
- Hold employees accountable for work performance, recognizing and rewarding individual and team contributions.

Improve the Way We Work...
- Find, share, and implement new ideas and best practices.
- Capitalize on government initiatives and reinvention laboratory status.
- Work closely with NUWC Division Keyport to draw from each other's strengths.
- Apply new organizational effectiveness concepts to make the Division more effective and efficient.
- Use cross- and intra-departmental reliance to capitalize on our strengths.
- Use performance measurement to assess cost-effectiveness and overall performance.
- Create incentives to eliminate wasteful or no-consequence work.
- Realize technical process improvements to enhance performance and achieve targeted cost/schedule reductions.
- Maintain competitive costs to customers.
- Establish and manage to appropriate business operating targets.
- Pursue technologies that enhance business effectiveness.

Provide Capable and Affordable Products...
- Support OPNAV and the Fleet in defining technical requirements.
- Exploit emergent technologies (e.g., simulation-based design, synthetic training environments, etc.) that enhance product quality.
- Improve communications with customers to quickly ascertain emergent Fleet requirements and to provide faster response.
- Devise and implement engineering practices and approaches that decrease cycle times and costs while enhancing product performance.
- Streamline or eliminate practices and processes that cause unnecessary delays in deployment or reduce effectiveness of our products.
- Pursue cross-departmental and external collaborations as a means to derive solutions that drive down costs and development times while improving product performance.
- Use a total systems engineering perspective in technical processes.

Innovate for the Future...
- Refine and apply warfare analysis methods and advanced concepts to better anticipate and assess military requirements.
- Create and deploy technical visions that drive and shape technology insertion opportunities.
- Collaborate with agencies and organizations that have strong potential to contribute to our technical knowledge.
- Pursue opportunities to leverage investments in technology.
- Encourage innovative technological approaches to undersea warfare challenges, allowing managed "risk-taking".
- Devise and utilize an employee development strategy that fosters the Division's growth as a learning organization.
- Develop a revitalization strategy for our facilities.

Balanced Performance Measures

- Customer Perspective
- Internal Business Perspective
- Learning and Growth Perspective
- Financial Perspective
- Employee Perspective

balance

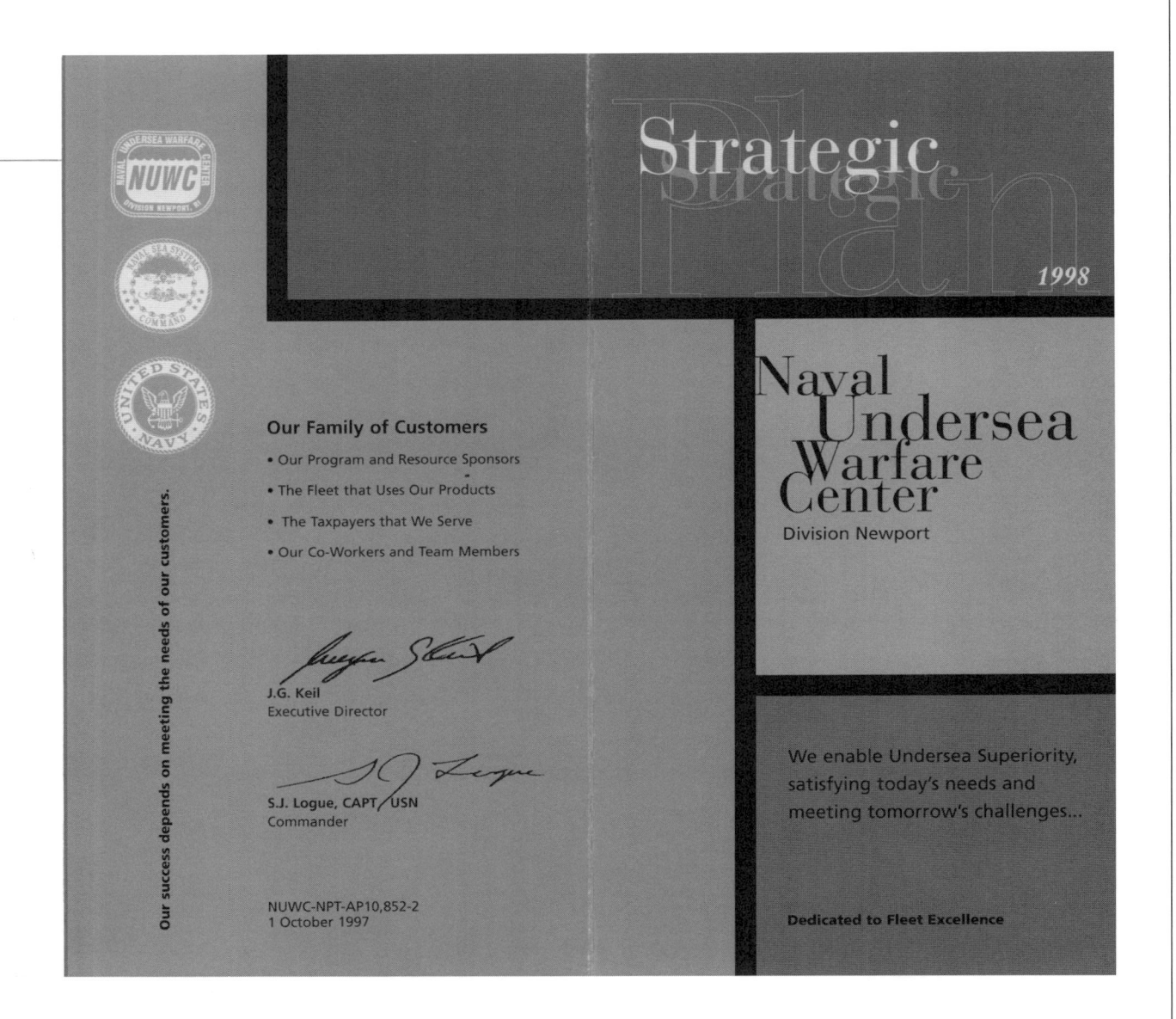

The Balanced Scorecard at the Naval Undersea Warfare Center

Strategic Plan 1998

Naval Undersea Warfare Center
Division Newport

We enable Undersea Superiority, satisfying today's needs and meeting tomorrow's challenges...

Dedicated to Fleet Excellence

Our Family of Customers
- Our Program and Resource Sponsors
- The Fleet that Uses Our Products
- The Taxpayers that We Serve
- Our Co-Workers and Team Members

J.G. Keil
Executive Director

S.J. Logue, CAPT, USN
Commander

NUWC-NPT-AP10,852-2
1 October 1997

Our success depends on meeting the needs of our customers.

Our Operating Principles

Our customers come first.
Working with our customers, we respond to the needs of the Fleet to ensure we provide the most effective and affordable undersea warfare products and services in a timely manner.

Our workforce is critical to our success.
We provide our workforce with the skill set, knowledge, motivation, and work environment to effectively accomplish our mission. We rely on our workforce to forge the future of the Division.

Diversity strengthens our creativity and teamwork.
We respect each other and our differences and recognize the value of our diverse backgrounds.

Improvement must be continuous.
We have a passion for excellence! We understand and support quality programs, and constantly work to enhance our processes, products, and services.

Teamwork is essential.
We cooperate, communicate, and collaborate, both internally and externally, to achieve the most effective products and services.

Innovation and creativity are crucial.
We seek new and innovative approaches to old problems and attack new challenges with imagination. We look outward for creative ideas to adapt to our use. We take manageable risks to field new technologies for effective solutions.

We are accountable.
We are honest, ethical, and accountable for all our actions.

We are committed to environmental stewardship and safety. We promote practices and attitudes that respect our environment and make our workplace safe and productive.

We are good citizens of our community.
We recognize our economic and social impact on the stakeholders in our communities. We adhere to the highest standards of citizenship and participate in charitable, educational, and community outreach programs.

NUWC NEWPORT DIVISION FIVE-YEAR PLANNING PROCESS

Figure 9–4 depicts the FY 2001–2005 five-year planning process, and Figure 9–5 presents the five-year planning schedule. The five-year planning plan of action and milestones (POA&M) is shown in Figure 9–6.

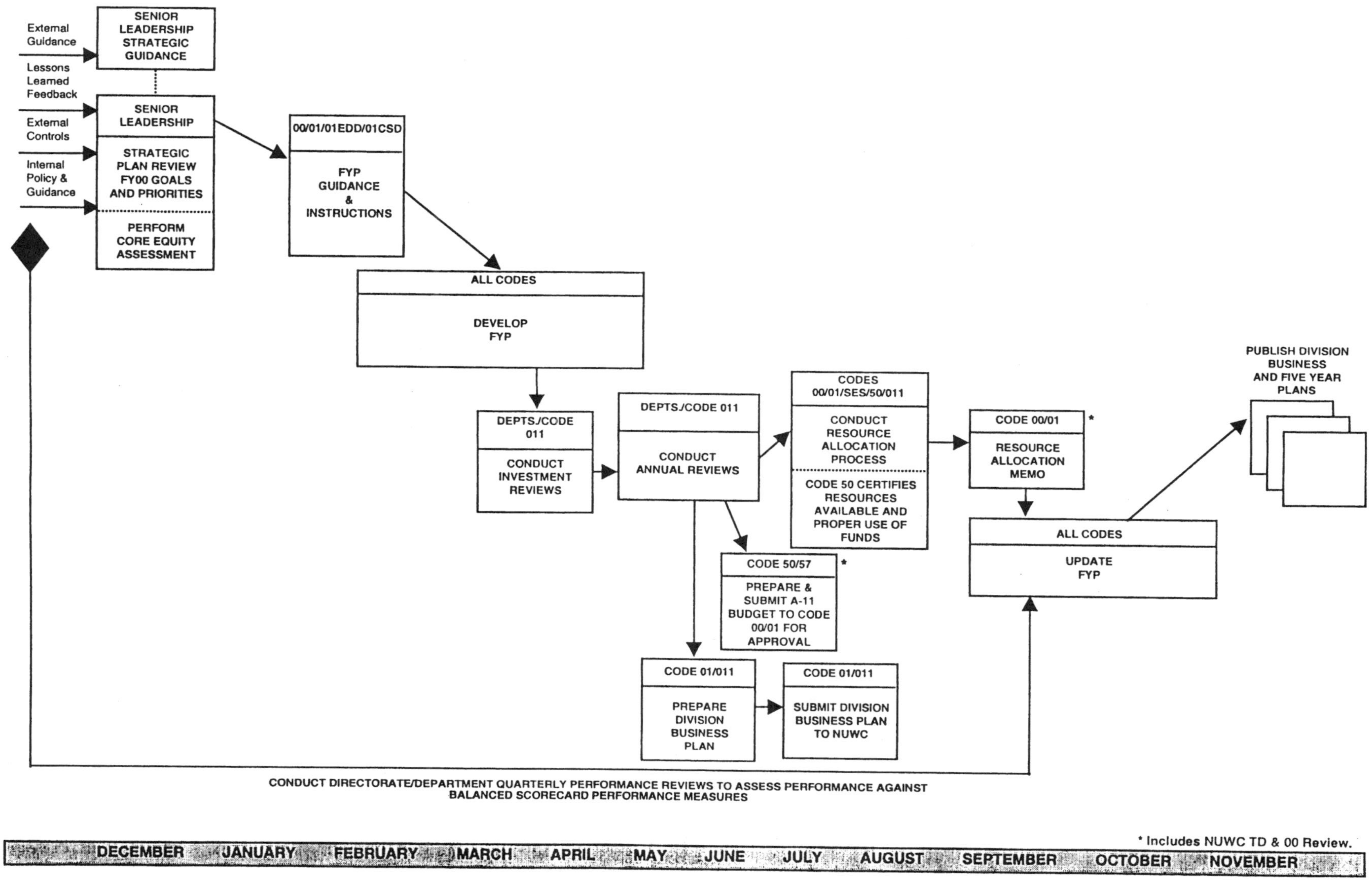

Figure 9–4. FY01–05 Five-Year Planning Process. *Source:* Head, Strategy Development Staff (Code 011), Naval Undersea Warfare Center, Division Newport, Newport, Rhode Island.

• Prepare Planning Guidance and Instructions	Dec–Jan
• Release Guidance and Instructions	14 Feb
• Develop Five Year Plan (All Codes)	Feb–May
• Conduct Investment Reviews (Round 1)	1–10 Mar
• Division Investment Proposals Due to Support Investment Process	24 Mar
• Conduct Investment Reviews (Round 2)	1–10 Apr
• Finalize Approved Investment Projects & Request Additional Documentation	20 Apr
• Conduct the Annual Review (All Codes)	5 May
• Prepare Business Plan and A-11 Budget for Review & Approval (NUWCNPT and NUWC CM Review)	May–Jun
• Finalize Division Business Plan for Submission to NAVSEA	Jul
• Conduct Resource Allocation Process	1 Jul–20 Aug
• Issue Resource Allocation Memo	1 Sep
• Update to Five Year Plan Data	Sep–Nov
• Publish Five Year Plans	Dec
• Conduct Quarterly Performance Reviews	Oct–Jan–Mar–Jul

Figure 9–5. FY01–05 Five-Year Planning Schedule. *Source:* Head, Strategy Development Staff (Code 011), Naval Undersea Warfare Center, Division Newport, Newport, Rhode Island.

	1st Qtr			2nd Qtr			3rd Qtr			4th Qtr		
	Oct	Nov	Dec	Jan	Feb	Mar	Apr	May	Jun	Jul	Aug	Sep
Final Division Business Plan/Document Core Equity Assessments/Sustainable Plan & Determine Investment Strategy		▲										
Prepare External Scan			▲	▲								
Release Guidance & Instructions					▲							
Directorate/Departments Develop Five Year Plans (All Codes)					△			▲				
Investment Proposal Submissions Due to Code 011 (24 Mar)						△						
Finalize Approved Investment Projects & Request Additional Required Documentation (April)							△—△					
Directorate/Departments Submit Five Year Plans to Code 011								△				
Conduct the Division Annual Planning Review								△				
Prepare Division Buinsess Plan and A-11 Budget for Review and Approval (May–Jun)*								△	△			
Conduct the Resource Allocation Process (Jun–Aug)								△			△	
Finalize the Division Business Plan for Submission to NAVSEA (1 Jul)										△		
Issue the Resource Allocation Memo—Directorates/ Departments To Update the Five Year Plans (8 Sep)*												△
FY01 Conduct Directorate/Department Performance Reviews—Quarterly	○			○			○			○		

*Includes NUWC TD & 00 Review.

Figure 9–6. FY01–05 Five-Year Planning POA&M. *Source:* Head, Strategy Development Staff (Code 011), Naval Undersea Warfare Center, Division Newport, Newport, Rhode Island.

"FIVE-YEAR PLANNING EXPLAINED IN ONE EASY LESSON"

The article that follows is reprinted from T. Edgar, "Five Year Planning Explained in One Easy Lesson," pp. 5–6, *NUWSCOPE,* Vol. 30, No. 3., March 2000.

How NUWC Operates as a Business

In a recent conversation about key business processes that are used at the Newport Division, Juergen Keil, the Executive Director, noted, "the Division five-year planning process is one of the most important cornerstones of our Strategic Management Process." The use of the annual planning process to craft agreement between the Commander and Executive Director and the directorate and department heads on the future course of the Division and their departments "makes us fairly unique among government activities."

All departments and directorates use this defined and systematic process (see box), which has been in place since 1981, to develop program and management plans for a five-year-planning window. The plans are used to document a variety of data including strategies, resource requirements, and the skills needed to support the current Navy, the future Navy, and the Navy after next.

Annual five-year planning process review

External Scan—documents trends and events that could impact Newport Division business activity.

Guidance development and distribution—based on scan data, external guidance and internal survey results, and used to guide plan preparation.

Plan preparation and submission—departments develop program and management plans in accordance with guidance.

Annual plan review meeting—provides a Division-wide view of resource requirements and an opportunity to discuss issues and share information.

Plan analysis—plans and review-meeting data analyzed to support resource allocation decision process.

Resource allocation—allocates indirect and G&A, core equity, sustainment initiative and associated investment funds, and sets performance targets.

Plan execution—departments do what is planned

Performance measure—performance monitored at Quarterly Performance Reviews and with the Balanced Scorecard.

The five-year plans are aligned with other products of the Division's strategic management process. These include the mission, vision, operating principles, and goals contained in the Strategic Plan that define the long-term vision of where the Division is going and how it is going to get there. The five-year plans have a tactical focus that provides program initiative and resource utilization plans that enable near-term progress toward strategic goal and vision attainment. And the accumulation of funding and work year projections, in turn, provide valuable input in the preparation of the Division's annual A-11 budget submission and are used to formulate stabilized work year rate was explained in a September 1999 *NUWSCOPE* article; the budget process will be discussed in a future *NUWSCOPE* article.

The development this year of the Division's first business plan, prepared in response to NAVSEA direction, was able to capitalize on the sound work used in the development of the Division's FY00–04 five-year plans. This year's planning guidance, which will guide development of the FY01–05 plans, has been modified to bring our five-year plan development in close alignment with our business plan development. This alignment will minimize the preparation burden placed on Division employees.

Five-year Planning Process

The process begins in the first quarter of the fiscal year with an external scan that documents key trends and events that shape the USW environment and can influence Division business activity. The scan includes data on policy and regulatory trends, market analysis, long-term Navy needs and requirements, and a quick-look at socio-economic factors that could impact the Division over the planning period. Scan data are integrated with the results of the Customer Survey and Employee Opinion Survey and with a synthesis of Navy and DoD strategic plans and associated planning guidance. This information, together with guidance from the Technical Director of NUWC, is used to establish five-year planning guidance.

Distribution of the five-year planning guidance in the second quarter of the fiscal year initiates the planning process. The guidance tasks directorates and departments to develop a comprehensive plan addressing all elements of running their business area. This includes defining overall technical/functional program direction, goals, business initiatives, resource requirements, training plans, strategic skill requirements, environmental plans, investment needs, and metrics with quantifiable targets. For the FY01–05 plan cycle, departments will also address core equity sustainment, business base trends, workforce effectiveness initiatives, and customer loyalty initiatives. These additions strengthen the alignment of the five-year plans with the new business planning process. The guidance requires consideration of and planning for all aspects of near- and long-term direction and needs. Plan development involves discussion with other Division departments, customers, suppliers, and stakeholders in the formulation of realistic and challenging goals and robust plans for execution in the planning window.

How the Plans Are Used

Following their completion by the directorates and departments, the plans are reviewed during the Annual Plan Review meeting, which is usually conducted in May. It is led by the Commander and Executive Director and involves senior managers from all directorates and departments. The meeting provides a Division-wide view of resource requirements identified in the plans. The review meeting, which provides a forum in which important issues are identified and discussed, best practices are shared, and the management team is informed of key program challenges and opportunities, starts the process of building a Division-level picture of the future.

Resource allocation is the next step in the process. It is based on an analysis of the information developed during the annual plan review meeting, knowledge about externally imposed resource constraints and mandates, and negotiations between Division and directorate and department leaders. Resources allocated through this process include: overhead and service cost center budgets (indirect and G&A), Division training budget and plan, staffing levels (including hiring), core equity sustainment initiatives and associated investment funds, and facility maintenance projects. In addition, operating targets for direct work year performance and productivity ratio are established. The Commander and Executive Director normally release the resource allocation memorandum in August; it documents resource allocation decisions and establishes resource utilization policies for the next fiscal year.

Performance Measurement

The Division took the lead among Navy activities in linking performance measurement with the planning process in 1994 when it developed an enterprise-level system of performance measures. The measures selected—Customer, Employee/Learning and Growth, Financial, Internal Business, and Stakeholder—have become the Division's Balanced Scorecard (BSC). They are used as indicators of the overall organizational health and to assess progress toward achieving the strategic goals. The BSC approach to performance measurement is an integral part of the strategic management process and since the 1997 planning cycle each directorate and department has arrayed its key measures into the five perspectives of the BSC. Quarterly review of Division, directorate, and department BSC metrics are conducted and provide an opportunity to assess, and if necessary redirect, action needed to keep the Division moving toward goal attainment.

On a quarterly basis, performance against the plan and against operating targets is assessed during the Quarterly Performance Review (QPR) conducted by the Commander and Executive Director with directorate and department heads. QPRs also address program highlights, the BSC metrics, customer survey data, safety and environmental initiatives, and core equity sustainment initiatives.

Why Do We Do All of This . . . ?

When asked, "Why do we do all of this planning? After all, plans and reality tend to diverge, especially in the out years," Keil responded: "The deliberative process that occurs during plan development and review provides value to our overall management process. We continue to use this systematic planning process because it enables a strategic conversation between Division leaders that prepares us to make smart business decisions based on consideration of a broad range of options that encompass customer, NAVSEA, and Navy concerns. By assessing future contingencies, articulating alternatives, and addressing resource requirements, the Division is better positioned to face organizational challenges and respond to them with coherent policies and plans." He concluded by saying that "documenting the plan development process and sharing it with the workforce helps to communicate business priorities and realities. The Five-Year Plans, together with the Division Strategic Plan and Business Plan, help employees understand where the Division is headed and how they can help the Division realize its goals."

So, if you have never read a Five-Year Plan, talk to your branch, division, or department head. Copies of previous years' plans are available in the Division's Technical Library. Business plan information was provided in articles in the January and February issues of *NUWSCOPE*. Your branch head soon will have a copy of the Business Plan that you can examine.

If you have questions or ideas about the annual five-year planning process, please contact Traci Edgar of the Corporate Strategy Development Staff.

"A JOURNEY OF CHANGE"

The following article, which appeared in Volume 2, Issue 2, of *PERFORM,* describes how NUWC used an aligned and cascading balanced scorecard to manage change.

Managing Change Through an Aligned and Cascading Balanced Scorecard: A Case Study

By Georgia M. Harrigan and Ruth E. Miller
Naval Undersea Warfare Center Division
Newport, Rhode Island

Introduction

In 1996, Naval Undersea Warfare Center Division Newport began a "Journey of Change" to respond to key customer feedback, to effect cultural change, and to position for the 21st century. This article discusses how the Division established and implemented a customer-driven Performance Measurement system that is critical to its mission and strategic plan and used it to define and communicate the business culture of the organization to support the Journey of Change. The Performance Measurement system was heavily influenced by articles in the *Harvard Business Review* by Robert S. Kaplan and David P. Norton ("The Balanced Scorecard - Measures that Drive Performance," January-February 1992; "Putting the Balanced Scorecard to Work," September-October 1993; and "Using the Balanced Scorecard as a Strategic Management System," January-February 1996), and by their book, *Translating Strategy into Action: The Balanced Scorecard.* NUWC Division Newport has used the Balanced Scorecard (BSc) approach for four full years and continues to use it. The organization has found that the BSc methodology allows the leadership to communicate strategic direction both externally and internally throughout the organization and to measure progress toward strategic goal attainment on a systematic basis.

The goal of this article is to present an integrated view of the theoretical and practical application of the BSc. Isolating only the theoretical perspective leads to an academic reading that presents the ideal scenario, without considering that the BSc application in an organization is a chaotic, messy, and complex job. Considering only the practitioner's view leads to a list of events because practitioners are so inundated that they often act without the 40,000-foot view or they neglect to take time for reflection. By combining the two perspectives, the authors intend to provide an informative and practical discussion, which will help other organizations apply the BSc methodology to their strategic planning and Performance Measurement initiatives.

This article is organized as follows. Section 1 is a general discussion of the relationship between a customer-driven Performance Measurement system and a customer-driven organization. Section 2 is a description of the development of the NUWC Division Newport Performance Measurement system. Section 3 provides the evolution of the scorecard and the results of two significant improvement efforts. Section 4 is a discussion of the effort to achieve strategic alignment both external and internal to the organization. Finally, Section 5 provides the "next steps" for the scorecard: how the system could be applied to create a "learning organization."

How a Customer-Driven Performance Measurement System Creates a Customer-Driven Organization

Premise: If an organization can establish and implement a customer-driven Performance Measurement system, it will have made great strides toward becoming a customer-driven organization.

This premise is based on the insight that structure influences behavior. The systems perspective tells us we must look beyond personalities and events and into the underlying structures that shape individual actions and create conditions in which a type of event becomes likely. Peter Senge[1] noted, "When placed in the same system, people, however different, tend to produce similar results."

The term structure does not mean the logical structure of a carefully developed argument or the reporting structure shown by an organization chart; it refers to a systemic structure, which is concerned with the key interrelationships that influence behavior over time.[2] This systemic structure is created with interconnected information-feedback loops. Feedback loops form the central structures that control change in all systems. All change takes place within the control of feedback loops.[3]

If this insight that "structure determines behavior" and the premise are accepted, then it follows that a customer-driven organization is the result of a customer-driven Performance Measurement system. Exhibit 1 illustrates this relationship by describing the steps an organization takes to develop and implement the system. To achieve a customer-driven organization, it is not enough to have a customer-focused mission; that mission is implicit to an organization because a mission is an organization's reason for being and must be clear and coherent. With this in mind, an organization defines its desired future state, its vision. Both internal and external factors define today's organization and determine what conditions or actions influence its ability to meet its mission, so the organization must consider the gap between today's organization and the desired future state—then it must develop strategic goals to bridge the two. The strategic goals translate the vision into specific outcomes that the organization must create to realize its vision and close the gap.

Once the mission, vision, and strategic goals are defined, the customer-driven Performance Measurement system can be developed. The organization defines actions (which Kaplan and Norton refer to as objectives) to further translate the goals. The actions (objectives) are grouped within five perspectives: financial, customer, internal business, employee/learning and growth, and stakeholder. The actions (objectives) provide a framework for many critical management processes and influence the operation of the organization and the delivery of products and services, in turn affecting customers, employees, stakeholders, and partners.

> *"Once the mission, vision, and strategic goals are defined, the customer-driven Performance Measurement system can be developed."*

Each specific action has one or more metrics associated with it, which provide an understanding of the status or the evaluation of the action. The actual measured values are gathered by feedback from customers, employees, and stakeholders. Each metric has an associated targeted value toward

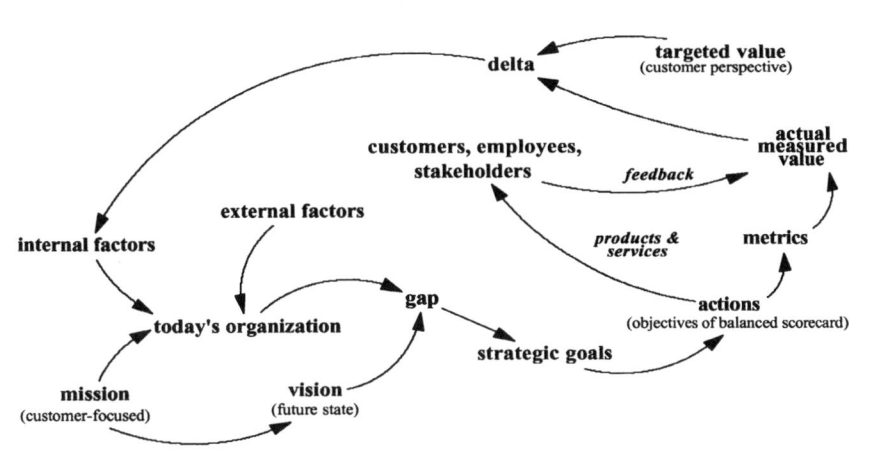

Exhibit 1: The Proces of Creating a Performance Measurement System

which the organization strives. In a customer-driven Performance Measurement system, these targeted values are developed from the perspectives of the customers, employees, and stakeholders by considering their needs and expectations.

Comparisons between the actual measured values and the targeted values reveal a delta. This analysis becomes available for the next iteration of defining the current state of the organization—it becomes an internal factor. The measures and values cause "internalizing" of the customer needs and expectations; hence a customer-driven organization is created.

Development of the NUWC Division Newport Performance Measurement System

NUWC Division Newport began exploring "Performance Measurement linked to enterprise performance and goals" around 1994, when performance reporting emerged as a major focus of the 1990s throughout government agencies. Significant legislation was passed during those years, most notably the Government Performance and Results Act (GPRA) of 1993. The GPRA stated: "…federal managers are seriously disadvantaged in their efforts to improve program efficiency and effectiveness, because of … inadequate information on program performance; and congressional policymaking, spending decisions and program oversight are seriously handicapped by insufficient attention to program performance and results."

The GPRA was not the only legislation passed; there was the Government Management Reform Act of 1994 and the Information Technology Management Reform Act of 1996, which required federal agencies to:

- strategically plan how they would deliver high-quality goods and services to their customers, and

- specifically measure their programs' performance in meeting those commitments.

Although the GPRA was intended only for the top, direct reports to Congress (i.e. DoD) and not for all organizational levels of the government, NUWC Division Newport used the law to build internal support for its Performance Measurement initiative. The concept of enterprise Performance Measurement was deployed organizationally through the Division's annual planning process. This 1994 initiative laid the groundwork for later BSc introduction and implementation throughout the Division's line and staff organizations. From 1994 to 1997, the Division collected and reported quarterly "Key Performance Indicators." The quarterly assessment consisted of eight metrics, which were primarily financial in nature but included several human resources and innovation measures. The goal of the assessment was to provide a single-page presentation of the health of the organization in an effort to improve organizational efficiency and effectiveness. The quarterly assessment reports were well received throughout the organization because before that time, although the data were always available, the information was not routinely synthesized for use in decision-making. The quarterly assessment report provided a cohesive look at the data; for example, hiring decisions could now be made by combining core competencies of the workforce with the business data forecasts to target employees with certain abilities.

In March 1997, NUWC Division Newport was introduced to the BSc concept and held workshop sessions to further the understanding of the BSc concept. The workshop sessions consisted of a short lecture and discussion on the background, theory, realities, and techniques involved in measuring what the organization does and how it relates to its goals and objectives. Then, teams formed and actually began developing scorecards—outcome measures and action plans.

To build the scorecard, the teams looked at five perspectives: the traditional four perspectives of the BSc (financial, customer, internal business, and learning and growth) and a government-added fifth perspective, employee. Adding the fifth perspective to the NUWC Division Newport BSc proved to be essential at that time because the Base Realignment and Closure activities were impacting at least

50 percent of the organization. Employees and work were being transferred and relocated to NUWC Division Newport from New London, CT; San Diego, CA; Norfolk, VA; and Orlando, FL. Leadership was trying to minimize the disruption, while addressing the challenge to craft a common culture from the distinct cultures joining the Newport site, by focusing on employees.

> **"The scorecard is not a substitute for a sound strategy, clear focus, and strong alignment energies within the organization."**

For each perspective, the process was to develop an objective related to the organization's mission. After these workshops, several of the NUWC product lines continued to develop their directorate or department scorecards. First drafts of these scorecards were submitted to Division management in August of 1997 as part of the yearly planning process (five-year plan). A Division-wide Balanced Performance Measures Team was formed in July of 1997 with the objective of developing the set of measures at the executive level for inclusion in the Division's strategic plan. In September of 1997 the scorecard was accepted by the senior leadership team and incorporated into the FY98 Strategic Plan. Although it was agreed that there were too many measures in this initial product, getting started and documenting the measures enabled NUWC Division Newport to surmount the initial hurdle and start the learning/experiential process. It was expected that through the use of the scorecard the "extra" measures would fall out during use or in the review process that is built into the strategic planning process.

This was just the beginning of the implementation, and the Division later realized that it was the "easy part" of the process. Successful implementation requires more than administrative structures, plans, and matrices. The scorecard is not a substitute for a sound strategy, clear focus, and strong alignment energies within the organization. The challenges to the organization, and specifically to top management, are developing faith in the organization's ability to achieve the goals, motivating it to do so, and focusing its attention long enough to internalize new capabilities.

The Evolution of the NUWC Division Newport Scorecard

NUWC Division Newport accepted that defining the measures to truly reflect the organization's strategy and vision is an iterative process in which continuous improvement is a critical and constant objective. The Division expected that the scorecard had to evolve if it was to be a viable and useful tool for the management of the organization. Integral to the Division's BSc process is a yearly assessment of the BSc—identifying problems/weaknesses in the process and key areas of improvements. To date, this yearly assessment process brought about two of the most significant impacts to the evolution of the NUWC Division Newport.

During the first yearly assessment, the key weakness identified werethe increasing number of measures and, more disconcerting, the ad-hoc fashion in which measures were being added. As the leadership and the external environment changed, new measures were gradually being added to the (already "too many measures") original scorecard. This was contrary to the process of considering the mission and defining objectives and measures that support the strategy of the organization. Furthermore there was a paradox: on one hand, the leadership was adding measures; but on the other hand, the leadership was asking that only the top-level measures, which require direct action on their part, be included. There was no mechanism to discern whether a new measure should or should not be added, and consequently the number of measures continued to grow. The root of the problem was the initial process used to develop the scorecard. It was done perspective by perspective and there was no consideration to defining how the perspectives, objectives or measures linked to each other. The absence of the linkage chart between the measures and objectives was what had allowed the ad hoc addition of measures. The first step was to begin linking the objectives within each perspective. The objectives were linked to define the cause-and-effect relationships. This exercise helped the team to further define the objectives and to consider which of them were truly related to the overall strategy and mission of the organization. It also became clear that the employee and the learning-and-growth perspective should be one perspective. Although emphasis on employees is a basic tenet at Division Newport, the objectives are inherently linked and cannot be viewed separately from the learning-and-growth perspective.

The next critical step in the process was to link the perspectives. This linkage defines the organization's strategy as it relates to the mission. Kaplan and Norton state: "The strategy is a set of hypotheses about cause and effect. The measurement system should make relationships (hypotheses) among objectives in the various perspectives explicit so that they can be managed and validated."[4]

The process to develop the hypotheses for the model that best describes NUWC Division Newport reconfirmed the team's earlier decision to combine the employee and learning and growth perspectives. The team also discovered a missing perspective: the stakeholder perspective. Up to this point, the stakeholder had been combined with the customer perspective. However, the team realized that although some customers may have been dual-hatted as stakeholders, there were clearly two different perspectives. Because NUWC Division Newport's mission involves national security, there are stakeholder interests that are vital for the success of the organization and are not entirely included in the customer perspective. Stakeholders, for example, include the Fleet, the sailor, Congress, and the U.S. taxpayers. The Fleet and the sailor can be included as customers, but customers are better described as the organizations and program managers that actually pay directly for the products and services offered by NUWC Division Newport (e.g., Program Executive Officers and the Naval Sea Systems Command).

The hypothesis that NUWC Division Newport accepted is shown in Exhibit 2. This model differs from the traditional industry model, where the financial perspective is the key driver (top of the cause-and-effect diagram). However, NUWC Division Newport's model cannot apply the traditional government model where the financial perspective (i.e., budget) is the foundation of the organization, because it is not an "institutionally funded" organization. NUWC Division Newport is part of the Navy Working Capital Fund and has to operate more like a business than do traditional government organizations.

An unexpected outcome of the hypotheses and the linkage chart was the emergence of three organizational themes: innovation, affordability, and customer first. The emergence of the three themes

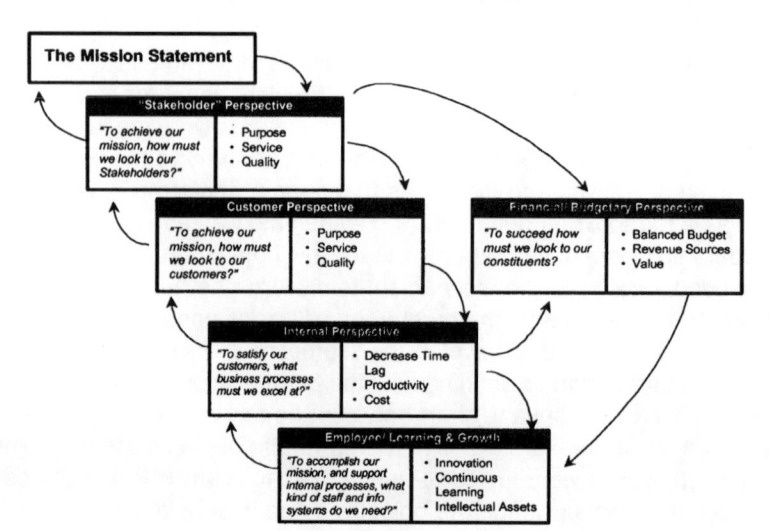

Exhibit 2: Tailored for NUWC Division Newport BSc Model

signaled to the team that the system of measures was fully aligned with the strategic direction of the Division and represented a critical validation of the scorecard construct. These themes, which were not prescribed, are the essence of NUWC Division Newport meeting its mission and represent the fundamental strategy concerns for the organization. This alignment provided the team with a sense of validation and additional merit to the Balanced Scorecard methodology.

> *"An unexpected outcome ...was the emergence of three organizational themes: innovation, affordability, and customer first."*

The second significant impact to the evolution was an unexpected outcome to our effort to improve the efficiency in administering the scorecard. In Fiscal Year 2001 NUWC Division Newport embarked on a BSc/Panorama Business Views (pbviews) pilot program whose purpose was to automate BSc data collection, maintenance, and reporting as much as possible, making it more efficient. Key personnel were introduced and trained in the use of the pbviews software product. The architecture was developed. Data from the Executive Business Information System is now automatically imported. Data from Customer and Employee Surveys was input. The data were the measure results, which were then compared to current Fiscal Year Targets and Stretch Targets (goals five years out). The pbviews system's architecture made it easy to view the progress to our strategic goals, through an intuitive "Red Yellow Green" Scoring. Furthermore this "rating" was then enhanced because the measure owners then provide analysis, commentary, and action plans (as required) for each measure. The unexpected outcome was that through this automation process we were able to gain a deeper understanding of our scorecard and the measurement process. Prior to this effort, the only expected outcome was the increased efficiency. However implementing the software helped us focus on the importance of target performance comparison and has led to the establishment of more challenging performance goals. It has also expanded the number of people with "first-hand" contact with the actual scorecard process.

Vertical Alignment and Empowerment

There is a widely accepted dichotomy between formulation and implementation of the organization's top-level goals. Senior managers formulate the goals, and the lower levels are expected to achieve them. Without a clear understanding of the organization's top-level goals and of the outcomes that are expected, employees are not positioned for success in attaining the goals. An effective Performance Measurement system can provide the necessary understanding.

Organizations need a clear and cohesive Performance Measurement framework that supports both the objectives and the collection of results. All levels of the organization must understand the framework, especially those entrusted with and expected to achieve performance goals and targets. They must clearly understand how success is defined and what their roles are in achieving that success. As a management instrument that translates an organization's mission and strategy into a comprehensive set of performance measures and also provides a framework for strategic measurement and management, the BSc can provide needed definition and structure to the organization.

NUWC Division Newport has found that the BSc methodology allows the leadership to communicate strategic direction internally throughout the organization to achieve top-down alignment. The results of the Employee Opinion Survey (EOS) provide data supporting the topto-bottom alignment of strategy that has been achieved using the BSc methodology.

The BSc methodology also supports external alignment. Exhibit 3 shows how the NUWC Division Newport mission and vision are linked to the missions of the organizations that are above NUWC in the hierarchy. In an ideal world the process of NUWC Division Newport's BSc development would have started with direction from higher Navy and higher Department of Defense scorecards. More often, as in the Division's case, there are no scorecards above the organization. However, by consid-

Exhibit 3: NUWC Division Newport Mission Statement Links to Other MIssions and Begins the BSc Process

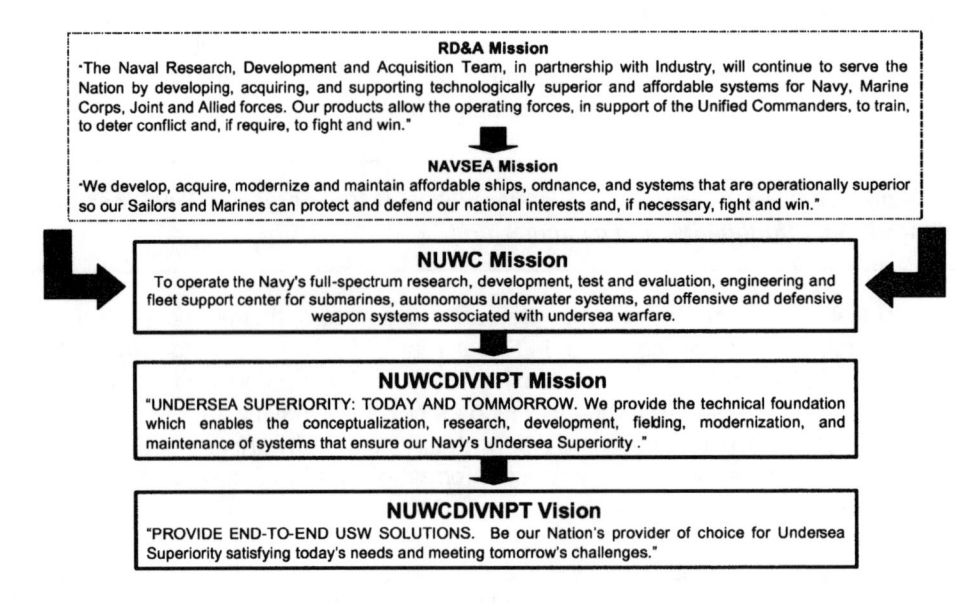

RD&A Mission
·The Naval Research, Development and Acquisition Team, in partnership with Industry, will continue to serve the Nation by developing, acquiring, and supporting technologically superior and affordable systems for Navy, Marine Corps, Joint and Allied forces. Our products allow the operating forces, in support of the Unified Commanders, to train, to deter conflict and, if require, to fight and win."

NAVSEA Mission
·We develop, acquire, modernize and maintain affordable ships, ordnance, and systems that are operationally superior so our Sailors and Marines can protect and defend our national interests and, if necessary, fight and win."

NUWC Mission
To operate the Navy's full-spectrum research, development, test and evaluation, engineering and fleet support center for submarines, autonomous underwater systems, and offensive and defensive weapon systems associated with undersea warfare.

NUWCDIVNPT Mission
"UNDERSEA SUPERIORITY: TODAY AND TOMMORROW. We provide the technical foundation which enables the conceptualization, research, development, fielding, modernization, and maintenance of systems that ensure our Navy's Undersea Superiority."

NUWCDIVNPT Vision
"PROVIDE END-TO-END USW SOLUTIONS. Be our Nation's provider of choice for Undersea Superiority satisfying today's needs and meeting tomorrow's challenges."

ering the missions of the organizations above, NUWC Division Newport was able to develop a scorecard that aligned with those of the external organizations once they developed their own BSc's.

Exhibit 4 provides an illustration of how the Balanced Scorecard in our chain of command, from the Undersecretary of Defense for Acquisition, Technology and Logistics (USD, AT&L) to ASN (RD&A) to the Naval Sea Systems Command to NUWC Headquarters to NUWC Division Newport to a NUWC Division Newport Technical Department, all aligns from the stakeholder perspective. The ASN (RD&A) has incorporated the BSC methodology in the 1999-2004 Strategic Plan. Although the terminology and the perspectives are different from NUWC Division Newport's, the general idea is similar. The

Exhibit 4: Cascading BSc's Align and Empower Organizations and Employees

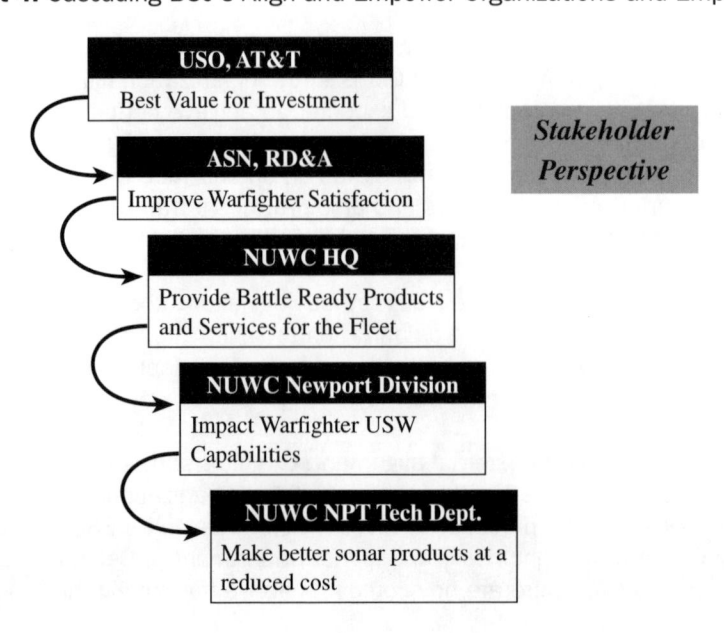

USO, AT&T
Best Value for Investment

ASN, RD&A
Improve Warfighter Satisfaction

NUWC HQ
Provide Battle Ready Products and Services for the Fleet

NUWC Newport Division
Impact Warfighter USW Capabilities

NUWC NPT Tech Dept.
Make better sonar products at a reduced cost

Stakeholder Perspective

Division has been able to align the objectives and perspectives for increased understanding of the actions it must take to contribute to the overall ASN(RD&A) strategy. This has often been described as "cascading" scorecards.

The authors advocate that it is unnecessary to have a one-to-one correspondence of each objective throughout the organization; however, where it is reasonable, the Division should have supporting objectives to contribute to the success of the Navy and Department of Defense. For example, the ASN (RD&A) has an objective to "decrease direct maintenance man hours per platform." Because this is not directly applicable to NUWC Division Newport, it would not make sense to force-fit an objective for the sake of uniformity. However, organizations can use the scorecards of organizations above them as guidance for their work, even though the measure is not explicitly on the scorecard. So by ASN (RD&A) providing their scorecards to NUWC Division Newport, the Division is able to become aware of ASN (RD&A)'s priorities and can check to ensure that organizations in the hierarchy are not pursuing projects that could have conflicting objectives. In other words, the ASN (RD&A)'s goal is to decrease direct maintenance man-hours per platform, so NUWC Division Newport, even though it is not monitoring this measure on the top-level organization's scorecard, should include maintenance man-hour measures in the product criteria so that they do not deliver products that increase direct maintenance man-hours per platform.

It is important to understand that the performance measurement system or BSc is not created—and does not exist—to control or measure the strategy, but rather acts as a lever to streamline and focus the strategy for overall breakthrough performance. To do this, the measures must have direct links to the strategic goals of the organization and must be focused to direct the attention of managers and employees to those factors that are expected to lead to competitive breakthroughs. The best Balanced Scorecards tell the story of the strategy so well that the strategy can be inferred by the collection of objectives and measures and by the linkages among them.[5]

> *"The challenges are to continue to learn how each objective, measure, and targeted value on the scorecard interacts with every other one."*

Next Steps

The Balanced Scorecard initiative at NUWC Division Newport is an evolving effort that will continue to present opportunities and challenges for improvement.

Using the scorecard for organizational learning

In this turbulent and competitive environment, the strategies are not linear or stable. The challenges are to continue to learn how each objective, measure, and targeted value on the scorecard interacts with every other one, and to consider the implications of achieving goals and objectives established in this ever-changing non-linear environment.

There are complex dynamics, and the BSc provides a framework for gaining an understanding of them. With its specification of the causal relationships between performance drivers and objectives, it allows management to evaluate the validity of strategy and quality of its execution, stimulating the managers to learn about the viability of the strategies.

The BSc allows the organization to think systemically about the strategy. For example, if employees and managers have delivered on the targeted measured values, then failure to achieve the expected outcomes is a signal that the theory underlying the strategy might not be valid. Managers should take such disconfirming evidence seriously and should reconsider their conclusions about market conditions, customer value propositions, competitors' behavior, and internal capabilities. This could result in reaffirmation of their belief in the current strategy, but it could also result in an adjustment to the quantitative values of the strategic measures. The team might conclude that they need a different strategy.[5] This learning that produces a change in people's assumptions and theories about cause-and-effect relationships is referred to as double-loop learning. It occurs when managers question their assumptions and reflect on whether the theory under which they were operating is still consistent with current evidence, observation, and experience.[6]

Left to its own devices, double-loop learning can take a very long time because it involves shifts in basic assumptions and beliefs, and these shifts occur only through experience over time. Computer simulation is a means to accelerate double-loop learning. A strategic feedback system can be designed to test, validate, and modify the hypotheses embedded in the strategy. In creating the strategic feedback system, the emphasis is on constructing cause-and-effect relationships. Dynamic computer simulations are required because cause-and-effect relationships are often far removed from the symptoms, both in time and in space, which limits the usability of simple correlation analyses. The human mind is also limited, and people can deal with only three or four variables at a time, and through only one or two time iterations. Most of us focus on the effect we want to create and then look for the most immediate cause to create that effect. The computer simulations can be used to play back management's view of the market, the environment, and the competition. Dynamic computer models can help with the discovery of other trigger points, separated in time and place from the desired effect, and because of human limitations these trigger points and insights will most likely be counterintuitive.

> *"A strategic feedback system can be designed to test, validate, and modify the hypotheses embedded in the strategy."*

Computer simulations will assist in the continued refinement and reflection on the balanced performance measures and are part of the organization's continuous improvement goals. An organization's ability to keep learning and developing will ensure that it continues to make excellent use of its resources, and that it will be appreciated by tomorrow's customers. It is a customer-driven organization.

Summary

The inclusion of the BSc in the NUWC Division Newport strategic management process provided the lever for implementation and assessment of planned organizational change. Much of the change derived from externalities, such as the end of the Cold War era, budget realities, and the resultant downsizing and consolidation of defense assets. Rather than take a reactive posture, however, Division leadership chose to effect change initiatives and to bring the entire workforce along on the journey. Today the Division is an organization that has made tremendous positive change and is an organization that is not complacent about the need for continuing adaptation to an accelerating rate and scope of change in the technological and business environments. As a strategic management tool used within the strategic management process, the BSc has enabled the definition of a road map and markers to effect the desired changes, both within the organization and externally, to redefine customer, supplier, and stakeholder relationships that are key to future organizational success. It is an essential element of the Division's "Journey of Change."

> *"As a strategic management tool used within the strategic management process, the BSc has enabled the definition of a road map and markers to effect the desired change."*

Georgia M. Harrigan leads strategic initiatives in the organizational transformation of the Naval Undersea Warfare Center Division, Newport, Rhode Island. These initiatives include support to the Office of Naval Research, in the area of Technology Insertion Strategies and Knowledge Management initiatives.

Ms. Harrigan has a Masters of Business Administration degree from the University of Rhode Island and an undergraduate degree in Mathematics from Boston College.

Ruth E. Miller, the Director for Strategy and Planning, is responsible for the NUWC and NUWC Division Newport's strategic management processes, which includes strategic planning, goal setting, Performance Measurement, operational planning, resource allocation, and the design and implementation of change strategies. Ms. Miller has a Masters of Business Administration from the University of Rhode Island's Executive MBA Program and an undergraduate degree in Political Science from Tufts University.

Ms. Harrigan and Ms. Miller have been invited to present the NUWC Division Newport experience with the Balanced Scorecard at a number of government and industry conferences.

End Notes

[1] Peter M. Senge, *The Fifth Discipline: Mastering the Art and Practice of the Learning Organization* (New York, NY: Doubleday 1990): 42.

[2] Peter M. Senge, *The Fifth Discipline: Mastering the Art and Practice of the Learning Organization* (New York, NY Doubleday 1990): 44.

[3] J.D. W Morecroft and ID. Sterman, *Modeling for Learning Organizations* (Portland, Oregon: Productivity Press 1994): 52,54.

[4] R.S. Kaplan and DR Norton, *Translating Strategy Into Action: The Balanced Scorecard* (Boston, MA: Harvard Business School Press 1996): 30.

[5] Robert S. Kaplan and David P Norton, "Using the Balanced Scorecard as a Strategic Management System," *Harvard Business Review* (January-February 1995): 75-85.

[6] Chris Argyris, "Teaching Smart People How to Learn," *Harvard Business Review* (May-June 1991): 99-109.

CHAPTER 10

The President's Management Agenda and Balanced Measures at the Internal Revenue Service

The Internal Revenue Service (IRS) has one of the broadest implementations of the balanced scorecard in the federal government. As the commissioner of the IRS embarked on the massive management and leadership task of turning the IRS around, he explained how he was going to modernize the IRS and significantly improve tax service to the American public.

Appearing before the Senate Finance Committee on January 28, 1998, he discussed the new mission of the agency. He stated that the modernized IRS would be guided by five principles. One of these five principles was to use balanced measures of performance. Prior to these changes, the system focused on IRS internal operations and failed to account for the taxpayers' viewpoint and satisfaction. The new balanced measures will take into account: (1) overall compliance by major taxpayer segment, (2) customer satisfaction, (3) employee satisfaction, and (4) continuous improvement.

The next several pages contain an excerpt from the commissioner's statement before the Senate Finance Committee and the goals of the IRS for the year 2000. A very detailed segment on the IRS Balanced Measurement System follows; it is adapted from the Internal Revenue Manual (IRM) 105.4. This application is somewhat unique in the federal government for several reasons. First, the entire agency of more than 100,000 personnel is subject to it. Second, Balanced Measures is one of the five levers of change for modernizing the IRS. Third, the measurement system focuses on what is important to achieve the strategic goals of the IRS. Therefore, the alignment of the measurement system with the mission of the IRS is impressive in the upper echelons of the federal government. Fourth, dollar measures of performance are not part of the measurement system. Finally, there is no ranking of offices.

The next several pages are a document, *Organizational Performance Management and the IRS Balanced Measurement System,* released in June 2000. It presents an update on the IRS Balanced Measurement System.

The IRS Balanced Measurement System elements are customer satisfaction, employee satisfaction, and business results. Business results consist of quality, quantity, and outreach. The IRS material is rich in detail on what the system is and what the system is not. The material provides much insight into why the system is used and what the IRS commissioner is trying to achieve in modernizing the IRS.

The chapter concludes with excerpts from the IRS 2003 performance plan, which show how the IRS is implementing the PMA.

COMMISSIONER'S TESTIMONY

The following material is adapted from *Statement of Charles O. Rossotti, Commissioner of Internal Revenue, Before the Senate Finance Committee, January 28, 1998,* www.irs.gov.

A Modernized IRS

Commissioner of Internal Revenue Charles O. Rossotti has developed a concept of a modernized American tax agency that will deliver significantly improved service to American taxpayers. The modern Internal Revenue Service will focus on the taxpayer's understanding and solving problems from the taxpayer's point of view. The new mission for the agency should be to help people comply with the law and ensure fairness of compliance.

The modernized IRS will be guided by five principles: understand and solve problems from the taxpayer's point of view, expect managers to be accountable, use balanced measures of performance, foster open, honest communications, and insist on total integrity.

The Goals of a Modernized IRS Will Reflect the New Focus on Taxpayers as Customers

Service to each taxpayer. The IRS will continue to make filing easier and provide first quality service to every taxpayer needing help. Taxpayers who may owe additional taxes or cannot pay what they owe will receive prompt, professional, helpful treatment.

Service to all taxpayers. The IRS will serve the American taxpaying public by increasing overall compliance and by increasing the fairness of compliance programs.

Productivity through a quality work environment. The IRS will increase employee job satisfaction and hold agency employment stable while the economy grows and service improves.

Achieving a Modernized IRS Will Require Significant Changes in Five Separate Areas

Revamped business practices. Business practices will be geared toward understanding, solving, and preventing taxpayer problems. Much greater emphasis will be placed on customer education and service. Compliance efforts will be forward looking to prevent most common taxpayer problems and will be geared toward early intervention to keep taxpayers compliant. Compliance tools will be reserved for only those who refuse to comply and will be used more sparingly.

Four operating units. Much of the current national office and regional office structures will be realigned to form management teams, each with end-to-end responsibility for serving a group of taxpayers with like needs. The four groups are: individual taxpayers with wage and investment income, small business and self-employed taxpayers, large business taxpayers, and employee plans/exempt organizations and state and local governments. Each organizational unit will have a tailored set of services to meet the needs of the taxpayers served by that unit. This organizational model, based on similar models in private industry, provides for fewer managerial layers and clear lines of responsibility. Currently, IRS managers are often responsible for administering the entire Internal Revenue Code across the full spectrum of taxpaying customers. Managers in the new business units will be able to focus on the specific needs of the taxpayers they serve.

Balanced measures of performance. Current IRS performance measures are oriented toward IRS internal operations and fail to account for the taxpayers' viewpoint and satisfaction. The new measures will be externally validated and will entail a balanced scorecard tied to the agency's goals. The new measures will take into account: overall compliance by major taxpayer segment, customer satisfaction, employee satisfaction, and continuous improvement.

Management roles with clear responsibility. By organizing around taxpayers with similar needs and issues, the management team for each of the four operating business units will be able to learn a great deal about the particular needs and problems affecting that group and be responsible for resolving those problems. The number of management layers in these new units will be fewer than the current levels of management, facilitating the implementation of new ideas, solutions, and better communications.

New technology. To support this business approach, the IRS is committed to move forward on upgrading and improving its technology through central, professional management, the establishment of common standards, and partnerships between the business units, the information technology professionals, and outside contractors.

The IRS plans to initiate a study to validate the concept for modernization and to plan for the implementation of the final plan. The study will involve extensive consultation with those involved with tax administration in this country both inside and outside the Internal Revenue Service. The IRS hopes to have this study phase done by this summer.

Improve Customer Satisfaction and Customer Service

The Internal Revenue Service (IRS) Customer Service Task Force found that our customers want fair, respectful, and courteous treatment; minimum contact with the IRS; easier, simpler forms and notices; easy access to help; and quick resolution of problems. In order to determine how we are doing, we developed customer satisfaction surveys for the major IRS business lines.

Goals
- Evaluate the results of the Customer Satisfaction Surveys for Fiscal Year (FY) 1999 and utilize these results to create measures of customer satisfaction for IRS and its major business lines as part of the balanced scorecard of performance.
- Minimize contacts with the IRS by rewriting by the end of FY 1999 the most frequently used taxpayer notices under the direction of a "notice gatekeeper."

Currently, the IRS processes over 215 million individual and business tax returns, with most of these transactions taking place on paper. The steady progress of the award-winning TeleFile program and other Electronic Tax Administration (ETA) initiatives gives a hint of the potential of electronic filing: less paper, no mail, an accuracy rate of 99 percent, faster refunds, and satisfied customers.

Goals
- Work toward making electronic filing truly paperless by piloting signature alternatives in FY 1999 and providing electronic payment options to taxpayers starting with Automated Clearing House (ACH) debit payments for balance due returns in FY 1999.
- Support and motivate the more than 85,000 Electronic Returns Originators (EROs) who provide electronic filing products and services to taxpayers and continue IRS' E-FILE campaign to better inform taxpayers and practitioners about the benefits of electronic filing. For FY 1999, increase the number of electronically filed individual returns filed through EROs to 21 million. Increase the number of individuals filing returns by phone (TeleFile) to over 6.6 million, which represents almost 27 percent of the 24.6 million taxpayers that are eligible to use this method of filing.
- If a complete and accurate tax return is filed and a taxpayer is due a refund, the IRS will issue a refund within 21 days if it was electronically filed and within 40 days if filed as a paper return.

Provide Better Telephone Service

The IRS runs one of the nation's most heavily used 800-number operations. In FY 1997, nearly 117 million callers reached the IRS by phone, up from 110.8 million in 1996 and 100.9 million in 1995.

Goals
- To make it easier for taxpayers to reach us, expand telephone service to 24 hours a day, 7 days a week by January 1, 1999. The IRS' goal is to provide this service with an access rate that will range from 85 percent to 90 percent for taxpayers calling the IRS and a tax law accuracy rate of 96 percent. We are currently working to improve our measurements for level of access and tax law accuracy. These measures will be revised and inserted here in the future.

Help Small Businesses

Small businesses are the fastest growing part of the national economy, and currently represent the overwhelming percent of all business tax returns. They are also the nation's largest private employer, accounting for 53 percent of private sector jobs and are the backbone of the wage reporting and withholding system. Everyone stands to gain by making it easier for them to fulfill their tax obligations.

Goals
- By the end of FY 1998, expand TeleFile to let many small businesses use their telephones to file quarterly federal tax returns and report employment taxes. In FY 1999, the IRS expects 1.2 million of an estimated 16 million eligible quarterly forms (Form 941) will be filed through TeleFile.
- To provide specialized products and services, especially in the area of electronic services for small businesses.

THE IRS BALANCED MEASUREMENT SYSTEM

The material that follows is adapted from Internal Revenue Service, "Chapter 2—The IRS Balanced Measurement System: A New Approach to Measuring Organizational Performance," in *Managing Statistics in a Balanced Measurement System,* Washington, D.C., Internal Revenue Service, September 15, 1999, Internal Revenue Manual 105.4.

[105.4] 2.1 (09-15-1999)

Overview

1) This chapter provides an overview of the IRS Balanced Measurement System and outlines how balanced measures, one of the five levers of change for modernizing the IRS, will be used to support a new approach to measuring organizational performance. This new measurement system focuses on what is important to achieve our strategic goals. The aim is to improve those processes that will make a difference. Dollar measures of

performance are not part of Balanced Measures and there will be no ranking of offices. The new organizational review process will be more forward-looking and will focus on actions taken to improve performance, not just the numeric measures results, i.e., the "numbers."

[105.4] 2.2 (09-15-1999)

What Is the IRS Balanced Measurement System?

1) The IRS Balanced Measurement System provides a means to:
   - Communicate organizational priorities, and better define what we need to focus upon as an organization.
   - Guide and motivate performance, and establish a linkage between performance goals and the organizational objectives.
   - Obtain feedback that will help us ascertain how well we are doing in meeting customer and stakeholder expectations and identify areas for improvement.
2) The elements of the Balanced Measurement System are Customer Satisfaction, Employee Satisfaction, and Business Results, with business results being comprised of measures of Quality and Quantity and Outreach. Each element represents an important aspect of the organization's goals and each is of equal importance in carrying out the Service's programs and functions. As such, any activity involving balanced measures, such as setting goals, assessing progress and evaluating results, must consider and address all elements of the Balanced Measurement System. Because some of these elements do not change as rapidly as others or require more time for data collection, the frequency of measures data availability may vary across the three elements. **However, such differences in the frequency of data availability do not reflect differences in priority.**

[105.4] 2.3 (09-15-1999)

Goals of the Balanced Measures Elements

1) The goals of the Balanced Measure elements are:
   - The goal of the Customer Satisfaction element is to provide accurate and professional services to internal and external customers in a courteous, timely manner.
   - The goal of the Employee Satisfaction element is to create an enabling work environment for employees by providing quality leadership, adequate training, and effective support services.
   - The goal of the Business Results element is to generate a productive quantity of work in a quality manner and to provide meaningful outreach to all customers.
2) Balanced Measures will be the measures used by the IRS to assess organizational performance at both the strategic level and the operational level. At the strategic level, such measures will be used to assess our overall performance in delivering on the mission and three strategic goals. Strategic measures would apply to the organization as a whole and to each of the major operating divisions in the modernized IRS. At the operational management level, measures are used to assess the effectiveness of program and service delivery of particular aspects of the organization, such as Customer Service, Collection, or Examination in the current organizational structure.

	Balanced Measures			
	Customer Satisfaction	Employee Satisfaction	Business Results	
			Quality	Quantity
Purpose/Goal	To serve customers professionally	To provide an enabling work environment	To do quality work	To work productively and to engage in proactive outreach activities designed to provide or enhance "top quality service" to all customers

[105.4] 2.4 (09-15-1999)

The Shift to Balanced Measures

1) The Balanced Measurement System has been developed as part of the effort to modernize the IRS and to reflect the Service's priorities, as articulated in the mission statement. This new approach to measurement will help shift the focus of individuals and the organization away from achieving a specific target or number to achieving the overall mission and strategic goals of the IRS.

2) Under the Balanced Measurement System, the IRS will still have and use performance results ("numbers"), but it will use these results much differently than it has in the past. Experience has shown that successful organizations cannot be managed by numbers alone. The numbers are only an indicator of past performance and, when considered by themselves, do not provide a complete picture of what is happening throughout the organization. IRS experience with various programs dealing with numerical performance goals over the past 40 years has shown that placing emphasis on one type of numeric goal can have an adverse impact on other important Service goals, e.g., productivity, quality case work, fair treatment of taxpayers, or employee satisfaction. The challenge given to the IRS through the Restructuring and Reform Act of 1998 was to develop an improved method of measuring performance that protects taxpayer rights, fosters quality service and considers the impact on employees. The Balanced Measurement System represents the IRS' response to that challenge.

[105.4] 2.5 (09-15-1999)

Balanced Measures and the IRS Management Model

1) The Service's management model represents a clear approach to managing our business and is directly linked to our mission, goals, and the Balanced Measurement System. The model is comprised of four elements: Plan, Do, Review, and Revise.

Elements of the Management Model

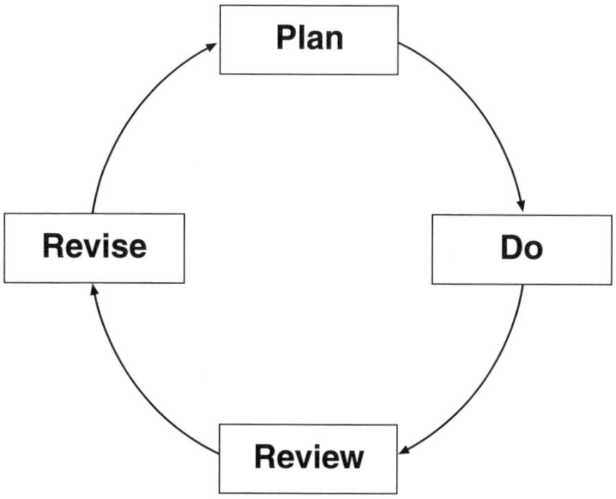

Plan: The "Plan" element "sets the strategy" and communicates areas of emphasis and what we will achieve with available resources. The Plan establishes clear direction, priorities, and goals. Balanced Measures are included in the plan as indicators of where we want to go and will help answer the question, "How will I know if I've achieved that strategy?"

Do: The "Do" element is the "day-to-day management" of activities.

Review: The "Review" element assesses the activities performed during "Do" against the plan. Emphasis will be on actions taken to achieve objectives as each manager "looks behind the numbers." The review focuses on conducting detailed analysis to identify the root causes of changes in performance and to determine appropriate corrective actions.

Revise: In the "Revise" element, measures and actions are modified based upon the reviews.

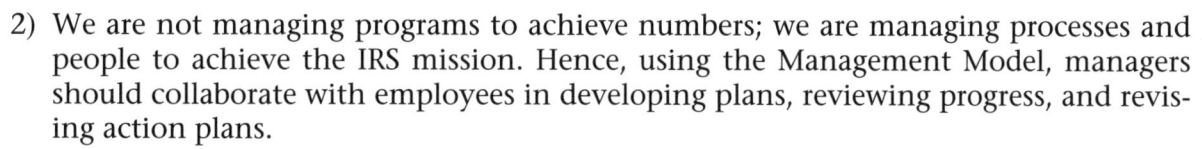

2) We are not managing programs to achieve numbers; we are managing processes and people to achieve the IRS mission. Hence, using the Management Model, managers should collaborate with employees in developing plans, reviewing progress, and revising action plans.

[105.4] 2.6 (09-15-1999)

Using Balanced Measures

1) The new Balanced Measurement System will enable the Service to:
   - Measure how an organizational unit has performed relative to its past performance.
   - Identify areas that need action to help improve performance, taking all the measures—Customer Satisfaction, Employee Satisfaction, and Business Results—into consideration.
   - Align and support various review processes so that there is communication throughout the organization.
   - Begin a dialogue between managers and employees that is focused on discovering and positively impacting the factors that influence performance.
   - Provide input to managerial performance appraisals, not serve as a direct evaluative tool.
2) For an example of the Balanced Measures identified for use in Examination, Collection, and Customer Service, see Exhibit 105.4.2–3.

[105.4] 2.7 (09-15-1999)

Diagnostic Tools

1) The IRS collects a great deal of additional information about programs and services, some of which had been used as performance measures in the past. Under the Balanced

Measurement System, only the approved set of balanced measures—both strategic and operational—will be used to measure organizational performance. NO OTHER INFORMATION OR DATA WILL BE USED AS MEASURES OF ORGANIZATIONAL PERFORMANCE. Indicators that are not designated as "Balanced Measures," hereafter referred to as "diagnostic tools," will be used to help analyze the factors that affect changes in the balanced performance measures in order to "get behind the numbers." The use of diagnostic tools provides a mechanism to analyze factors that influence performance and encourages dialogue about specific actions that can be taken by managers to improve customer satisfaction, employee satisfaction, and business results. No goals or targets will be set for diagnostic tools nor will they be used in individual performance evaluations.

[105.4] 2.7.1 (09-15-1999)

Examples of Diagnostic Tools

2) ... Diagnostic tools can include any type of data that is helpful in understanding what influences and impacts the balanced measures. In addition, it is permissible to use ROTERs as diagnostic tools. **In some cases, data used as a diagnostic tool for one organizational unit (i.e., cycle time) may be used as a balanced measure for a different organizational unit, and vice versa, as long as the measure conforms to the guidelines and restrictions set forth in Chapter 1.** A Reference Guide of Diagnostic Tools has been developed for Examination, Collection and Customer Service and this guidance is included in the respective functional chapters of IRM 105.4. However, the overall framework for the diagnostic tools translates to all functions and the guidance already provided for the Customer Satisfaction and Employee Satisfaction elements is relevant across most functions.

3) Diagnostic Tool Examples
- ROTERs (Records of Tax Enforcement Results)
- Results for individual questions on customer satisfaction surveys
- Results for individual questions on employee satisfaction surveys
- Cycle time
- Employee experience/training/skill levels (i.e., hours of training per employee, workforce mix, average educational attainment of newly hired employees)
- External factors (i.e., tax law, status of the economy)
- Employee absenteeism, turnover rates
- Physical resources
- Work policies
- Return closures per unit of effort
- Inventory level
- Survey rate
- Examined return disposition mix
- Workload mix
- No change rate
- Staffing resources (FTE appropriated, FTE realized, resource utilization)
- Results for individual quality standards/elements
- Wait time/transaction time
- Cost information

[105.4] 2.7.2 (09-15-1999)

How Not To Use the Diagnostic Tools

1) Examples of how not to use the diagnostic tools
   - Do not use diagnostic tools as performance measures
   - Do not set goals or targets for diagnostic tools
   - Do not use as individual performance measures (e.g., in an individual performance evaluation)
   - Do not use diagnostic tools for evaluative comparisons with other units. Use them to understand underlying factors that cause changes in the Balanced Measures

[105.4] 2.3 (09-15-1999)

Setting Goals/Plan Development

1) The IRS' traditional use of performance measures and goals has changed significantly with the introduction of the Balanced Measurement System. Balanced performance measures and goals will no longer be used as stand-alone evaluative tools. Instead, these performance measures and results will serve as indicators of progress the IRS is making organizationally in achieving its strategic goals and mission. They will be used to assess and refine the actions taken to improve customer satisfaction, employee satisfaction, and business results.
2) The establishment of goals and the development of plans must consider and address all elements of the Balanced Measurement System—Customer Satisfaction, Employee Satisfaction, and Business Results.
3) *Individual managerial or employee evaluations will not be directly tied to balanced measures results. Non-managerial evaluations will be based upon critical elements or performance standards as appropriate and the review of work performed. Managerial evaluations will be based on the actions taken in accordance with an agreed upon plan and performance standards. For managers responsible for an organizational component, the quantitative measurements of the balanced measurement system are one of the factors that should inform a performance appraisal. They are not to be used as a stand-alone evaluative tool. (Note: *This guidance does not apply to the "Pipeline" area of Submission Processing where individual quality/quantity information is used consistent with existing work agreements.)
4) There are two types of goals an organization can use to communicate priorities and guide performance, *qualitative and quantitative. Qualitative goals are general in nature and suggest a desired direction but do not establish a numeric target, e.g., "Improve Customer Satisfaction." Quantitative goals, hereafter referred to as numeric goals, are specific and do establish a specific numeric target, e.g., "Improve Customer Satisfaction from 70 Percent to 80 Percent." As the IRS makes the migration to the Balanced Measurement System, the goals used by the organization will tend initially to be more *qualitative than quantitative. As data become available for the new measures and as the organization begins to understand and adapt to the balanced approach, goals will then become more quantitative. (Note: *The term "qualitative" is not the same as the Quality measure in Business Results. "Qualitative" *describes the type of goal, not the type of measure.* For example, a qualitative goal for the Business Results Quality measure might be "Improve the Accuracy of Tax Law Information Provided to Taxpayers." A quantitative/numeric goal for the Business Results Quality measure might be, "Improve the Tax Law Accuracy Rate from 85 Percent to 90 Percent.")

5) Quantitative and numeric goals will be set for the balanced measures at the Service wide level to satisfy requirements of the Government Performance and Results Act and other legislation. They will be used by the Service to report on Agency progress in delivering its tax administration responsibilities. Additional numeric goals will be set no lower than the District/Division level to be used primarily for planning purposes. They cannot and will not be used to directly determine the evaluations of either organizational units or individuals. Qualitative goals, however, can be established down to the group level for use in Action Plans established during the formal plan development process.

6) Performance measures results and diagnostic tools will be used to analyze and track program progress and improvements against both quantitative and qualitative goals. Managers and employees are expected to use this information for planning purposes and for making revisions to actions that have been identified in support of the various goals.

[105.4] 2.9 (09-15-1999)

Using the Numbers

1) The Balanced Measurement System is about changing the way the organization uses numbers; it is not about eliminating the use of numbers. Without numbers, it would be very difficult to effectively manage the Service or gauge progress in meeting our tax administration responsibilities. However, unlike most other organizations, the work performed by the IRS has the potential to substantially impact the lives of citizens as well as their trust in government. As government employees entrusted with ensuring the public good, it is the responsibility of each employee to make certain that taxpayer rights are upheld and protected. For these reasons, the IRS must exercise great care and caution in how it uses measures and "numbers." It cannot support a business and management approach focused only on the achievement of certain numbers and targets. Past behaviors and practices that may have contributed to such an approach have to change. The Balanced Measurement System has been designed to help employees, both managerial and non-managerial, actively engage in an approach to management and measurement at the IRS that is focused on identifying and taking appropriate actions to improve performance and on diagnosing the underlying factors that have influenced organizational outcomes. Following is an explanation of how the use of numbers will change under the Balanced Measurement System.

[105.4] 2.10 (09-15-1999)

Setting Goals

1) Goals for organizational performance measures will be set under the Balanced Measures framework in the areas of Customer Satisfaction, Employee Satisfaction, and Business Results. However, numeric goals will be set only to the levels for which statistically valid results are available for all components of the Balanced Measurement System—currently to the District (Center)/Division level. Numeric goals for each measure should be set in consideration of the other balanced measures and established based on a review of previous year results, the anticipated mix of resources available, and the linkage to organizational priorities and initiatives. At levels below the District (Center)/Division level, only qualitative goals, such as "Improve Case Quality," can be established for the balanced measures and would then include a set of specific actions.

[105.4] 2.11 (09-15-1999)

Communicating/Sharing Goals and Results

1) As data requirements are met for all elements of the Balanced Measurement System, Service wide numeric and qualitative goals will be included in organizational documents that are distributed broadly both within and outside the organization such as the budget submission, the annual performance plan, and the Operations plan. As such, Service wide qualitative goals can be shared and discussed at all levels of the organization with both managerial and non-managerial employees. Service wide numeric goals, however, should only be shared and discussed with managerial and non-managerial employees when there is a legitimate business purpose for sharing such data, such as the organizational planning process. **In any instance when numeric organizational goals are shared, caution must be exercised to ensure that any such discussion does not imply or suggest numeric goals for an individual or organization.**

2) District (Center)/Division qualitative goals can be shared at all levels of the organization. **District (Center)/Division numeric goals, however, should only be shared and discussed with managerial employees at the levels for which there is a legitimate business purpose for sharing such data,** i.e., at the branch level for planning purposes. Furthermore, District (Center) Directors and Division Chiefs must exercise great caution in how they share numeric goals in order to avoid the numbers focused pressures that were felt under previous measurement systems and to ensure that any such discussion does not imply or suggest numeric goals for that branch. Such sharing of goals should be done in a way that *does not* encourage the competitive environment that existed previously among some organizational units whose efforts were directed at achieving numeric targets without carefully considering the impact on all elements of the Balanced Measurement System—Customer Satisfaction, Employee Satisfaction, and Business Results.

3) Determining the appropriateness of sharing a goal depends on whether there is a good business reason for using such a statistic. Consider the following when making this decision:
   - What is the business reason for communicating the Goal?
   - What is the business risk of not providing the Goal?
   - What is the potential undesirable outcome that could come from the misuse of the Goal?
   - What is the risk that the intended recipient would reasonably believe that the communication suggested a quota or goal below the District (Center)/Division level or for an individual? Regarding this last element, consider:
     A) The degree of organizational knowledge and understanding of the intended recipient(s)
     B) The organizational climate at the time and place of the communication
     C) The context in which the communication is to be made
     D) Any guidance on how the Goal can or cannot be used
     E) The manner in which the communication is delivered
     F) The expectation of follow-up with respect to the Goal and the nature of the expected follow-up
     G) The probable internal perception of the communication of the Goal
     H) The probable public perception of the communication of the Goal

4) Under this approach, it would be allowable for a District (Center) Director or Division Chief to share numeric goals with Branch managers for use in the development of action plans as long as that discussion covered all components of the balanced measures and was done as part of the organizational planning process. For example, in any given

year, the organization's need to balance performance across all elements of the measures may require greater emphasis on some elements and lesser emphasis on other elements so as to maintain balance. This information is directly helpful in developing the supporting action plans and determining the types of actions necessary to achieve balance.

5) Once the action plans are completed, results should be looked at periodically because the numbers serve as indicators of the impact that actions are having on organizational performance. The discussions that must follow, however, need to focus on the specific actions, the extent to which it seems they are working and whether there is a need to revise or recommend additional actions. **It would never be appropriate for a District (Center) Director or Division Chief to use any discussion of numeric goals or results as an opportunity to apportion, establish, or suggest additional numeric goals at the branch or group levels.** And, once again, caution must be exercised in any such discussion to ensure that numeric goals for individuals are neither implied nor suggested.

6) *Sharing Data*—In sharing data/results for balance measures, the following restriction applies. Under the Balanced Measurement System, an organizational unit is allowed to see its own results (data) and the results of organizational units at levels above and below (if applicable). An organizational unit is not allowed to see results that are identifiable to other units at the same organizational level. This restriction is intended to help eliminate the competitive environment that existed in some areas among groups, branches, and districts to achieve the highest numeric results without considering the appropriateness of the actions being taken or the impact of those actions on each of the elements of the Balanced Measurement System. **Furthermore, the performance of any one unit at any level of the organization should not be used as a standard by which the performance of any other unit would be evaluated.** The appropriate purpose for sharing balanced measures results and diagnostic tool data among organizational units is in conducting analysis, identifying potential areas for improvement, and exploring best practices.

[105.4] 2.12 (09-15-1999)

Evaluating Performance of an Organizational Unit

1) In evaluating the performance of an organizational unit, the numeric results achieved with any of the balanced measures can be communicated orally and in writing in an organizational review only to the level for which numeric goals were established for all components of the Balanced Measurement System, i.e., currently the District (Center)/Division level. Furthermore, at any time an organizational review is conducted, all components of the Balanced Measurement System must be considered and addressed. The inclusion of numeric results in an organizational review is only to provide a point of reference for a more detailed discussion of the impact of the actions that were taken to help achieve the IRS' mission and strategic goals as translated through the balanced measures. The reason for this restriction is to reduce the chance that the numeric results would be seen as the determining factor behind positive or negative organizational reviews, a situation that might cause the organization to regress to previous practices where organizational goals were inappropriately translated into individual goals.

2) Under this approach, it would be appropriate for an organizational review document for a Region or District (Center)/Division to display the numeric goals and results as long as they were provided in conjunction with a detailed discussion of the actions that

were taken to improve performance and, as appropriate, an explanation of the factors that may have influenced the final outcome. **It would not be appropriate for an organizational review to include specific measures results for organizational units below the District (Center)/Division level because no corresponding quantitative goals would be available from which the basis for such a numeric comparison could be made.** The discussions at those levels must be focused on action plans and related accomplishments, not numeric results.

[105.4] 2.13 (09-15-1999)

Evaluating the Performance of an Individual

1) In evaluating performance of an individual, the numeric results achieved with any of the balanced measures will never directly equate to the evaluation of any individual. Rather, a managerial evaluation must focus on the actions that were taken to improve performance in each area of the balanced measures. The numeric results are helpful only for making an initial assessment of the impact that those actions had on the balanced measures. The reason for this restriction is fundamental to the entire intent of the balanced measures approach and critical to changing behaviors. If individuals are held accountable solely for achieving specific numeric targets, the natural response is to focus attention on the numbers and not actions.

2) Using this guidance, it would be inappropriate for any written evaluation or performance discussion of an individual to reference a specific number, e.g., "John Smith, the Division Chief in District X, met the performance goals established in his performance plan. His office closed 500 more cases than the goal." An appropriate reference might be "John Smith, the Division Chief in District X, met the performance goals established in his performance plan. The agreed upon actions resulted in improvements in customer satisfaction, employee satisfaction, and business results." This overview would then be followed by a more detailed description of the specific actions that were taken toward achieving the goals.

[105.4] 2.14 (09-15-1999)

Day to Day Management

1) While numeric balanced measures goals will not be set below the District (Center)/Division level, numeric results for some of the balanced measures will be reported and statistically valid down to the branch level. The purpose for sharing numeric results at lower levels of the organization is to assist managers in the planning process, determine the impact actions are having on performance, and establish revised plans based on what is learned from the seven step process (see Section 2.15) to "get behind the numbers." Therefore, balanced measures results can be communicated throughout the organization when they are being used for an appropriate business purpose. However, in sharing results, the following restriction applies. Under the Balanced Measurement System, an organizational unit is allowed to see its own results and the results of organizational units at levels above and below (if applicable). An organizational unit is not allowed to see the results of other units at the same organizational level. This restriction is intended to help eliminate the competitive environment that existed in some areas among groups, branches, and districts to achieve the highest numeric results without

considering the appropriateness of the actions being taken or the impact of those actions on each of the elements of the Balanced Measurement System.

2) For example, a Division Chief completes a review of results for the balanced performance measures and observes that the Division is improving in the quality, customer satisfaction, and employee satisfaction areas but is experiencing declines in the quantity area. It would be appropriate for the Division Chief to meet with the Branch Chiefs and engage in a discussion about the performance of that Division and include references to the numeric results that have been achieved at the Division level. To make that discussion useful, the Division Chief could share trend information for the Division level results so that the Branch Chiefs can see the changes in performance for each balanced measure relative to the last data collection period, the previous year, etc. The focus of that discussion, however, must be on the actions taken and on "getting behind the numbers." The Division Chief might then say, "The action plans we established for our division are yielding positive results and are helping us meet our qualitative goals of improving customer satisfaction, employee satisfaction, and quality. However, we are experiencing a decline in quantity in comparison to the last quarter and in comparison to this time period last year even though we have the same mix of staffing and other resources. What do you think may be influencing this balanced measure element and how might we revise our plans to improve performance in this area?" **It would not be appropriate at any level, however, for a manager to distribute spreadsheets containing the balanced measures goals and monthly results to subordinate managers and then direct them to "improve performance."** Also, while the Division Chief would review the results of each branch for management purposes (e.g., to identify areas in which to focus attention, to identify best practices), the Division Chief should not share the numeric results of one branch with the others. If a best practice has been identified, it is allowable and encouraged for the Division Chief to share that practice with the other branches.

[105.4] 2.15 (09-15-1999)

Getting Behind the Numbers

1) Using balanced measures, "getting behind the numbers" is a seven step problem solving process as outlined below. Throughout this process, keep in mind that numbers are only a starting point and that, through analysis, implementation of a revised course of action is the objective.

[105.4] 2.15.1 (09-15-1999)

Receive Data

1) The first step is to obtain data. Data may be obtained from a variety of sources, examples of which are performance measures results (i.e., survey results, Quality Review Results, data on EMSS (Executive Management Support System)), data collected by the Taxpayer Advocate, and Diagnostic Indicators. In other instances, data may have to be locally developed.

[105.4] 2.15.2 (09-15-1999)

Define the Problem

1) In some cases, the problem may be obvious. In other cases, you will need to analyze the data to identify the problem.
2) If you suspect a problem, then ask the question, "What is the real problem?"
3) State the problem in objective terms. An accurately worded problem statement is important for the other steps in the process.
4) A good example is: "Taxpayers do not have a sufficient understanding of IRS procedures." Not: "IRS employees are not explaining our procedures sufficiently to taxpayers."

[105.4] 2.15.3 (09-15-1999)

Determine Potential Causes of the Problem

1) Determining potential causes requires research. Look at all the data available to you. Talk with your employees and peers, and search out potential causes.
2) Assess the possible causes. Don't jump to conclusions about the solution.
3) Evaluate causes and prioritize them based upon their impact on the problem.

[105.4] 2.15.4 (09-15-1999)

Define Courses of Action To Address Identified Causes: Balance Checking Matrix

1) In this step, you will be brainstorming to identify solutions that will address the most significant causes.
2) Think creatively. Write down all possible solutions. *Remember to include "do nothing" as a potential course of action and evaluate the impact of doing nothing in the Balance Checking Matrix.*
3) Once you have identified possible solutions use the Balance Checking Matrix . . . to consider their impact on all three balanced measures.
4) Remember, the Balance Checking Matrix is not a "decision matrix" in that you should not simply select the alternative with the most pluses. It is intended to ensure that each Balanced Measure area is considered. It also helps identify any Balanced Measure area where you may need to do something else to reduce possible negative impacts.

Courses of Action: Balance Checking Matrix

Indicate "+", "−", or "0" impact on measure and provide brief rationale for rating

Form 12302 (7-1999) Cat. No. 28073Z

Proposed Courses of Action (State specific cause being addressed)	Impact on Measure		
	Employee Satisfaction	Customer Satisfaction	Business Results
Course of Action 1			
Course of Action 2			
Course of Action 3			

A) When working through the matrix remember: For each alternative, assign a positive, negative, or neutral rating for the impact this alternative might have on each of the three balanced measures:
   - Positive impact with "+"
   - Negative impact with "–"
   - Neutral or no impact with "0"
B) Write out the justification for each rating. This helps to document your reasoning for subsequent evaluation if necessary. For example, if there is a negative impact on employee satisfaction, what is that negative impact?
C) In selecting a course of action:
   - Consider how the course of action supports the IRS mission and Strategic Goals.
   - Consider which course of action may be the most realistic/least costly to implement.
   - Collaborate with others on making the final selection.

[105.4] 2.15.5 (09-15-1999)

Determine a Course of Action

1) Select a course of action that will have the greatest impact on solving the problem in order to best support the IRS mission and strategic goals. Communicate the decision in terms of how it impacts employee satisfaction, customer satisfaction, and business results to ensure understanding that all three balanced measures were considered.

[105.4] 2.15.6 (09-15-1999)

Implement a Course of Action

1) Create a detailed action plan that identifies the steps to be taken in implementing the course of action.

[105.4] 2.15.7 (09-15-1999)

Track Effectiveness of the Course of Action

1) Your action plan should address how you intend to follow up and monitor the effectiveness of the selected course of action. This step reinforces the Review and Revise aspects of the Management Model.

[105.4] 2.16 (09-15-1999)

How Leaders Can Successfully Use the Balanced Measurement System

1) "What you do" speaks more loudly than what you say. There are many actions that can be taken to demonstrate commitment to Balanced Measures and to create a work environment that equally fosters Employee Satisfaction, Customer Satisfaction, and Business Results.
2) The first place to start is to clearly communicate your commitment by using the Balanced Measures approach in all your dealings with customers and employees. When making business decisions, ask "How will this impact customers, employees, and business results?"

3) Overall:
- Be a role model and let others see you using a balanced approach in decision-making.
- Communicate decisions in terms of how the decision impacts employee satisfaction, customer satisfaction, and business results.
- Mentor others. Help them make balanced business decisions, and assist them in developing plans to improve performance.
- Start rewarding, verbally and in writing, those who model the new behavior.
- Be an advocate with upper-level management for the issues outside of your control. Communicate to employees what you have done.
- Roll up your sleeves and get behind the numbers. Get involved.

[105.4] 2.17 (09-15-1999)

Additional Information on the Balanced Measurement System

1) For additional information about the IRS Balanced Measurement System, refer to the Balanced Measures site on the IRS Insider at: www.hq.irs.gov:80/programs/modern/measures/measures.htm.

Exhibit [105.4] 2–1 (09-15-1999). General Questions and Answers about the Balanced Measurement System.

Q1. How do these organizational measures link to individual front-line appraisals?

Individual appraisals of front-line employees will continue to be based on critical elements for their positions. The critical elements in some areas will or have been adjusted to more closely reflect the Service's new priorities as reflected in the Balanced Measures. All employee standards have been updated to reflect the retention standard for all employees that require the "fair and equitable treatment of taxpayers." Overall, evaluations of individual employees must be based on a review of actual work performed as judged against elements and standards and with consideration given to the specific facts and circumstances of each case.

Q2. How do these organizational measures link to individual manager appraisals?

The balanced organizational measures will be inputs to individual manager performance appraisals, but the focus will be on the actions taken to improve performance, not on the numbers. For FY 2000, the critical job elements for managerial employees are being updated to incorporate the balanced measurement system objectives.

Q3. What guarantees are there in the process to prevent managers from relying on "numbers"?

Managers will be expected to look not just at the measurement results but at the facts, circumstances, and specific situations in any area that the measures indicate warrant attention. Managerial expectations have been created to support this change and additional steps to reinforce the new approach include changes to the review processes and the individual performance management processes.

Q4. Will we compare our numerical results against prior years to assess progress?

Measurement results from 1 year will be compared with prior year results to assess progress. This does not mean that a manager's appraisal is determined by how much measures results change over the year. The results can change for numerous reasons, many of which are not under the control of the manager. The actions taken by the manager to improve performance will be what influences the manager's appraisal.

Q5. Why the change?

To better serve taxpayers, we needed to modernize the IRS, including our management practices. The Commissioner has articulated a new vision and mission. This vision focuses on three high-level goals: service to each taxpayer, service to all taxpayers, and productivity through a quality work environment.

Q6. How will we measure Customer Satisfaction?

The Customer Satisfaction measure is based on the customers' perceptions of the service they receive, as obtained through processes such as phone surveys or mail surveys. Survey responses to specific questions will provide the basis for identifying areas with the greatest potential for improvement.

Q7. How will we measure Employee Satisfaction?

There will be two surveys: (1) A Corporate Climate Survey of a sample of IRS employees to check on top level issues and test specific topical issues, e.g., the use of measures, and (2) An Employee Satisfaction Survey available to all IRS employees that will comprise the Employee Satisfaction Score.

Q8. How will we measure Quality in Business Results?

Quality will generally be based on independent review of closed cases or ongoing casework using many of the existing systems, e.g., EQMS—Examination Quality Measurement System, CQMS—Collection Quality Measurement System, CQRS—Centralized Quality Review System.

Q9. How will we measure Quantity in Business Results?

The quantity area of Business Results will consist of outcome neutral measures of production and resource data, such as the number of cases closed or work items completed, as well as a measure of customer outreach efforts.

Q10. When will we have balanced measures for all parts of the IRS?

The development and implementation of balanced measures is [sic] being completed in phases. In Phase I, completed in early 1999, the IRS focused on much of Examination, Collection, and Customer Service. In Phase II, taking place throughout 1999, the focus is on those components of the modernized IRS that are scheduled to roll-out first. In Phase III, which will get underway in late 1999 and early 2000, the remaining components not worked in Phases I & II will be addressed. Until balanced measures are developed across all parts of the IRS, managers and employees can continue to use existing performance measures as appropriate and keeping in mind the overall balanced approach set forth in this chapter.

Exhibit [105.4] 2–2 (09-15-1999). Glossary of Terms.

ACTION PLANS

Specific tactics/actions identified in each work unit, below the division level, to achieve and support the IRS' Business Plans and Operations Plans.

BALANCED MEASURES

Indicator of results for two or more measures considered of equal importance.

BUSINESS PLANS

Identifies major actions to be taken by a Region, Executive Officer for Service Center Operations (EOSCO), Chief, Customer Service Field Operations (CCSFO), District or Service Center in support/implementation of the Operations Plan and Strategic Goals.

BUSINESS RESULTS MEASURES

Indicators of the quality and quantity of work performed.

CUSTOMER

Any internal or external person or entity to whom you provide services.

CUSTOMER SATISFACTION MEASURE

An indicator of the level of overall satisfaction with service provided by the IRS as perceived by internal or external customers.

DIAGNOSTIC TOOLS

Indicators that are not designated as "Balanced Measures." They are used to discover the factors impacting changes in the Balanced Measures.

EMPLOYEE SATISFACTION MEASURE

An indicator of the level of overall satisfaction with the work environment as perceived by employees.

GOAL

A desired performance objective can be qualitative or quantitative (numeric).

IRS BALANCED MEASURES

Indicators of organizational performance for Customer Satisfaction, Employee Satisfaction, and Business Results.

OPERATIONS PLAN

A high level plan developed annually by the Chief Operations Officer and the Assistant Commissioners. It defines the priorities and identifies the actions that each Assistant Commissioner area will focus on for the upcoming year. The Operations Plan is the focus for the development of Business Plans and Action Plans.

ORGANIZATIONAL MEASURES

Indicators of the progress the IRS is making in achieving its strategic goals and mission.

OUTCOME NEUTRAL

Production or resource data that does not contain information regarding the tax enforcement result reached in any case, e.g., number of cases closed, level of service provided, assistance, and outreach efforts undertaken.

PERFORMANCE MEASURE

An indicator of results for an activity, process, organization, or program.

PERFORMANCE MEASURES RESULT

Numeric outcome of a measure for an activity, process, organization, or program.

QUALITY MEASURE

A numeric indicator of the extent to which completed work meets prescribed standards.

QUANTITY MEASURE

An indicator of outreach efforts, outcome neutral productivity, and resource utilization.

STAKEHOLDERS

Groups or individuals who have a vested interest in an organization. They can be internal or external to IRS.

STRATEGIC GOAL

A strategic goal defines how an organization will carry out its mission over a period. It is expressed in a manner that allows a future assessment to be made on whether the goal was or is being achieved. The goal may be of a programmatic, policy, or management nature.

Exhibit [105.4] 2–3 (09-15-1999). Balanced Measures for Examination, Collection, and Customer Service.

	Quality	Customer Satisfaction — Quantity* (Volume/Mix)	Employee Satisfaction	Business Results	
Examination Measures	Examination transaction survey score	Examination employee satisfaction survey score	EQMS score % Cases overage	Number of returns closed (by audit category) –Individual < $100K –Individual > $100K –Individual with schedule C or F –Business < $10 M –Business > $10 M Time spent on outreach (work in progress)	

	Customer Satisfaction	Employee Satisfaction	Business Results	
Quality	Quantity* (Volume/Mix)			
Collection Measures	Collection transaction survey score	Collection employee satisfaction score	CQMS Score % Cases overage % Offers in compromise processed within 6 months	Number of cases closed –TDA –TDI Time spent on outreach (work in progress)
Customer Service Measures	Toll Free –Transaction survey score	Toll Free –Employee satisfaction survey score	Toll Free –Quality (Tax Law and Accounts) –Timeliness	Toll Free –Level of service –Adherence to scheduled hours –Time spent on education/outreach (work in progress)
	ACS –Transaction survey score	ACS –Employee satisfaction survey score	ACS –Quality –Timeliness –Customer relations –Overage inventory	ACS –Level of service –Time spent on outreach (work in progress)
	Service Center Exam –Transaction survey score	Service Center Exam –Employee satisfaction survey score	Service Center Exam –Exam/ASFR Quality –Overage inventory	Service Center Exam –Exam/ASFR closures –Time spent on outreach (work in progress)

ORGANIZATIONAL PERFORMANCE MANAGEMENT AND THE IRS BALANCED MEASUREMENT SYSTEM

The material that follows is adapted from the Office of Organizational Performance Management, Internal Revenue Service, Department of the Treasury, *Organizational Performance Management and the IRS Balanced Measurement System,* June 2000, Publication 3561 (Rev. 6-2000), Catalog Number 28908N. It can be accessed on the IRS Web site (www.irs.gov/prod/news/measures.html).

ORGANIZATIONAL PERFORMANCE MANAGEMENT AND THE IRS BALANCED MEASUREMENT SYSTEM

The IRS will use balanced measures, comprised of both output and outcome measures[1], at both the strategic level and the operational level to measure organizational performance. At the individual level, critical elements and critical performance expectations that support and align with the IRS mission and balanced measures approach will be the basis by which employees are evaluated.

In September 1999, a Balanced Measures Regulation was issued to formally establish the IRS new performance management system. The issuance of the regulation, which followed a public comment period, sets forth the structure for measuring organizational and employee performance within the IRS. A copy of the regulation is available on the IRS Insider and the IRS Digital Daily (www.irs.gov).

At the strategic level, measures will be used to assess overall performance in delivering on the mission and three strategic goals. Strategic measures will apply to the organization as a whole and to each of the major operating and functional divisions in the modernized IRS.

At the operational management level, balanced measures are used to assess the effectiveness of program and service delivery of particular components of the organization.

The IRS has translated its mission into three strategic goals of service to each taxpayer, service to all taxpayers,

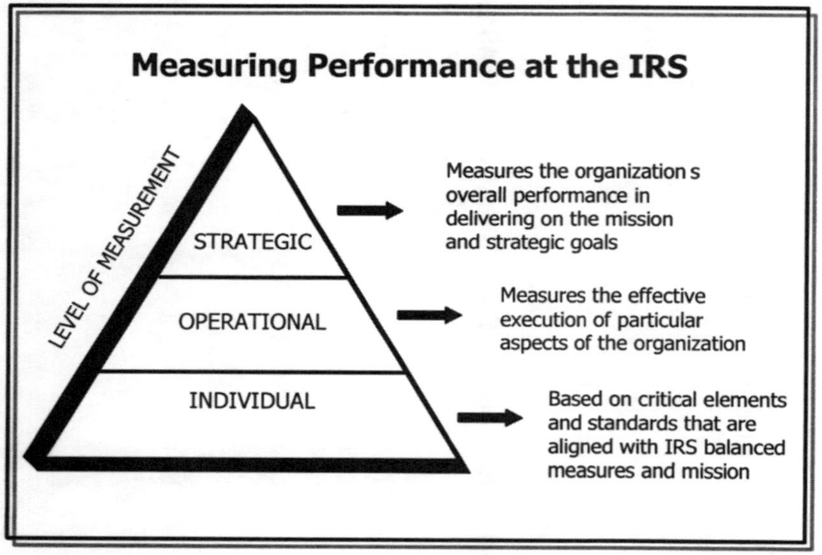

Measuring Performance at the IRS

- **STRATEGIC** — Measures the organization's overall performance in delivering on the mission and strategic goals
- **OPERATIONAL** — Measures the effective execution of particular aspects of the organization
- **INDIVIDUAL** — Based on critical elements and standards that are aligned with IRS balanced measures and mission

LEVEL OF MEASUREMENT

The IRS Balanced Measurement System has been developed as part of the effort to modernize the IRS and to reflect the Service's priorities, as articulated in the IRS mission. This new approach to measurement is intended to help shift the focus of individuals and the organization away from achieving a specific target or number to achieving the overall mission and strategic goals of the IRS.

To help ensure balance, each of the three components of balanced measures — customer satisfaction, employee satisfaction, and business results — will be carefully considered by the IRS when setting organizational objectives, establishing goals, assessing progress and results, and evaluating individual performance.

---

[1] Output measures reflect units produced or services produced by a program, e.g., cases closed, calls answered. Outcome measures reflect results – the changes or accomplishments that are achieved, e.g., customer satisfaction, employee satisfaction, quality.

The President's Management Agenda and Balanced Measures at the Internal Revenue Service   235

and productivity through a quality work environment. These three strategic goals are supported by the balanced measures as depicted in the next table. This framework will assist the IRS in describing how programs and initiatives tie to achievement of the mission and goals as reflected in improvements in the measurement results.

Relationship of Strategic Goals to Balanced Measures

STRATEGIC GOAL	BALANCED MEASURE
Objectives	
Service to Each Taxpayer • Make filing easier • Provide first quality service to each taxpayer needing assistance • Provide prompt, professional, helpful treatment to taxpayers in cases where additional taxes may be due	Customer Satisfaction
Service to All Taxpayers • Increase Fairness of Compliance • Increase Overall Compliance	Business Results (Quality, Quantity & Outreach)
Productivity through a Quality Work Environment • Increase employee job satisfaction • Hold agency employment stable while economy grows and service improves	Employee Satisfaction

OPERATIONAL LEVEL BALANCED MEASURES FRAMEWORK

Service to Each Taxpayer/Customer Satisfaction

The service to each taxpayer goal is measured from the customer's point of view. The goal of the Customer Satisfaction element is to provide accurate and professional services to internal and external customers in a courteous, timely manner. The customer satisfaction goals and accomplishments of operating units within the IRS are determined on the basis of customer feedback collected via methods such as questionnaires, surveys and other types of information gathering mechanisms. Information to measure customer satisfaction for a particular work unit is gathered from a sample of the customers served. Customers are permitted to provide information requested for these purposes anonymously. Customers may include individual taxpayers, organizational units or employees within the IRS and external groups affected by the services performed by the IRS operating unit.

Service to All Taxpayers / Business Results

The service to all taxpayers goal is gauged through a combination of quality, quantity and outreach measures. The goal of the Business Results elements is to generate a productive quantity of work in a quality manner and to provide meaningful outreach to all customers. The business results measures consist of numerical scores determined under the elements of Quantity and Quality.

- The quantity measures, which are to be used in conjunction with the quality, customer satisfaction, and employee satisfaction measures[2], provide information about the volume and mix of work products and services produced by IRS operating units and consist of outcome-neutral production and resource data. Examples include the number of cases closed, work items completed, customer education, assistance and outreach efforts undertaken, hours expended and similar inventory, workload and staffing information.

---

[2] The Balanced Measures Regulation restricts the use of quantity measures for organizational units with employees who exercise judgement with regard to enforcement of the tax law. Quantity measures may be used to set organizational goals or to evaluate organizational performance in these areas only if done in conjunction with the other elements of the Balanced Measurement System. (See section 801.2(b) of the Regulation.)

- The quality measures provide information about how well IRS operating units developed and delivered their products and services. The quality measures are determined based upon a comparison of a sample of work items handled by certain functions or organizational units against a prescribed set of standards that incorporate the customers point of view. Additional quality measures will gauge the accuracy and timeliness of the products and services provided.

Productivity Through a Quality Work Environment / Employee Satisfaction

The productivity through a quality work environment goal is assessed via measures of employee satisfaction. The goal of the Employee Satisfaction element is to create an enabling work environment for employees by providing quality leadership, adequate training, and effective support services. The employee satisfaction ratings to be given within the IRS are determined on the basis of information gathered via survey. All employees have an opportunity to provide information regarding employee satisfaction under conditions that guarantee them anonymity.

ADDITIONAL LINKAGES BETWEEN BALANCED MEASURES AND STRATEGIC GOALS

The relationship of operational performance measures to strategic goals as described above is intended to help illustrate the primary linkages between the measures and goals. The IRS recognizes that secondary linkages between the measures and the three goals also exist. For example, efforts to improve employee satisfaction in support of the productivity through a quality work environment goal often result in improvements to customer service thereby enhancing the *service to each taxpayer* goal. Similarly, quality efforts that improve the timeliness and accuracy of work performed not only result in improved business results and *service to all taxpayers* but can also result in improved levels of customer satisfaction and better *service to each taxpayer.*

USE OF ENFORCEMENT DATA

In addition to the balanced measures, the IRS collects a great deal of other information about programs and services that is useful for purposes of tracking, analyzing and reflecting the factors that affect overall performance. Some of this information, such as dollars collected, dollars assessed, liens filed, and seizures executed, are *records of*

Performance Assessment Framework

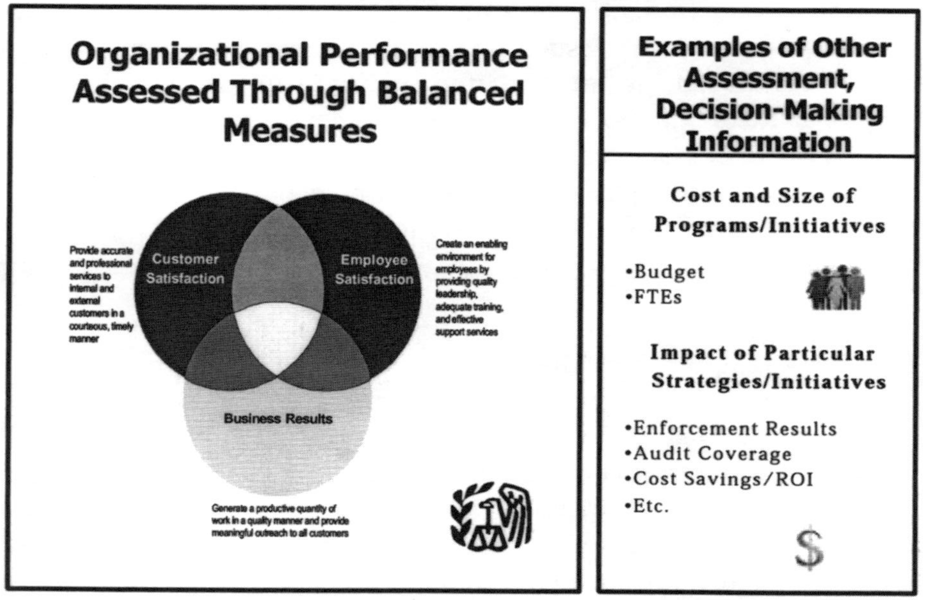

Organizational Performance Assessed Through Balanced Measures

- Employee Satisfaction: Create an enabling environment for employees by providing quality leadership, adequate training, and effective support services
- Customer Satisfaction: Provide accurate and professional services to internal and external customers in a courteous, timely manner
- Business Results: Generate a productive quantity of work in a quality manner and provide meaningful outreach to all customers

Examples of Other Assessment, Decision-Making Information

Cost and Size of Programs/Initiatives
- Budget
- FTEs

Impact of Particular Strategies/Initiatives
- Enforcement Results
- Audit Coverage
- Cost Savings/ROI
- Etc.

tax enforcement results which the organization is prohibited by law from using to evaluate or to impose or suggest production quotas or goals for any employee.

Therefore, in the IRS Balanced Measurement System, enforcement statistics are not measures of performance at either the operational or strategic level. Enforcement statistics are used, however, at a strategic level to make projections for and to assess the effectiveness of particular strategies and initiatives. Such information is intended to help illustrate the potential impact of resource and strategy decisions on factors that affect overall compliance, such as audit coverage.

DEVELOPING BALANCED MEASURES

At the Strategic Level

As described earlier, measures at the strategic level are meaningful for the service as a whole and for each of the operating and functional divisions. They will be comprised of measures such as burden, compliance, overall customer satisfaction and employee satisfaction, and productivity. Taxpayer burden and voluntary compliance, for example, are among the most important outcomes affected by IRS activities for which measurements at the strategic level are critical but also inherently difficult to develop. The challenge is in identifying valid and reliable ways to measure them.

To date, the balanced measures effort has focused primarily on the development of measures at the operational level. However, work began in FY 1999 and will accelerate in FY 2000 to develop strategic measures for roll-out in the modernized IRS during FY 2001. Once fully implemented, strategic measures will be used by the IRS in its annual performance plan at the Strategic Management Level and for each Operating Division and Functional Division.

At the Operational Level

The IRS is utilizing a four-step process for the development of balanced measures in each of its Operating Divisions and Functional Divisions. The total duration from start to finish of this process varies depending on the availability and usability of existing measures as well as the complexity and related system requirements of the final set of measures selected.

In Phase I, Conceptualization and Problem Definition, the measures team is convened, a charter and timeline is prepared, and a baseline of current measures, if applicable, is completed. The teams are comprised of national office and field IRS personnel and union representatives. In Phase II, Development, the team identifies a proposed set of measures for each element of the balanced measurement framework customer satisfaction, employee satisfaction, and business results. During this phase, best practice

Balanced Measures Development Process

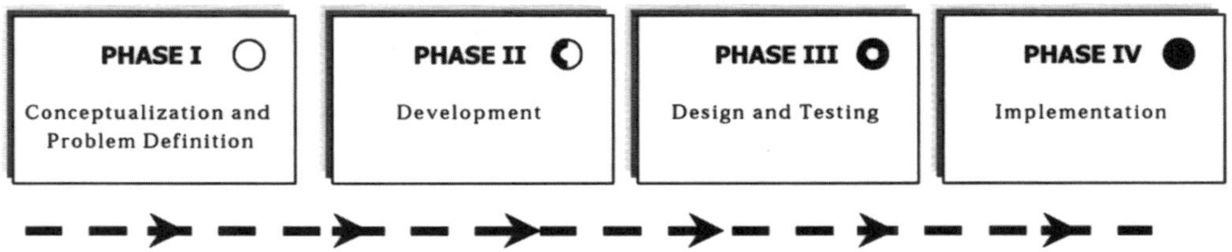

PHASE I	PHASE II	PHASE III	PHASE IV
Conceptualization and Problem Definition	Development	Design and Testing	Implementation

238   PRESIDENT'S MANAGEMENT AGENDA

reviews are conducted and a pro/con analysis is applied to each proposed measure. Phase II concludes upon approval of the proposed set of measures by the IRS Organizational Performance Management Steering Committee. For purposes of obtaining additional feedback on the proposed measures, information is also shared with external stakeholders and others via press releases and the IRS Digital Daily web site. In Phase III, Design and Testing, the approved measures are thoroughly tested and revised as necessary. An implementation plan is prepared for the final phase, Implementation. During implementation Phase IV, any management information system requirements and cost and personnel needs are resolved. Prior to rolling out the measures, a communication and training plan is completed and ownership of the measures is clearly established in the relevant Operating or Functional Division.

Exempt and Government Entities[3], Large and Mid-Size Business, Appeals, Taxpayer Advocate Service, Research, Statistics of Income, and additional Customer Service product lines. These measures are undergoing final design and implementation. Other measures teams underway in CY 1999 that are expected to have approved balanced measures in early CY 2000 include Information Systems, Criminal Investigation, Counsel, Submission Processing, and Agency Wide Shared Services. All remaining areas, including Small Business/Self-Employed and the Wage & Investment Operating Divisions, will commence measures development in CY 2000. For the Small Business/Self Employed and Wage and Investment Operating Divisions, much of the balanced measures work that has already been completed for the Examination, Collection, and Customer Service functions will be applicable. The Measures Development Progress table reports on progress for the Operating Divisions and Functional Divisions.

Measures Development Progress

Large and Mid-Size Business	●
Tax Exempt and Government Entities	●
Small Business and Self Employed*	○
Wage and Investment*	○
Information Systems	◐
Agency-Wide Shared Services	◐
Taxpayer Advocate Service	●
Criminal Investigation	◐
Appeals	◐
Counsel	◐
CORE	◐

KEY:
○ Not yet started or Phase I
◐ Phase II, Development Underway
◑ Phase III, Testing and Final Development
● Phase IV, Implementation   As of 12/99

*Much of the balanced measures development work already completed in Examination, Collection and Customer Service will be transferable and applicable to these Operating Divisions.

PROGRESS UPDATE

The IRS completed balanced measures development for the Examination, Collection and three Customer Service product lines in calendar year (CY) 1998. In CY 1999, additional balanced measures were approved for Tax

---
[3] Balanced measures were approved for most of the Tax Exempt portion of TE/GE. Additional measures work is yet to be done for the Coordinated Exam Program, Customer Account Services, and Government Entities.

6

The transition from the old ways of doing business to the new, modernized IRS will take time. The measures reflected in this document will help move the IRS in that direction and bring the organization a step closer to a truly balanced framework of measurements at the strategic and operational levels.

As the balanced measures are tested and used throughout the organization, lessons will be learned and refinements in the measures may be necessary. However, the basic concept of what needs to be measured customer satisfaction, employee satisfaction, and business results will remain stable and firmly grounded in the organizational design principles of the modernized IRS.

SUMMARY

In moving forward with the creation of a new organization focused on providing America's taxpayers top quality service by helping them understand and meet their tax responsibilities and by applying the tax law with integrity and fairness to all, it is essential that the IRS change how it measures organizational performance. Key to this change is the development of new, balanced measures that are aligned with the mission and strategic goals of the new IRS.

Management Challenge or High Risk Area: *Human Capital*

Issue

The GAO considers strategic human capital management as a high-risk area for the government, and the President's FY 2001 budget has added human capital to its list of Priority Management Objectives. Inadequate attention to strategic human capital management has created a government-wide risk of eroding the capacity of some agencies to perform their missions. Like many other government agencies, the IRS faces a range of serious personnel management issues, ranging from recruiting, training, and retaining employees to problems associated with the IRS' recent reorganization and modernization efforts. During FY 2001, the IRS struggled with a continuing need to properly staff, train, and provide adequate tools for employees.

Actions Planned or Underway

Changes to IRS' personnel management practices were key elements of the much larger restructuring of the IRS. The new flexibilities and authorities provided under RRA '98 have enabled IRS to attract, motivate, and retain the kind of employees needed to meet the challenge of modernizing the IRS, and to sustain long-term improved performance. Great progress has been made in using new flexibilities –as well as the creative use of existing authorities - to introduce streamlined, customer-focused personnel management policies, programs, and strategies that have paved the way for the overall IRS modernization program. A Workforce Transition Strategy using state-of-the-art techniques to match and shape the workforce to fit IRS' new organization was developed to provide advice, guidance, support, and oversight to all business units undergoing reorganization and/or restructuring. A competency-based evaluation and placement process used for filling GS-14 and 15 managers positions was developed. A Senior Manager Pay Band was established to more effectively address grade imbalances and to universally increase individual and organizational performance thresholds by ensuring that only truly outstanding managers advance to the top of the pay band.

Recruitment and relocation bonuses and retention allowances programs were redesigned to better serve the agency's efforts to recruit, relocate and retain employees in key positions. A group of employees was identified to serve as full-time recruiters for the next 18 to 24 months. Each recruiter has been assigned specific colleges and universities with whom they will establish an on-going relationship. A Human Resources Investment Fund (HRIF) was implemented to provide monetary assistance for training and education to enhance individual employee and organizational growth. Employee critical job elements and performance standards were aligned with our Service-wide Balanced Measurement System and five critical job elements common to all of our occupations for appraising individual employee performance were created.

The IRS will continue to address Human Capital issues through the following actions:

- Use the Senior Manager Pay Band system to more effectively allocate salary resources to promote and encourage individual and organizational excellence.
- Expand the pay band system to all front-line and mid-level managers.

- Expand the competency-based evaluation and placement process for mid and top-level managers, to include grade 12 and 13 Group Managers.
- Evaluate the pilot executive bonus system, which allows executives to determine a target bonus percentage for annual performance bonuses at the beginning of the performance year, for possible application to the rest of the executives in the IRS.
- Continue to offer an extensive array of Web- and computer-based training for employees via the Internet, Intranet, and by CD-ROM covering subjects such as communications, customer service, project management, finance, accounting, and leadership.
- Continue to provide an extensive array of executive development training activities that prepare our participants for top-level leadership positions.
- Continue to encourage executives establish relationships with either their Alma Mater or schools in their local areas.
- Continue partnerships with employee organizations to help recruiters establish relationships with community-based organizations.
- Continue the state-of-the-art advertising campaign that was established to promote the IRS as an employer of choice.
- Design a personnel demonstration project to improve the management of IRS' executive corps by introducing two types of executive-level positions, Senior Executive and Senior Professional. The dual-track executive categories will also allow us to better target training and education resources to the two distinct type of leaders, and give more flexibility in tailoring personnel management programs and strategies that best meet the needs of each group.
- Rehire retired federal executives on a part-time basis and allow them to receive the full combined value of their salaries and annuities.
- Make competitive and non-competitive term appointments in the Senior Executive Service for up to five years.
- Place executives hired from outside the Government in the eight hour annual leave accrual category, and allow them to receive advanced leave credits immediately upon appointment.
- Increase the maximum performance bonus that can be given to executives to 30% of base pay.
- Establish performance appraisal rating levels that are the same as those used for our other managers, and introduce a multi-year performance appraisal cycle.

FY 2003 IRS Annual Performance Plan
February 4, 2002

Major Management Challenges and
High Risk Areas

SA-22

Management Reforms

The President's Management Plan includes five government-wide initiatives: Strategic Management of Human Capital, Budget and Performance Integration, Competitive Sourcing, Improve Financial Management and Expand Electronic Government. In addition, OMB has identified four IRS management programs they believe are in most need of reform: Tax Compliance Measurement, Electronic Filing, Work Process Modernization and Technology Modernization. Progress toward addressing these reforms is addressed through IRS' existing program activities. Measures of IRS program activities serve to show progress in addressing the management reforms. Below is a cross-walk showing the relationship between the management reform and the program activities.

Management Reform	Pre-Filing	Filing	Compliance	Research & SOI	Information Services	Information Services Improvement Projects	Business Systems Modernization	EITC	Shared Services	General Management & Administration
Strategic Management of Human Capital										X
Budget and Performance Integration										X
Competitive Sourcing										X
Improve Financial Performance										X
Expanding Electronic Government		X					X			
IRS Tax Compliance Measurement				X				X		
IRS Electronic Filing		X					X			
IRS Work Process Modernization		X	X						X	
IRS Technology Modernization							X			

Table: Management Reform Cross-walk to Program Activity

Below are brief reports on the status of these reform efforts.

Strategic Management of Human Capital

IRS developed a five-year restructuring plan that involves a massive effort to establish a new mission and focus, build a new organizational structure, and streamline business practices. IRS is currently in the fourth year of the five-year restructuring initiative that has shifted the IRS from a geographically based organizational structure to one based on four customer-oriented operating divisions that correspond to key groups of taxpayers. The original five-year plan is being extended through FY 2004 to cover a major redesign of IRS' extensive call site operations, which will increase program specialization and improve the quality of assistance to telephone-based customers.

Organizational and mission changes have made IRS more "citizen-centered" by reducing the number of management layers, and freeing up personnel resources for redeployment to front-line customer support activities. The restructuring effort has removed five management layers, and moved decision making much closer to the customer. Although the full effect of these changes will take place over many years, IRS has already realized the following tangible benefits:

- Decreased the number of management layers by 50 percent in major field organizations.
- Reduced the number of mid- and top-level managers by approximately 500, or 25 percent.
- Moved aggressively to fill over 3,500 new front-line tax administration and customer service positions.
- Redeployed or voluntarily separated over 3,000 employees (mostly in staff/overhead positions) surplused by the restructuring.
- Shifted emphasis from compliance to pre-filing activities as a way to more effectively utilize personnel resources.
- Introduced a number of new personnel management flexibility's and tools to accommodate the new streamlined, flatter organizational structure, and to improve staff quality and performance.

In the area of human resources management, the IRS has adopted a strategic and systematic approach that includes a more sophisticated level of workforce planning, and an enhanced IRS- wide commitment to value and invest in its employees. A fundamental component of this new strategy is to view employees as Human Capital, a strategic asset to be enhanced. In this regard, the IRS has introduced a life-cycle management approach to human resources management that emphasizes the long-term value of its employees, and focuses on providing them the training, tools, structures, incentives and accountability to work effectively in the restructured IRS. This approach is future oriented, relies on workforce planning, involves investment, creates a performance-oriented culture, and aligns human resources management with the core IRS mission.

On August 17, 2001, IRS submitted its Report on IRS Restructuring to Treasury. This report provides a more detailed accounting of IRS' restructuring efforts and will be used by Treasury as part of the Departmental response to the Office of Management and Budget (OMB) request, pursuant to OMB Bulletin 01-07, for a five year restructuring plan.

Budget and Performance Integration

IRS has implemented and is refining a strategic planning, budgeting and performance management process designed to support management in determining strategic goals; establishing measures and targets; determining resource levels; and evaluating results. Performance measures are a critical component of the process. IRS has designated 73 critical operational performance measures from hundreds of existing measures. They are currently the best available measures for assessing progress towards accomplishing the strategic goals and objectives. In addition, they are balanced to emphasize customer satisfaction, employee satisfaction and business results

IRS is developing strategic measures of customer satisfaction, burden, payment compliance, filing compliance, reporting compliance, employee satisfaction and productivity. These measures will more clearly assess IRS success in achieving its mission, goals and objectives, and will be supported by the operational measures.

IRS is developing a pilot for the integration of budgetary resources and performance results for the Customer Service program. The IRS selected its toll-free program as a performance based budgeting pilot. The following chart shows quality and productivity program goal improvements for FY 2000 through FY 2003 for the toll-free program.

TOLL FREE QUALITY AND PRODUCTIVITY PROGRAM GOAL IMPROVEMENTS

MEASURE	FY 2000	FY 2001 W/O REFUND	FY 2001 WITH REFUND	FY 2002	FY 2003
CUSTOMER SATISFACTION
Customer Satisfaction	3.46	3.58	3.58	3.56 (SB/SE) 3.49 (W&I)	3.63 (SB/SE) 3.49 (W&I)
QUANTITY
Automated Calls Answered	49.7M	63M	68M	75M	66M
Assistor Calls Answered	32.9M	31M	32.5M	33.7M	36.8M
Assistor Services Provided	33.5M	34.5	35.8M	37.5M	40.8M
CSR Level of Service	59%	62%	55%	71.50%	76.30%
QUALITY
Tax Law	73%	74%	74%	78%	82%
Accounts Tax Law	60%	63%	63%	72%	78%

Note 1: Assistor Services Provided equals one call answered by each assistor. This is not true of Assistor Calls Answered because one call can be handled by more than one assistor.

Note 2: Began implementation of the screener strategy in FY 2000, but not all calls answered by screeners were captured in the Assistor Services Provided.

Competitive Sourcing

Federal agencies are required to complete public-private or direct conversion competitions for activities performed by the government that are listed on agencies Federal Activities Inventory Reform Act inventories. Agencies are to have completed action on 15 percent of the FTE listed on the FAIR Act inventory by the end of FY 2003. IRS has provided the Department of Treasury an Inventory of Commercial Activities and a separate report on inherently governmental positions.

In support of the 5% FY 2002 goal, the following areas will potentially be included in IRS's competitive sourcing program:

- A seat management pilot trial that provides for the periodic refreshment of desktops and laptops and the encompassing workstations.

- IRS' three Area Distribution Centers that specialize in the distribution of tax forms and publications and internal use printed material.

- Selected components of IRS' Agency Wide Shared Services organization that will be determined later.

At this time, IRS has not established firm targets for FY 2003 and beyond. However, IRS is exploring the potential to pursue further managed competition in the information technology area and the shared services area. Potential targets will be identified and assessed during the next three to six months.

Improve Financial Performance

IRS' most significant problems related to erroneous payments are found in the Earned Income Tax Credit (EITC) program. EITC is a refundable tax credit for low-income workers. Taxpayers receive this credit by filing a Federal Income Tax Return. Based on internal and external studies, IRS has determined that significant numbers of taxpayers claim the credit but do not meet the eligibility requirements. The reasons for these overclaims range from taxpayers making errors due to the complexity of the law to individuals who file false returns with bogus W-2s to claim the credit.

To address erroneous payments in the EITC program, IRS:

- Revised all taxpayer assistance products to emphasize determination of eligibility. The Form 1040 series instructions have been revised to enhance taxpayers' ability to determine eligibility.

- Implemented all statutory authority to correct returns with incorrect EITC claims when these errors can be determined during processing of returns. Research done by IRS indicates that taxpayers generally do not repeat these errors in subsequent year filings.

- Implemented a 'pre-refund' examination process. For those errors, which can only be corrected through deficiency procedures, IRS has begun selecting returns during the filing season and holding any refund until the completion of the examination.

- Developed a database that uses third party information such as child custody records to determine which returns to select for examination of questionable EITC claims.

- Implemented a multi year integrated strategy to educate tax return preparers regarding common EITC errors, to examine preparer practices, and to propose penalties as appropriate because more than 60 percent of all EITC returns are prepared by paid preparers.

- Continues to measure compliance with EITC statutes. The Tax Year 1999 EITC Compliance Study is scheduled to be completed by the Spring of FY 2002.

FY 2003 IRS Annual Performance Plan
February 4, 2002

To improve overall financial management, IRS is implementing two major systems: the Custodial Accounting Project (CAP) and the Integrated Financial System (IFS). CAP will provide a single, integrated repository of taxpayer account information and collections information to support custodial financial reporting; to produce an initial, critical component of an enterprise data warehouse; and to provide resolution of many long standing financial management weaknesses, including compliance with existing statues and regulations. CAP will provide a Taxpayer Accounts Sub ledger (TASL) and a Collections Sub ledger (CSL) that directly feed a standard government general ledger. TASL Build 1 will develop the data repository of taxpayer account information and integrate it with the general ledger, making TASL accessible for management analysis and reporting. IRS has completed the Architecture Phase of the CAP. The Systems Development Phase is scheduled to be completed in December 2002, with deployment of Build 1 of TASL scheduled for March 2003.

IFS is being designed to address material weaknesses in financial reporting and to bring the IRS into compliance with the Federal Financial Management Improvement Act (FFMIA). IFS will be deployed in two builds. Build 1 will contain the core financial elements, such as General Ledger, Accounts Receivable, Accounts Payable, Cost Accounting, payroll and funds control. Build 2 will provide for non-core systems, such as fixed assets, travel and procurement. The requirements phase of IFS is scheduled to be completed by November 2001, with procurement of software targeted for April 2002. Deployment of Build 1 is scheduled to be completed by October 2003 and Build 2 should be completed by October 2004.

Expanding Electronic Government

IRS is also expanding its Electronic Tax Administration (ETA) efforts to ultimately provide taxpayers the ability to easily, securely and inexpensively conduct all their interactions with the IRS electronically. E-Services, a Business Systems Modernization project, has been initiated to develop easy-to-use electronic products and services targeted at specific practitioner segments that inform, educate and provide service to the taxpaying public. In addition, e-Services will provide electronic customer account management capabilities to all business, individuals, and other customers in a safe and secure manner. IRS has also initiated improvement projects to make all forms and schedules for 1040 filers available electronically and to improve the content and layout of notices sent to taxpayers.

E-government includes a growing number of methods for procuring products and services, such as using electronic catalogs; reverse auctioning; and, increasing "Business to Government" interfaces. IRS is moving from its current legacy procurement systems to a web based request-tracking system and integrated procurement system. Successful implementation of these systems is critical and resources will be focused on this effort. Once completed, IRS will begin its e-government initiative and focus on applying Government to Business and Business to Government functionality. Requirements will be assessed and a market survey will be conducted to determine the current trends and practices in e-government. At a minimum, this will include:

- Reviewing customer and employee requirements related to e-government.

- Reviewing federal government requirements from OMB, GSA and others to ensure IRS is in concert with their direction [IRS is currently in compliance with the OMB's FY 2002 goal of posting appropriate solicitations on the government-wide point-of-entry website www.FedBizOpps.gov]

- Reviewing industry best practices and current trends.

Highlights of IRS' achievements in this area include savings of $17.3 million for FY 2001 through FY 2003, using reverse auctioning for the purchase of up to 95,000 laptop and desktop computers; and, generating over 500 FTE in savings and cost avoidance in FY 2003 through the use of e-filing and other "e" initiatives.

Chapter 11

Best Practices in Performance Measurement

This chapter presents an excerpt from an article detailing an in-depth study of the use of balanced measures in the federal government. It is adapted from the *National Partnership for Reinventing Government,* "Balancing Measures: Best Practices in Performance Management" (September 1, 1999), www.npr.gov.

"BALANCING MEASURES: BEST PRACTICES IN PERFORMANCE MANAGEMENT"

Executive Summary

When the Government Performance and Results Act was first implemented, many felt that government management was somehow "different," that the same rules that applied to the private sector could not apply to the public, or at least not in the same way. After all, government agencies do not have a bottom line or profit margin. However, recent efforts, as this study shows repeatedly, attest that is not true. The bottom line for most government organizations is their mission: what they want to achieve.

However, they cannot achieve this mission by managing in a vacuum, any more than can the private sector. More specifically, the roles of customer, stakeholder, and employee in an organization's day-to-day operations are vital to its success—and must be incorporated into that success.

In their groundbreaking *Harvard Business Review* article, Robert S. Kaplan and David P. Norton introduced the concept of the Balanced Scorecard to the private sector. This article, and subsequent works by them, discusses private sector efforts to align corporate initiatives with the need to meet customer and shareholder expectations. This study looks at how these efforts relate to, and are being replicated within, the public sector. It examines the ways and means by which government organizations are trying to include customers, stakeholders, and employees in their performance management efforts—to reach some *balance* among the needs and opinions of these groups along with the achievement of the organization's stated mission. All of the organizations that served as partners in preparing this report have had some level of success in doing this.

Our partners believe that, while there is no perfect fit of the Balanced Scorecard as envisioned by Kaplan and Norton with performance planning, management, and measurement within the public sector, this does not mean that the concept isn't useful in government planning—particularly with some tinkering and tailoring. So, public sector organizations with the most mature strategic planning processes—notably city and state governments—felt that the area of employee satisfaction, for example, translated better to the public sector when seen as employee empowerment and/or involvement.

Defining whom exactly the *customer* is can be a challenge for government agencies, especially for federal agencies with more than one mission. For example, the U.S. Coast Guard has both enforcement and a service mission—and consequently different customer bases. And even those agencies that have but a single mission, such as regulatory agencies like the Environmental Protection Agency, must take into account not only those with whom they deal on a day-to-day basis in their enforcement activities, such as major manufacturers, but also the citizen who is being protected by those enforcement activities. And the organization that provides a service or benefit, like the Social Security Administration, must distinguish between what the customer may want and what U.S. citizens may be willing to spend; that is, to balance their fiscal responsibilities to the taxpayer with their responsibilities to beneficiaries.

Other important lessons about balanced performance measurement gleaned from site visits and interviews with our best practice and resource partners include the following:

- Adapt, do not adopt: Make a best practice work for you.
- We are not so different after all: Public or private, federal, state, or local, there are common problems—and common answers.
- Leadership does not stop at the top, but should cascade throughout an organization, creating champions and a team approach to achievement of mission.
- Listen to your customers and stakeholders.
- Listen to your employees and unions.
- Partnership among customers, stakeholders, and employees results in success. Telling—rather than asking—these groups what they need does not work.

Why should you, a government leader, try to achieve a balanced set of performance measures—or what is often referred to as a *family of measures*? Here's what we found in our research: Because you need to know what your customer's expectations are and what your employee needs to have to meet those expectations. Because you cannot achieve your stated objectives without taking those expectations and needs into account. Most importantly, because it *works*, as can be seen from the success of our partners.

Therefore, you need to balance your mission with customer, stakeholder, and employee perspectives. How exactly do you go about doing this? These are the best practices we learned from our partners.

Establish a Results-Oriented Set of Measures That Balance[s] Business, Customer, and Employee

- *Define what measures mean the most* to customer, stakeholder, and employee by (1) having them work together, (2) creating an easily recognized body of measures, and (3) clearly identifying measures to address their concerns.
- *Commit to initial change* by (1) using expertise wherever you find it; (2) involving everyone in the process; (3) making the system nonpunitive; (4) bringing in the unions; and (5) providing clear, concise guidance as to the establishment, monitoring, and reporting of measures.
- *Maintain flexibility* by (1) recognizing that performance management is a living process, (2) limiting the number of performance measures, and (3) maintaining a balance between financial and nonfinancial measures.

Establish Accountability at All Levels of the Organization

- Lead by example.
- Cascade accountability: share it with the employee by (1) creating a performance-based organization, (2) encouraging sponsorship of measures at all levels, and (3) involving the unions at all levels of performance management.
- Keep the employee informed via intranet and/or Internet; don't rule out alternative forms of communication.
- Keep the customer informed via both the Internet and traditional paper reports.
- Make accountability work: reward employees for success. Supplement or replace monetary rewards with nonmonetary means, reallocate discretionary funds, and base rewards in a team approach.

Collect, Use, and Analyze Data

- *Collect feedback data,* which can be obtained from customers by providing easy access to your organization; remember too that "survey" is not a four-letter word.
- *Collect performance data* by (1) investing both the time and the money to make it right, (2) making sure that your performance data mean something to those that use them, (3) recognizing that everything is not on-line or in one place, and (4) centralizing the data collection function at the highest possible level.
- *Analyze data*: (1) combine feedback and performance data for a more complete picture, (2) conduct root-cause analyses, and (3) make sure everyone sees the results of analyses.

Connect the Dots

If your performance management efforts are not connected to your business plan (which defines day-to-day operations in a government agency) and to the budget (which is where the money is), then you will be doomed to failure because your performance measurement approach will have no real meaning to the people running, or affected by, the program. Planning documents must connect to business plans, and data systems and the budget process must be integrated with all these other factors. By doing so, you can create a strategic management framework which serves to focus the entire organization on the same mission and goals.

Share the Leadership Role

Leadership is a critical element marking successful organizations, both public and private. Cascaded throughout an organization, leadership gives the performance management process a depth and sustainability that survives changes at the top—even those driven by elections and changes in political party leadership. Two experts in the field, the Hon. Maurice McTigue, a former New Zealand cabinet member now working at George Mason University, and Dr. Patricia Ingraham of the Maxwell School at Syracuse University, emphasize in their teaching the importance of leadership in a political environment. Given the potential constraints such an environment can present, a successful public sector organization needs strong leadership that supports the adoption of balanced measures as a feature of organizational management and accountability.

Why Did We Do This Study?

For many years, leaders at all levels in the private and public sectors have searched for the right tools and techniques to help them create high-performing organizations. The Balanced Scorecard introduced in 1992 by Kaplan and Norton of the Harvard Business School galvanized and revolutionized the field. The Balanced Scorecard approach to performance management gained wide use and acclaim in the private sector as a way to build customer and employee data into measuring and ensuring better performance outcomes. It thus transformed the way private sector companies could achieve and analyze high levels of performance and was critical in revitalizing such companies as Federal Express, Corning, and Sears.

In August 1993, Congress passed the Government Performance and Results Act (referred to as both GPRA and the Results Act). Under GPRA, leadership in the public sector was legally obligated to address issues such as performance planning and management—as well as report on the results of those efforts. Many felt that government management was "different," that the rules of performance management and measurement that applied to the private sector could not apply to the public. After all, government agencies do not have a bottom line or profit margin.

Recent efforts have shown, however, that not only do the basic concepts apply to the public sector, they can also be used to create a successful organization. For example, agencies may not have a financial bottom line, but they do have goals and outcomes that can indicate success (e.g., reduction in pollution).

Other concepts apply as well, as was borne out by Executive Order 12862, signed by President Clinton in September 1993. This order requires federal agencies to determine from their customers the kind and quality of service they seek. In the same way that the private sector experienced noticeable changes by measuring beyond business results, government agencies have also begun to balance a greater constellation of measures by incorporating customer needs and expectations into their strategic planning processes. ***This balanced approach to performance planning, measurement, and management is helping government agencies achieve results Americans—whether customers, stakeholders, employees, or other—actually care about.***

Cities, states, and counties have actively adapted the balanced measures approach. Some federal organizations too have begun to pursue balanced measurement as part of ongoing efforts to improve efficiency, effectiveness, and customer service in their organizations. Abroad, similar activities have been taking place. The British government formed the Performance and Innovation Unit to, among other things, "promote innovative solutions that improved the effectiveness of policy, the quality of services and the responsiveness to users' needs." Also, the Service First Unit in the UK has been focusing on customer service issues for several years. Many Canadian government agencies—including Natural Resources Canada, the St. Lawrence Seaway Management Corporation, Atomic Energy of Canada, Ltd., and the Trademarks Office—have been working to link their customer service, performance management, and budget processes together.

At a time when new performance, budget, and strategic challenges to the public sector affect its current and future decisions, much can be gleaned from these various experiences with balanced performance measurement. Thus, Vice President Al Gore—after hearing three highly successful and diverse corporate leaders at a reinvention forum attribute balanced measurement of performance as critical to taking their companies to the top—charged the National Partnership for Reinventing Government (NPR) with identifying and studying best practices in using balanced measures in the public and private sectors.

Lessons We Learned

Overall, a balanced approach to performance measurement works and will improve organizational performance when used. Flexibility is the key. There is no "cookie cutter" approach, but there are elements and experiences reported here that can be useful and beneficial to all agencies.

- *Adapt, don't adopt.* A best practice generally cannot be adopted exactly the way it was done in another organization, but it can be adapted to fit your organizational needs and culture. Most of the organizations we interviewed have adapted the traditional Balanced Scorecard into a family of measures that is uniquely suited to their culture, their structure, their mission. In the final analysis, you must adapt an approach to fit *your* particular needs.
- *We aren't so different after all.* One of the most interesting discoveries for the team was the fact that the problems the different organizations were facing were not very different. Most struggled with the same issues: reducing the number of measures, validating and verifying data, establishing accountability and responsibility without being punitive, and—most importantly—trying to balance achievement of the organization's mission with the needs of customer, stakeholder, and employee. In many cases, merely defining the customer was an obstacle. Public or private, federal, state, or local, there are common problems—and common answers—in many areas.
- *Leadership doesn't stop at the top.* Leadership is important, but not just at the top levels; leadership by employees in solving problems and achieving mission is what makes for a most successful organization.
- *Listen to your customers and stakeholders.* You might be surprised to learn what is really important to them. The Oregon Department of Motor Vehicles was prepared to spend money on ways to provide faster service and shorter lines. Then it asked its customers what they wanted. *They* wanted a choice in the ID picture that would be laminated onto their license. Oregon listened and invested in better photographic equipment and provided a choice to the customer as to the picture to be used.
- *Listen to your employees and unions.* Employees have historical knowledge and experience at the day-to-day operations level. Don't underestimate the importance of this information and expertise. In addition, regarding the union, if it is part of the solution, it is no longer part of the problem. This precept is especially critical in achieving culture change within an organization.
- *Partner with customers, stakeholders and employees; don't control.* The more you partner with those who have a vested interest in the success of your organization, the more successful your organization is likely to be. Some of the most successful organizations work closely not only with customers and employees, but also with unions and legislators. Better communication results in an increased level of trust.

Most importantly, we learned that ***there is no such thing as a fixed and truly balanced set of measures***; instead, the ***process*** of balancing the needs of customers and employees against mission is a constant and living one, flexible and open to change.

The team learned a great deal from this study; we are pleased to share this knowledge with you. The practices listed here can be used, adapted, and implemented throughout the public sector. We hope this report will be seen as a tool to help everyone do their job better and more efficiently.

Balancing Measures: Why Should I Do It and What Does It Mean?

> Reflecting back on the long history of federal service, I never saw any single measure which could adequately describe an agency's performance. Use of the "scorecard," because it balances both internal and external stakeholder concerns, gives us a much more comprehensive, and balanced, picture of how we are doing. The measures we traditionally used tended to focus almost exclusively on internal processes. They also failed to measure three major areas: the real cost of doing business, the impact of the processes on the veteran-customer, and their impact on employees. Use of the scorecard balances our measures because it looks at both external and internal measures. They keep the organization focused on the vision and our stakeholders: veteran-customers, employees, and tax-payers. The scorecard measures provide a "line of sight" for every employee to see their contribution to organizational results.
> —Joe Thompson, Under Secretary for Benefits,
> Veterans Benefits Administration, Department of Veterans Affairs

Balancing measures is a strategic management system for achieving long-term goals. Senior executives in industries from banking and oil to insurance and retailing use balanced measures to guide current performance and plan future performance. They use measures in four categories—financial performance, customer knowledge, internal business processes, and learning and growth—to align individual, organizational, and cross-departmental initiatives and to identify processes for meeting customer and shareholder objectives.

Their experience has shown that *balancing a family of performance measures works*. This means that in each phase of performance planning, management, and measurement, the customer, stakeholder, and employee are considered in balance with the need to achieve a specific mission or result. This approach has worked in the private sector and is beginning to take firm root in government as well. While there is no exact formula for applying balanced measures, the goal of this report is to provide options and courses of action for use in and across the federal government. The experiences of those who have begun to use balanced measures provide opportunities for agencies to read about what has been successful for others, to choose applicable practices, and to improve performance to match the best in the business.

Are You a Driver or a Pilot? Instrument Panel versus Dashboard

Using balanced measures allows you to mirror the factors that you believe are critical to the success of your organization. "A good way to understand the balanced scorecard is to imagine yourself as the captain of a jumbo jet," write Robert Kaplan and David Norton in their groundbreaking article on the management tool in the *Harvard Business Review*. They continue:

> Imagine the flight deck and all the instruments, dials and gauges on the panel in front of you. These instruments tell you about the various parts of the plane and how it is flying. Reliance on the altimeter only would be foolish—you might know your altitude, but you would not have any warning about impending storms. You wouldn't look only at the radar, of course—how would you know when you were low on fuel?

Balanced measures serve as an *instrument panel* for your organization. They provide important information from different perspectives, creating a holistic view of the organization's health. They bring together on a single management report many of the disparate elements of the organization's agenda.

Another useful metaphor in discussing a balanced approach to performance management is the *dashboard approach*. Management, when resistant to change, will often complain that it cannot focus on everything at once, that the "powers that be" need to make up their mind about exactly what it is the leader is to look at. The answer to this is that being a good leader is like driving a car. After all, there are many gauges on the dashboard. While you are driving, you take note of the level of fuel (you don't want to run out of gas). You watch the water level (you wouldn't want to overheat the engine). In addition, if an emergency light were to come on, you would notice that as well. These all are secondary observations, however, to the driver's primary focus of moving the car safely in one direction while watching for obstacles in the road, including other drivers. That is exactly what a good leader in an organization should be doing. A balanced set of performance measures is like the gauges on the car; the mission is the destination.

Why a Balanced Approach?

Regardless of which metaphor you embrace, a balanced approach allows you to consider all the important operational measures at the same time, letting you see whether improvement in one area is achieved at the expense of another. Key indicators should tell you how the organization is doing. They will probably change over time to reflect shifting organizational goals. Performance levels can be reported on a monthly or quarterly basis. All levels of management, including field personnel, can participate in the reporting process; together, they provide a good idea of the health of the organization from a variety of perspectives. It is only with a balanced approach that leaders can create success throughout their organizations.

This proven approach to strategic management imbeds long-term strategy into the management system through the mechanism of measurement. It translates vision and strategy into a tool that effectively communicates strategic intent, and motivates and tracks performance against established goals.

A strategy is a shared understanding about how a goal is to be reached. Balancing measures allows management to translate the strategy into a clear set of objectives. These objectives are then further translated into a system of performance measurements that effectively communicates a powerful, forward-looking, strategic focus to the entire organization. In contrast with traditional, financially based measurement systems, *the balanced measures approach solidifies an organization's focus on future success by setting objectives and measuring performance from distinct perspectives.* The old method of management, which focused only on the bottom line, no longer works. If the customer, stakeholder, and employee are not part of the solution, they will forever be part of the problem.

Balanced across What Perspectives?

You need to look at your performance management from three perspectives: employee, customer, and business.

The *employee perspective* focuses attention on the performance of the key internal processes that drive the organization. This perspective directs attention to the basis of all future success—the organization's people and infrastructure. Adequate investment in these areas is critical to all long-term success. Without employee buy-in, an organization's achievements will be minimal. Employees must be part of the team.

Examples of Concerns from the Employee Perspective
- How do you get employees to see the federal government as an employer of choice?
- Focus on issues such as employee development and retention.

The *customer perspective* considers the organization's performance through the eyes of a customer, so that the organization retains a careful focus on customer needs and satisfaction. For a government entity, this perspective takes on a somewhat different meaning than for a private sector firm; that is because most public sector organizations have many types of customers. The private sector recognizes the importance of the customer and makes the customer a driver of performance. To achieve the best in business performance, the government, too, must incorporate customer needs, wants, and must respond to them as part of its performance planning.

Examples of Concerns from the Customer Perspective
- How do you want your customers to view you?
- Who are your customers? Is there more than one group?
- Are measures based on external customer input?
- Do your measures reflect the characteristics of good service (accessible, accurate, clear, closure, timely, respectful)?

The *business perspective*, like the customer perspective, has a different interpretation in the government than in the private sector. For many organizations, there are actually two separate sets of measures: the *outcomes*, or social/political impacts, which define the role of the agency/department within the government and American society; and the *business processes* needed for organizational efficiency and effectiveness.

Examples of Business Results
- How do you want your stakeholders and/or customers to view you?
- Are your measures outcome/results-based?
- Are the results something customers care about?
- Do you have real-time data for reporting purposes?

Together, these perspectives provide a balanced view of the present and future performance of the organization. A balanced set of measures allows leaders to think of their organization in its totality. ***There is no one "right" family of measures.*** The measures must reflect the overall mission strategy of the organization. They have to be the measures that drive the organization. In most cases, they are developed through an iterative, evolutionary process. You can have as many categories as you want, but the idea is to keep it as simple as possible so that your measurements can be global and quick.

For the team members of this study, the key challenge has been to determine what has to happen to make it possible for government leaders to manage through the use of a balanced set of measures.

Summary of Best Practices in Balancing Measures

In 1994, Vice President Al Gore gave a lecture as part of the Georgetown University Series on Governmental Reform in which he identified the characteristics of "The New Job of the

Federal Executive." Among those characteristics were "creating a team environment, empowering employees, putting customers first, and communicating with employees." Those characteristics are embedded in the best practices of our partners—especially in this area of performance measurement.

There is no generic set of balanced measures that can be applied as best practice to all functions of the public sector. Certain conditions, however, need to exist within an organization for a balanced approach to performance management to be successful:

- Strong leadership that supports the adoption of balanced measures as a feature of organizational management and accountability;
- The capability to communicate effectively throughout the organization and the organization's ability to communicate to decision makers; and
- The knowledge that customers, employees, and stakeholders are fully informed and that they understand and support the initiatives of the organization.

While an attempt to find a *one-size-fits-all* approach will not work, there are some generic principles that remain constant across all government organizations:

- *Good product or service.* Does the organization meet the consumer's need for goods or services or rectify a perceived wrong?
- *Good image.* How does public opinion view the organization? Are employees enthused by the public's perception of them?
- *Good availability.* Can customers get easy access and satisfaction? Is the organization ready and able to respond immediately to any reasonable challenge?
- *Good employer.* Are there high levels of staff retention, staff morale, and job satisfaction?
- *Continuous improvement.* Is there a continuous evaluation process to identify and implement improvements? Do the improvements benefit the product to the community?

A successful organization in the public sector will apply these principles to its strategic framework, which links performance planning, measurement, and reporting to day-to-day operations, balancing the need to achieve a stated mission with the needs of the customer, stakeholder, and employee. . . . [O]ur partners are doing just this as they:

- Establish a results-oriented set of measures that balances business, customer, and employee;
- Establish accountability at all levels of the organization;
- Collect, use, and analyze data;
- Connect the dots; and
- Share the leadership role.

CHAPTER 12

The Balanced Scorecard in Procurement—Two Case Examples

There are two good examples of the application of the BSC in the procurement function. The first is the very broad and detailed work of the Procurement Executives' Association (PEA). The second example comes from the Department of Transportation.

PEA GUIDE TO THE BALANCED SCORECARD

The material that follows has been adapted from the Procurement Executives' Association, *Guide to a Balanced Scorecard: Performance Management Methodology: Moving from Performance Measurement to Performance Management.* The full guide can be accessed on the Web site of the Department of Energy (www.pr.doe.gov/pmmfinal.pdf).

Performance Management Strategy

This chapter sets forth the definitional baselines for performance measurement and performance management, provides a brief overview of the goals of a performance management system, and discusses a conceptual framework for performance measurement and management.

1. What Is Performance Management?

There are wide ranges of definitions for performance objective, performance goal, performance measure, performance measurement, and performance management. To frame the dialog and to move forward with a common baseline, certain key concepts need to be clearly defined and understood, such as:

Performance objective. This is a critical success factor in achieving the organization's mission, vision, and strategy, which if not achieved would likely result in a significant decrease in customer satisfaction, system performance, employee satisfaction or retention, or effective financial management.

Performance goal. A target level of activity expressed as a tangible measure, against which actual achievement can be compared.

Performance measure. A quantitative or qualitative characterization of performance.

Performance measurement. A process of assessing progress toward achieving predetermined goals, including information on the efficiency with which resources are transformed into goods and services (outputs), the quality of those outputs (how well they are delivered to clients and the extent to which clients are satisfied) and outcomes (the results of a program activity compared to its intended purpose), and the effectiveness of government operations in terms of their specific contributions to program objectives.

Performance management. The use of performance measurement information to effect positive change in organizational culture, systems, and processes, by helping to set agreed-upon performance goals, allocating and prioritizing resources, informing managers to either confirm or change current policy or program directions to meet those goals, and sharing results of performance in pursuing those goals.

Output measure. A calculation or recording of activity or effort that can be expressed in a quantitative or qualitative manner.

Outcome measure. An assessment of the results of a program compared to its intended purpose.

2. Performance Management System Goals

A leading-edge organization seeks to create an efficient and effective performance management system to:

- Translate agency vision into clear, measurable outcomes that define success, and that are shared throughout the agency and with customers and stakeholders;
- Provide a tool for assessing, managing, and improving the overall health and success of business systems;
- Continue to shift from prescriptive, audit- and compliance-based oversight to an ongoing, forward-looking strategic partnership involving agency headquarters and field components;
- Include measures of quality, cost, speed, customer service, and employee alignment, motivation, and skills to provide an in-depth, predictive performance management system; and
- Replace existing assessment models with a consistent approach to performance management.

3. The Balanced Scorecard Methodology

Leading organizations agree on the need for a structured methodology for using performance measurement information to help set agreed-upon performance goals, allocate and prioritize resources, inform managers to either confirm or change current policy or program direction to meet those goals, and report on the success in meeting those goals. To this end, in 1993 the Procurement Executives' Association (PEA) created the Performance Measurement Action Team (PMAT). Their task was to assess the state of the acquisition system, to identify a structured methodology to measure and improve acquisition performance, and to develop strategies for measuring the health of agency acquisition systems.

The PMAT found that organizations were using top-down management reviews to determine compliance with established process-oriented criteria and to certify the adequacy of the acquisition system. This method was found to lack a focus on the outcomes of the processes used and was largely ineffective in obtaining dramatic and sustained improvements in the quality of the operations.

The PMAT did extensive research and made site visits to leaders in performance measurement and management in an attempt to identify an assessment methodology appropriate for federal organizations. The model chosen was developed by Drs. David Norton and Robert Kaplan—the Balanced Scorecard (BSC) model. As modified by the PMAT, the measurement model identified critical success factors for acquisition systems, and developed performance measures within the four perspectives discussed below. Agencies which implemented the PMAT model utilized generic survey instruments and statistics obtained from the Federal Procurement Data System and other available data systems to determine the overall health of the system and how effectively it met its performance goals.

The work done by the PMAT has formed the foundation for the BSC methodology presented in this Guide. The lessons learned, and the best practices and strategies resulting from the PMAT experience, were used to create an expanded and enhanced BSC model. The PEA believes this revised methodology to be the best for deploying an organization's strategic direction, communicating its expectations, and measuring its progress toward agreed-to objectives. Additionally, a 1998 study by the Gartner Group found that "at least 40% of Fortune 1000 companies will implement a new management philosophy . . . the Balanced Scorecard . . . by the year 2000."

The BSC presented in this Guidebook is a conceptual framework for translating an organization's vision into a set of performance indicators distributed among four perspectives: financial, customer, internal business processes, and learning and growth. Some indicators are maintained to measure an organization's progress toward achieving its vision; other indicators are maintained to measure the long-term drivers of success. Through the balanced scorecard, an organization monitors both its current performance (finance, customer satisfaction, and business process results) and its efforts to improve processes, motivate and educate employees, and enhance information systems—its ability to learn and improve.

4. The Four Perspectives of the Balanced Scorecard

Financial. In the government arena, the "financial" perspective differs from that of the traditional private sector. Private sector financial objectives generally represent clear long-range targets for profit-seeking organizations, operating in a purely commercial environment. Financial considerations for public organizations have an enabling or a constraining role, but will rarely be the primary objective for business systems. Success for public organizations should be measured by how effectively and efficiently they meet the needs of their constituencies. Therefore, in the government, the financial perspective emphasizes cost efficiency, i.e., the ability to deliver maximum value to the customer.

Customer. This perspective captures the ability of the organization to provide quality goods and services, the effectiveness of their delivery, and overall customer service and satisfaction. In the governmental model, the principal driver of performance is different than in the strictly commercial environment; namely, customers and stakeholders take preeminence over financial results. In general, public organizations have a different, perhaps greater, stewardship/fiduciary responsibility and focus than do private sector entities.

Internal business processes. This perspective focuses on the internal business results that lead to financial success and satisfied customers. To meet organizational objectives and customers' expectations, organizations must identify the key business processes at which they must excel. Key processes are monitored to ensure that outcomes will be satisfactory. Internal business processes are the mechanisms through which performance expectations are achieved.

Learning and growth. This perspective looks at the ability of employees, the quality of information systems, and the effects of organizational alignment in supporting accomplishment of organizational goals. Processes will only succeed if adequately skilled and motivated employees, supplied with accurate and timely information, are driving them. This perspective takes on increased importance in organizations, like those of the PEA members, that are undergoing radical change. In order to meet changing requirements and customer expectations, employees may be asked to take on dramatically new responsibilities, and may require skills, capabilities, technologies, and organizational designs that were not available before.

Figure 12–1 visually depicts the global BSC framework. . . .

BALANCED SCORECARD
STRATEGIC PERSPECTIVES

```
                        CUSTOMER
How do our customers                    What must we excel at?
see us?
          FINANCIAL —— MISSION   —— INTERNAL
                       VISION       BUSINESS
                       STRATEGY     PROCESSES

Do we get the best                      Do we continue to
deal for the Government?                improve and create value?
                        LEARNING
                         AND
                        GROWTH
```

Figure 12–1. The Global BSC Framework. *Source:* Adapted from Procurement Executives' Association, *Guide to a Balanced Scorecard: Performance Management Methodology: Moving from Performance Measurement to Performance Management,* www.pr.doe.gov/pmmfinal.pdf.

5. Implementing a Balanced Scorecard

A. **Collaborative efforts.** To realize the full benefits of the BSC, the PEA encourages the adoption of the BSC for all key agency functions.

- Implementing the BSC agency-wide will provide: (1) a common methodology and coordinated framework for all agency performance measurement efforts; (2) a common "language" for agency managers; (3) a common basis for understanding measurement results; and (4) an integrated picture of the agency overall.
- While implementing the acquisition BSC is an important first step, helping agencies to develop BSCs for additional functions (e.g., program, human resources, finance, IT) will strengthen the link among the acquisition system, those additional functions, and agency missions and goals. This will highlight how performance improvement initiatives in one area positively or negatively affect performance in another area. Also, this will promote cross-functional coordination of improvement efforts and help break down "stovepipes" in the agency.
- Acquisition executives may serve as advocates to promote the benefits of BSC agency-wide by advertising successful improvement efforts, and by discussing the BSC methodology in meetings with the Secretary, Administrator, or senior-level managers in other functional areas.
- The BSC will provide sound data on which to base business decisions, from allocation of available resources to future direction. This will enable the agency to manage its activities and its resources more effectively. For example, the BSC could form a common basis to support a business case for more resources.
- While we believe the Procurement Executive should promote the BSC's benefits and encourage its adoption beyond the acquisition realm, an agency can benefit even if it ultimately decides to adopt the BSC only for its acquisition function. The four perspec-

tives provide a useful framework for analyzing and understanding how acquisition supports accomplishment of the agency's mission. The information gained will help the agency assess how its acquisition system is performing, whether it is meeting its objectives, and whether it is moving in the direction envisioned in the FAR guiding principles. *As the key leader for the acquisition BSC, the Procurement Executive has a critical role in ensuring its successful implementation and use, and is responsible for setting into motion the steps recommended in this Guide.*

B. Pathway to success. A federal agency can take several steps to encourage support for BSC activities or any performance measurement and improvement efforts within its organization:

1. **Make a commitment at all levels—especially at the top level.** Research clearly shows that strong leadership is paramount in creating a positive organizational climate for nurturing performance improvements. Senior management leadership is vital throughout the performance measurement and improvement process. By senior management, we mean the organizational level that can realistically foster cross-functional, mission-oriented performance improvements—from senior operating or functional managers in the various acquisition and program offices throughout a federal agency, to the Secretary or Administrator of the agency. Senior management should have frequent formal and informal meetings with employees and managers to show support for improvement efforts and implementation initiatives. Also, they should frequently review progress and the results of improvement efforts.
2. **Develop organizational goals.** Goals need to be specified and publicized to provide focus and direction to the organization. Vision Statements and Strategic/Tactical Plans (including systematic ways to evaluate performance) are important for methodically planning acquisition performance improvements. To be meaningful, they must include measurable objectives along with realistic timetables for their achievement. For acquisition measures, it may be appropriate to use or build upon the performance principles and standards set forth in the Federal Acquisition Regulation (FAR) Subpart 1.102 to develop goals, whether they are stand-alone goals or a subset of larger, overarching organizational goals. Providing guidance on the best way to link acquisition goals to annual, mission-oriented GPRA performance plans is also essential. This will demonstrate that the agency is serious about acquisition improvement initiatives.
3. **Offer training in improvement techniques.** Training should be provided to appropriate personnel to help them properly make process improvements. The scope of training should include the operation of integrated project improvement teams; the role employees play in exercising sound business judgment, and the specific techniques for making process improvements (e.g., flowcharts, benchmarking, cause-and- effect diagrams, etc.). Comprehensive training is needed to expand employees' technical capabilities and to achieve "buy-in" for undertaking meaningful improvement efforts. Use of facilitators can provide "just-in-time" training to members of process action teams.
4. **Establish a reward and recognition system to foster performance improvements.** In our view, agencies should tie any reward and recognition system to performance improvement as measured by the acquisition BSC. Thus, employee incentives will tend to reinforce the organizational objectives being measured by the acquisition BSC. While handing out rewards to individual employees has its place, group reward and recognition systems are also needed to encourage integrated, cross-functional teams of employees, customers and managers to undertake acquisition performance improvement. Agencies may wish to consult with OPM and OMB for suggestions on the most suitable types of rewards and recognition (e.g., plaques, bonuses, etc.).

5. **Break down organizational barriers.** To overcome unfounded fears about the perceived adverse effects of performance measurement and improvement, we believe that the official uses of the acquisition BSC need to be spelled out to employees and managers. For example, it might be useful to invite representatives from the National Partnership for Reinventing Government (formerly known as the National Performance Review), Office of Federal Procurement Policy, the PEA Team, and the agency's own senior-level management to speak to key agency personnel on the purpose of undertaking customer surveys, performance measurement, and process improvement. These officials could explain that the performance measurement data is to be used to promote self-assessment, self-improvement, progress in acquisition reform, linkage to overall mission goals, and collaborative cross-agency benchmarking—not to take reprisals against individuals or organizations. Also, we recommend presentation of "success stories" that demonstrate the non-threatening nature of the BSC methodology, including how an agency can target areas most in need of improvement, benchmark against best-in-class organizations, and form integrated project teams to undertake performance improvements. Stakeholders must be shown that a cooperative effort toward performance improvement is the most appropriate course of action—that supporting the BSC is in their best interest.

6. **Coordinate headquarters and field office responsibilities.** Implementation should be a collaborative effort between an agency's lead corporate office (such as an acquisition management office at HQ) and its local (or field) offices. The offices should jointly decide on their respective roles and responsibilities relative to the BSC. In most cases, the lead corporate office is in the best position to provide leadership, oversight, and a well-defined methodology. The assignment of other roles and responsibilities will differ based on what is appropriate for the offices' circumstances, such as:

- How centralized or decentralized the offices are.
- The extent to which data are collected from a centralized information system or from local databases.
- The extent to which surveys are conducted centrally or locally.

Some PEA agencies have found that local acquisition offices are best suited for implementing the actual assessment process by generating quantitative data from appropriate sources, and by conducting surveys to obtain the necessary feedback for making procurement system improvements. The lead corporate office provides local offices the tools, training, software programs, and guidance they need to compile and examine their own results. This might include computer templates that help select survey samples, generate mailing labels, enter survey data, track survey data, and analyze survey data. The local offices also provide advice on accessing and compiling quantitative Management Information System (MIS) data; while the lead office encourages the use of existing quantitative data systems for multiple performance measurement purposes. Under this model, in partnership with the local offices, the lead corporate office:

- Assumes a leadership role in developing and refining the survey instruments to be used.
- Prepares generic cover letters.
- Facilitates the conduct of surveys at the local offices.
- Fosters local improvement initiatives (including benchmarking) resulting from the survey efforts.
- Monitors response rates, compliance with the required statistical methodology, and overall survey administration progress.

With a clearly defined methodology in hand, the local procurement offices in these agencies:

- Develop their own mailing lists.
- Select their own samples.
- Print and mail the surveys.
- Compile their own survey data.
- Track and analyze the office-unique survey results.
- Generate their own management information system quantitative data.

We recommend that there be an agreement among the lead corporate office and local offices to use a set of common measures, instruments, supporting computer templates and improvement strategies in line with PEA tenets. This agreement should rest firmly on a cooperative relationship between the corporate lead office and the local offices, in which both have worked closely together to design and build their BSC-based performance measurement and improvement system. In some cases, the agreement may give local procurement offices the discretion to use additional, office-specific measures.

C. Other key steps. What follows are some additional approaches that will help in successfully implementing a performance measurement and improvement system:

- **Demonstrate a clear need for improvement.** If you cannot demonstrate a genuine need to improve the organization, failure is a virtual certainty.
- **Make realistic initial attempts at implementation.** If your initial attempts are too aggressive, the resulting lack of organizational "buy-in" will limit your chance of success. Likewise, if implementation is too slow, you may not achieve the necessary organizational momentum to bring the BSC to fruition.
- **Integrate the scorecard into the organization.** Incorporating performance measurement and improvement into your existing management structure, rather than treating it as a separate program, will greatly increase the BSC's long-term viability.
- **Change the corporate culture.** To achieve long-term success, it is imperative that the organizational culture evolve to the point where it cultivates performance improvement as a continuous effort. Viewing performance improvement as a one-time event is a recipe for failure.
- **Institutionalize the process.** Creating, leveraging, sharing, enhancing, managing, and documenting BSC knowledge will provide critical "corporate continuity" in this area. A knowledge repository will help to minimize the loss of institutional performance management knowledge that may result from retirements, transfers, promotions, etc. . . .

How To Establish Performance Measures

This chapter provides a methodology for establishing performance measures within the four perspectives of the balanced scorecard approach and for ensuring that the measures fit within an overall management approach. . . .

How can an organization establish performance measures that make sense? There are many variations to the theme. As indicated earlier, we found the approach presented by Kaplan and Norton to be the most effective, particularly for ensuring that measures relate to the specific vision and mission of the organization. This approach is only one of many. Which method you use will depend on your organization, its culture, and its mission.

1. Define Organizational Vision, Mission, and Strategy

The BSC methodology, as with most performance management methodologies, requires the creation of a vision, mission statement, and strategy for the organization. This ensures that the performance measures developed in each perspective support accomplishment of the organization's strategic objectives. It also helps employees visualize and understand the links between the performance measures and successful accomplishment of strategic goals.

The key, as pointed out by Kaplan and Norton, is to first identify where you want the organization to be in the near future. Set a vision—a vision that seems somewhat out of reach. In this way, "[t]he Balanced Scorecard . . . provides managers with the instrumentation they need to navigate to future competitive success." (Kaplan and Norton)

2. Develop Performance Objectives, Measures, and Goals

Next, it is essential to identify what the organization must do well (i.e., the performance objectives) in order to attain the identified vision. For each objective that must be performed well, it is necessary to identify measures and set goals covering a reasonable period of time (e.g., three to five years). Sounds simple, however, many variables impact how long this exercise will take. The first, and most significant, variable is how many people are employed in the organization and the extent to which they will be involved in setting the vision, mission, measures, and goals.

The BSC translates an organization's vision into a set of performance objectives distributed among four perspectives: Financial, Customer, Internal Business Processes, and Learning and Growth. Some objectives are maintained to measure an organization's progress toward achieving its vision. Other objectives are maintained to measure the long-term drivers of success. Through the use of the BSC, an organization monitors both its current performance (financial, customer satisfaction, and business process results) and its efforts to improve processes, motivate and educate employees, and enhance information systems—its ability to learn and improve. Figure 12–2 . . . provides matrices used in the BSC methodology to help develop objectives and measures. The matrices are relatively straightforward and easy to understand. However, developing the contents of each matrix is the hard part.

When creating performance measures, it is important to ensure that they link directly to the strategic vision of the organization. The measures must focus on the outcomes necessary to achieve the organizational vision and the objectives of the strategic plan. When drafting measures and setting goals, ask whether or not achievement of the identified goals will help achieve the organizational vision.

Each objective within a perspective should be supported by at least one measure that will indicate an organization's performance against that objective. Define measures precisely, including the population to be measured, the method of measurement, the data source, and the time period for the measurement. If a quantitative measure is feasible and realistic, then its use should be encouraged.

When developing measures, it is important to include a mix of quantitative and qualitative measures. Quantitative measures provide more objectivity than qualitative measures. They may help to justify critical management decisions on resource allocation (e.g., budget and staffing) or systems improvement. An agency should first identify any available quantitative data and consider how it can support the objectives and measures incorporated in the BSC. Qualitative measures involve matters of perception, and therefore of subjectivity. Nevertheless, they are an integral part of the BSC methodology. Judgments based on the experience of customers, employees, managers, and contractors offer important insights into acquisition performance and results.

For example, while an agency will usually need surveys to gauge some elements of customer satisfaction such as timeliness of service, process-oriented measures such as acquisi-

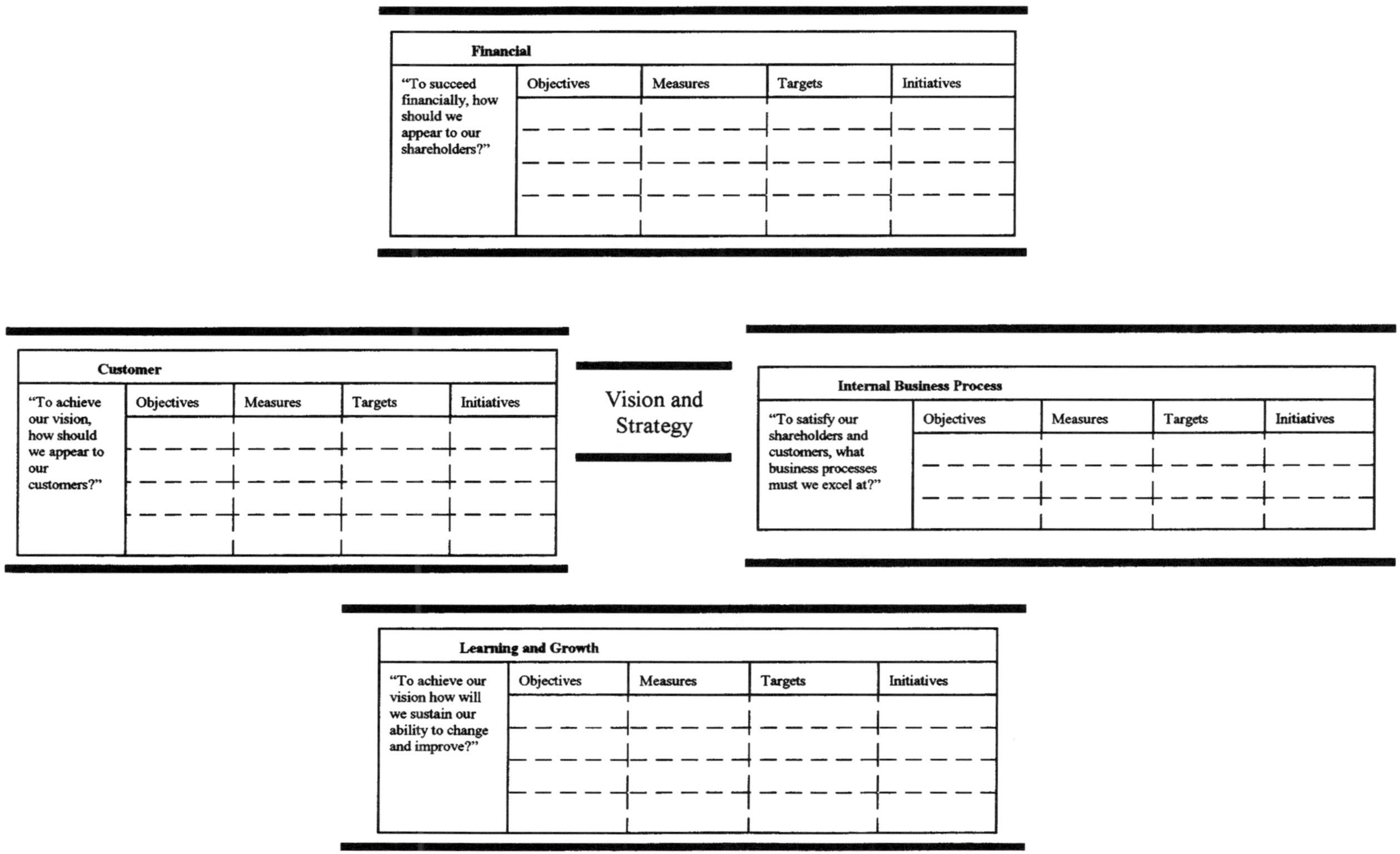

Figure 12-2. Matrices Used in the Balanced Scorecard Methodology. *Source:* Adapted from Procurement Executives' Association, *Guide to a Balanced Scorecard: Performance Management Methodology: Moving from Performance Measurement to Performance Management,* www.pr.doe.gov/pmmfinal.pdf.

tion lead time or contract delivery time may be used as supplemental quantitative indicators—they help explain the underlying reasons for survey performance results. Achieving a balance among quantitative and qualitative factors (as well as among process-oriented and results-driven measures) is crucial in developing a valid BSC methodology.

The evolution of all performance measurements should begin with an organization's Strategic Plan. Figure 12–3, "Integrating Performance Measurement with Other Business Strategies," is a model which depicts a timeline for the business strategies/processes and strategic events that could occur within an organization, and the integration of performance measurement (in this case, acquisition performance measurement) within the process. A synopsis of each follows:

- **Strategic plan.** The Strategic Plan is a five-year plan that extends (in the model) from FY 1997 to FY 2002. It is the one document that sets forth the overall direction, vision, and mission of the organization and recognizes the requirement to set performance goals and to identify measures to gauge progress toward these goals.
- **Performance plan.** To accomplish the Strategic Plan, an annual Performance Plan is developed. This plan defines the measures, activities, and goals that, when taken together, indicate how well the organization's overall goals are being achieved.
- **Budget process.** The budget defines the resources needed to accomplish the strategic goals. Within this process, senior acquisition managers (e.g., procurement heads) develop an acquisition budget strategy, which is an integral step to strengthening budgetary requests and obtaining the resources to meet strategic planning and performance goals.
- **Procurement performance measurement plan.** Following down the strategic planning process, more and more refined performance measures are utilized. This plan can be the document that provides the specific link to the Strategic and Performance Plans. The foundation of the Procurement Performance Measurement Plan stems from the goals, objectives, and measures of the Strategic and Performance Plans.

Many models exist for translating the performance measures of the organization into an individual's performance plan. One of our participating agencies is employing the model shown in Figures 12–4 and 12–5. Figure 12–4, "Performance Management Framework," depicts how strategic initiatives can flow from the agency strategic plan down to an acquisition organization's strategies and then into objectives, measures, targets, and initiatives. This figure becomes the foundation for developing performance plans. Figure 12–5, "Employee Performance Management," shows how the performance measures, using the BSC framework, can be developed following the flow-down of strategic guidance from the agency level down to the individual acquisition official performance plan level. By tying an individual's performance appraisal to the organization's strategic goals, it helps employees understand the vision, mission, and goals of the organization, and motivates employees to work as a team to support initiatives that directly relate to the corporate goals by rewarding them for organizational accomplishments and not just individual achievements.

3. Evolve with Experience

Finally, it takes time to establish measures, but it is also important to recognize that they might not be perfect the first time. Performance management is an evolutionary process that requires adjustments as experience is gained in the use of performance measures. . . .

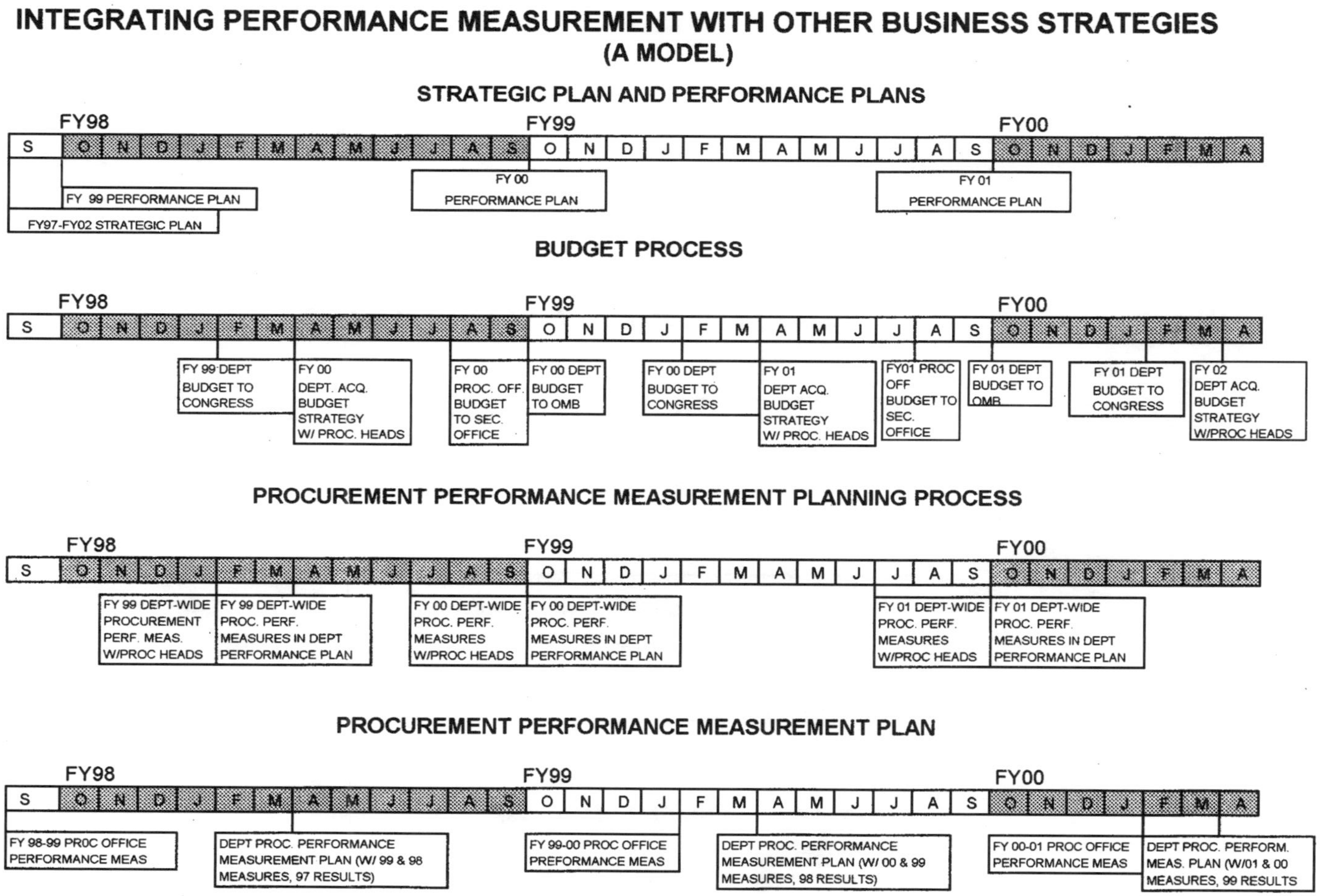

Figure 12-3. Integrating Performance Measurement with Other Business Strategies: A Model. Source: Adapted from Procurement Executives' Association, *Guide to a Balanced Scorecard: Performance Management Methodology: Moving from Performance Measurement to Performance Management,* www.pr.doe.gov/pmmfinal.pdf.

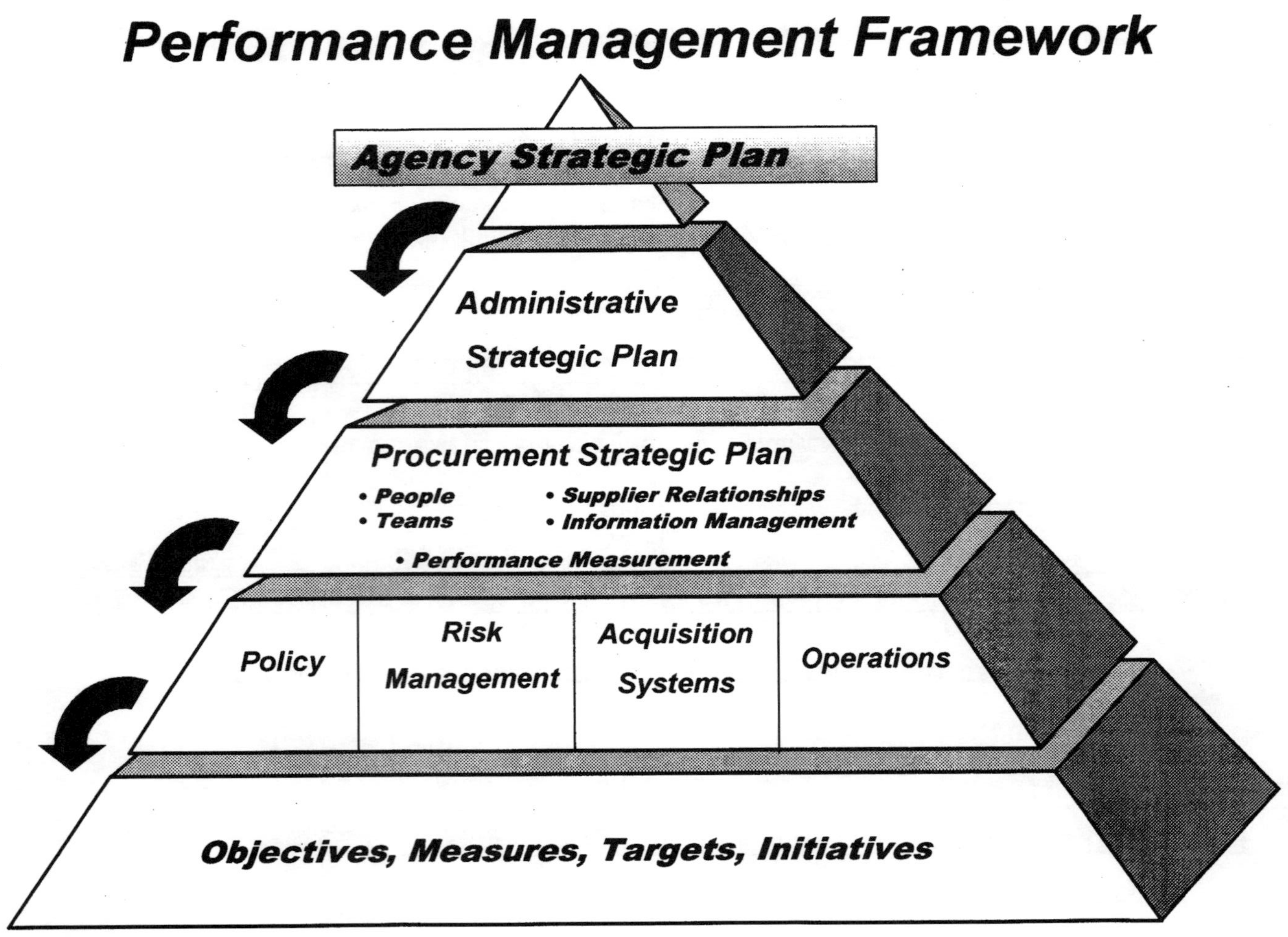

Figure 12-4. Performance Management Framework. *Source:* Adapted from Procurement Executives' Association, *Guide to a Balanced Scorecard: Performance Management Methodology: Moving from Performance Measurement to Performance Management,* www.pr.doe.gov/pmmfinal.pdf.

Employee Performance Management

AGENCY STRATEGIC PLAN

Strategic Priorities:
•

Programs | Measures

ADMINISTRATIVE STRATEGIC PLAN

Strategic Priorities:
- Risk Management
- Integrated Policy and Planning
- Development and Diversity

- Information Technology
- Financial Management
- Customer Service

Responsibilities | Measures

PROCUREMENT EXECUTIVE PERFORMANCE PLAN

Strategic Priorities:
- Customer Satisfaction
- Effective Service Partnership
- Minimize Administrative Cost

- Acquisition Excellence
- Information for Strategic Decision Making
- Quality Workforce

Customer	Financial	Internal Business Process	Learning and Growth
- % Customer Satisfaction w/ Timeliness - % Customer Satisfaction w/ Quality - % Customer Satisfaction w/ responsiveness, cooperation, and communication to meet mission	- Cost to Spend Ratio - Cost avoidance through use of purchase cards - Prompt payment interest paid vs. total $ disbursed	- Ratio of protest upheld at GAO and COFC - # of actions using electronic commerce - % achievement of Socio-economic goals - % Competitive procurement of total procurements	- Extent of reliable management information - % of employees meeting mandatory standards - % of employees satisfied with the work environment - % of employees satisfied with the professionalism, culture, values and empowerment

Figure 12-5. Employee Performance Management. Source: Adapted from Procurement Executives' Association, *Guide to a Balanced Scorecard: Performance Management Methodology: Moving from Performance Measurement to Performance Management*, www.pr.doe.gov/pmmfinal.pdf.

Data Collection

In Chapters Three and Four, we identified a variety of measures that may be used in an acquisition balanced scorecard. Some of the measures fall within the purview of quantitative metrics, while others are of a more qualitative nature. In this chapter, we discuss the key ground rules for collecting reliable performance data to track these quantitative and qualitative measures.

1. Basic Principles

Whether data are quantitative or qualitative, applying the two basic data collection principles identified below will help an agency to obtain reliable data in the most efficient manner. Using these principles, an agency may find synergies between existing, separate systems. Defining links where data collection serves multiple purposes can improve efficiency, support partnerships among organizations, and provide a framework for future system improvements.

A. Use existing data sources to the extent feasible. Many agency management information systems already collect reliable quantitative data, which are useful for acquisition performance measures; and agencies likely have large investments in these systems. These systems include financial, personnel, and administrative systems, as well as contractual information systems. Contractual information systems encompass agency feeder systems to the FPDS, as well as electronic commerce databases (e.g., GSA's Electronic Commerce Online Statistics Reporting System).

For example, the agency may already track measures on workforce training and education as part of a contracting officer warrant program. Also, some data necessary for an acquisition measure may be regularly captured and reported through a management information system that supports another agency function, such as finance or small business. An agency's existing quantitative data typically cover a broad spectrum—from workforce quality, procurement lead-time, and extent of compliance with socioeconomic goals to the use of electronic commerce, contract protest records, and competition statistics.

Moreover, qualitative data from existing acquisition surveys may be used to support BSC efforts. Some agencies have designed and already use acquisition-specific surveys. Much of the data collected by those surveys will be useful for the BSC with little or no change. In some cases, other agency survey instruments collect acquisition-related data. For example, an agency-wide employee survey may collect information useful for the learning and growth element if the acquisition-related information can be segregated. The agency should avoid duplicative surveys and maximize the use of results from a minimum number of surveys.

Data in an automated system should be used directly from that system instead of having to re-enter it into a separate system that supports the BSC. Using existing data sources for multiple reporting purposes improves data reliability by minimizing the potential for errors in repetitive data entry. It also minimizes the burden of data collection and training, thereby promoting greater acceptance of the BSC. Of course, agencies need to ensure that all users have a common understanding of each shared data element.

B. Automate data collection where possible. While many agencies have management information systems that are partially automated, we encourage the expanded use of automation to compile important quantitative data, where efficient and cost-effective. Moreover, as technology evolves, we expect more and more surveys to be administered electronically (e.g., using e-mail hyper-linked to the Web) with automated qualitative survey results going directly into applications that gauge performance. Automation will tend to save time, reduce error rates, and obviate the need for separate data entry and verification.

However, to ensure the validity of automated surveys, data reliability standards must still be maintained, survey recipients must have equal access to relevant electronic media (e.g., e-mail; Web, etc.), and the corporate culture must be technologically sophisticated enough to make survey participants willing to apply this new medium to surveys. For example, if an agency's contractors were to receive an electronic version of a survey; print it in hard copy; and return the completed hard-copy survey by mail (instead of completing and returning the survey on-line) the advantage of using the automated process would be lessened. More important, if contractors are not receptive to an electronic survey process, they may simply delete the initial automated survey transmission—leading to poor response rates. In light of these factors, we recommend that automation be used on a selective basis for internal surveys (i.e., employee, customer, or manager surveys) and only sparingly for external (contractor/vendor) surveys. In addition, e-mail alert notices and reminders will be instrumental in achieving adequate response rates, especially for automated external surveys.

2. Survey Methodology

If the basic principles identified above are followed, agencies will be able to compile management information for quantitative metrics in a rather straightforward fashion. However, since collecting qualitative data is much more demanding, you may wish to avail yourselves of the following overview of survey methodology to help you maintain data integrity.

A. Survey populations & instruments. . . . As explained in Chapter Four, the PEA has decided to collect core, common performance data on a variety of measures—some of which are compiled using surveys. The sample survey instruments address core, common performance objectives (e.g., Customer Satisfaction, Employee Satisfaction, etc.). They also build upon the survey instruments developed under the original PMAT model, are basically equivalent to one another in content, and lay a firm, consistent foundation for cross-agency benchmarking. However, each participating agency retains the flexibility to tailor the survey instruments to meet its own needs.

The sample survey instruments address different types of measures, and involve different types of participants. Under the "Learning and Growth" perspective, the Procurement Employee Survey addresses the core measures of Quality Work Environment and Executive Leadership. It reflects questions the agency should ask office employees, supervisors, and managers. Under the "Customer" perspective, the Procurement Customer Survey targets the core measures of Timeliness, Service/Partnership, and Quality. It reflects questions the agency should ask customers internal to the agency who use items or services delivered by contract (direct internal customers). The questions also apply to customers outside the agency who generate requirements (direct external customers).

In addition, some agencies use a Self-Assessment "survey" to capture qualitative data for the core performance objective of "Information Availability for Strategic Decision-Making" under the "Learning & Growth" perspective, as well as other measures such as Mission Goals or Contract Administration. (It is worth noting that some agencies also include optional quantitative metrics under the Self-Assessment umbrella). The self-assessment survey questions are for contracting office managers, who may call upon lower level supervisors for their contributions. Also, some agencies use a Contractor/Vendor Survey in order to better understand their vendors' (i.e., industry partners') perspective about the efficiency, timeliness, quality, and cooperation of agency acquisition and program offices—thus promoting the incorporation of best industry standards into agency acquisition practices.

B. Survey design. Surveys should be designed in accordance with current research techniques. For example, survey instruments should be brief, with only very basic information requested to measure satisfaction and to obtain feedback on areas that may require improvement. Agencies would do well to: formulate simple and direct questions; avoid open-ended questions; make the questionnaire answerable within 15 minutes; group questions into categories for ease of response; assure anonymous responses; present the questions in a user-friendly booklet form; and pre-test the questionnaire to ensure minimal respondent burden and facilitate as high a response rate as possible. Pre-testing the survey instruments will allow agencies to eliminate or revise questions as necessary, add material that the representative respondents strongly believe should be included, and improve the overall quality and utility of the instruments.

Using a Strongly Disagree to Strongly Agree (or equivalent) rating scale, examples of simple and direct survey questions might include the following:

- "My work schedule is flexible." [Quality Work Environment, under Employee Survey]
- "Customers respect my procurement office." [Executive Leadership, under Employee Survey]
- "Obtains products/services when I need them." [Timeliness, under Customer Survey]
- "Deals with me in a courteous, business-like manner." [Service/Partnership, under Customer Survey]
- "Obtains high-quality products/services." [Quality, under Customer Survey]

Incorporating background questions (e.g., business category; type of product or service) will allow for later multivariate statistical analysis so that an agency may assess whether differences in categories of respondents' backgrounds help explain differences in responses to individual questions (e.g., whether contractor satisfaction varies by type of business organization). This information will help agencies to better target opportunities for acquisition system improvements. Moreover, it is recommended that a "comments" section be added at the very end of the survey for obtaining respondents' observations on good practices and procedures, descriptions of problem areas, and recommendations for solving those problems. A "comments" section often contributes to receiving higher response rates.

C. Statistical survey methodology. Survey procedures are needed to make sure that agencies obtain sound statistical data. Reliable data depend heavily on selecting representative survey participants, targeting the proper sample size, and obtaining reasonably high response rates. Thus, the methodology that follows is designed to ensure that individual agencies conduct the BSC surveys according to accepted statistical standards. Since developing and implementing statistical survey procedures is an exacting discipline, please bear in mind that some of the terminology used below may get somewhat technical at times. You may wish to consult with a trusted statistician to guide you through any unfamiliar statistical terrain.

In general, each participating agency should plan to take a 50 percent sample for populations of 1,000 or fewer—based on a hypergeometric distribution—to achieve precision of plus or minus 3 percent at the 95 percent confidence level. [Unlike a normal distribution, a hypergeometric distribution applies to very small populations.] For example, if we receive survey results indicating that 58 percent of customer survey participants strongly agree that some acquisition function is performed well, then we can say that between 55 percent and 61 percent of customers feel that way—58 percent plus or minus a 3 percent margin of error. Also, the 95 percent confidence level indicates that our survey results would be obtained in 95 out of 100 cases.

A normal distribution should be used for any populations larger than 1,000. Systematic random sampling (selecting every nth one from an alphabetical list of the population names) should be used to ensure representative survey results. At least a 50 percent survey response rate is needed to obtain the full range of opinions and minimize non-response bias. Relaxing the requirements for response rates, confidence levels, and systematic random sampling would significantly reduce the reliability of survey data—thus, degrading the integrity of the resulting improvement process—including benchmarking within or between agencies.

Agencies may need to stratify their employee, customer, and contractor populations to obtain representative samples. Stratified sampling consists of separating the elements of these populations into mutually exclusive groups (called strata) and randomly selecting samples from those strata. Stratification is especially important when it is expected that answers to survey questions may differ significantly from one stratum to another in the population (e.g., commercial firms vs. non-profit organizations, in the contractor population). It would ensure that each employee, customer, or contractor stratum is reflected according to its relative size in the population. Sampling from the overall population without stratification is more likely to result in some strata being over-represented and other strata under-represented in the survey. Without stratification, there is a risk of obtaining misleading survey responses and drawing the wrong conclusions.

For example, if an agency's contracting office expects that its contract specialists, purchasing agents, policy staff, supervisors, managers, and clerical staff would basically provide different answers to key Employee Survey questions, then it should stratify its employees by categories for sampling purposes. Also, if employee answers to survey questions are expected to differ between headquarters and field office locations, then the employees should also be broken down geographically for sampling purposes. Stratified sampling is not much more difficult to accomplish than simple random sampling. Neither survey data collection nor analyses are affected by the choice of a sampling procedure. . . .

D. Using focus groups and point-of-service questionnaires. Before bringing this chapter to a close, it would be appropriate to comment briefly on the extent to which focus groups and point-of-service questionnaires play a role in qualitative data collection. As far as point-of-service surveys are concerned (i.e., surveys done at the point where services are provided to customers), we believe that they have a legitimate place in an agency's arsenal of performance measurement tools. However, many agencies use a census to capture this type of performance information—for each and every transaction with a customer. While the information is compiled on a real-time and comprehensive basis, there's a down-side to its use: the process tends to be burdensome on the customers, and response rates tend to be lower than normal. In light of this, we recommend that agencies sample their point-of-service transactions (to reduce burden), as well as follow-up with their point-of-service survey participants (to ensure adequate response rates). Under extenuating circumstances (e.g., inability to achieve adequate response rates), it may be necessary to consider making the completion of the questionnaire a condition of the transaction. However, if the questionnaire is at all burdensome to complete, this contingency may have unintended consequences, i.e., alienation of valued customers.

With respect to focus groups, we feel that it is inherently wrong to use them as a substitute for formal survey efforts. Focus group opinions offer only anecdotal information, and are not necessarily representative of the views of the overall population of customers, employees, managers, or contractors. However, focus groups may complement or support formal survey efforts in a variety of ways. For example, agencies may use them to generate ideas for the development of survey instruments, pre-test survey instruments, implement organizational improvements downstream, etc.

DEPARTMENT OF TRANSPORTATION'S PROCUREMENT BALANCED SCORECARD

The next good example of the balanced scorecard in procurement is the implementation by the Department of Transportation (DOT). The material that follows has been adapted from the *Department of Transportation's Procurement Balanced Scorecard*, May 1999. The full article can be found at www.dot.gov/ost/m60/scorecard/ppmsrev.htm.

The Department of Transportation has a Procurement Performance Management System that links the GPRA requirements to procurement through a balanced scorecard measurement approach. Major portions of the article are included here.

Contents

DOT's Procurement Performance Management System Policy Principles
   Introduction
   Purpose
   Waivers
   Implementation
   Procurement Performance Management System Timeline
DOT's Procurement Performance Management System
   Introduction
   Acquisition's Strategic Path
   Procurement Performance Planning Model
DOT's Balanced Scorecard for Acquisition
   Background
   DOT'S BSC Methodology
   Key Business Drivers for Enhanced Performance
   Choosing Measurements
DOT's Three Pathways to a Balanced Scorecard
   Introduction
   The Three Pathways to DOT's Procurement BSC
   Deriving the BSC
Using Balanced Scorecard Results To Manage Performance
   Introduction
   Using BSC Results for Managed Performance
   Action Plan for Improved Performance
   Future Success
Attachments
   A—FY00 DOT-wide Procurement Performance Measurements
   B—Survey Pathway
   C—Management Information System Pathway
   D—Diagnostic Pathway
   E—Tools for Assessing Performance
   F—References and Resources

DOT'S Procurement Performance Management System Policy Principles

Introduction

This document establishes the policy principles for DOT's Procurement Performance Management System (PPMS), which links the requirements of the Government Performance and Results

Act (GPRA) to procurement through the use of a Balanced Scorecard (BSC) measurement approach. DOT has chosen the BSC as its tool to gauge procurement's performance progress and to manage the risk inherent in the fiduciary responsibilities of the procurement manager. *It is also this methodology that will be used to report DOT's procurement performance under GPRA.*

The Procurement BSC contains measurements in three separate pathways, each of which connects and flows with the other. These Pathways are:

- The *Survey Pathway* uses the Performance Measurement Assessment Tool (PMAT) methodology.
- The *Management Information Systems (MIS) Pathway* uses information systems (e.g., Contract Information System) to collect data.
- The *Diagnostic Pathway* mainly uses a process and/or results-oriented assessment to evaluate performance. . . .

Purpose

The acquisition community holds a great fiduciary responsibility to the public. With the obligations of millions of dollars, we must ensure that we make wise use of public resources and act in a manner that maintains the public's trust. This includes exercising discretion, using sound business judgment, and complying with applicable laws and regulations. The purpose of this document is to set forth DOT's procurement BSC methodology, the policy principles relating to the BSC, and measurements that will flow from DOT's strategic plan to the PPMS. These measurements will gauge the performance of our fiduciary responsibility as well as gauge our progress toward our goal of becoming a world class acquisition system. The Procurement Management Council has overall responsibility for developing and maintaining the PPMS and may charter subgroups (e.g., Procurement Information Exchange Council) to help carry out this responsibility.

Procurement Performance Management System Policy Principles

- The BSC measurement approach will be the tool used to assess our performance.
- DOT wide measurements will be used.
- Operating Administration (OA) measurements (beyond the DOT wide measurements) may be used by the OA as a whole or by individual offices for their own unique needs. Data for these measures will be collected and analyzed by the OA/office utilizing the measure.
- The collection and plotting of data and submittal of the Balanced Scorecard Report to the OAs will be performed by the Senior Procurements Executive's (SPE's) office.
- An annual meeting will be held between the SPE and PMC member to discuss the OA's unique BSC results and procurement strategies. Meetings with OA field offices may be held upon request of the PMC member.
- No publication, dissemination, or comparing individual OA results will be done without prior consent of the PMC member or their representative.

OA includes the Transportation Administrative Service Center (TASC).

Waivers

Any requests for exceptions to this document shall be submitted through the HCA to the SPE. The request is to contain sufficient detail to clearly explain the basis of the request, procedures sought to be waived, and any recommended alternative action.

Implementation

This document applies to all OAs and is to be implemented by the HCA as shown in the following timeline.

Procurement Performance Management System Timeline

FY99

ACTION	TIMELINE
FY99 Budget	Completed Jun 1997
FY99 Performance Plan	Completed Sep 1997, updated Sep 1998
FY99 BSC Development	Completed Mar–Apr 1999
FY99 BSC Data Collection • Surveys • MIS	Nov–Dec 1999 Jan 2000
FY99 Performance Report and Management Plan/Input to GPRA	Mar 2000

FY00

ACTION	TIMELINE
FY00 Budget	Completed Jun 1998
FY00 Performance Plan	Completed Sep 1998, to be updated Sep 1999
FY00 BSC Development	Jan–Mar 2000
FY00 BSC Data Collection • Surveys • MIS • Diagnostic	Nov–Dec 2000 Jan 2001 Jan 2001*
FY00 Performance Report and Management Plan/Input to GPRA	Mar 2001

FY01

ACTION	TIMELINE
FY01 Budget	Jun 1999
FY01 Performance Plan	To be completed Sep 1999 and updated Sep 2000
FY01 BSC Development	Jan–Mar 2001
FY01 BSC Data Collection • Surveys • MIS • Diagnostic	Nov–Dec 2001 Jan 2002 Jan 2002*
FY01 Performance Report and Management Plan/Input to GPRA	Mar 2002

*To be conducted every three years as a minimum or over the course of three years (e.g., OAs with multiple field offices).

Future timelines will follow the above FY01 timeline escalated by one year.

DOT's Procurement Performance Management System

> Coming together is a beginning.
> Keeping together is a process.
> Working together is success.
> —Henry Ford

Introduction

Uncertain times brought us face-to-face with the reality of fewer resources and less money to accomplish our mission. In 1995, to help combat these budgetary cuts, we replaced our formal Procurement Management Reviews with a less costly and less resource-intensive performance measurement system based largely on surveys provided to relevant acquisition personnel. The Performance Measurement Assessment Tool (PMAT), as this survey tool is referred, provided us with a method to assess the state of our procurement system. From the PMAT came our current use of the Balanced Scorecard (BSC) as the method by which we are deploying our strategic direction, communicating our expectations, and measuring our improvement progress. This resulted in a tool that emphasizes prevention rather than detection.

There were many statutes that impacted our choice of using the BSC to view our performance. They include: the Government Performance and Results Act (GPRA) of 1993, the Federal Acquisition Streamlining Act of 1994, the Government Management Reform Act of 1994, the Federal Acquisition Reform Act of 1995, and the Information Technology Reform Act of 1996 (the Clinger-Cohen Act). Each of these statutes, in some form, required agencies to strategically plan how they will deliver high-quality supplies and services to their customers, and specifically measure program performance in meeting their strategic commitments. DOT's strategic commitments follow many paths.

Acquisition's Strategic Path

In planning our strategic commitments, we have the opportunity through the Procurement Management Council (PMC) to look at the needs of each operating administration and consolidate the common requirements of the whole into ONE strategic objective. This is especially beneficial in the budget process where a ONE DOT approach can advance and support our budget requests. When developing our business strategies and integrating them within our planning processes, it is important that PMC members request and receive input from their field offices especially those having unique business arrangements (e.g., fee-for-service organizations). Our overall path to the BSC flows from GPRA as shown below. . . .

DOT's Strategic Path to the Balanced Scorecard
Strategic Plan—>Performance Plan—>Budget—>Performance Agreement—>
Balanced Scorecard

A synopsis of each follows:

- **DOT Strategic Plan.** The Strategic Plan is a five-year plan. It is the one document that sets forth the overall direction, vision, and mission of our agency and recognizes the requirement to set performance goals and to identify measures to gauge progress toward these goals. The acquisition portion of the Strategic Plan is under the heading "Resource and Business Process Management Strategy." . . .
- **DOT Performance Plan.** To accomplish the Strategic Plan, an annual Performance Plan is developed. This plan defines the measures, activities, and goals that, when taken together, indicate how well the agency's overall goals are being achieved. The acquisition

portion of the Performance Plan is under the heading "Resource and Business Process Management Strategy." ...

- **Budget Process.** The budget defines the resources needed to accomplish the strategic goals. Within this process, senior acquisition managers (e.g., procurement heads) develop an acquisition budget strategy which is an integral step to strengthening budgetary requests and obtaining the resources to meet strategic planning and performance goals.
- **Performance Agreement.** A Performance Agreement is used to translate and flow down the goals and objectives of the Executive Branch through the Departments. For DOT, this top-down approach is illustrated as follows (titles may vary depending upon organizational structure):

President
⬇ Secretary of Transportation
⬇ Assistant Secretaries & Administrators of each OA
⬇ Office Directors
⬇ Office Managers/Supervisors
⬇ Employees

The goals of the Performance Plan are achieved through the efforts of DOT personnel by tasks outlined in their Performance Agreement. The achievement of these goals can be reflected in the individual's annual Performance Appraisal. By tying the appraisal to the organization's strategic goals, personnel can more fully understand the vision, mission, and goals of the organization and be rewarded for organizational accomplishments rather than just individual achievements.

Balanced scorecard-procurement performance measures. Following down the strategic planning process, more and more refined performance measures and/or tasks are utilized. These measurements are contained in [Appendix C].

The following "Procurement Performance Planning Model" illustrates how performance measures (using the BSC framework) can be developed utilizing the flow-down of the DOT strategic guidance.

Procurement Performance Planning Model

DOT Strategic Plan

Strategic Goal: Foster innovative and sound business practices as stewards of the public's resources in our quest for a fast, safe, efficient, and convenient transportation system.

⬇

DOT Performance Plan	
Goal: To create a world class acquisition system.	
Strategic Objectives: • Develop an acquisition workforce that meets the demands of the 21st century • Make doing business electronically our standard resulting in lower operating costs. • Improve acquisition customer satisfaction.	
Measures:	
Increase % of workforce meeting Clinger-Cohen educational requirements by 5% and training requirements by 50%.	Achieve a customer satisfaction rating of 85%.

Achieve a purchase card usage of 87.5% of simplified acquisition actions.	Increase use of Electronic Commerce by 5%.
Achieve Employee Satisfaction rating of 80%.	

⇩

DOT's Balanced Scorecard

Goal: To create a world class acquisition system.

Strategic Objectives:

• To improve Customer Satisfaction.	• To make doing business electronically our standard resulting in lower operating costs.
• To improve Employee Satisfaction.	• To facilitate procurement programs that effectively apply and comply with law and regulation.
• To have business integrity, fairness, openness.	• To fulfill public policy objectives.
• To have a quality workforce meeting statutory standards.	

Measures by Perspectives:

Customer	Employee	Internal Business Process (IBP)	and Growth	Finance
–% satisfied w/ timeliness.	–% of overall employee satisfaction	–Extent IBPs facilitate program that effectively applies and complies with law and regulation	–% of employees meeting mandatory standards	–Amount of cost avoidance by using purchase cards
–% satisfied w/ quality	–% satisfied with professionalism, culture, values, empowerment	–% competitive procurement of total procurements	–Extent of reliable management information	–% of prompt pay paid vs. $ dispersed
–% satisfied w/ responsiveness, cooperation, etc. to meet mission	–% satisfied with the work environment	–% of actions using electronic commerce		–% of $ obligated for commercial items

DOT'S Balanced Scorecard for Acquisition

> Balance suggests a steadiness that results when all parts are properly adjusted to each other, when no one part or constituting force outweighs or is out of proportion to another.
> —Webster's Third New International Dictionary

Background

In 1993, the interagency Procurement Executives' Association (PEA) created the Procurement Measurement Action Team. Their task was to assess the state of the acquisition system, to identify a structured methodology to measure and improve acquisition performance, and to develop strategies for measuring the health of agency acquisition systems.

The Team found that organizations were using top-down management reviews to determine compliance with established process-oriented criteria and to certify the adequacy of the acquisition system. This method was found to lack a focus on the outcomes of the processes used and was largely ineffective in obtaining dramatic and sustained improvements in the quality of the operations.

The Team did extensive research and made site visits to leaders in performance measurement/management to identify an assessment methodology appropriate for federal organizations. The Team chose a model developed by Drs. David Norton and Robert Kaplan—the Balanced Scorecard (BSC)—because it is:

- Focused on high impact measures
- Intended to be easy and economical to use
- Balanced with emphasis on prevention rather than detection
- Customer-oriented and cross-functional
- Empowering to the procurement organization to make improvements
- Designed to compare the quality of service

The work done by this Team has formed the foundation for the BSC methodology used by DOT's acquisition community. A subsequent team was formed in 1998 by the PEA to develop a guide to a BSC. This document, "Guide to a Balanced Scorecard Performance Management Methodology," was considered a valuable resource for this document.

DOT'S BSC Methodology

DOT's BSC is a structured methodology for using performance measurement information to gauge our progress in and to help us reach our goal of creating a world class acquisition system. To achieve balance in examining the health of our organization, five overarching perspectives are used for our success. These are:

Acquisition's Five Overarching Perspectives

- Customer
- Employee
- Internal Business Processes
- Learning and Growth
- Finance

Key Business Drivers for Enhanced Performance

Within these perspectives, we focus on specific performance areas or key business drivers considered critical to DOT's acquisition function. The areas for heightened performance are:

- Cost
- Quality
- Timeliness
- Quality Work Environment
- Public Policy Fulfillment
- Integrity, Fairness, Openness
- Innovation and Streamlining
- Statutory and Regulatory Application and Compliance

These performance areas are aligned with the guiding principles of the Federal Acquisition Regulations System (Part 1) and are used by world class purchasing systems, both public and private.

Choosing Measurements

> Begin with the end in mind.
> —Stephen Covey

Once the key business drivers are chosen, it is necessary to select a method for gauging the progress toward our goal. We have selected the use of measurements as our indicators for improvement and using measurements under the five perspectives creates a balanced approach. This forms the foundation for DOT's Balanced Scorecard. (See [Appendix C] for a listing of DOT's procurement measurements.) While goals are critical to the measurement effort, a baseline normally must be developed. This may require research, experience or benchmarking with others to set the baseline necessary for determining a realistic measurement goal.

The measurements chosen are linked to DOT's Strategic Plan and focus on the outcomes necessary to meet the Plan's goals. DOT's BSC uses measurements that focus on our goal of creating a world class acquisition system. In his book, "Keeping Score," M.G. Brown provides us with some of the guidelines we consider when choosing our measurements. They include:

Measurement Guidelines

- Measures should be linked to the factors needed for success: key business drivers.
- Measures should be a mix of past, present, and future to ensure that the organization is concerned with all three perspectives.
- Measures should be based around the needs of customers, shareholders, and other key stakeholders.
- Measures should start at the top and flow down to all levels of employees in the organization. Measures need to have targets or goals established that are based on research rather than arbitrary numbers.

We also consider a number of other factors including:

- Operating administration unique needs (each OA has the opportunity to choose additional measures as needed)
- The availability and accuracy of data systems
- The impact on available resources

DOT'S Three Pathways to a Balanced Scorecard

> Even if you're on the right track, you'll be run over if you just sit there.
> —Will Rogers

Introduction

Once the key business drivers are identified and the appropriate measurements developed, it is necessary to decide how performance information will be gathered and evaluated. For DOT, the three tools used for collecting data are: surveys, management information systems, and diagnostic assessments. Each of these methods has been translated into pathways for developing and calculating measurement results. These three pathways contain the measurements, that when linked together, form DOT's Procurement Balanced Scorecard (BSC).

The Three Pathways to DOT'S Procurement BSC

The pathways to our BSC utilize the three methods we have available for collecting quantitative and/or qualitative data. Our pathways were named after these three methodologies.

- Survey Pathway (mainly Qualitative)
- Management Information System (MIS) Pathway (Quantitative)
- Diagnostic Pathway (Qualitative and/or Quantitative)

Each pathway interacts and links with the other as shown:

- The *Survey Pathway* uses the Performance Measurement Assessment Tool (PMAT) methodology.
- The *MIS Pathway* uses information systems (e.g., Contract Information System) to collect data.
- The *Diagnostic Pathway* mainly uses a process and/or results-oriented assessment to evaluate performance.

Operating administrations have significant flexibility in using the three pathways. Each, however, have core measurements from which evaluations are taken. These measurements are discussed under each path. . . .

Deriving the BSC

When the measurement results of the three pathways are linked, it provides us a full view of our progress in reaching our goal. However, before these links can be made, certain steps must be followed. These are:

- Collect the measurement data
- Compute the rating for the measurement
- Link the measurement results in graph or chart form to obtain a visual perspective

Data collection. Each of the three pathways uses a different method for collecting data.

- The *Survey Pathway*, which uses mostly qualitative data, utilizes surveys with electronic data entry capability to receive its data. The data is normally inputted by the customer, employee, and manager, and compiled by the Senior Procurement Executive's (SPE) office.
- The *MIS Pathway*, which uses quantitative data, utilizes various automated data information systems including the Contract Information System and Electronic Posting System. The data is normally inputted by the user and compiled by the SPE's office.
- The *Diagnostic Pathway*, which may use qualitative data to supplement quantitative data, mainly utilizes a manual or hands-on approach to gauge performance. Normally, the information is generated by acquisition personnel and the data compiled by independent evaluators.

Linking the measurement results. Once the data is collected and a score for each measurement is derived, the results will be displayed as a SCORECARD in chart or graph form. The charts may show results for specific measurements in the same overarching perspective, in similar functional areas, in areas having direct impacts on another, or grouped together to form a picture of the total health of the acquisition function. As much as possible, the charts will provide benchmarking data between an individual OA's measurement results and the DOT wide goal/results.

Using Balanced Scorecard Results To Manage Performance

> If there's a way to do it better . . . find it.
> —Thomas A. Edison

Introduction

We have used *performance measurement* as a method to evaluate our progress toward improving our acquisition system. *Performance management* goes a step further. It uses the results of our measurements to make positive change in the way we do business, by helping set performance goals and prioritize resources, by informing us of the need to either confirm or change current policy or program direction, and by sharing results.

For DOT, procurement performance management begins by evaluating the results of our Balanced Scorecard (BSC)—our integrated performance measurement system. *The BSC offers us the ability to consolidate, into one management document, a picture of our progress in areas needing top-level performance while also showing us if improvement in one area is causing a shortfall in another.*

Using BSC Results for Managed Performance

Role of the senior procurement executive's (SPE's) office. The SPE will, in partnership with the PMC, set DOT wide measurement goals.

The SPE's office is the point for accumulating and transferring DOT wide and OA data into a BSC chart(s) that visually depicts an OA's progress. The SPE will hold annual meetings with each PMC member (or field office representatives as requested by the PMC member) to present these DOT wide measurement results as it relates to the OA and the Department as a whole. During these meetings, management strategies for improvement will be explored which may include researching and applying the successful practices of other OAs.

The SPE's office will perform a number of outreach efforts pertaining to performance measurement. Externally, DOT will periodically participate in the benchmarking of common measurements with other Departments. When this occurs, the SPE's office will provide the results of the other Departments (along with the DOT wide results) to the OAs for internal benchmarking purposes.

Evaluating the scorecard. Understanding what a particular result really means is important in determining whether or not it has value. Collecting data by itself is not useful information, but when viewed from the context of our goals and objectives, it can be very useful. Proper analysis is imperative in determining whether or not the measurements are effective and the results are contributing to our objectives. By the use of the three pathways to the BSC—Survey, MIS, Diagnostic—we can use data to determine the level of progress we are making in reaching our goal. But how can this data be used and what do the results mean? When looking at the data results, some insight may be gained by asking the following questions:

- Does the data indicate any performance trends over time? If so, how is the trend data looking and does it reveal a shortfall in one area because of a gain in another? By comparing current and past results, we can determine if we are on the proper course.
- Were performance goals met? If not, explore what inhibited successful performance.

- Were performance goals exceeded? If so, perhaps other benefits to the organization can be gained such as operating cost reductions. Sharing such information may also spread the gain to other OAs.
- How did we compare with participating organization(s)? (Used when benchmarking.)
- Can the data be used to improve performance in areas other than the one(s) assessed or can it pinpoint specific areas for consideration? Data can help identify specific areas within the larger assessed area that need attention.
- Where should improvement efforts be focused to achieve the greatest or most needed return? Many times the amount of available resources dictates the need to focus on particular areas that will provide the most return for the resource investment.

Importance of trend data. To evaluate our performance level, trend data is perhaps the most critical of all. The more data available for a particular measurement, the better are the chances of getting an accurate picture of the progress toward our goal. While our BSC mainly uses annual data, there are many measurements, especially in the MIS Pathway, that can be reviewed on a monthly or quarterly basis. This data can provide a larger data base from which to gauge performance and to alert us to any fluctuations in performance that may need to be examined.

Key to success. The key to success is to achieve as much balance as possible for all measures on the BSC. If one measure has a deep fluctuation, care must be taken not to change too drastically to get performance back in line because it may cause problems in areas critical to a particular operation. Being able to use the measurement results to make good management decisions is the foundation of performance management. Attachment E [see Appendix C] provides a number of performance assessment tools that may be helpful when making decisions for improvement.

Action Plan for Improved Performance

Sharing results. As with any performance management system, feedback is vital for the system to grow and flourish. Retaining results without sharing them, especially among its participants, is a sure way to kill this type of system. Conversely, to share and inform, is to nurture and promote the system. Feedback can be accomplished in many ways such as through electronic mail, briefs, newsletters, and conferences. Not only is it critical to let respondents and any other interested parties know the measurement results, but it is also important to work with them to develop strategies that will be employed for improvement.

Strategies for improvement. Once measurement results are analyzed for both the DOT wide and OA measures and the areas needing improvement determined, it is time to determine the strategies needed to achieve our desired results. One of the best methods for determining the necessary strategies is to partner with your customer and/or employees. Those affected by the process are normally the best ones to reveal what needs to be done. The objective is to have the strategies lead to the goals/outcomes desired. It is those goals/outcomes that feed into the Government Performance and Results Act report.

Goal setting. Every measure needs to have an associated goal in order to know where to head, how fast to go, and when the destination is reached. Of critical importance, is to have clear, quantifiable goals for those measures contained in the Strategic and Performance Plans. When determining goals for either DOT wide or OA unique measures, the following, as required by the Government Performance and Results Act, should be considered:

- The identification of the goals in an objective, quantifiable, and measurable form;
- The operational processes, skills and technologies, and resources such as human, capital, and information needed to meet the goals;

- The basis for comparing measurement results with the desired goals; and
- The means for verifying and validating the measurement results.

Future Success

The success of our Procurement Performance Management System (PPMS) is dependent upon many factors. These include:

- Demonstrating strong support for the System at all levels of management
- Integrating procurement's critical measures into DOT's Strategic and Performance Plans
- Spreading the word as to what performance measurement and performance management is, its purpose and its benefits
- Ensuring the data (e.g., Contract Information System data) is accurate and reliable
- Promoting participation in completing surveys and other evaluation tools
- Sharing results and providing feedback to participants to help nurture and promote improvement through performance management
- Using measurement results and partnering with your customers to determine the strategies for improvement
- Translating management strategies into action for improved outcomes
- Setting goals and benchmarking results.

As we progress on our improvement journey, we expect the system to grow and become more effective. Any comments or suggestions to help lead this growth are welcome.

CHAPTER 13

The Balanced Scorecard in Human Resources at the Department of Energy

This chapter presents a very detailed and effective example of how the Department of Energy (DOE) developed and applied the BSC approach to the human resources (HR) function. The DOE HR Council commissioned the HR Performance Measurement Project Team to develop a systems approach to measurement. The team accomplished that objective with the aid of the Strategic Effectiveness Group, LLC and its president, John Hirsch.

On November 4, 1998, Mr. Hirsch presented a briefing on this effort. The material that follows is adapted from that briefing developed by Mr. Hirsch and Joseph Montgomery. It is presented with the permission of John Hirsch. (*Note:* Sections One and Three of the briefing are presented here; Section Two can be found in Appendix A.)

STRATEGIC MEASUREMENT SYSTEM FOR DOE CONTRACTOR HUMAN RESOURCES (SMS^{HR}): A COMPREHENSIVE APPROACH TO TAILORED STRATEGIC HR PLANNING

Introduction—A New Approach to Contractor Oversight

Through the advent of contract reform and the implementation of performance-based contracts, the Department of Energy (DOE) has determined it must redefine its oversight role in the area of Contractor Human Resources to embrace the principle of strategic management found in private industry.

The role of Human Resources (HR) in the commercial environment is evolving to the level of a strategic partner with line management in the development and accomplishment of key business goals. A central component of success for a strategic HR organization is a comprehensive, performance system which establishes goals tied to the entire organization's mission and provides feedback on the impact of and value added by HR. The SMS^{HR} is DOE's initiative to increase the effectiveness of the HR function, aligning it with both the contractor's corporate needs and those of the DOE field office and HQ.

To accomplish this objective, in 1998 the DOE HR Council commissioned the Human Resources Performance Measurement Project Team to develop a systems approach to measurement. The team established a set of criteria:

- *Activity to Result*—Emphasize the "bottom line" and results of performance, not just performance itself
- *Process to Substance*—Emphasize substantive issues, not procedural efforts unless required by statute or regulation
- *Subjectivity to Objectivity*—Emphasize objectivity while identifying strategic perspectives. HR performance measures have been traditionally "soft" which is the converse of most non-HR circumstances (e.g., Balanced Scorecard)

- *Involvement in Oversight*—Increase program oversight by de-emphasizing "daily" involvement and maintain focus on "for cause" circumstances

Additionally, in consideration of the diversity of site missions, the varying levels of HR sophistication needed, and the differences in the amount of collaboration experienced at various sites, the Project Team agreed with the RL approach that the design of any program developed should meet the following requirements:

- *Dynamic and Incremental*—Program should be phased in without an implementation "end-state"
- *Flexible and Adaptable*—Program should allow for and reflect individual circumstances of each prime contractor and measure both business management excellence and sound human resource practices
- *Collaborative*—Program should reinforce mutually developed expectations between DOE and contractor HR counterparts
- *Simplistic*—Program should be as uncomplicated as practicable
- *Accommodate*—Program should accommodate the "Balanced Scorecard" at the prime contractor level

Within the general parameters of SMS^{HR} the Project Team with the aid of the Strategic Effectiveness Group, LLC, an organizational improvement consulting team, prepared this report. The recommendations serve as a blueprint for the creation of a complex-wide process for strategic HR planning utilizing the Balanced Scorecard as its measurement oversight tool.

- Section One, "Creating an HR Balanced Scorecard," explains the logic of the process and presents the step-by-step methodology for creating a plan and the resulting scorecard.
- Section Two, "Applying the Model: Creating a BSC for a Hypothetical Hanford Contractor," is a case study that brings the process to life with examples from a variety of Hanford situations.
- Section Three, "Overview of the Balanced Scorecard," explains the purpose of the BSC and its linkage to strategic management including mission, vision, and business strategy.

Note: These three sections are prepared in a format that can be used for overhead transparency presentations.

The HR Council's expectation is that all contractor HR organizations, in collaboration with their DOE Contracting Officer, will use the process described herein to create a BSC. The process is designed to provide a product that is tailored to the particular needs of each individual operation. It is designed to focus the participants on a few key activities that will make a real difference in assisting the contractor organization in fulfilling its DOE site mission. Oversight is enhanced through specific measures that determine whether the HR function has been successful in meeting its targets. Underlying the entire process is a key assumption: the BSC is implemented in a collaborative fashion. It anticipates that interactive discussions occur throughout the process, so that the resulting BSC marries the needs of the contractor's line organization, its HR department, DOE's local program office, and contracting officer.

Section One Creating an HR Balanced Scorecard

What Are the Anticipated Requirements?
- Use of the Balanced Scorecard approach
- Contractor measures that:
- Link with contractor & DOE mission/
- Vision/strategy

- Include customer satisfaction
- Show cost and efficiency of
- Business systems
- Assess relevant aspects of
- Organizational culture
- Show compliance with laws, regulations
- A self-assessment plan (BSCA)
- A self-assessment report, based on data collected
- Participation in surveillance, validation activities by Field Office

Benefits of an HR Scorecard ("What's in It for Me?")
- Improves the HR contribution to the "bottom line"—in a visible fashion
- Gives HR a direction and strategy
- Improves the teaming relationship with DOE HR
- Makes HR look great to senior/line management
- Provides strong rationale for DOE "push backs"

Potential Concerns about the HR Scorecard ("What Is This Going To Cost Me?")
- HR will need to think strategically and in terms of contribution to the corporate mission
- Elevates DOE involvement above transactions
- Will probably require extra effort at relationship building with DOE HR
- HR will need to set priorities, disengage in some low value-added tasks

Overview: Creating an HR BSC
1) Create an HR mission, vision, strategy that are aligned with corporate and DOE Field Office HR mission, vision, strategy
2) Consider DOE, contractor drivers; identify desired organizational characteristics to support corporate, DOE HR strategies
3) Compare current status with applicable Best Practices to establish appropriate standards
4) Set performance targets for key characteristics needing change
5) Determine actions/tactics to achieve goals
6) Create measure(s) for each tactic. Specify mechanics of data collection, analysis
7) Sort measures into BSC quadrants; prioritize measures; select one or two measures for DOE oversight purposes

Preliminary Steps in BSC Preparation

Step 1

Business and Environmental Drivers

DOE Field Office HR Mission Vision Strategy Corporate Mission Vision Strategy	**DOE HR Tactics** **Corporate Tactics**	**Contractor HR Analysis:** Based on Corporate and DOE HR Mission/Vision/Strategy, and DOE and Contractor Drivers: 1. What is Appropriate HR Mission, Vision, Strategy? 2. What Type of Org. Does HR Need to Help Create?
Collaboration between Corporate and DOE Program Office	Field Office HR Collaborates with Contractor HR Director to develop Its Tactics	DOE HR and Corporate Review the Analysis as a Reality and Alignment Check

RELATIONSHIPS

Understanding Field Office and Contractor HR Drivers

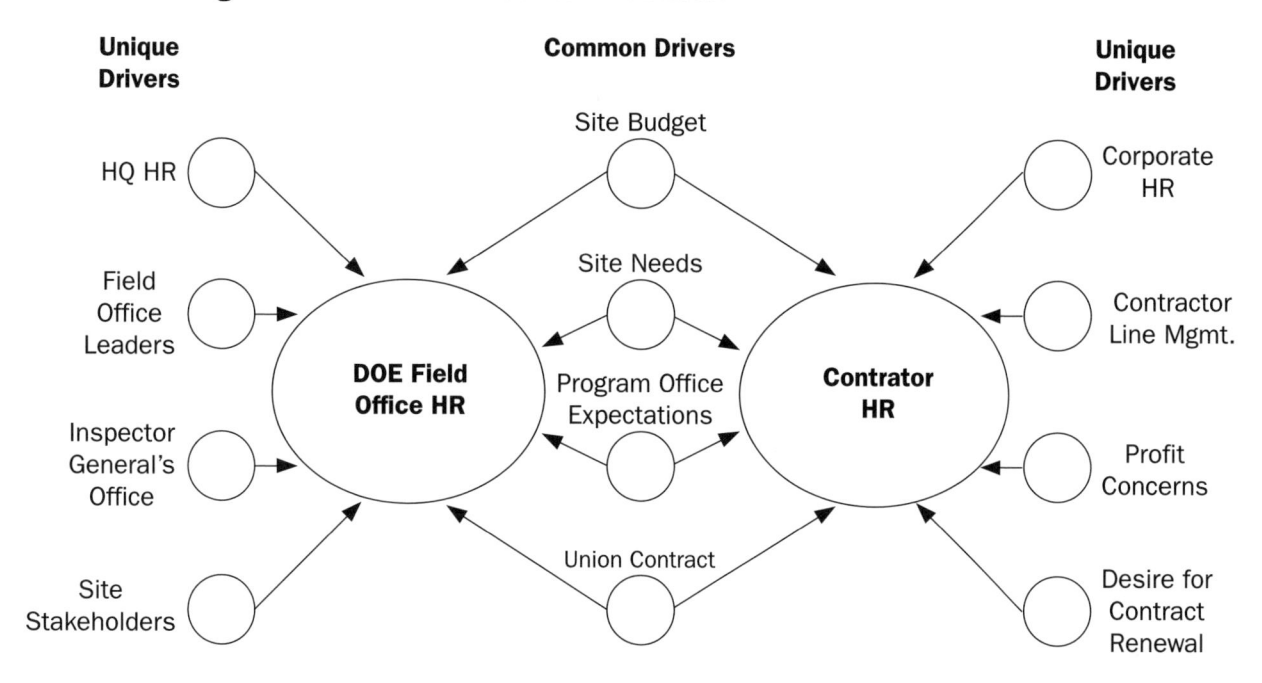

Unique Drivers

- HQ HR
- Field Office Leaders
- Inspector General's Office
- Site Stakeholders

Common Drivers

- Site Budget
- Site Needs
- Program Office Expectations
- Union Contract

DOE Field Office HR ↔ **Contrator HR**

Unique Drivers

- Corporate HR
- Contractor Line Mgmt.
- Profit Concerns
- Desire for Contract Renewal

Using Desired Org. Characteristics To Drive Assessments, Goals, Tactics, and Measures

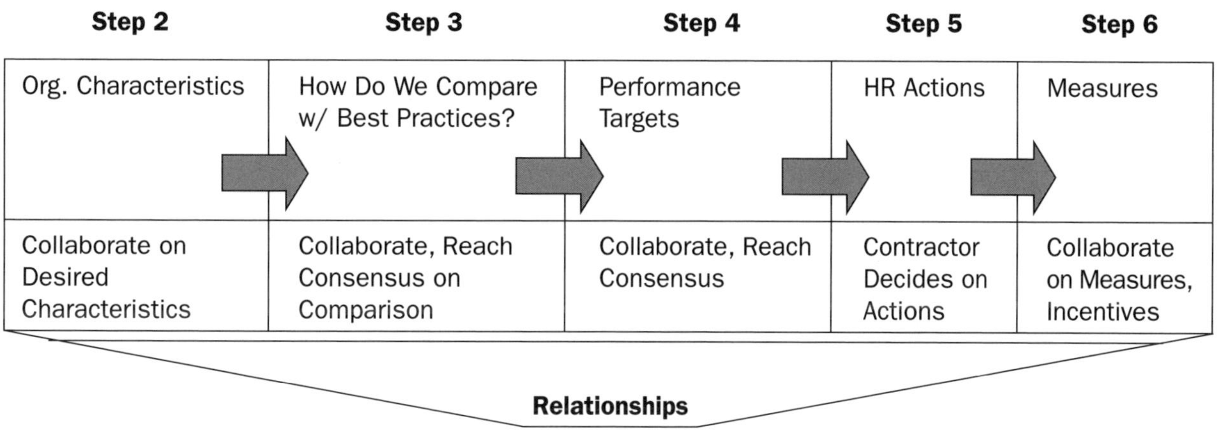

Step 2	Step 3	Step 4	Step 5	Step 6
Org. Characteristics	How Do We Compare w/ Best Practices?	Performance Targets	HR Actions	Measures
Collaborate on Desired Characteristics	Collaborate, Reach Consensus on Comparison	Collaborate, Reach Consensus	Contractor Decides on Actions	Collaborate on Measures, Incentives

Relationships

Establishing the "Mechanics"

Step 6 Continued

Measure:	How is data collected?	How often?	Who collects?

Sort Measures into a Draft BSC

Work Processes	Culture
Customer Satisfaction	Finance

Section Three Overview of the Balanced Scorecard (BSC)

Purpose of the BSC
- Indicates system-wide effectiveness, not just financial results
- Links long-term strategies with short-term actions, goals/objectives
- Builds consensus on what's important
- Communicates what's important to all levels
- Assesses degree of success of the strategy
- Builds staff alignment, accountability

Examples of Measures

Customer Satisfaction	Survey of responsiveness, quality, technical capability, overall satisfaction; number of complaints, lost customers
Culture	Survey of staff perceptions of innovation, professional dev . . . , resources; new capabilities; values, operating principles
Effective Work Processes	Cycle time, processing time, scrap/waste, output, inventory, queue time, setup time (includes white collar processes)
Financial Success	Business volume, ROI, backlog, growth in assets, capital-to-asset ratio, operating expenses

A Caution
The BSC must be built upon a sound mission, vision, and strategy. Creating a random collection of measures or using what looks good (or is popular) will not lead to success. (Kaplan & Norton, 1992, 1996)

The Strategic Management System

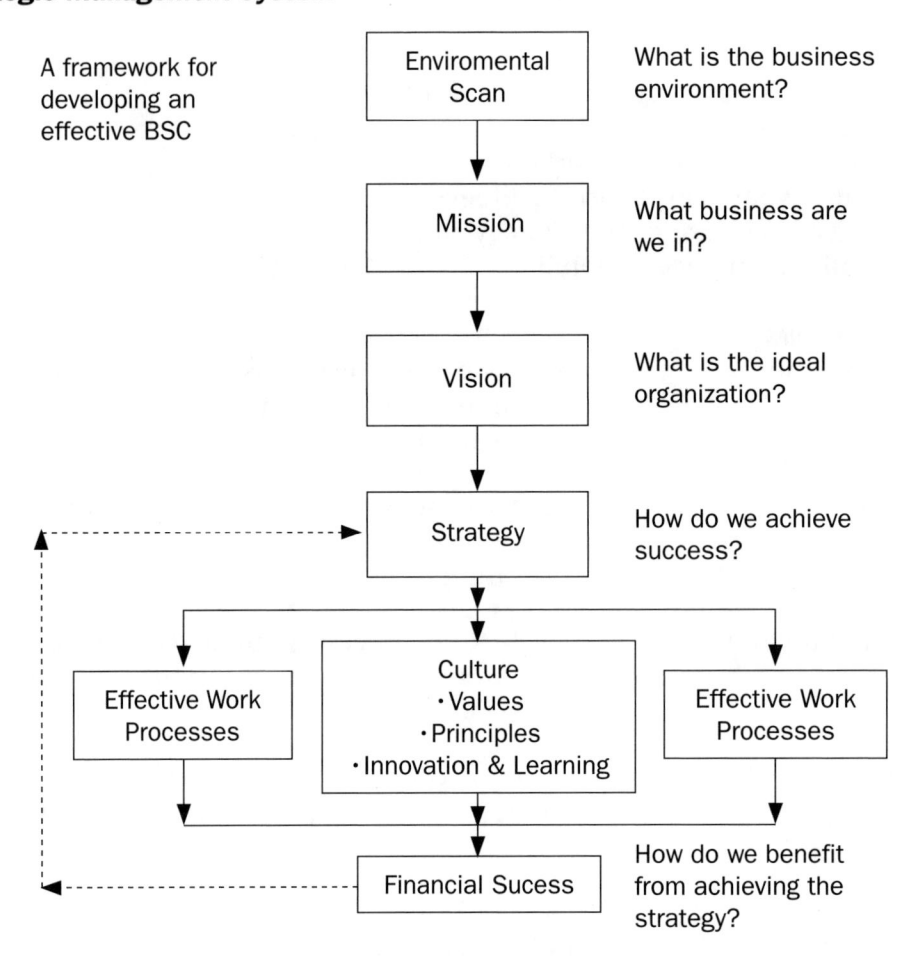

A framework for developing an effective BSC

- **Enviromental Scan** — What is the business environment?
- **Mission** — What business are we in?
- **Vision** — What is the ideal organization?
- **Strategy** — How do we achieve success?
  - Effective Work Processes
  - Culture
    - Values
    - Principles
    - Innovation & Learning
  - Effective Work Processes
- **Financial Sucess** — How do we benefit from achieving the strategy?

© Copyright, Strategic Effectiveness Group™, 1998

The Private Sector BSC

Work Processes · *Innovation* · *Operations* · *Post-sale service*	Culture · *Key values* · *Operating principles* · *Innovation* · *Learning*
Customer Satisfaction · *Market share* · *Customer retention* · *Customer acquisition* · *Customer satisfaction* · *Customer profitability*	Finance · *Revenue growth & mix* · *Cost reduction/productivity imp.* · *Asset utilization/investment strategy*
	**Note: bullets indicate possible topics for measure development**

Environmental Scan
- Asks customers, suppliers, stakeholders, staff, management how they view your performance
- Based on interviews, focus groups, surveys
- Requires valid, unbiased information
- Creates a clear understanding of how each group sees you
- Creates a "systems" view of the business

"Mission" Answers the Questions:
- What business are we in?
- What are we paid to provide?
- What is our value-added?
- What is our role in the organization or the market?

A sound definition of mission has *great power* to align and motivate the entire organization.

Vision
- Describes the ideal organization—one that is incredibly successful at achieving the mission
- Includes creative thinking about work processes, customers, the culture, relationships, quality, profit, professional development, etc.
- Involves a consensus of the management team, staff about the desired future

Business Strategy
- A clearly stated hypothesis about what is required for organizational success. "If we do . . . then we will succeed."
- Drives the measures used on the BSC

Strategies for Success
1) Be the leading edge innovator, technology provider, product leader
2) Be the low cost producer/supplier
3) Be the most tightly linked, integrated with the customer
4) Leverage off of unique characteristics:
   - Unique product
   - Unique, specific customers
   - Unique production characteristics
   - Unique technology
   - Unique sales approaches
   - Unique distribution features
   - Access to key natural resources

Characteristics of Sound Strategy
- Choose a single strategy—"straddling doesn't work"
- Be the best in that area
- Achieve at least minimal acceptable performance in the other three areas
- Base all actions, activities on that strategy
- Maintain flexibility—be open to opportunities

All Measures Derive from Strategy
- Finance: Are we achieving our financial objectives? Is the strategy showing bottom-line improvements?
- Customer: How is the customer reacting to our strategy? Are we providing the value-added defined by our strategy?
- Work process: Are we operating effectively, efficiently to achieve the strategy?
- Culture: Are we creating the values, skills, attitudes needed to achieve the strategy?

CHAPTER 14

Utilizing the Balanced Scorecard Tool in the Public Sector

This chapter is a detailed slide presentation used in OPM training courses from GAO. It covers a wide variety of uses for the balanced scorecard.

Dr. Sharon L. Caudle of GAO developed the presentation that follows. The presentation has been adapted for use here with Dr. Caudle's permission. The opinions expressed are her own and do not reflect the official position of GAO.

Utilizing the Balanced Scorecard Tool

Sharon L. Caudle, Ph.D.
Senior Analyst, Office of Strategic Issues
U.S. General Accounting Office
441 G St., NW MS2440C
Washington, DC 20548

A Government Scorecard Framework

Public Stewardship — To meet the legislative intent, how should we provide effective policy and resource stewardship for our stakeholders and society at large?

Clientele Impact — To achieve our mission, how should we serve and impact our clientele--those who receive our products, services, funding, or our regulatory intervention?

Day to Day Processes — To meet our public trust and clientele impact commitments, how should we effectively work internally and externally through extended, effective business processes?

Human Capital Support — To meet out commitments, how should we identify, secure, and sustain employee and delivery partner commitment, knowledge, and skills?

Enabling Support — To meet our commitments, how should we craft the right organizational alignment and technological support?

Government Scorecard Perspectives

Public Stewardship — Policy and Resource Stewardship
- Program policy in line with legislative mandates and directives
- Funding in line with results expectations
- Financial integrity policies and practices

Clientele Impact — Accountability to Clientele Needs
- Direct product, services, funding impact
- Regulatory compliance, problem-solving, intervention impact

Day to Day Processes — Extended Business Processes
- Internal/external business process innovation capabilities and improvements
- Collaborative, productive relationships

Human Capital Support — Employee and Delivery Partner Commitment, Skills, Development
- Employee, delivery partner skills, expertise retention and development
- Employee, delivery partner empowerment
- Employee, delivery partner commitment

Enabling Support — Organizational Alignment and Technological Support
- Organizational roles/structure fit with results
- Investment, impact of needed technology

Examples: Broad Scorecard Perspectives

- **Public Stewardship**: Reduce and avoid costs due to fraud and incorrect billings

- **Clientele Impact**: Increase number of children in foster care adopted into a permanent home

- **Day to Day Processes**: Reengineer grants management business process to improve service to partners and costs and delay

- **Human Capital Support**: Implement workforce analysis findings to build skills matching agency mandates

- **Enabling Support**: Streamline agency organizational layers and align resource location with partners' support needs

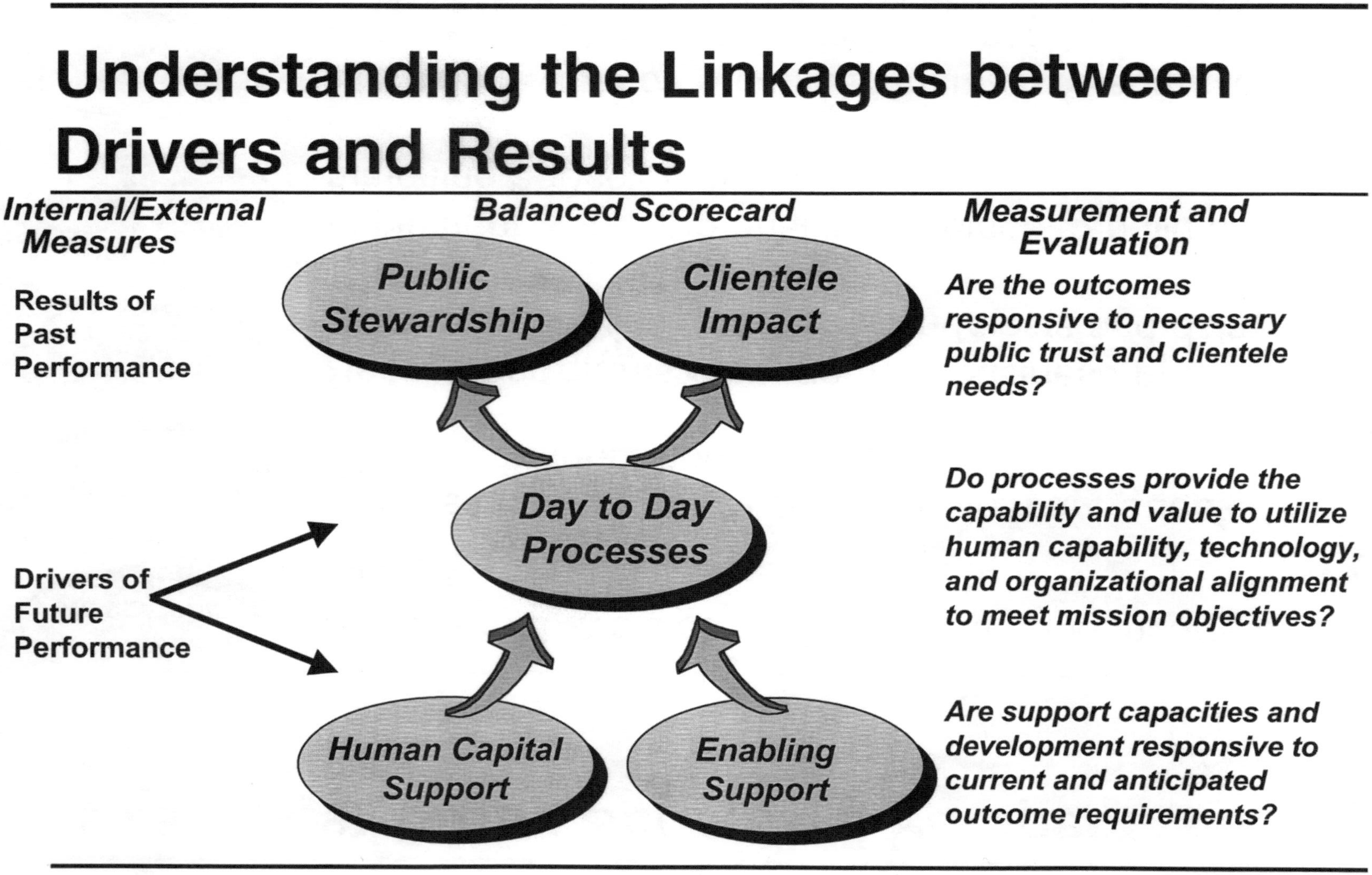

Understanding the Linkages between Drivers and Results

Internal/External Measures	Balanced Scorecard	Measurement and Evaluation
Results of Past Performance	**Clientele Impact**	Are the outcomes responsive to necessary public trust and clientele needs?
	Day to Day Processes	Do processes provide the capability and value to utilize human capability, technology, and organizational alignment to meet mission objectives?
	Public Stewardship	
Drivers of Future Performance	**Enabling Support** / **Human Capital Support**	Are support capacities and development responsive to current and anticipated outcome requirements?

City of Charlotte 2000 Corporate Balanced Scorecard

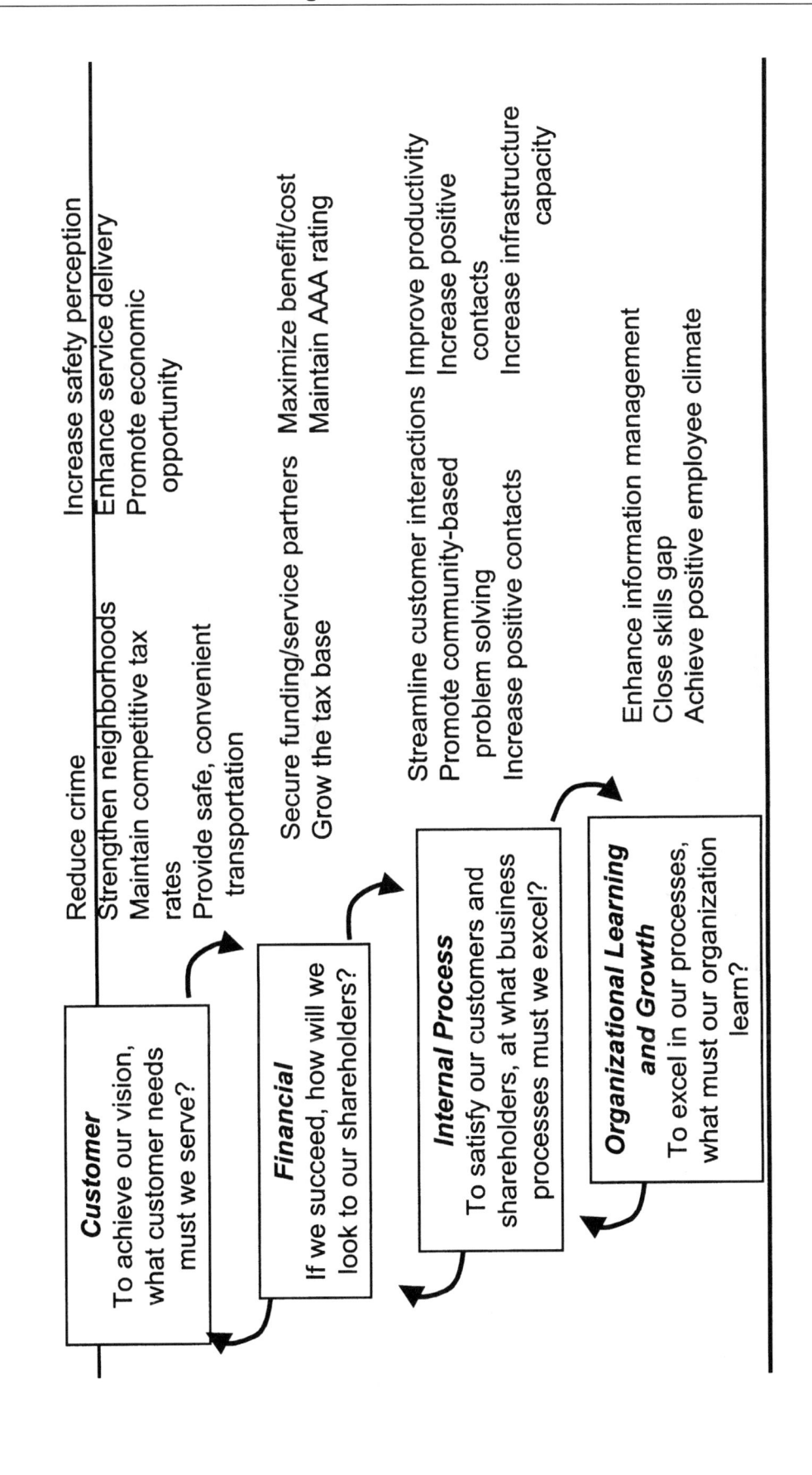

Customer
To achieve our vision, what customer needs must we serve?

- Reduce crime
- Strengthen neighborhoods
- Maintain competitive tax rates
- Provide safe, convenient transportation
- Increase safety perception
- Enhance service delivery
- Promote economic opportunity

Financial
If we succeed, how will we look to our shareholders?

- Secure funding/service partners
- Grow the tax base
- Maximize benefit/cost
- Maintain AAA rating

Internal Process
To satisfy our customers and shareholders, at what business processes must we excel?

- Streamline customer interactions
- Promote community-based problem solving
- Increase positive contacts
- Improve productivity
- Increase positive contacts
- Increase infrastructure capacity

Organizational Learning and Growth
To excel in our processes, what must our organization learn?

- Enhance information management
- Close skills gap
- Achieve positive employee climate

Charlotte Linkage Model and Measures

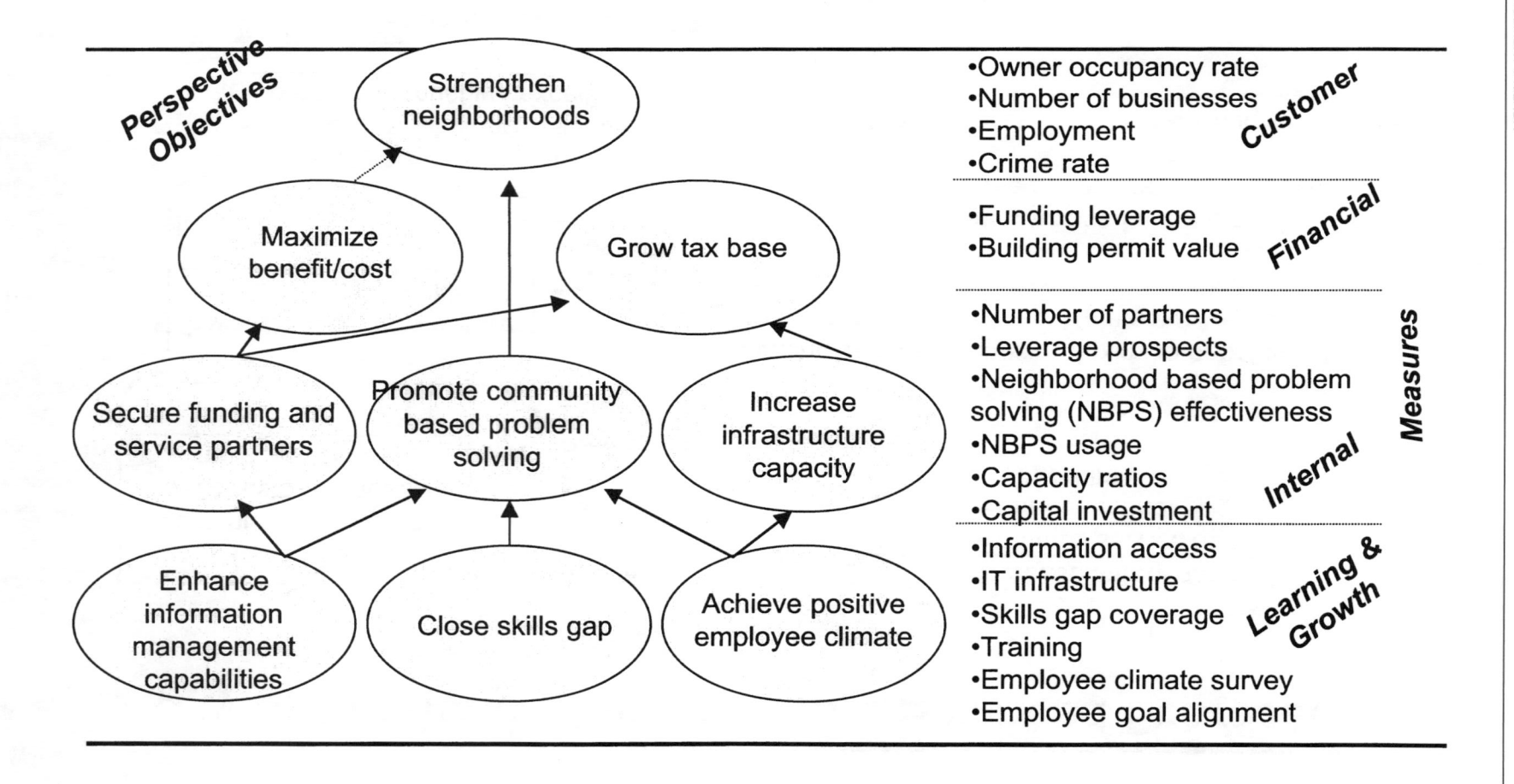

Perspective / Objectives

- Strengthen neighborhoods
- Grow tax base
- Increase infrastructure capacity
- Maximize benefit/cost
- Promote community based problem solving
- Achieve positive employee climate
- Close skills gap
- Secure funding and service partners
- Enhance information management capabilities

Measures

Customer
- Owner occupancy rate
- Number of businesses
- Employment
- Crime rate

Financial
- Funding leverage
- Building permit value

Internal
- Number of partners
- Leverage prospects
- Neighborhood based problem solving (NBPS) effectiveness
- NBPS usage
- Capacity ratios
- Capital investment

Learning & Growth
- Information access
- IT infrastructure
- Skills gap coverage
- Training
- Employee climate survey
- Employee goal alignment

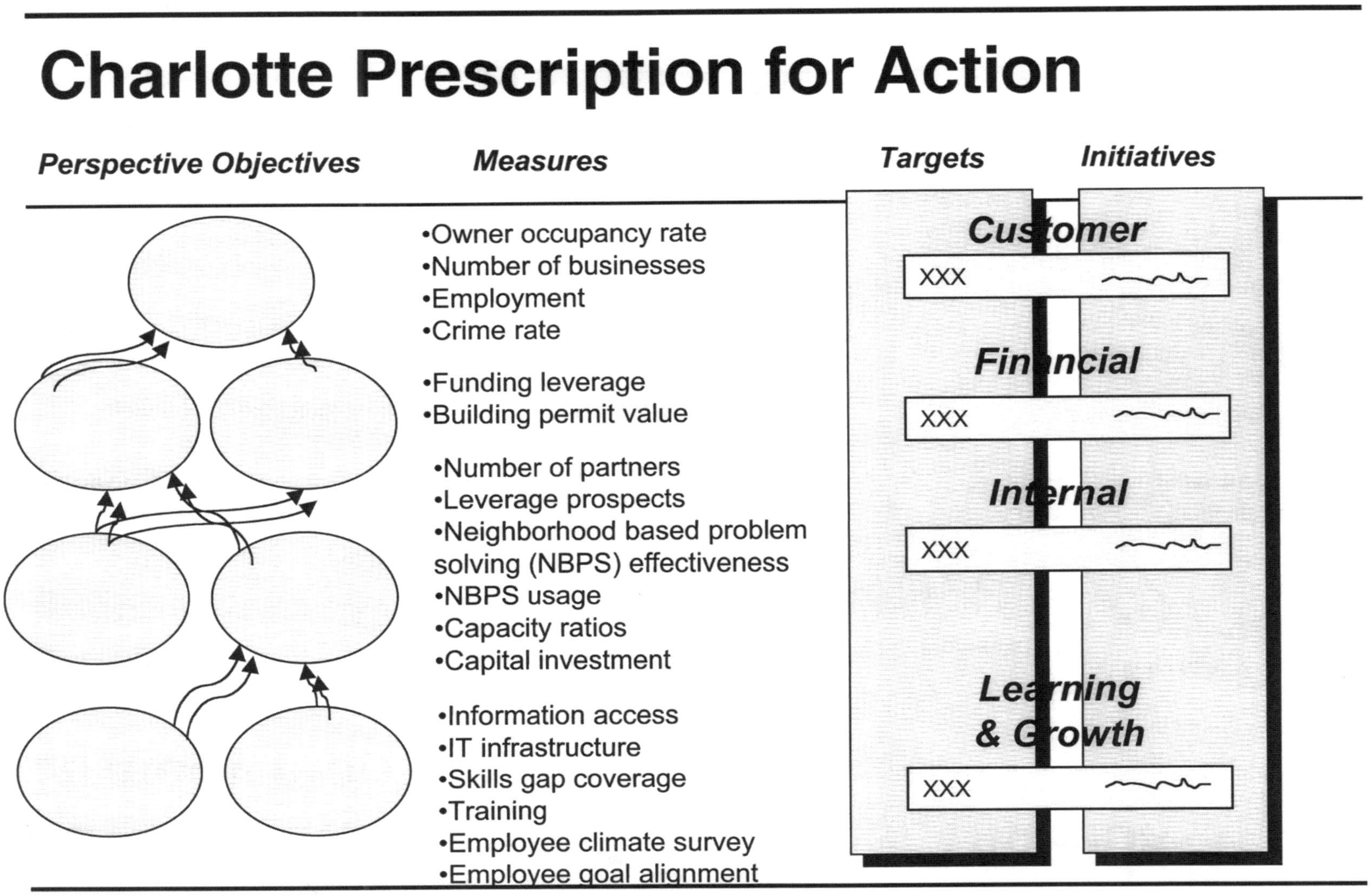

Charlotte Prescription for Action

Perspective Objectives	Measures	Targets	Initiatives
	• Owner occupancy rate • Number of businesses • Employment • Crime rate	**Customer** xxx	
	• Funding leverage • Building permit value	**Financial** xxx	
	• Number of partners • Leverage prospects • Neighborhood based problem solving (NBPS) effectiveness • NBPS usage • Capacity ratios • Capital investment	**Internal** xxx	
	• Information access • IT infrastructure • Skills gap coverage • Training • Employee climate survey • Employee goal alignment	**Learning & Growth** xxx	

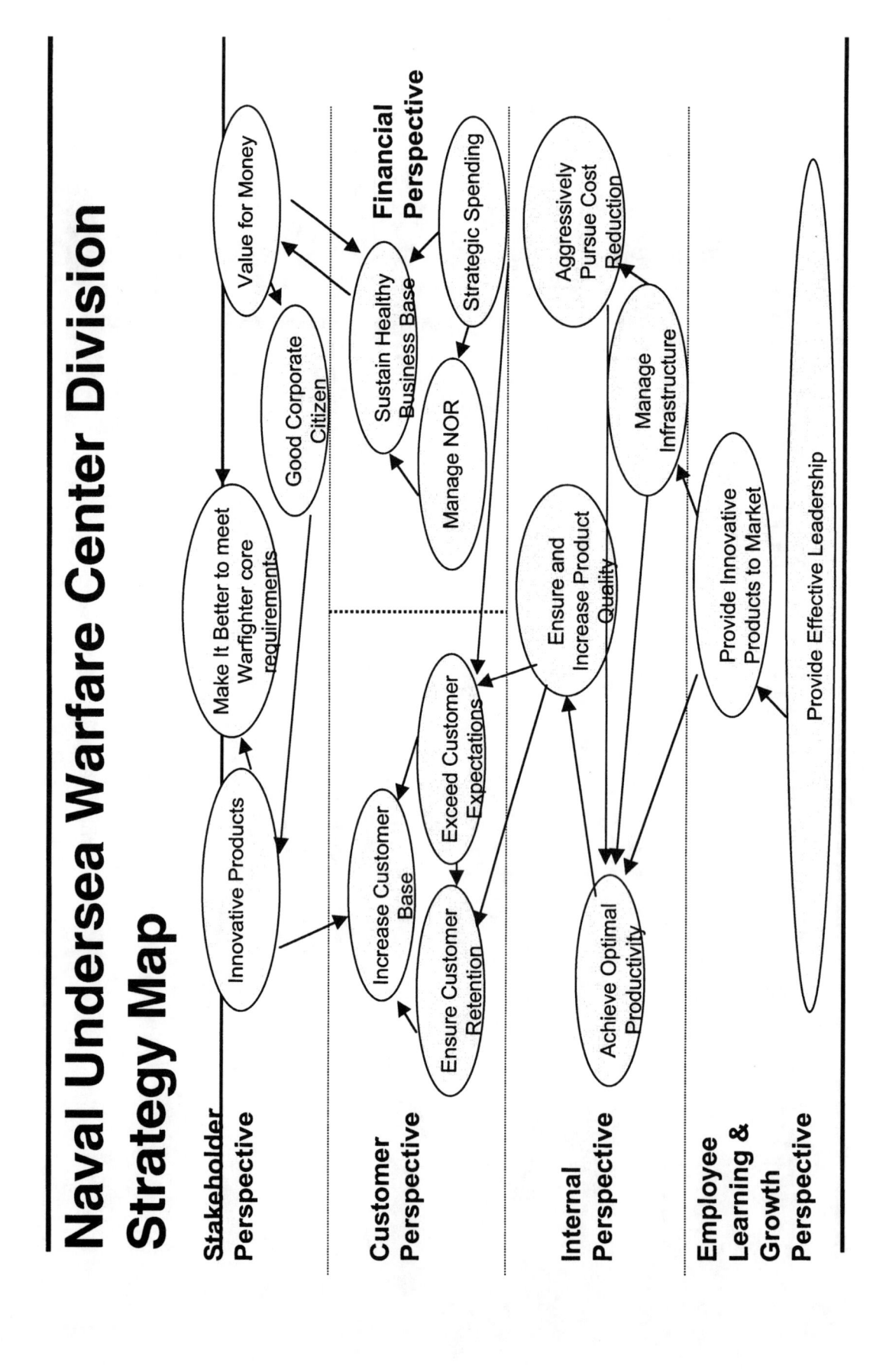

Naval Undersea Warfare Center Division Strategy Map

Stakeholder Perspective
- Value for Money
- Make It Better to meet Warfighter core requirements
- Innovative Products
- Good Corporate Citizen

Financial Perspective
- Sustain Healthy Business Base
- Strategic Spending
- Aggressively Pursue Cost Reduction
- Manage NOR

Customer Perspective
- Increase Customer Base
- Exceed Customer Expectations
- Ensure Customer Retention

Internal Perspective
- Ensure and Increase Product Quality
- Manage Infrastructure
- Achieve Optimal Productivity
- Provide Innovative Products to Market

Employee Learning & Growth Perspective
- Provide Effective Leadership

NUWC Customer Objectives, Definitions, Measures

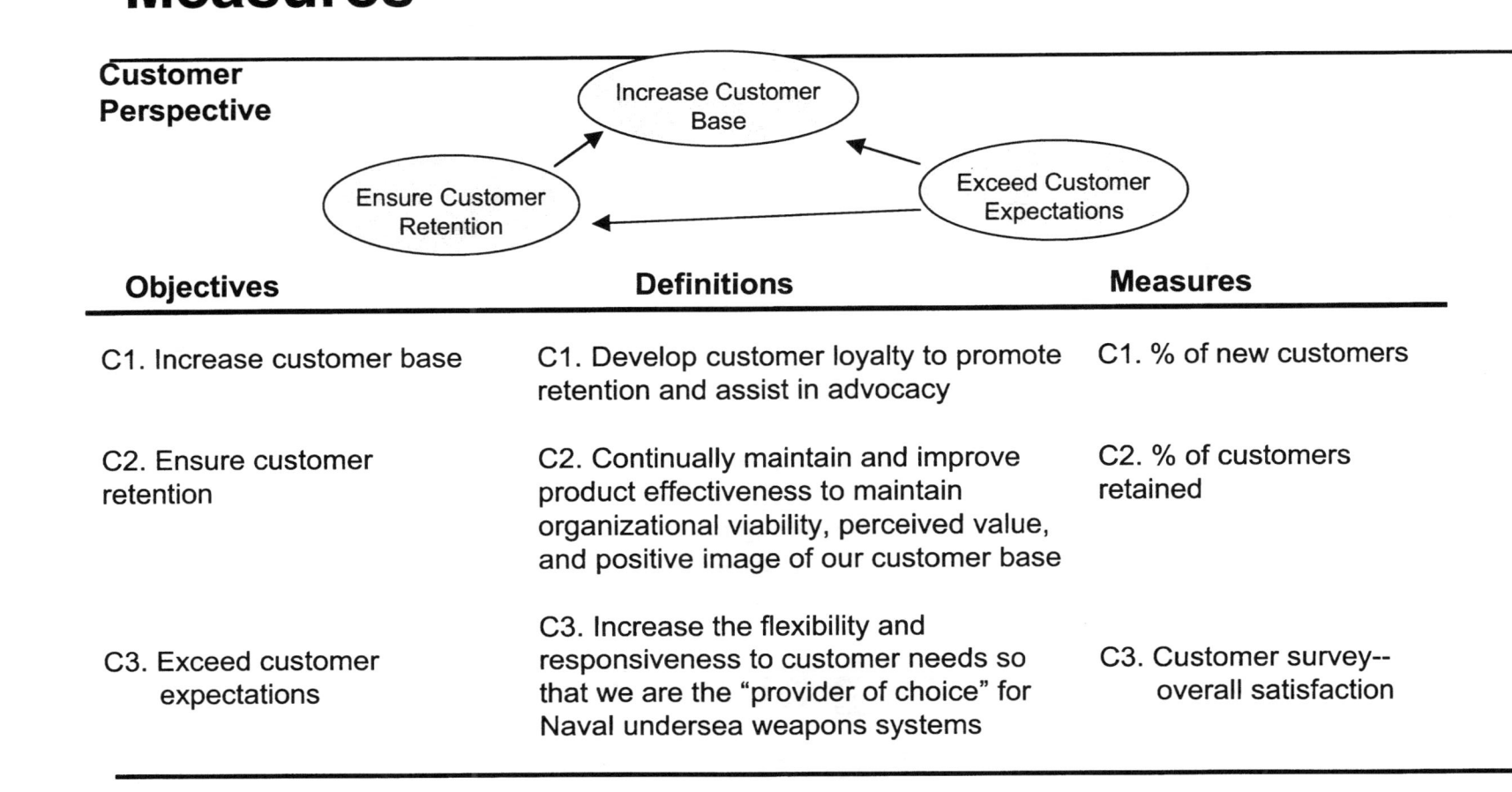

Customer Perspective

```
    Increase Customer
         Base
        ↗    ↘
Ensure Customer   Exceed Customer
   Retention       Expectations
```

Objectives	Definitions	Measures
C1. Increase customer base	C1. Develop customer loyalty to promote retention and assist in advocacy	C1. % of new customers
C2. Ensure customer retention	C2. Continually maintain and improve product effectiveness to maintain organizational viability, perceived value, and positive image of our customer base	C2. % of customers retained
C3. Exceed customer expectations	C3. Increase the flexibility and responsiveness to customer needs so that we are the "provider of choice" for Naval undersea weapons systems	C3. Customer survey-- overall satisfaction

310 PRESIDENT'S MANAGEMENT AGENDA

NUWC Employee/ Learning & Growth Perspective Cascading Example

Division Mission and Vision — Hierarchical Scorecards

Division Newport Objectives*
- Enhance support for Innovative Initiatives
- Provide Innovative Products
- Maintain Flexible Workforce that can Innovate

DivNpt Measures*
- % of OH budget spent on Innovation
- Non-mandatory Training Hours
- # of Patent Disclosures

Directorate/ Department (D/D) Objectives*
- Develop advanced concepts and technology to address evolving Navy needs
- Create a focus on reduction of system total ownership cost
- Increase partnering with industry and academia
- Become recognized as a team player

D/D & Individual Measures*
- Number of Proposals submitted
- Number of Publications and Presentations
- Number of Patent Disclosures
- Number of CRADAs
- Workshop/ Symposium Attendance

Individual Contributing Factors and Expectations
- Innovation and Initiative
  - Geared toward delivering high-quality sonar products
- Team Work
- Continuous improvement

* *Only the Objectives and Measures directly applicable to Individual Performance are listed*

Charlotte Department of Transportation: Alignment

	City Scorecard	CDOT Scorecard
Customer Perspective	• Strengthen neighborhoods • Enhance service delivery • Provide safe, convenient transportation	• Maintain the transportation system • Operate the transportation system • Develop the transportation system • Determine optimal system design • Improve service quality • Strengthen neighborhoods
Financial Accountability Perspective	• Secure funding/service partners • Maximize benefit cost	• Expand non-city funding • Maximize benefit/cost
Internal Process Perspective	• Improve productivity • Increase positive contacts • Increase infrastructure capacity	• Increase infrastructure capacity • Secure funding/service partners • Improve productivity • Increase positive contacts
Organizational Learning and Growth Perspective	• Enhance information management • Close skills gap • Achieve positive employee climate	• Enhance automated information systems • Enhance field technology • Close skills gap • Empower employees

Charlotte Department of Transportation: Measures

Customer Perspective Objective	Lead Measure	Lag Measure
C-1 Maintain the transportation system	**C-1 Repair Response**: repair response action **C-1 Travel Speed**: average travel speed by facility and selected location	**C-1 High Quality Streets**: condition of lane miles at 90 rating
C-2 Operate the transportation system	**C-2 On-Time Buses**: public transit on-time	**C-2 Safety**: city-wide accident rate; # of high accident locations
C-3 Develop the transportation system	**C-3 Programs Introduced**: newly introduced programs, pilots, or program specifications	**C-3 Basic Mobility**: availability of transit
C-4 Determine optimal system design		**C-4 Plan Progress**: % complete on 2015 Transportation Plan
C-5 Improve service quality	**C-5 Responsiveness**: % of citizen complaints and requests resolved at the CDOT level	**C-5 Commute Time**: average commute time on selected roads
C-6 Strengthen neighborhoods	**C-6 Issue Response**: defined situations where CDOT identifies, responds to neighborhood traffic and mobility issues	**C-6 Neighborhood-Oriented Programs**: programs implemented through community-based problem solving

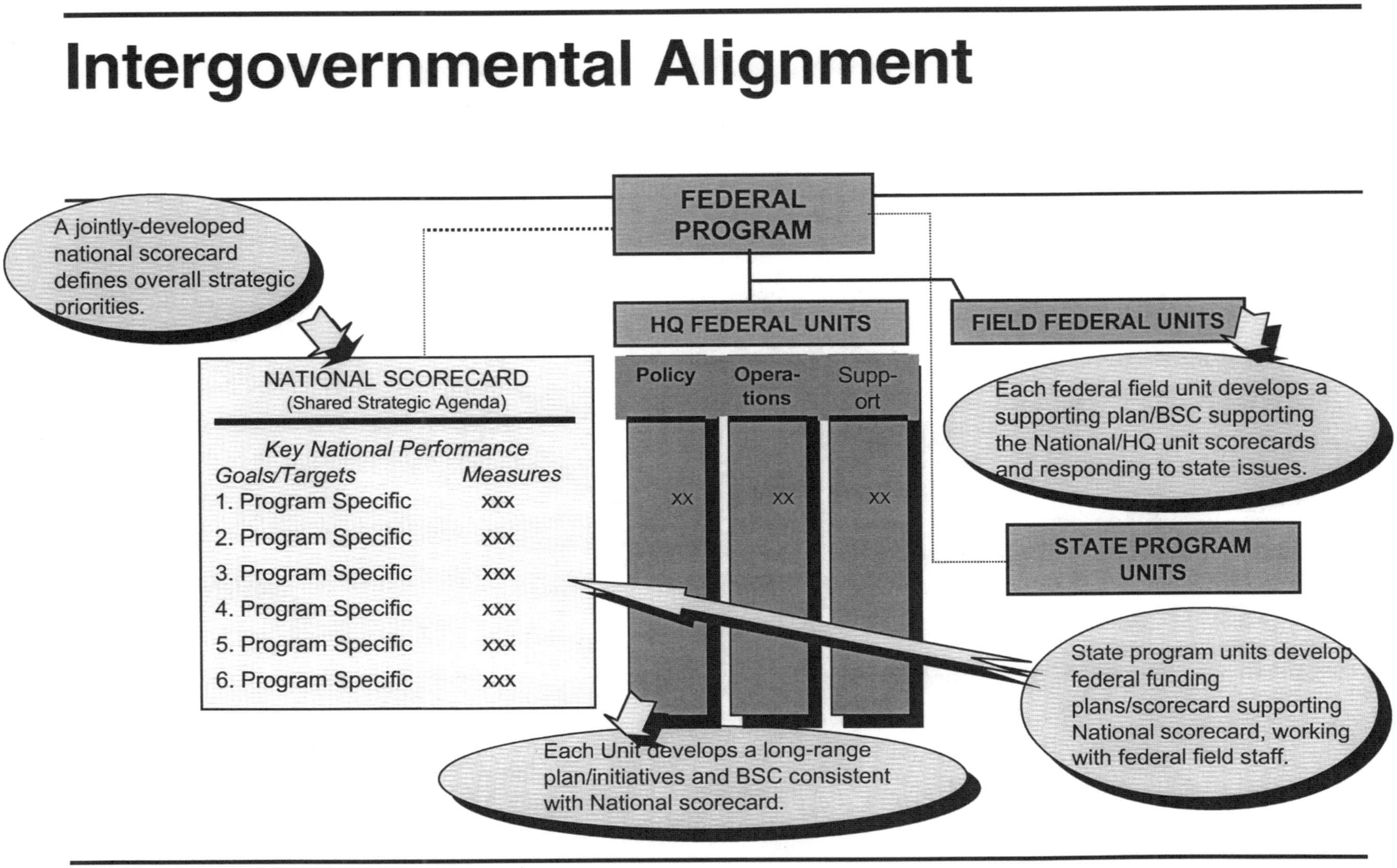

Utilizing the Balanced Scorecard Tool in the Public Sector

Intergovernmental Alignment

A jointly-developed national scorecard defines overall strategic priorities.

NATIONAL SCORECARD
(Shared Strategic Agenda)

Key National Performance
Goals/Targets   Measures
1. Program Specific   xxx
2. Program Specific   xxx
3. Program Specific   xxx
4. Program Specific   xxx
5. Program Specific   xxx
6. Program Specific   xxx

FEDERAL PROGRAM

HQ FEDERAL UNITS
Policy | Operations | Support
xx | xx | xx

FIELD FEDERAL UNITS

Each federal field unit develops a supporting plan/BSC supporting the National/HQ unit scorecards and responding to state issues.

STATE PROGRAM UNITS

State program units develop federal funding plans/scorecard supporting National scorecard, working with federal field staff.

Each Unit develops a long-range plan/initiatives and BSC consistent with National scorecard.

Strategy Map Linkages

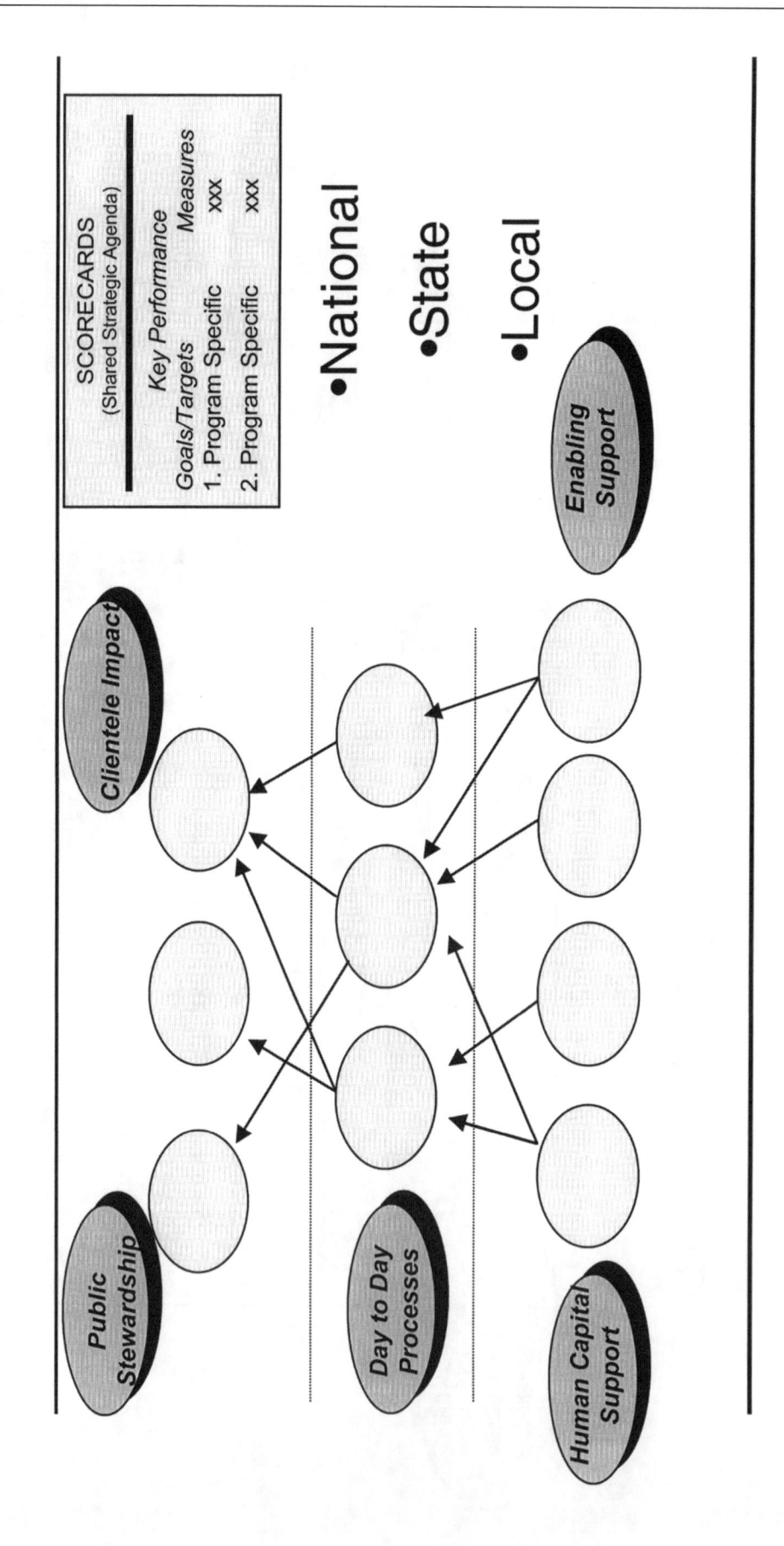

Clientele Impact

Public Stewardship

Day to Day Processes

Enabling Support

Human Capital Support

SCORECARDS
(Shared Strategic Agenda)

Key Performance Goals/Targets	Measures
1. Program Specific	xxx
2. Program Specific	xxx

- National
- State
- Local

National and State Scorecard Matching

National Scorecard

Public Stewardship
- Increase underserved children screened and receiving early intervention health care
- Reduce state error rates in financial accounting

Clientele Impact
- Increase the quality of statewide early intervention needs assessment and action planning

Day to Day Processes

Human Capital Support
- Increase number of health care providers who have pediatric expertise
- Provide technical assistance on identifying/tracking state service gaps

Enabling Support

State Scorecard

- Achieve targets for the number of eligible children under six who receive early intervention and primary health care
- Achieve clean financial audits

- Implement statewide protocol for early intervention needs assessment
- Increase uniform and evidence-based guidelines for pediatric screening
- Decrease local grant approval process for pediatric care funding

- Increase number of graduates from State University in pediatric primary care specialties
- Increase number of local clinics with capacity to track pediatric screening needs

Shared Commitment

GPRA Vital Components: Questions

Mission and Goals
- Does the mission define a public need defined in statute? Is it results-oriented?
- Are the goals related to the mission and cover the agency's major functions, operations, and crosscutting efforts with others? Are they results-oriented? Can their performance be assessed?

Measurement and Evaluation
- Are systems in place to produce reliable performance and cost data to set goals, evaluate results, and improve performance?

Means and Strategies
- Are the means and strategies linked to the goals and managers' and staff day-to-day activities and the efforts of delivery partners?
- Is it clear how the agency will align its activities, core processes, work force, and other resources to support mission-related outcomes?

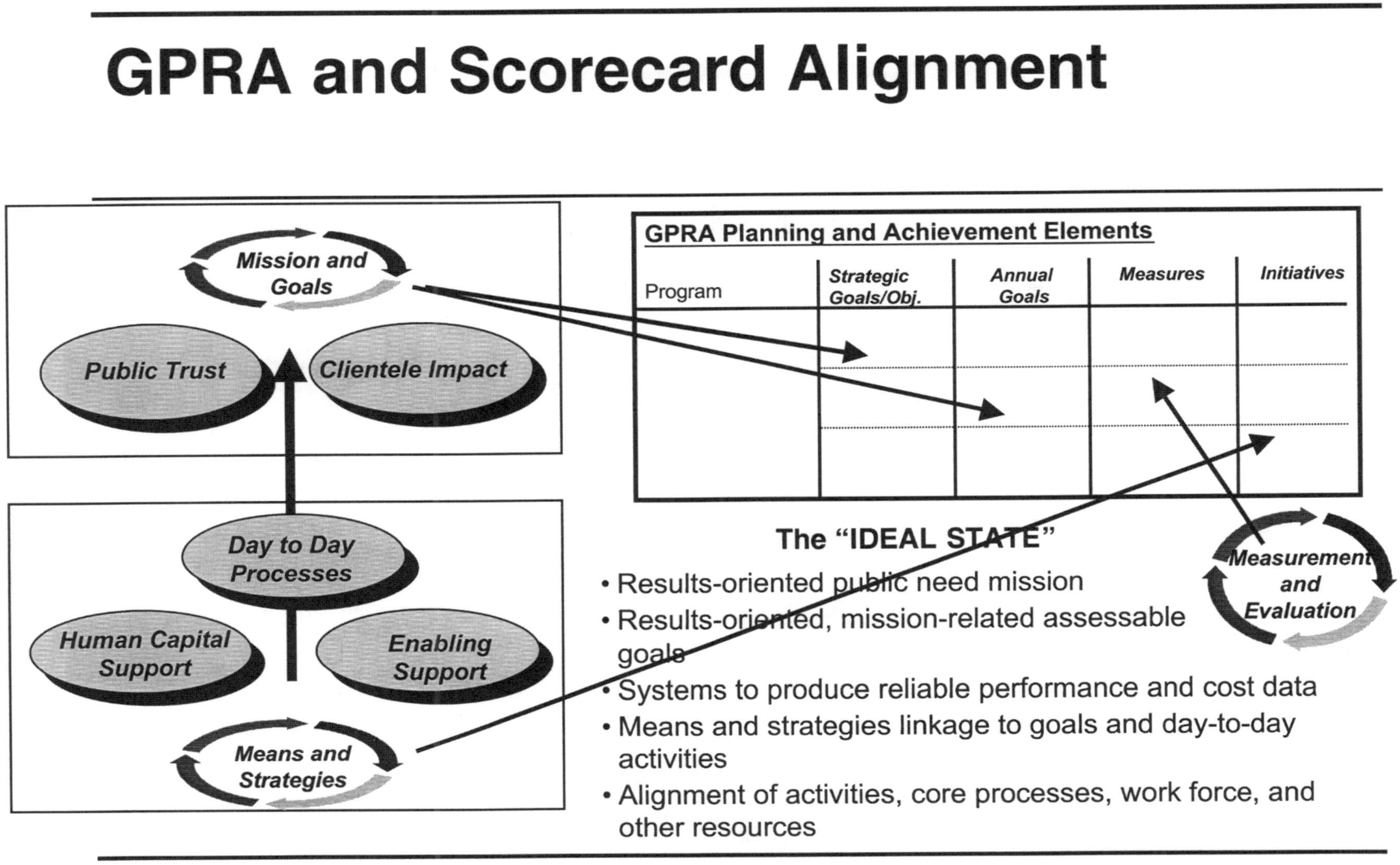

GPRA and Scorecard Alignment

GPRA Planning and Achievement Elements

Program	Strategic Goals/Obj.	Annual Goals	Measures	Initiatives

The "IDEAL STATE"
- Results-oriented public need mission
- Results-oriented, mission-related assessable goals
- Systems to produce reliable performance and cost data
- Means and strategies linkage to goals and day-to-day activities
- Alignment of activities, core processes, work force, and other resources

Measurement and Evaluation

Mission and Goals — Clientele Impact, Public Trust

Day to Day Processes — Enabling Support, Human Capital Support

Means and Strategies

Senior Executives: Balanced Measures

- An approach to performance measurement that balances organizational results with the perspectives of groups such as customers and employees

- Agencies define the measures, determine the appropriate balance, and decide an implementation method

- SES critical elements and performance requirements must be consistent with the agency's strategic plan.

ORGANIZATIONAL RESULTS

EMPLOYEE PERSPECTIVES

CUSTOMER SATISFACTION

OTHER MEASURES

CHAPTER 15

The Future of the Balanced Scorecard in the Federal Government

The balanced scorecard or balanced measures are in use at varying levels of organizations and at varying levels of effectiveness across the federal government. The breadth of use and effectiveness should only increase over time. The President's Management Agenda should provide impetus to use the BSC in enterprise situations.

One of the major inhibitors to growth and effective implementation of GPRA has been the somewhat "spotty" support of top management in many federal organizations. The PMA and the current OMB budget process should change this.

In many respects, the increased use of the balanced scorecard and balanced measures should be expected in the various functional areas of federal government organizations. They not only have a more precise view of what is required of them for successful operations but also are more manageable in many situations. The procurement function has been under pressure to provide faster and more effective customer service for a long time. Therefore, it is not surprising that procurement entities have gone a long way in developing the balanced scorecard as a measure of their success. On the other hand, trying to get large federal organizations to take on strategy and performance measurement with stakeholders, customers, and all sorts of different inputs to the process is potentially much more varied and complex.

Table 15–1 reflects the various measurement perspectives of the federal organizations discussed in this book. The first is the Kaplan/Norton[1] approach, followed by organizational perspectives and functional perspectives.

Table 15–1 Federal Government Balanced Scorecard Analysis—Measurement Perspective

Kaplan-Norton	Financial	Customer	Internal	Learning & Growth	
DFAS	Financial	Customer	Internal Business	Learning & Growth	
FAALC	Financial Stakeholder	Customer		Learning & Growth	
NUWC	Financial	Customer	Internal Business	Learning & Growth	Employee
IRS	Business Results	Customer Satisfaction		Employee Satisfaction	
Report on Performance	Business	Customer	Employee		

---

[1] Robert S. Kaplan and David P. Norton, *The Balanced Scorecard* (Boston: Harvard Business School Press, 1996).

DOT Procurement	Financial	Customer	Internal Business Practice	Learning & Growth	Employee
DOE HR	Financial	Customer Satisfaction	Culture	Work Processes	

This book provides a wealth of information on how the concepts of the balanced scorecard and balanced measures have developed in the federal government. This book also reflects how the President's Management Agenda supports and is supported by the BSC. Now is the time to build on this foundation and develop more effective federal government organizations.

APPENDIX A

Balanced Scorecard for a Contractor

The information presented in this appendix is adapted from a November 4, 1998 briefing by John Hirsch and Joseph Montgomery of the Strategic Effectiveness Group, LLC (see Chapter 13). It is presented with the permission of Mr. Hirsch.

SECTION TWO APPLYING THE MODEL: CREATING A BALANCED SCORECARD FOR A HYPOTHETICAL HANFORD CONTRACTOR

Preliminary Steps in Balanced Scorecard Preparation

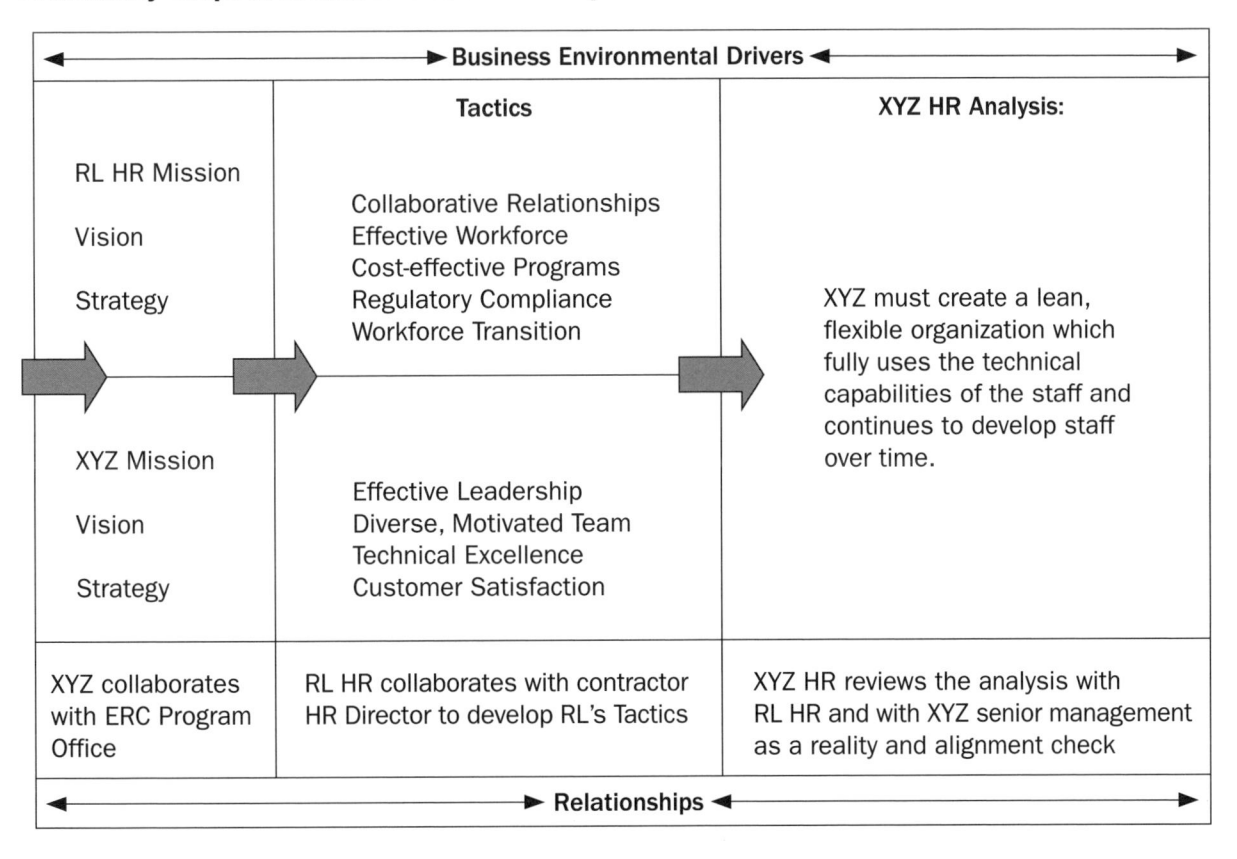

← → Business Environmental Drivers ← →

	Tactics	XYZ HR Analysis:
RL HR Mission Vision Strategy	Collaborative Relationships Effective Workforce Cost-effective Programs Regulatory Compliance Workforce Transition	XYZ must create a lean, flexible organization which fully uses the technical capabilities of the staff and continues to develop staff over time.
XYZ Mission Vision Strategy	Effective Leadership Diverse, Motivated Team Technical Excellence Customer Satisfaction	
XYZ collaborates with ERC Program Office	RL HR collaborates with contractor HR Director to develop RL's Tactics	XYZ HR reviews the analysis with RL HR and with XYZ senior management as a reality and alignment check

← → Relationships ← →

Understanding RL HR and Contractor HR Drivers

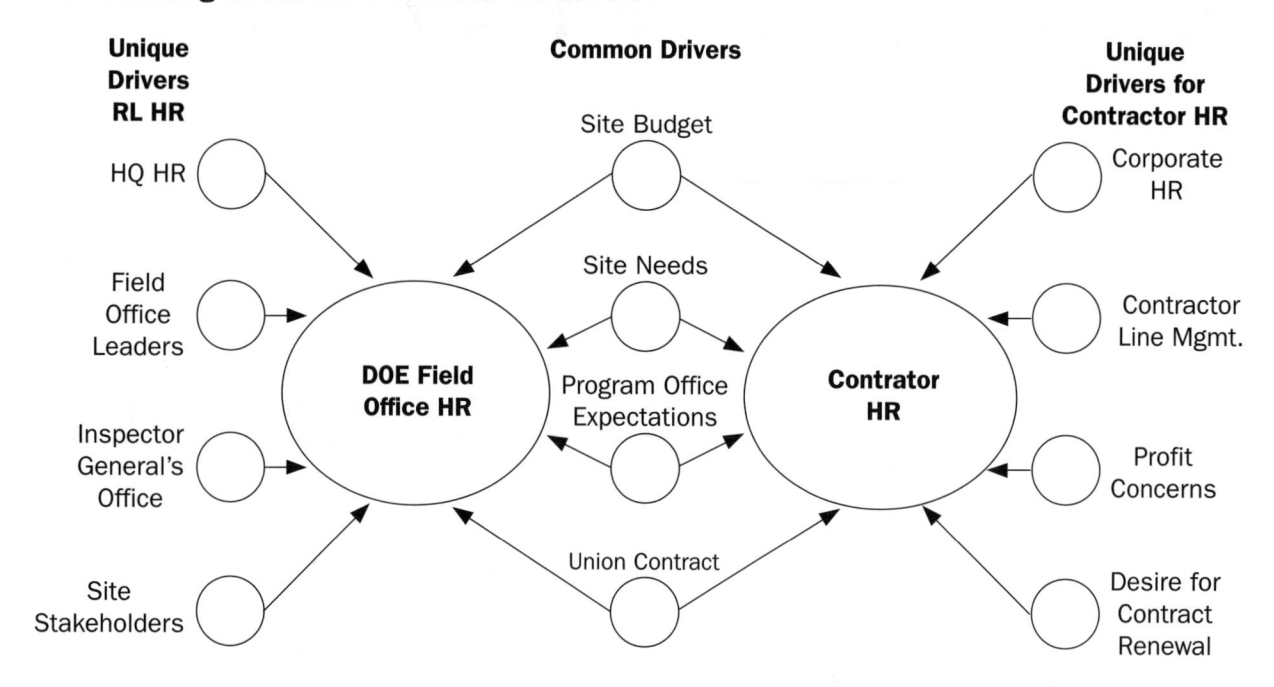

Unique Drivers RL HR
- HQ HR
- Field Office Leaders
- Inspector General's Office
- Site Stakeholders

Common Drivers
- Site Budget
- Site Needs
- Program Office Expectations
- Union Contract

Unique Drivers for Contractor HR
- Corporate HR
- Contractor Line Mgmt.
- Profit Concerns
- Desire for Contract Renewal

DOE Field Office HR ↔ Contrator HR

Using Desired Organizational Characteristics To Drive Assessment, Goals, Tactics, and Measures

Org. Characteristics	How Do We Compare w/ Best practices?	Performance Targets	HR Actions	Measures
Empowered Teams Productive workforce Strong culture, values Low overheads				
XYZ HR and RL HR collaborate on desired characteristics	XYZ HR and RL HR collaborate, reach consensus	Collaborate, reach consensus	XYZ decides which actions it wishes to take	Consensus on the measures, incentives

◄──────────── Relationships ────────────►

Possible Missions for Contractors

- Environmental restoration/cleanup
- Research and development
- Defense production
- Each mission will require its own distinct vision of success, strategy, and tactics

(XYZ mission is environmental restoration and cleanup)

Aligning XYZ Mission, Vision, Strategy

	XYZ	**RL–HR**
Mission	Assess and clean up hazardous contamination	As a public steward, oversee contractors to provide the workforce needed for effective, efficient cleanup
Vision	Highly efficient, effective, technically advanced, partnering, leadership, teamwork	Collaborative relations w/all parties; capable, cost-effective workforce, compliance w/regs. and goals of workforce transition
Strategy	High tech. with strong customer linkages, project mgmt. skills	Tightly linked w/customers & suppliers (contractors)

Primary Tactics to Support Strategy

XYZ Tactics for Innovation Strategy
    Developing Effective Leadership
    Creating a Diverse, Motivated Team
    Ensuring Technical Excellence
    Building Customer Satisfaction

RL-HR Tactics for Tight Linkages Strategy
    Creating Collaborative Relationships
    Promoting an Effective Workforce
    Promoting Cost Effective Programs
    Requiring Regulatory Compliance
    Requiring Workforce Transition

Aligning XYZ Mission, Vision, Strategy

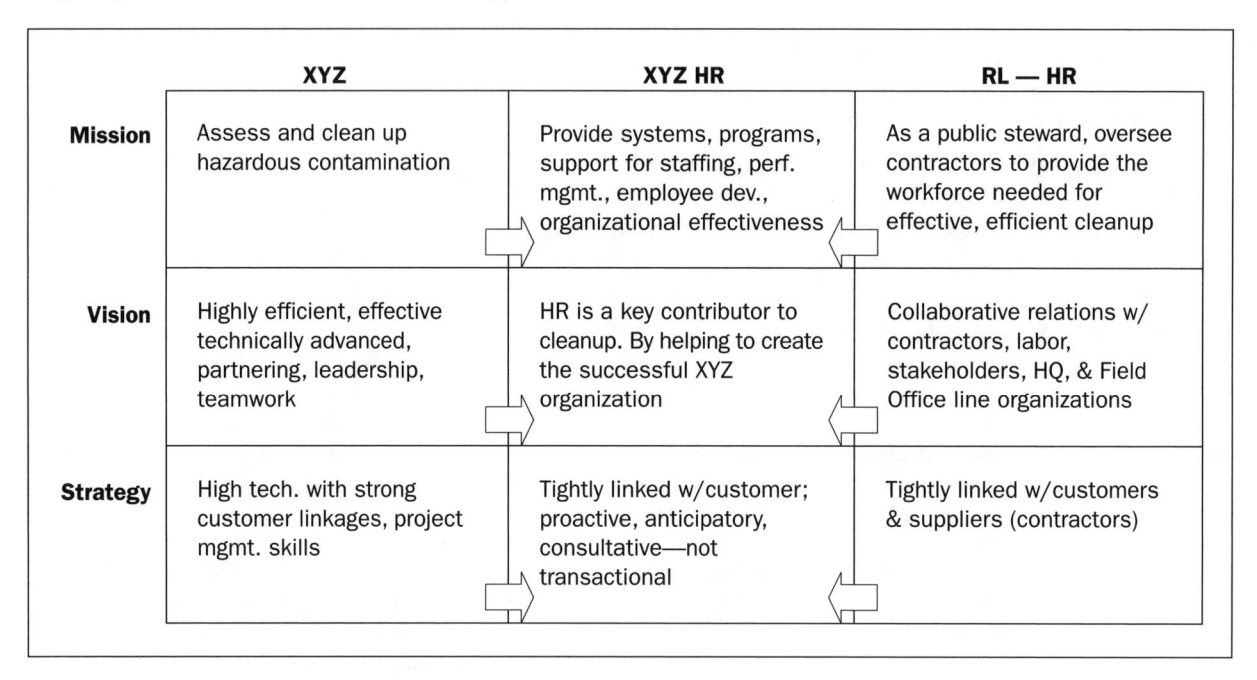

	XYZ	XYZ HR	RL — HR
Mission	Assess and clean up hazardous contamination	Provide systems, programs, support for staffing, perf. mgmt., employee dev., organizational effectiveness	As a public steward, oversee contractors to provide the workforce needed for effective, efficient cleanup
Vision	Highly efficient, effective technically advanced, partnering, leadership, teamwork	HR is a key contributor to cleanup. By helping to create the successful XYZ organization	Collaborative relations w/ contractors, labor, stakeholders, HQ, & Field Office line organizations
Strategy	High tech. with strong customer linkages, project mgmt. skills	Tightly linked w/customer; proactive, anticipatory, consultative—not transactional	Tightly linked w/customers & suppliers (contractors)

XYZ Organizational Characteristics Desired for Success of Mission

1. Decentralized, highly flexible empowered project teams that share skills and functional support via a matrix structure
2. Workforce which is very productive and has right KSAs
3. A culture which focuses on:
   - Performance guided by strong values: safety, integrity, innovation, and quality
   - Employee development: know-how for good performance on current job, planning for next job
   - Rewards & recognition for performance/results
   - Regular measurement of performance
4. Low overheads: low ratio of support to productive labor and lower costs of staff

Desired Organizational Characteristics Drive HR Assessment, Goals, Tactics, and Measures—Example

Organizational Characteristic	How Do We Compare to Best Practices Applicable to This Site?	Perf. Targets	HR Actions	Perf. Measures	BSC Quadrant
Empowered Flexible Teams	• Highly effective, but need to improve sharing staff expertise across projects • Some self-managed teams (SMTs)	• Maintain effectiveness but 10% greater sharing • 10% more SMTs	• Establish baseline • Create tracking mechanism • Develop reports to recognize sharing managers	• Survey of project mgr. perceptions; • % staff on >1 project • # SMTs	Work processes
Low Overhead	Generally favorable, except 15% above market comparator for all benefit costs	Reduce benefit costs by 10% next year	• Increase insurance deductibles • Increase stop-loss • Study other benefit programs for later actions	Deductible % Increase • # programs evaluated • Benefits expense factor	Finance
Effective Reward and Recognition Program	• Current programs are ad hoc, lack formalization • R&R programs need to be strategically tied to achieving the mission, reinforcing the business strategy, producing the desired results	• Formalized programs in place • Direct links w/strategy, desired outcomes, & culture	• Form line/HR employee team to design program • Obtain Gvt/DOE approval • Obtain union support as necessary • Implement program • Communicate to staff	• % time over schedule • Survey—mgmt, staff perceptions • $ value of awards (per capita) • # staff recognized (% of total)	Culture
A workforce that has the right KSAs for current jobs and is building skills for transition to the next job	• Workforce has right skills for today, but inadequate attention to the next job • Need meaningful, individualized development plans for exempt staff with most resources to high-potentials • Need planned skill enhancement programs related to new technologies for hourly staff	• Effective planning for next job • Mentoring for high potentials • Skill progs. in place	• Create a tailored, all staff dev. program • Obtain sr mgt approval • Pilot train hi-pots to create plan • Establish union/mgt team to develop skills program • Pilot with one skill	• % of hi-pots with dev. plans • Line mgt. sat. with dev. process • Pilot group sat. with perceived enhancement of skills	Culture

Organizational Characteristic	How Do We Compare to Best Practices Applicable to This Site?	Perf. Targets	HR Actions	Perf. Measures	BSC Quadrant
Support functions aligned with line organizations	Some alignment, especially in election/recruiting; HR tends to take on "policeman" role with line to get compliance with rules, rather than true service orientation. Tendency for adversarial relationships to result.	Line perceives step-function improvement in support orientation of "X" %	• Assess support orientation of each HR service area • Create a plan for achieving alignment in main functions • Assign accountable staff to each project • Solicit line input • Solicit line fdbk on progress	Survey—line perceptions of support for their needs; progress perceived	Culture

Sort Measures into a Draft BSC

Work Processes	Culture
• Project manager perceptions of sharing technical expertise* • # staff on >1 project	• % time over schedule for R&R • Survey—staff perceptions of R&R, development process* • $ value of awards, # recognition • # hi-pots with plans • Pilot group satisfaction
Customer Satisfaction	**Financial Goals**
• HR role effectiveness:* survey—executives; managers; employees; DOE-RL	• Increase in deductibles • # benefits programs evaluated • Benefits expense factor* • Budget for improvement projects • Revenue/FTE; expenses/FTE

*Indicates measures incentivized by DOE

Summary

- Contractor HR organizations will be asked to create an HR BSC
- The BSC requires a logical, step-by-step development process that focuses on how HR supports organizational needs
- There are several decisions to be made, including desired level of performance compared with Best Practices
- The BSC development process provides major benefits to the HR function

Index

A

assessing program performance, 56–60
asset utilization/investment strategy, financial theme, 4

B

balanced performance measure (BPM), 165
balanced scorecard (BSC)
　creating for contractor, 321–327
　future of, in government, 319–320
　importance of, 3, 8
　merging with President's Management Agenda, 41–42
balanced scorecard tool, utilizing in public sector, 299–318
best practices, performance management, 249–257
BPM. *See* balanced performance measure
BSC. *See* balanced scorecard
budget
　integrating with performance, 41
　relationship to strategic plan, 1
Bush, President George, 2

business perspective, performance measures, 165
business strategy, private sector
　alignment, 8
　customer perspective, 4–5
　employee capabilities, 6–7
　empowerment, 8
　financial perspective, 3–4
　information system capabilities, 7–8
　internal business perspective, 5–6
　learning and growth perspective, 6–8
　motivation, 8

C

Caudle, Dr. Sharon L., 299
citizen-centered government, 2
Clinton, President Bill, 1
competitive sourcing, 41
contractor, creating balanced scorecard for, 321–327
core measurement outcomes, 5
cost reduction/productivity improvement, financial theme, 4
customer acquisition, 5

customer perspective, performance measures, 165, 319–320
customer profitability, 5
customer relationship, 5
customer retention, 5
customer satisfaction, 5
customer value proposition, 5

D

Defense Finance and Accounting Service (DFAS)
　Corporate Balanced Scorecard, 110–120
　creation of, 95
　measurement perspective, 319–320
　Strategic Plan, 96–109
Department of Energy (DOE), 289–298
Department of Transportation, 276–287, 320
DFAS. *See* Defense Finance and Accounting Service
documents, mandated, 1
DOE. *See* Department of Energy

E

earnings before interest and taxes (EBIT), 7

electronic government, 41
employee capabilities, 6–7
employee perspective,
  performance measures,
  165
employee productivity, 7
employee retention, 7
employee satisfaction, 7
employee surveys, 7

F

Federal Aviation
  Administration Logistics
  Center (FAALC)
  measurement perspective,
    319–320
  Strategic Plan for 1994,
    121–125
  Strategic Plan for 1997,
    126–135
  Strategic Plan for 1999-
    2002, 136–149
  Strategic Plan for 2003-
    2007, 150–164
financial performance,
  improving, 41
financial perspective,
  performance measures,
  165, 319–320
financial themes,
  relationship to business
  strategy, 4
fiscal year (FY), 165
Five-Year Planning
  Explained in One Easy
  Lesson, Naval Undersea
  Warfare Center, 199–201
future, of balanced
  scorecard, 319–320
FY. See fiscal year

G

General Accounting Office
  (GAO), 1–2, 299–318
governing with
  accountability, 43–55

Government Performance
  and Results Act of 1993
  (GPRA), 1
grow stage, private sector
  life cycle, 3
Guide to a Balanced
  Scorecard, Procurement
  Executives' Association,
  259–275

H

harvest stage, private sector
  life cycle, 3
Hirsch, John, 289, 321
HR. See human resources
human capital, strategic
  management of, 41
human resources (HR), 289

I

image and reputation, 5
information system
  capabilities, 7–8
internal perspective,
  performance measures,
  165, 319–320
Internal Revenue Service (IRS)
  Balanced Measurement
    System, 216–233
  Commissioner's
    Testimony, 213–216
  Internal Revenue Manual,
    213
  measurement perspective,
    319–320
  Organizational
    Performance
    Management, 233–248
  *Organizational Performance
    Management and the IRS
    Balanced Measurement
    System,* 213
internal value chain
  analysis, 5
IRS. See Internal Revenue
  Service

J

Journey of Change, Naval
  Undersea Warfare Center,
  202–211

K

Kaplan, Robert S., 3–8, 319–
  320

L

learning and growth
  perspective, performance
  measures, 165, 319–320

M

market share, 5
market-based government, 2
measurement perspective,
  balanced scorecard, 319–
  320
Montgomery, Joseph, 289,
  321

N

National Aeronautics and
  Space Administration
  (NASA)
  Performance Plan, 66–73
  PMA Action Plans, 74–94
*National Partnership for
  Reinventing Government,*
  249
Naval Undersea Warfare
  Center (NUWC)
  Five-Year Planning
    Explained in One Easy
    Lesson, 199–201
  Journey of Change, 202–
    211

measurement perspective, 319–320
Newport Division Five-Year Planning Process, 196–198
Newport Division Strategic Plan Brochure, 1998, 193–195
Newport Division Strategic Plan, 1998, 177–192
planning, use of, 165
Strategic Management Process, 175–176
Strategic Plan, 1998, 165–175
Newport Division Five-Year Planning Process, Naval Undersea Warfare Center, 196–198
Newport Division Strategic Plan Brochure, Naval Undersea Warfare Center, 193–195
Norton, David P., 3–8, 319–320
NUWC. *See* Naval Undersea Warfare Center

O

Organizational Performance Management and the IRS Balanced Measurement System, 213

P

PEA. *See* Procurement Executives' Association
performance drivers, 5
performance plan, 1
performance reports, 1
President's Management Agenda (PMA)
 balanced scorecard, merging with, 41–42
 importance of, 2, 8
 text, 10–39
private sector life cycle, 3
procurement
 Guide to a Balanced Scorecard, Procurement Executives' Association, 259–275
 Procurement Performance Management System, Department of Transportation, 276–287
Procurement Executives' Association (PEA), 259–275
product/service attributes, 5
program assessments for FY 2004, 61–64

R

results-oriented government, 2

revenue growth and mix, financial theme, 4
revenue per employee, 7
Rossotti, Charles O., 213

S

Senate Finance Committee, 213
Strategic Effectiveness Group, 289, 321
strategic information coverage ratio, 7–8
Strategic Management Process Naval Undersea Warfare Center, 175–176
Strategic Measurement System for DOE Contractor Human Resources, 289–298
Strategic Plan, Naval Undersea Warfare Center, 165–175
strategic plans, long-range, 1
surveys, employee, 7
sustain stage, private sector life cycle, 3

U

United States Government FY 2004 Budget, 43–64